One hundred years after Marshall McLuhan's birth, Elena Lamberti explores a fundamental, yet neglected aspect of his work: the solid humanistic roots of his original 'mosaic' form of writing. In this investigation of how his famous communication theories were influenced by literature and the arts, Lamberti proposes a new approach to McLuhan's thought.

Lamberti delves into McLuhan's humanism in light of his work on media and culture, exploring how he began to perceive literature not just as a subject, but as a 'function inseparable from communal existence.' Lamberti pays particular attention to the central role played by Modernism in the making of his theories, including the writings of Ford Madox Ford, James Joyce, Ezra Pound, and Wyndham Lewis. Reconnecting McLuhan with his literary past, *Marshall McLuhan's Mosaic* is a demonstration of one of his greatest ideas: that literature not only matters, but can help us understand the hidden patterns that rule our environment.

ELENA LAMBERTI is a research professor in the Department of Foreign Langt~~ ~~~ ~~~ ~~~ Literature at the University of Bologna.

ELENA LAMBERTI

Marshall McLuhan's Mosaic

Probing the Literary Origins
of Media Studies

UNIVERSITY OF TORONTO PRESS
Toronto Buffalo London

© University of Toronto Press 2012
Toronto Buffalo London
www.utppublishing.com
Printed in Canada

ISBN 978-1-4426-4013-9 (cloth)
ISBN 978-1-4426-0988-4 (paper)

Printed on acid-free paper

Library and Archives Canada Cataloguing in Publication

Lamberti, Elena
Marshall McLuhan's mosaic : probing the literary origins of media
studies / Elena Lamberti.

Includes bibliographical references and index.
ISBN 978-1-4426-4013-9 (bound).   ISBN 978-1-4426-0988-4 (pbk.)

1. McLuhan, Marshall, 1911–1980 – Criticism and interpretation.   2. Mass
media and literature.   I. Title.

P92.5.M3L344 2012   302.23092   C2011-906833-8

University of Toronto Press acknowledges the financial assistance to its
publishing program of the Canada Council for the Arts and the Ontario Arts
Council.

Canada Council   Conseil des Arts   ONTARIO ARTS COUNCIL
for the Arts   du Canada   CONSEIL DES ARTS DE L'ONTARIO

This book has been published with the help of a grant from the Canadian
Federation for the Humanities and Social Sciences, through the Aid to
Scholarly Publications Program, using funds provided by the Social Sciences
and Humanities Research Council of Canada.

University of Toronto Press acknowledges the financial support of the
Government of Canada through the Canada Book Fund for its publishing
activities.

*To Martin,
my husband, who IS the difference*

But the writing in Aphorisms hath many excellent virtues, whereto the writing in Method doth not approach. For first, it trieth the writer, whether he be superficial or solid: for Aphorisms, except they should be rediculous, cannot be made but of the pith and heart of sciences; for discourse of illustration is cut off; recitals of examples are cut off; discourse of connection and order is cut off; descriptions of practice are cut off ... So there remaineth nothing to fill the Aphorism but some good quantity of observation: and therefore no man can suffice, nor in reason will attempt, to write Aphorisms, but he that is sound and grounded ... Secondly, Methods are more fit to win consent or belief, but less fit to point to action ... And, lastly, Aphorisms, representing a knowledge broken, do invite men to inquire farther; whereas Methods, carrying the show of a total, do secure men, as if they were at furthest.

Francis Bacon, *The Advancement of Learning*, 1605

If the doors of perception were cleansed
Every thing would appear to man as it is, infinite.

William Blake, *The Marriage of Heaven and Hell*, 1790–3

Contents

Acknowledgments

My first thank you acknowledges all those authors who have written about Marshall McLuhan. Whether or not I am in agreement with what came before, those authors and their ideas form the broader ground for my volume.

I owe a great debt of gratitude to my home university — Alma Mater Studiorum – Università di Bologna, and to my colleagues and staff at the Dipartimento di Lingue e Letterature Straniere Moderne and the Facoltà di Lingue e Letterature Straniere. Together, they constitute an enriching environment in which to work and learn. I am grateful to the late Giovanna Franci, who supported this project at the beginning and who passed away too soon and unexpectedly. I am very grateful to Cecilia Ghetti for her outstanding support and help with this work. I am also very indebted to my students, who enthusiastically continue to prove that 'literature is not a subject but a function inseparable from communal existence,' as per McLuhan's lesson. In particular, I'm grateful to Giulia Albertazzi, Giulia Del Pittore, Alessandra Mastroianni, Monica Rossi, Tommaso Santi, and Margherita Suardo, whose engaging participation in my class on 'Literature, Art, Communication: Marshall McLuhan's Mosaic' in the academic year 2008–9 renewed my enthusiasm.

Some of the research for this book was developed as part of an international project called 'The Marconi Galaxy: Technology, Culture, Myth-making,' generously co-sponsored by the Institute for Advanced Studies at the University of Bologna, the Guglielmo Marconi Foundation (Bologna), the Italian Cultural Institute (Toronto), the Robarts Centre for Canadian Studies (York University, Toronto), the Mobile Media Lab (Concordia University, Montreal, and York University, Toronto), and the Social Sciences and Humanities Research Council of Canada. I extend my gratitude to these collaborating institutions, to their directors, and to the colleagues who took part in the project: Dario Braga, Maria Cioni, Barbara Crow, Gabriele Falciasecca, Seth Feldman, Giuliana Gardellini, Cecilia Ghetti, Michael Longford, Sanja Obradovic, Robert Prenovault, Kim Sawchuk, Martin Stiglio, and Barbara Valotti.

The celebrations for the centenary of Marshall McLuhan's birth provided an additional opportunity to assess the ideas discussed in this book. I am grateful to all involved in the European and international network 'McLuhan100.' I owe a collective debt of gratitude to the team of colleagues involved in the events we hosted in Bologna, with the assistance of the Canadian government and with the outstanding support of the Canadian embassy in Rome: Giovanna Cosenza, Mirco Dondi, Roberto Farnè, and Paolo Granata. I am very grateful as well to the doctoral students whose work facilitated the organization of all our events in Bologna: Roberta Cadei, Alice Casarini, Francesco Barbieri, and Monica Rossi. My gratitude goes to all convenors and fellow panellists at the 'McLuhan100' events, which I was lucky to attend in Canada, the United States, and Europe. My special thanks to Marco Adria and Katherine Adams (University of Alberta, Edmonton), and to Stephen Kovats and Michelle Kasprzak (Transmediale, Berlin).

Many 'humanists' have guided me throughout this project. It was both delightful and revealing to discuss with them today's role of the humanities. Linda Hutcheon's comments on the volume prospectus offered the most generous encouragement one could expect at the beginning of the writing adventure. Max Saunders, Jason Harding, Paul Edwards, Alan Munton, and Brett Neilson offered fundamental help at different stages. Paul Hjartarson, Linda Morra, Adam Hammond, Wayne DeFehr, Gregory Betts, Paul Tiessen, and Kristin Fast formed a great 'modernist team' at the MEA Conference, University of Alberta, 2011; it was an honour to join their group and to discuss McLuhan and modernism with them. I could rely on Peppino Ortoleva, Dominique Scheffel-Dunnand, Gerald O'Grady, and Domenico Pietropaolo to provide solid criticism and intellectual interaction, helping me figure out a series of uncanny questions. Melba Cuddy-Keane and the MRRG group at the University of Toronto welcomed me at their series of seminars, where I could learn from them while sharing my ideas on modernism and media studies. Thank you to the faculty and staff of the Department of English, University of Toronto, and to the staff at the Robarts Library, who facilitated my research and my academic life in Toronto. Master John Fraser of Massey College has offered support through deeds and encouraging words on many occasions since 1997, when I first landed in Canada. I owe him, his wife, Elisabeth, Massey College, and all *Masseyites* a great deal. And also since 1997, Barry Callaghan and Claire Weissman Wilks have offered both intellectual and emotional shelter to me — constantly and with great generosity. From them, I have learned much about Canada, and the Canadian and international literary and artistic scenes. Grazie.

I am also very grateful for the institutional support I received from York University, and especially from the Robarts Centre for Canadian Studies, under the direction of Daniel Drache and Seth Feldman. In addition to Daniel and Seth, I want to thank all the colleagues at York with whom I have discussed my project over the past five years: Gabriella Colussi-Arthur, Julia Creet, Chris Doda, Robert Drummond, Vicky Drummond, Rishma Dunlop, Shelley Hornstein, Janine Marchessault, Ron Pearlman, Roberta Sinyor, Priscilla Uppal. Thank you to the staff of the Scott Library, for welcoming me and assisting me all through this project. My special gratitude goes to Clara Thomas and John Lennox, who were the first to welcome me at York University; they made me feel at home from the very first day. I am particularly grateful to B.W. Powe, also at York University, for his comments and feedback on an earlier version of this book: his acute criticism helped to better focus my writing and ideas. Grazie Bruce!

Coming from the 'literary planet,' Lance Strate's generous 'lessons' on media ecology and media studies offered me a way out of the theoretical labyrinth more than once. I am very grateful to him and to all the colleagues at the Media Ecology Association who have patiently listened to my artsy investigations, sharing comments and criticism. Lance also introduced me to general semantics and the work of Alfred Korzybski; there is some interesting overlapping between McLuhan's ideas on language and those of Korzybski, but they have not been discussed in this volume. *On the Binding Biases of Time,* Lance's book, offers a great kick-off for further investigations in that direction (and much more).

In Toronto, I am particularly grateful to Adriana Frisenna, Italian Cultural Institute, and all the staff of that institution for their constant support and encouragement. My gratitude also goes to all those with whom I have shared conversations and ideas while working on this project in Canada, in particular, Guido and Anna Condotta, Maria, Mark, and Rafi Lewis, Rosemarie Nielsen, Irani and Francis Zarb, Joyce and Tony Santamaura, Caroline and Alberto Di Giovanni, Hege and Emanuele Lepri, Alorani and Cecil Hahn, Konrad Eisenbichler, Patrizia and Umberto Villani, Giorgio Mitolo, and Tony and Cristiano De Florentis. Jane Freeman helped enormously on Shakespeare and his treatment of the 'Fool,' as well as being a very passionate friend and colleague. Peter Eliot Weiss and Michael Sweeney were constant points of reference, always finding time to listen, answer, ask, and provoke. Grazie.

I reserve a special thought for Eric McLuhan, who has incessantly taught me a lot, not only about Marshall but also about literature and the humanities, providing new, fresh, and often amusing insights on so many different narratives. Thank you also to Stephanie McLuhan, who read and commented on the volume prospectus, and to Michael McLuhan for his generous help with sources and ideas.

The University of Toronto Press was an outstanding team to work with. Siobhan McMenemy, acquisition editor, welcomed me and my project and followed each phase with great enthusiasm and support. Frances Mundy, associate managing editor, Shoshana Wasser, marketing coordinator, Ken Lewis, copy editor, and Chris Reed, publicist, were the most patient and intelligent team one could have hoped for. I am very grateful also to the Canada Council for their financial assistance, which turned this project from theory into a reality. I owe an immeasurable intellectual debt to the anonymous readers for their comments on the first draft of my manuscript, as well as to all members of the various editorial boards who have contributed to turning that draft into its final shape.

Each author knows that a book is always the result of a series of conversations juxtaposing personal and professional spheres. So-called 'academic research' is often at its best in non-academic situations, when one relaxes and talks about the work in progress in new, unexpected ways. I want to thank all those who contributed to create the perfect 'thinking/writing environment' outside of libraries and university offices: Martin Stiglio, Renata, Giampietro, Nicola, and Nicoletta Lamberti, Paolo and Athos Tamburini, Maria, Oliva, Pietro, Massimo, Maurizio, and Anna Magri, and their newly arrived Nera (Azzurra), Marta Martelli, Paolo, Irma, and Davide Battilani, Cecilia Ghetti, Monica Notari, Ester Zago, Simona Mambrini, and Elisabetta Menetti.

Maria Cioni was the first to read my manuscript; her help, support, intelligence, and generosity made this project possible. Maria, I learned from you more than I can express in words: your encouragement and bright insights are a token to your marvellous mind and to our friendship.

David Sobelman is the *deus ex machina* of this volume. He was there long before it was conceived, as through the years our conversations and correspondence played a major role in exploring Marshall McLuhan's 'poetics.' Later, as a story-editor, David helped me to shape my ideas into a narrative, to turn my (Italian) academic language into a more natural language: from 'theory-telling' to 'story-telling' was his immeasurable lesson. David, thank you for teaching me an important lesson: to respect all readers, which is the truer ethic of all forms of communication.

I am grateful to the following for their consent to quote: Michael McLuhan for Marshall McLuhan's quotations, *Copyright, The Estate of Marshall McLuhan*; Professor Renzo S. Crivelli and Dr Roberta Gefter Wondrich for excepts from my essay 'Vivisecting Society: Joycean Heuristic in Marshall McLuhan's *The Mechanical Bride*' (*Prospero*, VI-MIM); the Wyndham Lewis Memorial Trust (a registered charity) for quotations from Wyndham Lewis; Hampton Press for excerpts from Michael A. Moos, 'The Hypertext Heuristic: McLuhan Probes Tested (A Case for Edible Spaceship),' in Lance Strate and Edward Wachtel, eds, *The Legacy of McLuhan* (Cresskill, NJ: Hampton Press, 2005), and Casey Man Kong Lum, ed., *Perspectives on Culture, Technology and Communication* (Cresskill, NJ: Hampton Press, 2006); University of Toronto Press for all quotes from *The Gutenberg Galaxy* and *The Laws of Media*.

MARSHALL McLUHAN'S MOSAIC
Probing the Literary Origins of Media Studies

Prologue

'April is the cruellest month ...'

It was a nice morning in early April 2006, and I had arrived at the university in good time for my office hours. Nobody was there and I had the room all to myself; I treasure those silent minutes before you open the door and let the students in to discuss some titles in your course syllabus, their ideas for new essays, and their problems with academic curricula. That morning, in the silence of my office, I took some time to adjust to that space, I sipped my second cup of coffee while turning on my computer, and I stretched a little bit on my chair to make sure that all of my body was with me; then, after a quick scan of my mail, I felt ready to slip into some noise again. I opened the door. Students had finally arrived; their procession to my desk soon started. Everything looked like every other morning at the university: same old problems, and same old answers. Then, all of a sudden, one of my students posed a question which banged into my literary ears: 'Professor, can you please tell me how many pages out of this novel I have to read in order to pass your final exam?' The soft tone of that student's voice did not mitigate the echoes of the explosion I continued to hear in my head and to feel through my body well after he had posed his question. It was a nice morning in early April, and even though I had dutifully followed all my morning rituals, I was not prepared for that unexpected blast.

Some of you may not quite understand why I was so bothered; some may think that it was the student's 'minor effort / maximum result' philosophy which annoyed me. No, it was a deeper bang. To fully appreciate it, you have to realize that I not only teach American and Canadian *literature*, but that my faculty at the University of Bologna is, in fact, the

Faculty of *Modern Languages and Literatures*. I mean, it is a faculty fully inscribed in the humanities, dedicated to literary, cultural, and linguistic studies. If someone who had freely enrolled in that specific faculty was able to ask such a question, what about all those who were taking other programs instead? Where does literature stand in our society if even those who have chosen it as their field of study diminish both the pleasure and the importance of reading a novel?

That morning, I realized that I had been adapting to my closed educational system, that I had become the servo-mechanism of my own figure as a scholar. I had therefore made a terrible mistake: I had assumed that the students I welcomed in my classes shared not only my passion but also my own approach to literature, no matter their age, no matter the different educational environment they had experienced. Why otherwise choose literature at a time when other programs assure you a better potential for a wealthier life? It was a nice morning in early April; but April is the cruellest month, as T.S. Eliot taught us, and that morning I realized, like the narrator of *The Waste Land*, I was covered in forgetful snow and winter had kept me warm.[1] It was time to shake that numbing though protective blanket off.

This book stems out of that experience and my ensuing need. It stems out of my shaking off the snow which prevented me from truly seeing what was in fact evolving in front of me: inevitably, the digital revolution had reshaped the human factor, changing the way people learn, live, and experience. Today, literature is one (and not even the most popular) among other media taking part in the process. It is not true that a digitalized novel is the same novel as the printed one. We approach and read it in a different way. And I like both ways because each of them triggers a different knowledge and understanding in me. But I belong to a dying species. I was trained in a hybrid post-literate society still moving towards a post-secondary-orality phase which is now about to enter its prime. Contrary to my experience, my students were born and raised in the new post-TV media environment. I am not that old in comparison to them if I think of my age; but I am much older than them if I think of my media educational environment: in the past twenty-five years, our world has moved fast in terms of 'mass technology' or 'technology for the masses.'

This book is not meant to foster a battle between those who read traditional books and those who do not; it is not written with the intention to praise literature against new media. Environmental change cannot be halted through a blind defence of personal principles and affections. This is what I have learnt while shaking off the forgetful snow that my habits had laid down on me. I had a good master: Marshall McLuhan, a professor of English who is now remembered mostly – if at all – as a media guru. I never met the man in person. I met many of his disembodied versions though, always enjoying his storytelling and wit in video-recorded interviews and conferences. But the Marshall I love most is the Marshall I met through his books. It is there that I met the professor of English. It is through his books that he taught me the greatest lesson of my life as a literary scholar: 'Literature is not a subject but *a function* – a function inseparable from communal existence.'[2] How could I forget it for so long? Because I was caught in the university whirlpool: too much aesthetic, too much politics. Not much time to stop and look at the whole moving picture: wrong from the start!

It is time for us, scholars and students in the humanities, to reclaim Marshall McLuhan and learn from him. He never approached literature as a subject; he literally *applied* literature to the observation of his actuality. To explore such a perceptual concept, this book will investigate the literary origins of Marshall McLuhan's media studies. The *mosaic* is the tool he designed to help us to connect to our evolving actualities. And it is to his writing we must return to fully appreciate the potentialities of literature as a function. The media guru was born in a literary soil. To appreciate this, it would help to reconsider the role literature can still play inside our digital age. My book is my way to pay homage to Marshall McLuhan *the professor of English* who through his mosaic has taught me to escape from the isolation of my academic ivory tower, to put on my world and to better understand my students. In other words: he has encouraged me to shift to the control tower. He has taught me Francis Bacon's lesson, to look backward, *to enquire farther*. To fully appreciate the media guru, we have to return him to his literary roots. To fully understand our *mediascapes*, we have to reconsider literature, not as a subject, but truly *as a function*.

Look Backward, Enquire Farther

Sometimes we must take a step back to achieve a better leap forward. After two decades of semi-oblivion, Marshall McLuhan was brought back by the late 1990s because the world was now experiencing a technological revolution which made many of his visions come true: the planet had shrunk into a global village; the Internet medium was the new message; individuals were living outside their bodies, on air or through the Web. Looking through the rear-view mirror of knowledge and experience, I noticed that a new generation of media scholars was welcoming back Marshall McLuhan and his media probes, with thumbs up. Today, broadly speaking, not only have we resurrected him but we have also turned him into the Patron Saint whose apocryphal gospel is evoked to lend credibility to old and new theories on media. Some among the proselytes of the World Wide Web seem to act as new e-prophets eager to explain the old guru, what he foresaw, and even what he would say today. I perceive this as an attitude which looks back, not to enquire farther, but to confirm a closed vision of both the man and his theories. It is a reassuring attitude 'more fit to win consent or belief, but less fit to point to action,' to quote Francis Bacon's *The Advancement of Learning*. All along that span of time, little attention has been given to Marshall McLuhan's prose; too much attention has been given to his ideas on media, in most cases extrapolating them from a broader setting. As a result, McLuhan's complex *logos*, his linguistic *probes* and *aphorisms*, have been fragmented and reduced to captions accompanying the Saint's holy picture, like something taken for granted as a part of folklore that merits no further investigation. No matter how good and honest the intention, the long-term result of this renewed interest can only be one: the archetype will be retrieved only through little clichés, and once more, the original *ground* (the integral McLuhan) will be lost and fragmented into many *figures* (his various interpretations).

In this book, I propose to move back in order to enquire further. In this book, I will not discuss *what* McLuhan said; instead, I probe *how* he said what he said, and, most important, I probe how he came to elaborate and to structure his original form of communication. It is my intention to better appreciate McLuhan's true legacy, and in that sense, this book should be taken as an exegesis in progress. I move from the *literal* to the *structural*,[3] to encourage a different approach to McLuhan's work based on the architecture shaping his own *form of writing*. I plan to look through the rear-view mirror of McLuhan's works and literary roots to move forward towards a renewed understanding of his media studies; and through that, towards a better appreciation of our media environment. My goal is to contribute to rethinking, in the long run, the whole cosmogony constituting his thought and recompose the fragments (the various interpretations and misinterpretations of his thought). Retrieving this structural dimension can, in fact, open the way to new questions,' which, in turn, will lead to a renewed perspective not only on McLuhan but also on how we look at our own media environment. Does that sound like an ambitious goal? Yes. But, as the Canadian poet Rishma Dunlop wrote: 'The time for the ordinary is not possible anymore.'[4]

The way I see it, retrieving the structural can reveal what is perhaps McLuhan's greatest legacy: a different *forma mentis*. This is a new frame of mind conducive to a different approach to *knowledge*, wherein knowledge can be perceived as a *continuum* to be investigated in all its complexity. A very serious approach which, nevertheless, is also extremely playful. I still marvel thinking that Marshall McLuhan was at first a professor of English who based his investigations of the media upon a literary paradigm, namely, the one provided by Edgar Allan Poe in his famous short story 'A Descent into the Maelstrom.'[5] That simple story teaches us to look at the final effect, and work it backward until we find the original cause. It teaches us to be a witty Sherlock Holmes and curious explorers, to use our imagination and approach our world with cleansed doors of perception. McLuhan learned and applied that lesson all through his life.

This book will challenge previous binary perspectives on McLuhan (as a critic you were supposed to be either *for* or *against* him) by attempting to suspend biases and judgments of the validity of his theories on media.[6] Taking a step back, I will probe the *form* of McLuhan's writing, his so-called *mosaic*, which McLuhan introduced at the beginning of his second published volume, *The Gutenberg Galaxy* (1962):

> *The Gutenberg Galaxy* develops a mosaic or field approach to its problems. Such a mosaic image of numerous data and quotations in evidence offers the only practical means of revealing causal operations in history.[7]

Can this mosaic offer some suggestions on how to approach our complex and hyper-dynamic (or pseudo-dynamic) reality? Returning to the literary roots of McLuhan's media studies will help us to answer this question.

As a professor of English, Marshall McLuhan suspended his disbelief and speculated, provocatively and joyfully, about the new man-made environment. As a professor of English, he learned his lesson from James Joyce and other modernist masters, and used language as an old/new tool to read his times; and, as a professor of English, he tried to turn *logos* into a powerful probe *per se*. Do not read McLuhan only as the prophet of the electric age. Read him as a Shakespearian 'witty-foolish orator'[8] because, as James Joyce wrote, 'The war is in words and the wood is the world.'[9]

In this book, I will tell you more about my own journey as a literary scholar through McLuhan's wordy wood, because I truly enjoyed my exploration, as I trust you will too. The wood you will explore through this book does not look like a dark forest, but more like a garden maze whose mysteries will be slowly revealed; while walking through it, you yourself will gently shake off your forgetful snow and, once out, will stop to contemplate the maze from a literary viewpoint, appreciating the labyrinthine figure and its entangled patterns. Play with them. Trust the image of McLuhan I want to show you. Listen to him. Read his books. He is a great storyteller. Have confidence in him even when he drives you crazy and forces you along detours, when you want to rush and he forces you to slow down. Take a step back, stop and look, not with your eyes, but *through all your senses*. As soon as you adjust to McLuhan's literary landscape, you will start to look at things in a different way; you will see them as they truly are and learn how to see *through* them. You will see the grammarian through the guru, literature through technology, and the humanities through media. You will see through the literary origins of McLuhan's media studies, and, from there, you will set off on new explorations of your own. You will learn to apply McLuhan and understand why literature is not a subject but a function inseparable from our communal existence.

1 A Renewed Approach to Marshall McLuhan's Poetics

From Figure to Ground

The anthropologist Edmund (Ted) Carpenter, Marshall McLuhan's lifelong friend and colleague, wrote that 'knowledge of media alone is not sufficient protection from them,' a fact, he explained, that also applied to the man who taught us how to understand media: 'The moment Marshall McLuhan shifted from private media analyst to public media participant, he was converted into an image media manipulated & exploited.'[1] One-hundred years after his birth, we have now the occasion to return McLuhan from figure (his media image) to ground (the complex bringing together of his media investigations as well as his scholarly formation) by probing his mosaic and, through that, assessing the literary roots of all his discourses on media.

The year 2011 marked, in fact, the hundredth anniversary of McLuhan's birth; this occasion certainly brought renewed attention to both the man and his work, and a reappraisal of his theories and role as an intellectual in the twentieth century. The ensuing international setting of institutional, academic, scholarly, and public events offers a great opportunity to reconsider McLuhan as a whole. This situation is strongly encouraged by the technological age in which we are living now: the *electric age* that McLuhan started to explore from the early 1960s has evolved into our digital age and has become fully visible as an environment, so much so that today it is easier for us to access McLuhan's ideas than it was for those who read his books or listened to him in real time. We are familiar with McLuhan's name, we quote his *slogans* ('the medium is the message,' 'the global village'), and have accepted him as 'the high priest of popcult and metaphysician of media';[2] McLuhan and his slogans are in fact environmental elements of our digital realities. Against such a context, this volume offers instead a counter-environment to the overwhelming image of the media guru, retrieving McLuhan as a professor of English.

There are only a few studies on the same subject.[3] None of these studies, though, specifically investigates the making of McLuhan's mosaic in the light of precise literary models; nor do they propose comparisons of McLuhan and some major modernist writers through a cross-reading of media theories, pop culture, and other avant-garde experiments. Generally speaking, McLuhan's humanistic roots are constantly referred to as a fundamental ground for his media analysis, but critics seldom dig themselves into it. It is an enterprise full of labour, but it is a much needed one, as it can contribute to various fields of studies: not only media studies, but also modernist studies, cultural studies, literary studies and criticism, and, of course, communication studies. In most of these areas, in fact, we are witnessing an epistemological crisis, which often translates into the need to explore new approaches to old subjects in order to understand the making of new cultural and social matrixes worldwide. I trust that this volume will contribute to both the discussion and the development of new theoretical approaches by bringing together different signs and contexts, and therefore encouraging an ecological perspective not only to McLuhan or media studies but also to more traditional fields of knowledge. I would consider it a great achievement if this volume speaks to the curiosity of a general audience rather than just academics. But inside as outside the academic world, I approach communication not simply as an area of study – a subject – but as a human activity performing an essential function. Communication is first and foremost a social practice that involves each of us; and, in any communicative process, we want to actively master the cultural, social, artistic, political, and technological phenomena that constantly mould and change our different actualities. I also hope that my story in this book will bring students to stop enquiring about the number of pages, but to figure out instead the number of times they should have to read a novel to fully *make it function*.

This book is not written by a media theorist, my field of study being literature and literary criticism. I have approached McLuhan as a humanist exploring the electric age, that is, the age of *secondary orality*. *Secondary orality* is one in a series of terms (*electric age, Narcissus narcosis, rear-view mirror perspective, acoustic space, tactility*, and others) pertaining to the fields of McLuhan or media studies which I will be using in this volume and whose meaning will be unravelled step by step as my narrative progresses.

I have learned to use these terms myself, no matter my own field of study, because they well define our media environment. These terms should not be confined to specialists' domains but should be part of our common knowledge, because they help us to clarify and render our actuality. It is through language that McLuhan taught us how to understand the way new media reconfigure our world in the *image* of a global village. Through language, he probed how cultural, societal, and communicative dynamics shift inside a highly technological environment. Through language, he tried to awaken us and alert us to the difficulties of grasping the long-term effects of all technological innovations on our senses and on our realities. How was McLuhan able to 'see' and to 'understand' ahead of others, from the 1950s, situations which are all too obvious to us today? What turned him into a sagacious visionary or media prophet? My answers are precise. It was his humanistic background, his passion for literature, and his capability of developing a way of simultaneously *looking at* and *through* things based on his life-long training in the humanities.

By definition, a 'humanist' is: (a) a believer in the principles of humanism; (b) one who is concerned with the interests and welfare of humans; (c) a classical scholar; (d) a student of the liberal arts; (e) a Renaissance scholar devoted to humanism. McLuhan was all these definitions at once: he wrote his PhD dissertation on the English Renaissance, offering a deep analysis of the liberal arts of the trivium (grammar, rhetoric, dialectics); as an intellectual, he believed in the liberal and lay principles of humanism and was deeply concerned with the interests and welfare of humans in his own time. Being a humanist, McLuhan's ideas of *welfare* and *interest*, though, did not concern merely the material side of human existence, but also the intellectual and the emotional; his own interest in media derived from the need to fully understand the impact that evolving technological, cultural, and sociological processes were having on us humans. Freedom, independence, and free will result from knowledge and understanding of what is really going on around us, as he clearly assumes in the introduction to his first published book, *The Mechanical Bride* (1951).

As a humanist, McLuhan knew how to read books. A book is a system of signs and symbols carefully arranged, as all grammarians, rhetoricians, and dialecticians well know. Being a humanist living in the electric age, McLuhan used his knowledge of the liberal arts to read the signs and symbols of the new Book of Nature, 'to set the reader at the centre of the revolving picture created by these affairs [mechanical agencies of the press, radio, movies, and advertising] where he may observe the action that is in progress and in which everybody is involved.'[4] In his later writings, he was never as explicit again. From *The Gutenberg Galaxy* (1962) onward, he only shared his own *reading process* of the world. 'He repeated insistently that we should stop saying "Is this a good thing or a bad thing?" and start saying "What's going on?"'[5] As recalled by his son and collaborator Eric, as a humanist, he opted for Francis Bacon's *broken knowledge* and *aphorisms* – which he actualized through his thorough investigation of the great modernist masters – so to encourage his readers to enquire farther by themselves:

> Aphorisms, as Francis Bacon said, are incomplete, a bit like cartoons. They are not filled-out essay writing that is highly compressed. The aphorism is a poetic form that calls for a lot of participation on the part of reader. You have to chew on an aphorism and work with it for a while before you understand it fully ... My father deliberately chose this form of statement because he wanted to teach, not tell or entertain.[6]

McLuhan's broken knowledge aimed to turn his readers into active agents in the communication process, to develop their own reading strategies of the ongoing situations and, therefore, their own actions and reactions. It was his way to act in the interests and welfare of all humans.

The process of reading (a book, the world) is what is at stake here; and in McLuhan it transposes to the process of writing because his writing simply translates his reading process. While reading his writing, you also read the world or the situation he is processing: his mosaic is, in fact, a form which defines McLuhan as a 'post-secondary orality' humanist or media theorist – a definition which, in the following chapters, this volume posits and explores in the light of his scholarly background, as well as of his life-long curiosity concerning all human productions.

What Was THAT? McLuhan's 'Little Point'

In Henry James's novella 'The Figure in the Carpet,' Hugh Vereker, a renowned writer, tells the narrator (himself a writer who has just published a review of Vereker's last novel) that all his critics have missed his 'little point':

> By my little point I mean – what shall I call it? – the particular thing I've written my books most *for*. Isn't there for every writer a particular thing of that sort, the thing that most makes him apply himself, the thing without

the effort to achieve which he wouldn't write at all, the very passion of his passion, the part of the business in which, for him, the flame of art burns most intensely? Well, it's *that!*[7]

The 'thing for the critic to find,' insists Vereker is 'like a complex figure in a Persian carpet,' but he firmly refuses to tell the puzzled narrator what that figure looks like: he has to find it for himself. *Tormented* by the new challenge, the narrator starts his own search to no avail; he shares this puzzle with his friend George Corvick, who, instead, solves the mystery during a long trip to India and wires his fiancée, Gwendolyne, 'Eureka. Immense,' without saying 'what it is.' His secret discovery will be revealed only to Gwendolyne after they marry; a secret that Gwendolyne herself will preserve after her husband's premature death. Neither her second husband nor the narrator will ever be told 'what it is,' and they will both be left with their suspended curiosity after Gwendolyne's own death.

In 1996, when reading *The Gutenberg Galaxy* for the first time, I felt like the narrator in James's novella: it was an unusual, fascinating book, and though I could not *understand* most of it, nevertheless it *resounded* through me. The more I read it, the more it echoed in my mind: I knew there was something 'particular' in McLuhan's writing, but I continued to miss 'his little point'; I could not see his figure in the carpet. It was only several weeks later, while reading *The Interior Landscape: The Literary Criticism of Marshall McLuhan*, that I could shift to George Corvick's perspective and say: 'Eureka. Immense.' Reading McLuhan's literary criticism not only helped me to better understand the work of my favourite modernist masters (James Joyce, Wyndham Lewis, Ezra Pound are among those discussed in that book), but it also helped me to better understand 'what IT was' in *The Gutenberg Galaxy*: while reading their fiction and poetry, McLuhan had also started to read *through* the modernists' experiments with language and form; he had, in fact, *put them on*. He had so fully grasped their literary implications that he had used them to elaborate his own 'particular thing,' his own form of writing: the mosaic. *Well, it's THAT!*

When reading McLuhan, *form* is as important as *content*, just as it is when we read Joyce, Pound, Lewis, or Eliot. Translating THAT into *mcluhanese*, we could say that THE MEDIUM IS THE MESSAGE. As a literary and a modernist scholar, understanding McLuhan's teachings on literature, as well as on 'media as environments,' and to realize that those teachings had solid roots in his humanistic background was my epiphany.

As I later discovered when digging deeper into 'McLuhan Studies,' his years at Cambridge in the 1930s, his passion for literature and the arts, his appreciation of I.A. Richards's practical criticism, his true passion for the detective story as a genre, are facts acknowledged in various studies, biographies, and essays on Marshall McLuhan. And yet, mentioning Cambridge when discussing McLuhan has become a sort of semantic leitmotif, which nevertheless is not fully explored. All those who have written about McLuhan acknowledge that he was mad about books; we have come to know the authors he championed, and to recognize the importance of his humanistic background. However, we seem to still miss how all THAT played a major role in the making of McLuhan as a media scholar. In this book, I investigate this semantic leitmotif and show that McLuhan's literary roots are the substance of his original *poetics* as a media theorist or, even better, as a grammarian of media, as well as a media ecologist; in turn, they can become the substance of our own search, as citizens and ecologists, to understand the effects of our own mediascapes.

Pointing to Action: This Book

A renewed approach to McLuhan's *poetics* requires first of all acknowledging what we understand by the term *poetics*. My own understanding of this term follows Umberto Eco's definition of a poetics as the *operative project* that pervades a specific work and that leads to a given *form*, at once 'original' and 'traditional,' that is linked to other pre-existing forms.[8] Moving forward from this definition, I argue that Marshall McLuhan's *poetics* is far more complex than normally recognized, especially as far as *form* is concerned. Whereas his operative project is well known – to investigate the impact of new media on human consciousness and environment, so as to foresee, reveal, and eventually counterbalance the related side effects – the *form*, which shapes and gives new functional potential to such a project, is still underestimated. Not only is McLuhan's writing discontinuous; it also is pervaded by countless literary references and *exempla* derived from different artistic expressions. In reading his media analysis and investigations, one perceives that literature and the arts are playing a pivotal role in the shaping of McLuhan's writing technique. What might not be immediately evident is how that happens and for what purpose.

Literature and the arts, in fact, constitute a sort of constant *fil rouge*, a constantly unspooling thread, connecting in time McLuhan's media explorations. '*Mosaic*' or '*field approach*' is the term McLuhan himself employed to define these explorations. Mosaic was also his way of rendering them. That is his writing technique. In the following chapters, both these terms will be questioned and explored. As Donald F. Theall clearly acknowledged in his last book on McLuhan: 'What remains relatively unlearned from that figure [McLuhan's image as a "media guru" or as a "pop icon"], with its strengths and weaknesses as a pop poet bridging modernism and postmodernism, is the vital importance of the arts and literature and their history to the understanding of technology, culture, communication, artefacts and the processes of human perception. What he took to be most important was seldom perceived with the depth of understanding he would have wished. This is particularly true of the importance of arts and literature and the quintessential position he attributed to them as foreseeing the future.'[9] As a response to such a statement, my book investigates his form of writing as an operative tool stemming from the humanities and steering his own actuality.

In Part One of this book – 'The Mosaic' – I offer an investigation of McLuhan's form of writing, approached as a systemic cognitive tool through the unveiling of four different masks that, through time, we have put on Marshall McLuhan: the media oracle, the media guru, the modernist, the media/techno fan. This investigation cross-reads McLuhan's passion for the humanities in the light of his boundless intellectual curiosity, which embraced literature, the arts, anthropology, philosophy, and the hard sciences and social sciences alike. Further, it demonstrates that, since the early 1950s, McLuhan adapted the ancient *paideia*, or the process of educating individuals, to evolving new forms of communication, as well as to new forms of artistic expressions, as a way to read reality anew. As generally acknowledged by Donald F. Theall, Philip Marchand, Glenn Willmott, and Janine Marchessault, and Richard Cavell in their seminal though very different works on McLuhan,[10] ancient grammar, rhetoric, and dialectic are the basis of McLuhan's explorations. They combine with avant-garde experiments in a form which intends to transcend the limits of the printed page and to involve the reader in a new, dynamic vortex of situations and speculations. I will examine how the mosaic is conceived as an original 'verbo-voco-visual' form of writing (that is *acoustic* and not *linear*), at once involving the human sensorium not simply as a 'visual' experience, but as a 'tactile' (or participatory) process.

In Part Two – 'Modernist Ascendancies' – I will further investigate McLuhan's modernist roots in the context of the poetics of four main modernist writers: Ford Madox Ford, James Joyce, Ezra Pound, and Wyndham Lewis. As we will discover, each of these writers exemplifies a precise moment in the development of McLuhan's approach to media studies. Ford Madox Ford, the 'writers' writer,' stands as a gate opener: he introduced the idea of a *new form* to be searched and developed as a cognitive and conscious response to new societal matrixes. Ford taught McLuhan that form is as important as content, always insisting on the importance of studying and learning from other writers and intellectuals. James Joyce, the 'successful devotee of the rhetoric of the second sophists,'[11] helped McLuhan to forge new tools to explore reality, and to develop an *operative model* to the study of new environments: vivisection through language, understanding and epiphany through a playful and provocative combination of words. Ezra Pound, *the better craftsman*, showed McLuhan how to popularize the operative model through a clever combination of literature/art and popular forms of communication: from Confucius to crosswords, from Dante to The Press, he showed how to twist 'kulchur' to one's own *desiderata*. Finally, Wyndham Lewis, the enemy *par excellence* and the vorticist by nature, unveiled the substance of *new communicative processes* and offered a new theory of art as communication: he retrieved space against time and suggested how the Earth had now become ONE place, or, as McLuhan later said, 'a global village.' These chapters discuss how McLuhan came to develop his own style as a media scholar; they investigate his assertion in *The Interior Landscape* that provided the original epiphany that made me see McLuhan in a new light:

> After a conventional and devoted initiation to poetry as a romantic rebellion against mechanical industry and bureaucratic stupidity, Cambridge was a shock. Richards, Leavis, Eliot and Pound and Joyce in a few weeks opened the doors of perception on the poetic process, and its role in adjusting the reader to the contemporary world.
> *My study of media began and remains rooted in the work of these men.*[12]

What an amazing sentence that is! Take your time and read it over and over until its insightful simplicity resonates within you. The poetic process – literature, the arts, creative thinking – is McLuhan's preferred strategy for 'adjusting the reader to the contemporary world.' This idea constitutes the core of McLuhan's own *poetics*; it constitutes the principle that guided him in his complex attempt to read the world-in-progress. McLuhan found the tools for his explorations in communication through the literary and artistic tradition; it was his way of shaping his operative project and making it unique. It is therefore not by chance that in 1963 he called his new research centre at the University of Toronto 'Centre for Culture *and* Technology,' unequivocally linking the *two cultures*, the humanistic and the scientific, into a unique educational project. He pursued a strategy of exploration which is appreciated today as a prescient vision; however, it was much opposed at the time. Media ecology itself is a field of studies which originated in McLuhan's literary studies, and a field which was further explored and consolidated by scholars also sharing a humanistic approach to knowledge.

Finally, in Part Three – 'Applied McLuhan' – I will employ McLuhan's grand narrative on media and its operative model discussed in *Laws of Media* – the tetrad – as a strategy to cross-read literature and cinema, through an analysis of David Cronenberg's movie *Videodrome*, J.G. Ballard's novel *Crash*, and Cronenberg's film adaptation of the latter. It is my way of probing the making of the Marconi Galaxy through literary and media productions whose storytelling offers an interesting strategy to observe and identify, that is, to perceive and render, the making of two juxtaposing environmental situations. It also is a way to cross-read media, literary, and film studies as a way to mutually enlighten the development of evolving cultural models. In other words, it is a way to apply McLuhan to the humanities in the attempt to encourage an ecological approach to different fields of studies and communicative genres.

The above paragraphs introduce the operative strategy of my book. As far as form is concerned, I was tempted to employ McLuhan's discontinuous mode: after all, am I not writing this volume to praise McLuhan's mosaic and its potentialities? I then resolved to write in a more traditional way because my goal here is to make you *see*, to make you *hear*, and to make you *feel* and *think about* the literary origins of McLuhan's media studies. As I said before, as a literary scholar, I am genuinely interested in following the path connecting McLuhan's literary studies – and especially his investigations of some modernist masters – to his media explorations. I think that to probe McLuhan's *mosaic* constitutes a way to reinforce an apparently obsolete statement; namely, *literature matters*. It matters even in a world in which technological and economical forces seem to be the overwhelming factors. I want this message to reach my students, and I want this message to also reach politicians and decision-makers at a time when the humanities are first on the list of grant cutbacks. I do not want to achieve my goal by shocking or provoking my readers through a form which could be dismissed simply as being another McLuhanesque imitation, that is, an artificial verbal mockery somehow aping McLuhan's style. I am not so arrogant as to compare myself to McLuhan, and, after all, I have my own 'poetics.' (Not to mention the fact that, at present, not many in the control rooms of power appreciate the potentialities of artistic forms of communication, no matter how amusing or interesting they are.) *McLuhanese* is a language full of potential to achieve a better knowledge of our own actuality. But to appreciate such a language, you need first to be aware of and familiar with its etymology and grammar. This is what I will be discussing, and McLuhan himself will help me: the thread out of the maze is all his own. Throughout this volume, I will juxtapose quotations from his works, some of his puns and aphorisms, with my own writing in pursuit of a progression of effects leading to the true substance of McLuhan's mosaic and of his media studies. My hope is that my own writing strategy will help to shake off the forgetful snow from a few desks in the control rooms of power.

That said, before diving into McLuhan's vortex of words and exploring his so-called nonsensical prose, it is important to further dig and reveal the ground of my own approach to his poetics.[13]

Digging the Ground

One aspect of the 'myth' of Marshall McLuhan, central to the 1960s, was blown out of proportion: that of the eminent 'pop-philosopher,' the 'defender' or 'enthusiast' of the new electric media. Since he spoke of the end of the Age of Printing, it was generally assumed that he was an adversary of the Gutenberg Galaxy. This 'mythical construction' of the media guru is in fact a gross oversimplification, and it denies the complexity of his work – a complexity which is immediately recognized by readers who acknowledge that McLuhan was first and foremost a professor of English. As a professor, he was steeped in the Classics, and the Thomistic tradition, as well as the Romantic and the Symbolist achievements; as a professor, he was aware of the late modernists' formal experiments and used such experiments to give shape to his own 'formal frame.' McLuhan experimented in a unique way, combining in his sharp aphorisms an ancient oral tradition and a modern artistic search. McLuhan's detractors have been constantly perplexed or confused by his prose, by his hybrid style, and used it against him to also diminish his ideas on media. Most detractors referred to his language as 'nonsensical mcluhanese.'[14] I would rather call it McLuhan's *poetical prose*.

At the start of his career as an English professor, Marshall McLuhan wrote an anthology of poetry for high schools; a dissertation entitled 'The Place of Thomas Nashe in the Learning of His Time'; an Introduction to H. Kenner's *Paradox in Chesterton*; and essays entitled 'Pound, Eliot and the Rhetoric of *The Waste Land*,' 'Maritain on Art,' 'Poetic vs. Rhetorical Exegesis,' 'From Eliot to Seneca,' 'Kipling and Forster,' and 'Edgar Poe's Tradition' – a few of a very long list of titles that he published. This list in itself proves, as Eugene McNamara has written, that '… literature has mattered to Professor McLuhan … Despite the wider range of awareness implicit in his probes of the impact of new media on our modes of perception, the angle of vision, the interior landscape, remains the same. It is basically humanistic.'[15]

Literature matters. And it matters even more as a function than as a subject. McLuhan always used literature and the arts in at least two different yet complementary ways. As a media 'explorer,' he openly turned to *belles lettres* in order to prove his own statements; by so doing, he conferred to imaginative writing and visual arts the role of *exempla* from which to derive ideas and attitudes to be used as a better approach to perceive one's own time. As a literary critic, and as a professor of English, he investigated the formal achievements of different authors and poets, and related them to the new idea of 'sensibility' then evolving. McLuhan acted as a grammarian in search of new ways of observing and rendering ideas capable of counterbalancing the numbing effects of a constantly reshaping cultural environment.

Among the literary exempla he employed, the most famous is certainly the one I mentioned in my prologue; it derives from Edgar Allan Poe's 'A Descent into the Maelstrom,' and McLuhan already quotes it in the preface to *The Mechanical Bride*,[16] to introduce his method of observation. He would employ it throughout his life, over and over, as a metaphor to translate his approach to new media. For those who might not be familiar with it, let me recall the story of 'A Descent into the Maelstrom.' After the sinking of his small fishing boat and being thrown into the Maelstrom, a sailor manages to survive because he *stops to observe* the way the liquid vortex works. He notices that the spiralling water slowly swallows all objects; but he also notices that some objects hit the bottom and then flow upwards to the surface. He decides to grab onto an object that is floating upwards, and hold onto it as it spirals to the surface. By so doing, in spite of the danger and the unknown, the sailor adopts a new approach to a new situation, and saves himself: 'Poe's sailor saved himself *by studying the action* of the whirlpool and *by co-operating* with it.'[17]

Following a similar approach, from *The Mechanical Bride* onward, McLuhan studied the action of new media, cooperated with them, and tried to find strategies to counterbalance their overwhelming impact. From Poe's literature comes an example suggesting, through imagination, new possible strategies of perception and reasoning which, as he said, can help readers play 'at the centre of the revolving picture,' to 'observe the action that is in progress and in which everybody is involved,'[18] and to learn how to interact effectively with their own environment.

Hey, Marshall McLuhan, What Were You Doin'?

'Inherent in the artist's creative inspiration is the process of subliminally sniffing out environmental change.'[19] But the critic's (and reader's) task is to pour over every word, every statement, and work out its meaning. If it is true, as Ezra Pound wrote and as McLuhan believed, that 'literature is news that STAYS news,'[20] then it is vital for any critic to approach literature in a new way, as a probing instrument capable of alerting one to one's own environment. The modernist writers and poets were among the first to sniff out the ongoing change and to be alert to the risk of intellectual and cultural hypnosis. They tried to 'render their own time in the terms of their own time'[21] through a constant investigation of language, rhetoric, and artistic potentialities. For McLuhan, too, to find a form mirroring '[his] own time' became the challenge; in turn, the *mosaic* became his peculiar answer to that challenge.

As a whole, a mosaic creates a pattern in which the assembled components reveal an image which is larger than its parts. By cooperating with it, we can appreciate not only the final image, but also the way the various components have been assembled, that is, its art and craft. This is true also for McLuhan's *mosaic*: we must engage it to appreciate both its art and its craft to see its larger image. It is built upon discontinuous thoughts and relies on juxtaposing gaps which we have to approach with a new mental attitude. It relies on linguistic and conceptual combinations which are both playful and meaningful, as we shall later discover. Nevertheless, since the 1960s, the morphology of McLuhan's *mosaic* – combining literary references with anthropological, philosophical, and scientific observations, and discussing the effects of new media on various environments – has always triggered extreme and dichotomous reactions either *for* or *against*. Generally speaking, critics found McLuhan's ideas interesting and innovative, but they also found it difficult to cope with such a disruptive form of writing. In particular, critics reacted against McLuhan's lack of lexical coherence, against his use of analogy and discontinuity as opposed to the logic and linearity of traditional critical discourse.[22] They were also critical of his *puns* and *aphorisms*, often interpreted as verbal tricks used to disguise the lack of a precise and coherent point of view, and the absence of a serious scholarly background.[23] Yet, today, reading McLuhan's *mosaic*, taking into account the impact that modernist poetics had on it, as well as the implications of so-called 'discontinuous prose,' often related to postmodern critical and creative discourses, suggests the possibility of developing a new way of perceiving what was then dismissed as '*nonsensical mcluhanese.*' As Northrop Frye (McLuhan's 'antagonist' at the University of Toronto in the 1960s) noted:

> In the Sixties, both the anti-intellectuals who wanted to hear that they had only to disregard books and watch television to get with, and the activists pursuing terror for its own sake, found much to misunderstand in McLuhan. He was hysterically celebrated in the Sixties and unreasonably neglected thereafter ... So it is perhaps time for a sympathetic rereading ... and reabsorption of McLuhan's influence ... McLuhan raised questions that are deeply involved in any survey of contemporary culture, and in any attempt to define the boundaries of the emerging theory of society that I call 'criticism' in its larger context.[24]

Following Frye's suggestions, it is important to reconsider not only McLuhan's questions, but also his way of *articulating* them, since 'his criticism in its larger context' (as well as his more specific 'literary' criticism) is shaped and rendered in a new form: his *mosaic*.

As we shall see throughout this volume, from the structural point of view, the *mosaic* displays the same technique of discontinuity commonly considered typical of modernist (and, even more so, postmodernist) forms of narratology; in this sense, as both Theall and Willcott have agreed, McLuhan bridged modernism and postmodernism. As in all great modernist writers, McLuhan's writing process – his formal frame – is also an active part of the cognitive process. Again, like the modernist writers, McLuhan was a 'conscious writer,' aware of his rhetorical tools, and knew how to use them to achieve precise effects.[25] His prose was conceived to play with readers, not just trick or captivate them.

Yet, even today, for the general public and many academics, the mention of McLuhan's name immediately triggers a series of stereotyped responses which offer an overly simplified rendering of both the man and his ideas: the 'high-priest of pop-cult,' 'the global village,' and, of course, 'the medium is the message.' Unfortunately, each of these responses sounds more like a label than a real *image*, as Ezra Pound has defined it: 'An image is that which presents an intellectual and an emotional complex in an instant of time.'[26] Instead, they sound like formulas repeated to consolidate a given truth that no one bothers to question; taken together, they constitute a shared heritage based on perceptual clichés. In 'nonsensical mcluhanese,' they have turned into *figures* without a *ground*.

Those figures, that is, those clichés, have affected our reception of McLuhan, especially in Europe, where the slogans often appeared before the original books were available in translated editions.[27] Through time, the stereotyped responses have become the point of departure for all discussions about McLuhan and his ideas. In actuality, reading McLuhan's volumes is not even so important; what matters is to take a side pro or against him or, even, to metabolize the received responses in order to then reverse or trivialize their implications. It is an old story: from archetype to cliché, a sort of 'one-way road' leading from original statements to crystallized interpretations used to interpret both the messenger and his message.

Oh, What a Seer He Was!

Let's try and reassess McLuhan's role both as a man of letters and as a media scholar by replacing the old interpretative 'pop-clichés' with more articulated literary terms. This will permit me to introduce a different viewpoint from which we can later approach his media explorations and his experiments with form and language. Given his understanding of modernism, the image of T.S. Eliot's Tiresias in *The Waste Land* is particularly apt for that purpose, that is, to discuss McLuhan as a man of letters witnessing the making of a highly technological mass society. In this poem, Eliot re-elaborates classic myths to alert us to what the poet sees as the present-day condition of human beings; the crowd flowing over London Bridge in the first part of the poem stands, in fact, as a sad metaphor for a lost humanity marching towards a future which looks as desolate as the waste land around them. In particular, the figure of Tiresias – the prophet of Apollo who was transformed into a woman for seven years before regaining his masculinity, who was turned blind by Athena after he had seen her naked, and who was then compensated by the same goddess with the gift of clairvoyance – appears at the very core of the poem as the blind seer who speaks in the voice of integrity and reveals 'the substance of the poem':

At the violet hour, when the eyes and back
Turn upward from the desk, when the human engine waits
Like a taxi throbbing waiting,
I Tiresias, though blind, throbbing between two lives,
Old man with wrinkled female breasts, can see ...

In his sad vision, Tiresias sees a scene of ordinary life, the encounter of a typist and a 'young carbuncular man,' engaging in a dinner based on food in tins and leading to a sexual intercourse based on indifference. As T.S. Eliot himself explains in his notes to his work, Tiresias is the central character in his poem, the one who provides meaning and cohesion among the five sessions.[28] I borrow Eliot's rendering of Tiresias and his notes to introduce McLuhan as a *classic* intellectual, well trained and educated in the old style, but living in a new electric era which he explored. Although he was a mere spectator, he nevertheless became the *seer* alerting those who were looking without seeing, and who were hearing without listening. McLuhan, too, did not tell if what he saw was good or bad; he only showed and probed what was going on.

Contrary to Tiresias, though, McLuhan's foresight was not a goddess's gift, but the result of a specific sensorial training acquired through years of studies and of practice as a professor of English teaching younger generations of would-be literary 'geeks.' Conscious of the existing linguistic and cultural barrier between himself and his students, McLuhan started to learn the grammar of the new age and to approach the reality of new media as if it were a text. It is therefore more appropriate to speak, not of 'prophecies,' but of 'explorations' when discussing his works. Like Tiresias, McLuhan was not distracted by sight; like Tiresias, he learned how to rely on other senses as well. He was not affected by the perceptive disease that he called the Narcissus Narcosis:

The youth Narcissus mistook his own reflection in the water for another person. This extension of himself by mirror numbed his perceptions until he became the servomechanism of his own extended or repeated image ... He was numb. He had adapted to his extension of himself and had become a closed system.[29]

McLuhan was not distracted by the mirror effect, he was not mesmerized by extended or repeated images. Like the blind Tiresias, he was aware of the system as a whole because he perceived it as an evolving process. Combining this assumption with the literary image makes us appreciate

McLuhan as a 'seer.' McLuhan/Tiresias, *though blind, can see* things that other people can no longer (or not yet) see, as they are themselves made blind or numbed, *that is,* 'suspended in their understanding' ('... *when the human engine waits* ...') by a society which is in between two moments ('... *at the violet hour* ... ,' the twilight), rapidly moving from the mechanical to the electric age, that is, from the literate to the post-literate age. Their blindness is a paradoxical consequence of their preserving a more *visual* approach to their environment at a time when new media are turning it into a more and more *acoustic* one: they still rely on *the eye* rather than on *the ear.* They have lost a harmonious balance among all senses and are distracted by their own distorted visions. On the contrary, McLuhan/Tiresias has chosen to play with the new situation and dives into the new media-induced acoustic space; he replaces the eye with the ear and perceives and renders new phenomena through a renewed interplay of the other senses. He has learned from the poets to open his 'doors of perception' and to grasp the ground behind the figure. The limit, the handicap ('... *though blind* ...'), is turned into an exploratory tool; it is flipped into its reverse, as per one of McLuhan's four laws of media: What does a medium produce or become when pressed to an extreme? It flips into its reverse.[30] McLuhan/Tiresias is therefore urged to develop new ways to perceive his times and to render the results of his explorations: he chooses discontinuity (Francis Bacon's aphorisms, or T.S. Eliot's 'fragments'), simultaneity, and analogy as opposed to linearity and perspective; he retrieves the oral (tribal) circle and dismisses the visual (Renaissance) line. It is a change which enables him 'to see': '*I Tiresias, though blind, ... can see* ...'

The image of Tiresias also introduces McLuhan's role, not as a media *explainer,* but as a media *explorer.* Tiresias stands for the atavistic symbol of curiosity, the challenge to given knowledge; he stands for the artist investigating old situations through new cognitive and emotional patterns. Having been both a man and a woman, Tiresias embodies the androgynous, a mythical incarnation which brings the opposites together ('... *throbbing between two lives* ...'), male and female ('... *old man with wrinkled female breasts* ...'), reason and instinct, and therefore feels and perceives the infinite: Tiresias *can see.* In *The Waste Land,* Tiresias's vision is somehow apocalyptic and seems to implicitly acknowledge the impotence of the artist facing the making of the new mass society. Even though Tiresias perceives the scene and foretells the rest, he cannot stop the crowd flowing over London Bridge, marching towards their alienated destiny. Tiresias stands for a world which is confronting change, but he himself cannot halt such a change, nor can he force people to act one way or the other; whatever he wishes the world could be, he is there to show that world *as it is.* In a similar way, McLuhan – who candidly confessed to his interviewers that, generally speaking, he did not like change – was aware of the ongoing change. He refused to go with the flow and observed the movement from a still outpost: literature, the humanities.

In T.S. Eliot's poem, the *food in tins* laid out by the *typist* in Tiresias's vision is a metonymical object, that is, an object standing for a whole mass society now rendered as a by-product of new cultural, technological, and political forces which the seer can only foretell. A few years later, artist Andy Warhol will further explore that same metonymy in his famous paintings of cans of Campbell soup. Writing after Eliot and before Warhol, in *The Mechanical Bride,* McLuhan too criticizes mass society as a by-product of various agencies. Advertising, cartoons, market surveys, the press, cars, and machines are the elements forming the folklore of the industrial man that McLuhan ironically reveals and deconstructs while trying to instill a critical attitude in his readers. It is a sort of positive and playful challenge which we do not always find in the modernist works, where fear and contempt for the emerging mass society often prevail; it is also a unique moment in McLuhan's works, as he later will focus only on the dynamics of change and not on its moral evaluation. It is important to stress once more that after *The Mechanical Bride,* McLuhan dropped all judgments and concentrated on the complexity of the processes induced by new media, now explored through language and with an artist-like attitude. By so doing, he moved in the opposite direction from the crowd that, in T.S. Eliot's *Waste Land,* is flowing over London Bridge and appears like the living dead; he decided to be in the moment, to fully inhabit the present:

> McLuhan recognised that most people live in the rearview mirror – moving ahead in time but actually living in the past. 'People never want to live in the present' he said. 'People live in the rearview mirror because it's safer … They've been there before, they feel comfortable.' For McLuhan, the key to understanding the future was simply to focus on the present.[31]

McLuhan illuminated the future by perceiving the present; he read through the more visible clichés to reach the hidden archetypes. However, it is unfair to just condemn the crowd for moving along the safer path provided by shared clichés. Clichés are the common patterns of our age, which often translate into *revivals* and repetitions of ideas and situations.

Reducing something too complex down to something more accessible and universally recognizable reassures us. It has always been like that. As both Eric Havelock and Walter J. Ong have argued,[32] to read what is still unknown to us – whether an object or a more abstract experience or a feeling – through what we already know by naming it in a familiar way is a process which accomplishes a fundamental mimesis and performs a cohesive social function. However, if we are not well equipped to question and appreciate the substance of the cliché, our critical attitude can easily be turned into (or deceived by) commonly accepted views, that is, received ideas; and, as Matthew Arnold taught us, received ideas can lead to cultural and intellectual mediocrity. We cannot but acknowledge that, in time, accepted ideas are less reassuring for the crowd than for the corporate agencies which, in fact, control the flow of information. We have therefore an additional reason to return McLuhan's *slogans* to their true substance as *aphorisms*.

The Electric/Eclectic Humanist

Together with Wilfred Watson, McLuhan wrote a book called *From Cliché to Archetype*,[33] which, as Philip Marchand explained, considered the ways in which clichés flip into archetypes and vice-versa; the book 'attempted to articulate the process whereby those clichés retrieved from the scrap heap of the past became archetypes of the present.'[34] Consistently, McLuhan always tried to resist hollowing out words; he made a big effort, and took pleasure, in challenging what was commonly and too easily accepted, or proven. As a humanist, he inverted the direction and moved constantly towards the archetype, so much so that his so-called slogans are, in fact, polysemic aphorisms built upon a precise combination of words. Ironically, it was the wider *ground*, namely, his cultural context, forged more and more by evolving forms of instantaneous information, which proved detrimental to a more profound investigation of his witty prose. In the age of instantaneous information, the process was reversed once more, and McLuhan's learned puns were turned into slogans for that very age; he was 'converted into an image media manipulated & exploited,' recalls Carpenter.

Let's reverse that process. In the 1930s, as a student at Cambridge University, McLuhan investigated the potentialities hidden in the use of language. Writing his PhD dissertation on 'The Place of Thomas Nashe in the Learning of His Time,'[35] he began to discuss the progress of the liberal arts and of the *trivium* from pre-Socratic philosophers to English

Renaissance. From the time of his doctoral work to his university professorship in the United States and then in Canada, he wrote several literary essays, most of them on proto-modernist or modernist masters; however, he also published essays and a book on American advertising.[36] Similarly, in the period 1953–7, he was one of the editors of an interdisciplinary journal, *Explorations*, envisaging 'a series that will cut across the humanities and social sciences by treating them as a continuum.'[37] The essays McLuhan published in this journal show him using his literary background to investigate the new media environment. Thus, from the very beginning, literary criticism has been a fundamental component of McLuhan's ecological, eclectic, and probing approach to media analysis.

The above helps to understand why, inside the domain of media studies, media ecology is the only field that places McLuhan at its centre. Even though, as Casey Man Kong Lum writes, 'media ecology is the cumulation of the collective wisdom of many thinkers from many disciplines ... [and the] intellectual whole of media ecology is greater than the sum of its theoretical parts,'[38] Marshall McLuhan is commonly accepted as one of the founding fathers. Lum himself acknowledges that 'in a personal communication (March 1999), Postman credited McLuhan as the first person to use the term,' while indicating Postman as 'the person to first use it publicly.'[39] However, more important than establishing a philology of the term, is the realization that McLuhan stays at the centre of media ecology because his humanistic approach to media and society made him appreciate and explore 'media as environment,' that is, 'ecologically.' As Lum convincingly argues in his historiography of media ecology, that field emerged as a 'Theory Group' or as an 'Invisible College'[40] in the wake of scholars such as McLuhan, Postman, and Ong, whose works and ideas attracted other scholars also sharing a humanistic approach to knowledge. As an invisible college first, and as a university program at NYU's School of Education later, from the 1960s the media ecology group encouraged and consolidated interdisciplinary forms of investigation and research in line with those that McLuhan had started to pursue with Carpenter and others through the journal *Explorations*. His humanistic approach became his trademark in the field; so much so that media ecologists have named him 'The Modern Janus' who 'looks both to the past and future and unites them in a common vision':

His methods are really an outgrowth of the education in Practical Criticism he received at Cambridge in the 1930s, which he applied ever afterward in trying to get people to recognize all technologies as media and all media as uttering or extensions of ourselves. Once they are thus perceived, we can have some control over them, just as we can rhetorically control our other utterances. Rather than being a prophet of a New Age of media bliss, McLuhan used poetic technique and provided the probe, figure-ground analysis, and the tetrad as a heuristic for determining the effects of media change, so as to anticipate and counteract the worst of them.[41]

As James C. Morrison clearly points out in the above passage, the roots of McLuhan's original poetics are already revealed in his doctoral dissertation on Thomas Nashe. The peculiarity of this work lies in the fact that the history of the *trivium* is narrated from the point of view of the grammarian, because 'exposition and interpretation of stated doctrines are grammatical problems; and derivative philosophy and almost all histories of philosophy are the product of grammarians.'[42] Again, in *Laws of Media*, a volume conceived together by Marshall and his son Eric and published posthumously in 1988, you read that 'the *trivium* is our concern: all three of its elements are arts and sciences of language.'[43] Both quotations invite us to turn to the professor of English who managed to use his well-learned humanistic background from the very beginning to the very end of his scholarly life. While at Cambridge, following the example of I.A. Richards and F.R. Leavis, he investigated the precepts of practical criticism. He constantly considered all sorts of art productions, all literary and artistic *signs* – high and pop culture were perceived as man's 'artefacts' alike – as phenomena both produced by and returning to a precise environment, as *figures* at once deriving from and reshaping a much wider *ground*. His intention was to contribute to a cultural Renaissance opposing mediocrity and accepted ideas, inviting his readers to share the responsibility of living in a world constantly remade by technological change.

McLuhan's mosaic is therefore shaped by two important concepts that, combined with his formative background, deeply pervade his way of functioning, his *modus operandi*. Curiously, these two concepts themselves constitute the foundations of both the traditional scientific method and the artistic one, although this may not be immediately obvious when applied to McLuhan. I am referring to the concepts of *observation* and *identification* in the sciences, that is, *perception* and *rendering* in the arts.

McLuhan's *observation* and *identification*, his ways of *perceiving* and *rendering* his world, somehow straddle both the sciences and the humanities. They are built upon an artist-like use of imagination, intuition, and language; however, he applied them with a probing (and playful) attitude to all cognitive fields, to all forms of knowledge, to all media (generally taken as both products and extensions of man and of his faculties). As Derrick de Kerckhove has pointed out, McLuhan explored 'an area of knowledge usually reserved to human sciences through artistic methods and through the articulation of language.'[44] It is exactly *the articulation of language* which is important in McLuhan's *mosaic*. In this context, language is to be understood as an *arché* unifying *forma et substancia* (literally *form* and *substance*), thus becoming the cognitive agent which shaped his original aphoristic style, at once combining an ancient knowledge with avant-garde formal experiments. McLuhan was a humanist acting inside the electric age, pursuing an eclectic approach to knowledge and actuality, collecting materials from various fields and cultural languages; his holistic and inclusive approach to mobile situations (often dismissed as trivial generality) aimed to reveal new social patterns, that is, to point to the various larger figures in the carpet. Consistently, his form of communication was *humanistic*, at once *eclectic* and *electric*: he borrowed from literary and artistic traditions, and elaborated his findings into an original discourse whose fuzzy syntax puzzled those who could not chew on his aphorisms.

Learning the Grammar

The stamp of nonsensical mcluhanese, often used to denigrate McLuhan's form of writing, might stem from a peculiar, if not biased, approach to the work of the Canadian critic. Rigorous theoreticians have discriminated against McLuhan by choosing to hone in on the eccentricity of his critical analysis and evaluations. At the same time, McLuhan's explicit eclecticism or *generalism* has often been openly opposed to scholarly precision and method. In short, critics preferred to approach his mosaic academically, applying consolidated scholarly paradigms of reading and writing and dismissing the formal novelty as nonsense. Perhaps we might get the same kind of response if we approached Joyce's *Finnegans Wake* assuming it was George Eliot's *Middlemarch*.

To understand McLuhan's *grammar*, we have to start by questioning our approach to his writing. Let us decide to dive into the 'nonsensical prose' and cooperate with it. To do that, let us acknowledge first that McLuhan's passion for language and its cognitive aspects[45] urged him to experiment with new rhetorical strategies, combining intellectual and emotional aspects. After all, at Cambridge, McLuhan had studied with I.A. Richards, the critic who had theorized[46] the distinction between 'scientific truth or statement' and 'emotive utterance':

It will be admitted – by those who distinguish between scientific statements, where truth is ultimately a matter of verification as this is understood in the laboratory, and emotive utterance, where 'truth' is primarily acceptability by some attitude, and more remotely is the acceptability of this attitude itself – that it is not the poet's business to make scientific statements. Yet poetry has constantly the air of making statements, and important ones; which is one reason why some mathematicians cannot read it. They find the alleged statements to be false. It will be agreed that their approach to poetry and their expectations from it are mistaken.[47]

In the same essay, Richards underlines how words operate at once as sensorial stimuli and as symbols. He affirms that they form the tools that the poet must use to 'give order and coherence; that is, freedom to a set of experience.' Words are 'the skeleton,' the 'structure by which the impulses which make up the experience are adjusted to one another and act together.'[48] In his book *McLuhan, or Modernism in Reverse*, Glenn Willmott gives extensive proof that both Richards and Leavis had a major impact on McLuhan's thought.[49] If we apply Richards's idea of *poetical truth* to McLuhan's *nonsensical writing* in that context, and assume that McLuhan's statements require first an emotive response and only then a rational analysis, it becomes evident that in some readers the gap between the *form* of the communication and the *method* of perception has caused heuristic potentialities implicit in McLuhan's language to be missed (as well as mistaken). To recover these potentialities, we must accept his writing as a new genre of critical discourse, a sort of *hybrid pastiche* releasing new energy when we cooperate with it. By juxtaposing more traditional statements to aphoristic lines and puns, the mosaic joyfully retrieves the ancient pedagogical and formative properties of both literature and the arts.

We have to remember that McLuhan considered the media environment as a man-made artefact which has precise effects on the individuals who live in it (and through it), and which must be perceived as any other artefact: 'The new media are not bridges between man and nature: they are nature.'[50] Consistently, since the early 1950s, McLuhan insisted on the fact that it was necessary to apply 'the method of art analysis to the critical evaluation of society.'[51] From the very beginning, the *form* shaping his writing was conceived according to artistic paradigms: readers are asked to actively interact with each line, with each sentence, with each juxtaposition, in order to work out the first and most obvious level of meaning (the evident cliché or slogan), as well as the hidden levels (the larger pattern, the figure in the carpet, *that* 'little point'). In McLuhan, as in all poetry, readers are part of the process of communication; they take their place at 'the centre of the revolving picture'[52] in a printed environment which, as we shall see, is nevertheless very similar to the one induced by new media. As McLuhan pointed out in a famous letter he wrote to Harold Adam Innis in the 1950s: 'The whole tendency of modern communications whether in the press, in advertising or in the high arts is towards *participation in a process*, rather than apprehension of concepts.'[53]

According to Willmott, 'McLuhan developed a critical theory in the 1940s and 1950s which negotiated between higher modernism and American consumer society, and which found its model in [Eisenstein's] theory of cinema,' among others.[54] The underpinning idea is that our artificial world can be better perceived through a montage that suggests complex articulations embedded in the formal frame. McLuhan, after Poe, called it *pattern recognition*, a process which starts with a *poetic approach*, that is, with our acceptance of emotive utterances, which can be analysed afterwards. Richards argues:

> In the poetic approach the relevant consequences are not logical or to be arrived at by partial relaxation of logic. Except occasionally and by accident logic does not enter at all. The relevant consequences are those which arise through our emotional organization. The acceptance which a pseudo-statement receives is entirely governed by its effects upon our feeling and attitudes. Logic only comes in, if at all, in subordination, as servant to our emotional response.[55]

In a high-tech environment, the notion of taking into consideration 'our emotional response' as a possible point of departure to understand reality seems a bit odd. However, it has become more and more difficult to rationally master and process the amazing amount of data we continue to receive through media. As soon as we learn how to approach bits of information, they are already obsolete; each time we concentrate on what looks like useful details, we risk missing the whole ground surrounding and producing them. Unfortunately but inevitably, we often respond to the increasing information overload by scanning it or browsing through it. Our selection is seldom the result of careful stock-taking; more often, due to time constraints and the massive amount of data, we do not dig into the information flows, but surf them. Literally, *we stay on the surface of things*.

Being ready to learn strategies for approaching new data and new environments in a different way can surprise us and offer an unexpected way out. Poe's sailor himself was astonished by the playful element in his new strategy of observation that enabled him to survive. While recalling it, McLuhan insists that to apply a poetic approach to new artificial landscapes becomes an appealing and often amusing strategy through which we can indeed overcome the 'Narcissus narcosis.' It could guide us out of the media maze and counter cultural hypnoses; it can teach us how to move from cliché to archetype.

Like Ford Madox Ford, whom McLuhan learned to appreciate through Ezra Pound, the Canadian critic has often been accused of inaccuracy as far as his sources and data are concerned. However, if we take the emotional response as our point of departure, it is no longer so relevant if McLuhan reinterprets facts and turns them into new anecdotes or puns. Instead, it becomes more important to take into consideration the effects of his *mosaic*, of his peculiar *discourse*, on us as imaginative readers. It also becomes more important to investigate *how* McLuhan appeals to our emotional organization and, consequently, to our ability to turn the original emotion or intuition into a strategy, into data, into ideas, into *our own original way of thinking*. After all, Ford Madox Ford himself used to repeat that a critical attitude is best achieved through 'indirect means': the mosaic does not teach us *what* to see, think, or believe; instead, it teaches us *how* to engage with complexity by making us participate in the process of discovery.

Post-literate 'Paideia'

As new media-induced environments reshape us, affecting our sociological and anthropological constructs, we, in turn, must rethink our traditional ways of perceiving and rendering linear and sequential categories into simultaneous and discontinuous ones. But, at the same time, we must find a way to recompose bits of information into a complex, intelligible pattern. The *mosaic* aims precisely at that. It is conceived as 'the only practical means of revealing causal operations in history,'[56] and McLuhan uses his *mosaic* to question traditional ideas of *knowledge* and to move the reader from a *linear* (logical, ordered, exclusive) to an *acoustic* (non-logical, simultaneous, inclusive) perspective.

Yet, from the point of view of many of the specialists who were looking at the same world, but who shared a different idea of knowledge, McLuhan made an explicit and unforgivable mistake. He crossed the borders of different domains without exhibiting the right passport. He turned upside-down what had been effectively established by centuries of serious schooling, suggesting new modes of exploration based on the shocking association of apparently disparate ideas and topics. He experimented with interdisciplinarity before interdisciplinary studies were the fashion. And, even worse, he appeared to enjoy it! Most critics accused him of being too enthusiastic about all that was new; quite ironically, he was in fact acting on the basis of very ancient and traditional paradigms. As we will discover, in the never-ending battle of books, McLuhan stood for the ancients, not for the moderns, because his idea of knowledge was rooted in the arts of the *trivium* and was strongly shaped by a grammarian's approach. His media theories derive, in effect, from that knowledge of the trivium and are developed through its application. 'By surpassing writing we have regained our WHOLENESS, not on a national or cultural but cosmic plane,'[57] he wrote, as early as 1954. Being a grammarian, McLuhan's vocation was to explore such wholeness, looking for *connections through differences* acting on a cosmic plane.

McLuhan elaborated a new way of looking at our habitat. He combined his scholarly background and knowledge of contemporary literature and art, including the new pop culture, to explore what was going on around him and to alert his readers to the ongoing cultural processes. Starting with *The Mechanical Bride*, he showed us that only an *integrated approach* brings together the different domains which contribute to our understanding of the *wholeness* of the then electric, and now Internet and digital, age. Consistently, he insisted that in the information age, the specialist is an anachronism, someone who, according to him, 'never makes small mistakes while moving toward the grand fallacy.'[58] He reconsidered the idea of education and refused the compartmentalized academic methods of investigation, since they no longer mirrored the new reality. To observe the electric simultaneity through the rear-view mirror of linearity would imply relying upon a distorted version of reality. For McLuhan, the time had come to change spectacles and adopt new lenses. What is fascinating to discover is that McLuhan's *new spectacles* were in fact the ancient trivium.

In his books, McLuhan applies the modernist lesson and uses avant-garde experimental works to explore and draw parallels between the new media-induced landscape and ancient forms of societies and educational patterns. *The Gutenberg Galaxy*, for example, retrieves some of the tenets explored in his doctoral dissertation, as well as Bacon's lesson, and establishes the *mosaic* as a form at once retrieving and triggering knowledge.[59]

At the same time, in his public lectures, he continuously discussed the role of education in a mass society. In particular, he encouraged a 'totally new approach'[60] leading to a 'global education program that will enable us to seize the reins of our destiny.'[61] Such a program would serve, not to homogenize people's thought ('to win consent,' in Bacon's words), but, on the contrary, to induce a critical attitude to media in general. McLuhan considered higher education as the necessary tool to counterbalance cultural homologation; by higher education, he meant a *classic* education. The ancient *paideia*, a Greek term meaning 'to educate,' is associated with the idea of a rounded cultural education pursued in the light of a public life engaged in the public good and interest. *Paideia* is therefore the tool that McLuhan postulated as the only one capable of counterbalancing the subliminal effects of new media on the human sensorium. For McLuhan, literature and the arts were the instruments through which the ancient *paideia* could be retrieved. His laws of media are based on such pedagogical principles and form a post-literate tool enhancing *paideia*. As I will discuss later, they are a carefully conceived system of observation based on the combined action of the *trivium*, with a special emphasis on the 'evocative power' of words.

McLuhan's *mosaic* is fully inscribed within such an educational philosophy; it challenges the idea that knowledge proceeds through a progressive line and refutes the idea that new knowledge results from the mere accumulation of data and concepts. As a discontinuous form, the mosaic forces readers to shift from a visual (linear) to an acoustic (all-at-once) perspective; by so doing, the mosaic teaches us to acquire a simultaneous vision of multiple phenomena, all acting simultaneously, in the here and now, and constantly affecting each other.

Setting McLuhan's mosaic and his educational philosophy in his own time, we can recognize that he had set off on a very difficult mission. His most celebrated books (*The Gutenberg Galaxy*, 1962; *Understanding Media*, 1964) came out just a few years before the countercultures of the 1960s exploded worldwide. Knowledge was instrumental to the preservation of traditional institutions; the classroom was a place where you went to listen to your teachers and to learn notions by the book and not to question them. In the 1960s, when McLuhan established his famous Monday-night seminars at the Coach House, at the University of Toronto, his classroom looked instead like an *agora*, a *piazza*, rather than a traditional classroom. His lessons were not conceived as a lecturer's one-way monologues, but as *probes* challenging students and listeners to think about his media observations; as a professor, he wanted to *turn them on*. Those who attended his seminars still remember them as both engaging and entertaining; also, they recall how, a few years later, when McLuhan had become renowned worldwide, they attracted VIPs and many celebrities to the Coach House. At the Centre, McLuhan and his notorious guests urged the students to provocatively join them in their explorations. He invited them to approach literature and the arts as tools facilitating the sensorial and cognitive shift from the ivory tower to the control tower. What McLuhan suggested in those seminars is that curiosity and creativity are the perfect antidote to all fear of change. He often reminded them of Poe's sailor, of his adventure in the maelstrom, and of the way he used rational detachment and amusement to overcome terror.

Our amusement and our visions rely upon our will to play the game. Humour played a central role in the elaboration of McLuhan's poetics. Verbal and conceptual playfulness pervades all his books and interviews, contributing to the accusation that he lacked scholarly integrity, rigour, and method. Inevitably, inherent to this poetical mosaic is the acceptance of serious play with its suspended logic. After all, when we observe a painting by Franz Marc or read a book by Lewis Carroll, we know there are no blue horses, no speaking rabbits; and yet, it is through the suspension of disbelief and through one's association with remote and discordant events that an epiphany takes place.

From Integral Awareness to Storytelling

McLuhan ventured with an artist-like attitude into a new territory, seeking objective correlatives to express his experiences of it:

> When Sputnik went around the planet, nature disappeared, nature was hijacked right off the planet, nature was enclosed in a man-made environment and art took the place of nature. Planet became art form.[62]

In fact, while speaking as a scholar, McLuhan nevertheless behaved as an *artist* challenging the given rules. He knew that 'the artist cannot be the prudent and decorous Ulysses, but appears as a sham. As sham and mime he undertakes not the ethical quest but the quest of the great fool. He must become all things in order to reveal all. And to be all things he must empty himself.'[63] Consistently, he insisted that 'at play man uses all his faculties; at work he specializes.'[64] This aphorism is, in fact, the synthesis of a complex philosophy of education which McLuhan derived from his study of the *trivium* and from St Thomas Aquinas. According to St Thomas, in fact, intuition, that is, the *simplex apprehensio* – the first, pure, original, and even irrational perception of a new idea – comes better to minds cleared from too specialist *a priori* biases. Only afterwards can man start to reflect on this intuition through thought and reasoning, and thus move to the *reflexio ad phantasmata* phase, literally turning back to sense images. The final *giudizio* – the final conception, statement, or truth – is in fact shaped through this careful process of probing and testing the first intuition by means of *fantasie*, fantasies expressed through words. A playful attitude facilitates our intuition, stimulating pattern recognition and helping us to open up our doors of perception. It also helps us to approach knowledge with an *inclusive* rather than exclusive attitude.

Through his daily investigations, McLuhan encouraged an interdisciplinary cross-reading of the humanities and sciences; he opposed disciplinary boundaries and subdivisions which, in fact, stood as old, anachronistic ways of looking at the new environment, preventing us not only from seeing but also from understanding what was happening right under people's noses. Instead, McLuhan's playful descent into the electric maelstrom enabled him to reveal the ongoing reversal of a process which, starting from the Middle Ages, had brought writing, and then printing, to contain, control, and shape language, communication, and – inevitably – thought, since words are metaphors uttering our inner world. McLuhan perceived the reversal of literacy into post-literacy and the secondary orality launched by the electric media. It took centuries to move from orality to literacy, but less than a century to shift into the secondary orality of instantaneous information. McLuhan's critical agenda was to point out that the arts, literature, and higher education were key factors for understanding that shift and its implications. His definition of the artist, in fact, stems from a solid conviction that the artist is a person who grasps the consequences of his observations and actions; it is based on his (ancient) idea of post-literate *paideia*:

> The artist is the man *in any field, scientific or humanistic*, who grasps the implications of his actions and of new knowledge in his own time. He is the man of integral awareness.[65]

McLuhan proposes here a way to overcome the traditional dichotomy that opposes C.P. Snow's two cultures, sciences and humanities. *Integral awareness*, embedded in the artist image, is an attitude profitable for all scholars, all people, men and women, in *any field*. Each term in the quotation is carefully chosen in order to convey the potentialities embodied by such an image: *Integral*, that is, unifying *forma* and *substancia*, form and substance, ground and figure, at once connecting all things and being all things; but also, at a deeper level, 'integral' means untouched, pure, entire, intact, as to suggest an unbiased, childlike attitude of approaching knowledge, displaying both curiosity and playfulness. *Awareness*, that is, the alert condition which should be shared by anyone engaged in any form of investigation. Finally, the *artist* image, itself the symbol of a new *forma mentis*, based also on the use of imagination as a passe-partout attitude opening all doors leading to the discovery of the new environmental dynamics.

Sir Peter B. Medawar, a biologist who won the Nobel Prize for Medicine in 1960, wrote:

> Imagination is the energizing force of science as well as of poetry ... To adopt a conciliatory attitude, let us say that science is that form of poetry (going back now to its classical and more general sense) in which reason and imagination act together synergistically. This simple formal property ... represents the most important methodological discovery of modern thought.[66]

Here, Sir Medawar himself retrieves the idea of a common ground between the sciences and humanities, based on the fact that reason and imagination forge both poetical perception and scientific observation; it is in the process of identifying and rendering that the two fields seem to diverge. 'We all tell stories,' continues Sir Medawar, 'but the stories differ in the purposes we expect them to fulfil and in the kinds of evaluations to which they are exposed.'[67]

As previously noted, I.A. Richards spoke of 'scientific truth or statement' and 'poetical truth or pseudo-statement,' asserting that the former needs to be proved, while the latter is accepted for what it is. Yet *statement* seems to implicitly suggest that there is a deeper and fundamental level in which reason and imagination, sciences and humanities, scientific truth and poetical truth, meet. This deeper level is language, or – even better – *storytelling*. As Sir Medawar reminds us: 'We all tell stories.'

Words are the most unique man-made artefacts, and language and the stories we tell act as the unifying agent:

> Words are complex systems of metaphors and symbols that translate experience into our uttered or outered senses. They are a technology of explic-

itness. By means of translation of immediate sense experience into vocal symbols, the entire world can be evoked and retrieved at any instant.[68]

This is an idea Marshall McLuhan – the *electric* grammarian, a modern Janus – took from the ancient doctrine of the Logos, also known as the Doctrine of Names, the founding language for both physics and metaphysics. Together with his son Eric, he extended this Doctrine into a 'New Science,' which subsequently resulted in their *Laws of Media*, based on an applied probing model called the *Tetrad*. The tetrad is deeply rooted in the Logos: in it and through it, the ancient whole is recomposed, and the two halves, speech and reason, are once more combined and allowed to regain their primordial gnoseological function.

The tetrad is presented as a verbal heuristic device built upon four questions: What does each medium, each human artefact, enhance? What does it displace? What does it retrieve? To what does it reverse if pushed to an extreme? Just like the metaphor, the tetrad provides the tool to approach and perceive the essence of our new man-made environment; it works like an all-embracing, unifying verbal equation for reading and revealing *landscape*, that is, *our planet* perceived and rendered as *an art form*. Language is turned into the cognitive medium, the *arché* to which everything returns. McLuhan's *Laws of Media* invites us to turn into storytellers, to translate our observations into communication; it invites us to cooperate in a process through language. That's how the so-called *nonsensical mcluhanese* reveals itself as anything but *nonsensical*. The puns, the aphorisms, the paradoxes are acoustic, all-embracing warning signals. As I said before, they form a poetical prose built upon a serious combination of various liberal arts by McLuhan the humanist. His verbo-voco-visual words attack us, warn and alert us, forcing us to respond, to counteract; in other words, *to be awake*. Just like Joyce's language, McLuhan's language constantly plays with us and, in reverse, ends up troubling us. The mosaic, as its probing will show, is a carefully conceived form of exploration built upon several correspondences with other pre-existing and coexisting forms and epistemological paradigms. It is a form that shaped and enabled McLuhan's operative project and, in so doing, remains perhaps his greatest legacy, a sort of *mcluhanesque memorabilia* for our *post-secondary orality age*.

PART ONE

The Mosaic

2 Towards Post-Secondary Orality: The Mosaic

Embodying McLuhan

I never met the real McLuhan; I only met his many disembodied personalities, as many among you must have. We can, in fact, distinguish two main categories of discarnate McLuhan: the *real* – so to speak –and the *mediated*, that is, the various audio/video recordings of Marshall McLuhan, and the various literate recollections you find in all the books, biographies, or essays which have been dedicated to him worldwide. While the real discarnate versions speak to you and to your own imagination and ideas directly, the mediated ones have led to the various interpretations of both the man and the intellectual that critics or aficionados have popularized through time. We all have *memories* of McLuhan; we all have met him in one or more of his immaterial forms, consciously or unconsciously. Did you not meet him in Woody Allen's movie *Annie Hall*, where he interprets himself in one of the most renowned cinematic cameos? Or did you meet him as the Patron Saint of *Wired* magazine? Perhaps you met him on the air or on TV through the many slogans for the age he coined? Not to speak of those of you who certainly met him in class as a name attached to ideas and theories of communication and media. Depending on our age or interests, we have constructed our own McLuhan through a cross-reading of his immaterial presences.

As in the case of Vitangelo Moscarda in Luigi Pirandello's last and famous novel, *One, No One and One-Hundred Thousand*, McLuhan has become what we have made of him; we have put various masks on him, and we have looked at him through those masks. But each of these masks only reveals one side of his more complex *persona*, which, in fact, we still have to bring together. Let's start by bringing the discarnate McLuhan back to his materiality by allowing the man to return from his many avatars. In other words, let's retrieve McLuhan's existent body, his *living persona*. This is what I want to do in this part of the book: I want to invite you to transubstantiate his various masks into his written body, his *mosaic*. We will discover that while the substance, the key elements, and the function of the mosaic clearly relate to McLuhan's humanistic roots, its form develops from various communicative strategies which in fact relate to four among the various masks we have put on him and which, after all, are those which represent his most famous avatars: the *media oracle*; the *media guru*; the *modernist*; the *media* or *techno fan*. The mosaic embodies them *all at once*; hence, the mosaic also transcends the whole of these four discarnate versions of McLuhan. The mosaic is the embodiment of McLuhan's integral awareness; it is what makes us understand the function of his own storytelling; it is what engages us into a reading process which cannot be separated from our communal existence.

What is, in fact, a mosaic? If you think of it, we can associate different meanings with this term: the mosaic can be an art form (the Roman mosaics, or the Byzantine mosaics); or a multicultural approach to societal and cultural phenomena (the Canadian mosaic); or a type of pavement (a mosaic floor). These are just a few obvious examples pertaining to different domains: the artistic or the aesthetic one; the sociocultural and the political one; the most pragmatic one of construction and applied design. And yet, if you think of it, they all have something in common: their operative structure. All these ideas of mosaic in fact translate into a material or conceptual form based on fragments – or tiles or *tessere* – that are discrete units whose assemblage creates a figure which acquires meaning through the interplay with its own ground. By so doing, a pattern is created, which, in turn, is revealed through our active observation. Pattern recognition is the way we approach all mosaics: we look for the overall design that the careful assemblage of the various pieces brings to light, something which transcends their sum. Pattern recognition engages us, requires our will to cooperate with the structure; it turns us into detectives capable of seeing the narrative of a Roman or a Byzantine mosaic, as well as of a multicultural one, or even of a mosaic floor. Engaging with a mosaic, we participate in the process of giving meaning to what we experience. This is true for all that we define as *a mosaic*, including McLuhan's form of writing: it is a form which encourages an active participation from all seers, readers, spectators, who have to find the figure in the carpet, which is, in fact, *what connects figures and ground*.

While interfacing McLuhan's various masks, we find that his *mosaic* also makes us experience knowledge, and experience both him and his context *through* knowledge; it makes us progress towards a meaningful overall effect. As we shall see, McLuhan's mosaic cross-reads cultural traditions. It pursues a field approach to various problems and situations, and gives substance and materiality to its designer's intellectual originality. In later chapters, I will unveil the role played by each of the four masks in the making of the embodied McLuhan, that is, in the making of McLuhan's mosaic. Here, I introduce its substance (its hybrid conceptual structure), its tiles or *tessere* (the *probes*), and its function (how it operates and to what intent).

Casting the Hybrid

Doubtless, McLuhan was a great storyteller and a fluent orator. He enjoyed talking and lecturing about his process of discovery, and, when turning to literacy, he often elaborated on ways to render his 'stories.' This on-the-spot rendering was always based on a peculiar witty combination of his oral skills, his humanistic background, and his study of avant-garde art and fiction. Throughout his books, he probed the actuality of new media, but he also simultaneously reconceptualized these probes on the more traditional printed page, which he would turn into an original literate interface that recreated the electric orality he foresaw coming up in the immediate future.

McLuhan's explorations of language were not driven simply by the will to charm and seduce his audience, or to attract a variety of readers; through his writing, he was seriously aiming to master and render the complexity of the ongoing changes he was probing. As mentioned in my introduction, his *Laws of Media* translate into a probing device – the Tetrad – which combines orality and literacy in an effort to address the up-coming effect of computers and their effective way of bringing about a new phase of orality. I will return to this idea later on in this chapter, as well as in the third part of this book. What is interesting to note at this stage is how both McLuhan's mosaic (the final result of his experiments with form and language) and his laws of media (the final result of his media explorations) are conveyed as literate tools retrieving more ancient forms of communication, which are also apt in rendering the new electric interactivity. They both rely upon a hybrid substance which combines old and new educational and communicative strategies.

McLuhan's mosaic is therefore a non-linear form of writing which reconfigures the linear alphabetic form in order to give the written page a tactile and multi-sensorial dimension. Such a page is designed as a '*verbo-vocal-visual*' interface. The mosaic is a literate form capable of also translating the new '*verbomotor* culture' of our time, to use an expression coined a few years later by the scholar who theorized about the effects of our secondary orality, Walter J. Ong (who himself was one of McLuhan's students in the 1940s):

> Much in the foregoing account of orality can be used to identify what can be called *verbomotor* cultures, that is, cultures in which, by contrast with high-technology cultures, courses of action and attitudes toward issues depend significantly more on effective use of words, and thus on human interaction, and significantly less on non-verbal, often largely visual input from 'objective' world of things … We are expanding its use here to include all cultures that retain enough oral residue to remain significantly word-attentive in a person-interactive context (the oral type of context) rather than object-attentive.[1]

McLuhan's mosaic mirrors the new way people addressed their 'courses of actions and attitudes towards issues,' based more and more on collective interplay (person-interactive context) and less and less on solitary activities (object-attentive context). With that idea in mind, the modernist example, for McLuhan, was fundamental for at least two main reasons: it offered models of experimentation with new forms; and, yet, it also inscribed those same experiments inside a broader literate and cultural continuum. In this sense, the modernist literary roots of McLuhan's media studies constitute a link between tradition and innovation, both when perceiving the traditional and when rendering it anew in his observations.

Therefore, we should not be surprised to discover that McLuhan's favourite modernist masters are those who engaged with tradition and who combined old and new literary and artistic patterns into bold and original structures; that is, those who were not afraid to translate their own actuality, but who did not imagine it as existing in a cultural and historical vacuum. Certainly, he was fascinated by the explorations of late avant-garde movements, but his search also emanates from the study of those early proto-modernist writers who, at the turn of the previous century, started to question fictional and representative canons within a timeless literary and artistic 'sacred wood,' to use T.S. Eliot's famous definition of what literary tradition is.

Henry James, as early as 1884, suggested that there is 'no limit to [the novelist's] possible experiments, efforts, discoveries, successes,'[2] introducing the technique of the *limited point of view* as opposed to the more traditional one of the *omniscient narrator*. Following his example, Joseph Conrad and Ford Madox Ford developed new rhetorical devices undermining the ideas of unity and linearity still employed by more traditional Victorian novelists.[3] A few years later, Ezra Pound's imagism and T.S. Eliot's *fragments* and *objective correlatives* further explored the potentiality of formal discontinuity to render their own reality. And yet, even though the motto *make it new* stays as a lasting mark of modernist experiments, the very idea of 'new' pursued by all these writers moved from a carefully chosen tradition of reading the best, and from a constant study of previous literary productions.[4] Their *discoveries* were in fact the result of a continuous *re-discovery* of forgotten or other far-away traditions, the result of a constant dialogue between past and present literary achievements. T.S. Eliot and Ezra Pound were great admirers of Italian literature of the origins, from Dante to Petrarch to Boccaccio; Ford Madox Ford wrote one of the first volumes of comparative literature, enlightening readers from Confucius' day to his own in his *The March of Literature* (1938); Confucius and Eastern traditions were also part of Pound's literary and philosophical interests; James Joyce prided himself of being a living encyclopedia. The works of these writers are pervaded by countless references to what was there before, the voices of the dead poets disguised inside new phrases, echoing in original works of art, and engaging their present.

In a similar way, McLuhan's mosaic combines the need to experiment and open up a form of critical writing to new communicative devices pertaining to his own time (from ads to slogans to visual puns and other cultural devices); his knowledge of ancient rhetorical strategies and traditions acted as a catalyst. More specifically, he went back to the liberal arts of the *trivium*, which he retrieved through the study of both the Patristic tradition and the English metaphysical poetry of the seventeenth century. By so doing, as a hybrid, his mosaic combined various communicative codes and broke established academic canons. The mosaic no longer belongs to the school of method which, according to Francis Bacon, is 'more fit to win consent or belief, but less fit to point to action'; the mosaic does not guide the reader towards the acquisition of an established truth, but it engages the reader in a process of discovery which can be fulfilled only through an active desire to cooperate with the text. Like most modernist writings, McLuhan's writing is an *open text*, a sort of *writing in progress* which acquires always different meanings depending on the act of reading, and thus on the readers, who are thereby transformed into co-producers of meaning. McLuhan defined this process of continuous interplay and exegesis as a 'do-it-yourself participation on the part of the reader.'[5] It is possible to envisage here a similitude to an idea of learning pertaining to a different historical moment, the one beautifully captured by Raphael's painting *The School of Athens*. Even though it dates back to the Renaissance – a period which McLuhan considered as the moment in history celebrating the eye and sight over all other senses, that is, the moment in which Gutenberg's fragmented man was in his prime – Raphael's painting takes us into the heart of an ancient educational system based, not on the passive acceptance or memorization of learning, but on continuous investigations and never-ending dialogues among pupils and masters. The painting contains several references to Aristotle's *Metaphysics*, and portrays almost all major philosophers together, sharing the same space and in conversation with each other: Aristotle himself, Plato, Diogenes, Socrates, Parmenides, Epicurus, to name but a few. Pagan philosophy and Christian theology are brought together through knowledge, and the new students are invited to 'Seek Knowledge of Causes': the 'do-it-yourself participation' on the part of the students is based on the direct interplay with the philosophers' universal ideas, flowing in the air through conversations, preserved in books through time, and constantly retrieved and actualized through their study. Come to think of it, we can also find a parallel with our own actuality, at a time when the World Wide Web has become – for better or worse – our new School of Athens. When browsing the Web, we access knowledge in a direct way and freely assemble various data, news, ideas, and information available to us in the here and now; we are masters of our own interplay. In both the Athenian and our current learning situations, the responsibility to provide a meaning is ours: both the master philosophers and the Web give us a set of learning tools we have to investigate for ourselves. We decide if we want to stop at a first level of knowledge which stands before us, or enquire further. In both situations we are, in fact, interfacing with knowledge; as scholars at the School of Athens, or as surfers of the Web, we are the users reconnecting ideas, fragments, and various other bits we come across. We are the ones who decide how much effort we want to make to move forward in our knowledge. In a similar way, we are the interface between knowledge and ignorance when engaging with the hybrid substance of McLuhan's mosaic. We decide how much effort we want to make to learn through its discontinuous structure.

Substantial Discontinuity

Those of you who have some familiarity with more recent literary theories (from postmodernism to the evolution of the lyric essay), as well as with hypertext theories, will immediately appreciate the substance of McLuhan's mosaic discontinuity. Those of you who have not, will nevertheless find it easier than in the past to grasp the same concept, since today most media surrounding us are in fact exploiting discontinuity as an operative form: the world of instant information is itself a mosaic of data that we have to connect somehow. Discontinuity, intertextuality, and juxtapositions are, in fact, well-known rhetorical strategies of postmodernist critical discourses and narratives, as well as of electronic and digital forms of communication. At the same time, they stand at the core of most communicative strategies typical of our own daily routines, as we inhabit real and virtual landscapes whose narratives are based on assembling discontinuous modes. We might not immediately be aware of it because of the way we now inhabit discontinuity, and not just in terms of 'landscape' (as in the case of the constant juxtaposition of messages we experience when walking along our city streets, one coming after the other in various disconnected forms: images, sounds, or smells); we have, in fact, *put on* discontinuity. Our life palimpsests are more and more based on shared multi-tasking philosophies that shift us from one role to the next without even noticing. We are constantly urged to connect to something or someone, to link or network; we are urged to overcome discontinuity by behavioural patterns based on juxtapositions and interconnections.

This situation, which we experience through our daily routine, brings together the above mentioned literary theories and the model of the hypertext, something which also connects to our investigation of McLuhan's mosaic; in particular, it enables us to assess the latter's originality as a precursor of would-be forms of communication, as well as of literary and technological theories and applications. In the latest edition of his most well known book, hypertext guru George P. Landow writes that '… over the past several decades literary theory and computer hypertext, apparently unconnected areas of enquiry, have increasingly converged,'[6] precisely because of their elaboration of non-linear forms. This idea of a discontinuous form of writing, which today we accept and study as one mode of critical discourse, as well as a typical strategy of electronic communication, was still a novelty among scholars and university professors (though not among avant-garde artists) when McLuhan started to employ it outside the domain of the arts *stricto sensu*; hence, the strong reaction against a language which did not comply with the established rules. Glenn Willmott, for example, has convincingly discussed McLuhan's works as a cross-road connecting modernist and postmodernist trends, so much so that today we can read his mosaic as a form which has anticipated later postmodernist forms of *écritures*. Contrary to later schools of criticism, though, McLuhan's experiments with language do not respond to the need to address political or social vindications; instead, the goal is to remain detached and objective while exploring actuality as a complex ground resulting from the interplay of technological, sociological, and cultural factors. For instance, new historicism, cultural materialism, cultural studies, and postcolonial and gender studies have developed new formal structures in order to respond to established forms of literacy and discourse that are overwhelmingly biased historically, culturally, racially, or according to gender (*ex-centricity* being a clearly defined strategy employed by several postmodernist approaches).[7] However, McLuhan's new form of writing responds more to the need of conveying a new sensibility, a new environment *as it is*. His goal is, in fact, not to foster a political cause or to bring forward some criticism of the way new media or cultural and educational trends progress in relation to actuality. Rather, he wants to alert his readers to the new interactive psychodynamic processes induced by all technologies and forms of communication.

Similar also to computing, McLuhan's mosaic is based on *discontinuous* rather than on *continuous* structuring. Even though, as I will later discuss, there are some substantial differences between the mosaic and the hypertext, these two forms share similar fortuitous patterns. As readers, we can decide how to orient our own reading, and we can decide if we want to follow the table of contents (the menu) or if we want to start *in medias res*. When approaching McLuhan's books, we are free to direct our own explorations just as we do when navigating hypertexts. As I will show below, McLuhan's mosaic is in fact built around *probes*, which are conceived as 'verbo-voco-visual' *aperçus*, that is, hypertextual and multi-sensorial textual fragments; these probes operate as 'lexia' (to use Barthes's definitions) or 'windows' (to use a term we all understand as Internet users) introducing a complex set of issues through a paratactic structure based on an aphoristic-like technique. His writing is therefore characterized by an overwhelming intertextuality (and hypertextuality) which forces readers to explore a much more complex ground, against which single words or probes are set as three-dimensional figures to be read in depth. Intertextuality acts both within the very text (variations and repetitions of the same original concept) and outside it (juxtapositions of quotations and images from other texts or domains, implicit links with a broader set of sources, as well as with a broader context). Also, the brevity of each probe perfectly matches the attention span of today's readers, which – statisticians tell us – is decreasing constantly. However, the density of the probe, its aphoristic and paratactic structure, as well as its connection to the paradoxical, aims to counterbalance its brevity by encouraging a deeper and more engaging investigation. It is not by chance that McLuhan also called these probes *glosses*, employing a term used in biblical exegesis to explain passages in the text, a term which was also used to indicate marginal notes in manuscripts and printed versions of texts both in the classic and the vulgar tradition. A *probe* or *gloss* is a dynamic rhetorical device envisaged as a textual addition that creates a series of related patterns of knowledge inside and outside the text itself. If readers read *through* the probe – that is, if they see it as a window opening on a broader (textual and contextual) landscape – they read *in depth*, investigating and discussing possible meanings, links, and further implications. If they skip from a probe to the next one quickly, they can just have fun and use the mosaic as a form of amusing diversion which, nevertheless, can induce unexpected associations and, in time, even understanding and knowledge. After all, humour was a favourite tenet of McLuhan's form of communication.

Hence, to my mind, the *probe* or *gloss* constitutes the fundamental component of McLuhan's mosaic. The probe is used to convey a broken knowledge as in the aphoristic tradition; even if it often sounds like a formula, it forces you to become an active player. It is comparable to one of the many *fragments* modernist writers forged against their ruin to respond to the coeval chaos, the frightening change they were witnessing. The probe is in effect McLuhan's rhetorical device aimed at triggering intertextuality and operating as a link to other textual and contextual situations. Each probe introduces a set of apparently unrelated questions which are often conveyed in a paradoxical – and therefore provocative – way, and which readers are asked to explore. In time, McLuhan developed different types of probes, moving from traditional aphorisms to paratactic constructions involving also images, but the function of the probe remains the same: to provoke and engage the readers, and to encourage a different approach to situations by turning readers into 'active players' interfacing a substantial discontinuity.

What's in a Probe?

The probe constitutes the functional tile of McLuhan's mosaic; it is the smaller unit which is assembled to convey a pattern, to turn the fixity of the printed page into an acoustic experience. Those of you who were born in the age of the Internet will immediately appreciate the multimedia dimension of McLuhan's printed page; but only a few among those who confronted McLuhan's writing as early as the 1950s or early 1960s did: when approaching McLuhan's mosaic style of writing, readers were in fact confronted by a page which no longer reassured 'literate people,' as it no longer translated the act of reading into an ordered or rational process. McLuhan's pages no longer assimilated 'utterance to the human body,' a metaphor which returns us to a well-known entity. As Ong noted, traditionally texts

> introduce a feeling for 'heading' in accumulations of knowledge: 'chapter' derives from Latin *caput*, meaning 'head' (as of the human body). Pages have not only 'heads' but also 'feet,' for footnotes. References are given to what is 'above' and 'below' in a text when what is meant is several pages back or farther on. The significance of the vertical and the horizontal in texts deserves serious study.[8]

McLuhan undertook such a study, combining his literary and his media studies; he reconceptualized writing in the light of technological and environmental shifts. If you think about it, investigating the meaning of 'the vertical and the horizontal in texts' demands that we question the point of observation, the perspective we adopt when approaching things; it concerns our involvement as readers. The page that resembles the human body is a page which we can observe as an outer landscape while keeping our inner landscape detached. Even better, it is a page which separates the knower from the known and induces introspectivity. This works very well if we conceive knowledge and wisdom as progressive accumulations of data which we can store for later usage. In this way, reading becomes an act of epistemological stock-taking, an activity that fits literate civilization. But such a linear approach to knowledge no longer works as well in the electric or in the digital age, where information overload renders total accumulation impossible. Consistently, McLuhan's pages no longer resembled a human body: they lost the head and feet, and they lost their traditional 'physicality,' just as the 'discarnate human beings' of the electric age were losing their sense of body by extending their psyches into cyberspace.

Acting at the forefront of new technological revolutions, McLuhan's mosaic develops from a different metaphor, no longer a biological one, but a technological one: the *probe*, a flexible object through which we can carry out explorations not only outside but also inside different bodies. Pages written around probes incorporate readers into the text's landscape: readers of the mosaic are no longer external observers; they are inside the evolving picture. This means that readers do not have to approach McLuhan's printed page as *a thing*, but rather as *an event* in which the act of reading is integral to a participation in the process of discovery. From the late 1960s, the hippie movement 'got' and celebrated McLuhan's form of communication better than other audiences, the idea of 'happening' being at the core of its life philosophy. Needless to say, the appreciation coming from the countercultures of the young rebels did not contribute to the appreciation of McLuhan's scholarly work; it only gave more emphasis to one of his most ambiguous and celebrated masks, that of the media guru. Instead, the probe is an element which leads to a more complex interaction, as it is through the probe that we are invited to enter the text: it is the interface between us and the broken knowledge in the text.

While the rhetorical questions that open each chapter of *The Mechanical Bride* play a similar role, it is not until *The Gutenberg Galaxy* that the *probe* is introduced as a fundamental component of McLuhan's mosaic. In that book, probes are explicitly defined as 'glosses' and are particularly recognizable since they are juxtaposed with McLuhan's discussions and visually framed as if they are independent from the main written corpus. This is a visual strategy that places the probes at once *both inside and outside the text*. This mode of juxtaposition is paratactic and analogical and forces the reader to look for connections among probes/glosses and between a probe/gloss and the previous/following paragraphs, or the previous/following quotations. Readers can decide to stop at the probe/gloss and work with it as if they were probing a riddle, pouring over its potentialities in depth, trying to unveil the aphoristic lines before moving forward (or backward). They can also read it as a textual continuum, or even jump from one probe/gloss to the next, skipping the more discursive parts.

Readers are encouraged to approach the book at their own speed and pleasure: they are free to jump across pages; they are not required to read the text in a sequential way. In other words, the text works horizontally, but also vertically and in depth – as if it were a sort of alphabetically conceived 3-D. This is possible thanks to the evocative power of the text consciously assembled by McLuhan. Readers can also open the book at random and start to speculate on the probe/gloss they find, just as they might open a book of psalms, aphorisms, riddles, or meditations. In other words, we are invited to contemplate, or speculate, or entertain ourselves with the text we find on the page. The difference between a conventional sequential page and McLuhan's mosaic page is that the reader is sent to a ground that is not the abstract world of linear logic, or religion, philosophy, or wisdom, but the evolving, and by now far more tangible, electric world – which is currently our own blurring actuality. Readers are induced to approach the mosaic page and the world it relates to *analogically* and by indirect means. Such a world is not described in a didactic way. It is not offered as the content of the explorations (and, surprisingly enough, in *The Gutenberg Galaxy* McLuhan discusses mostly the complexity of the printing age, not of the electric age); instead, the mosaic page triggers a participatory (that is, inclusive) process. Irrespective of the content discussed, readers are engaged in an act of reading which aims to replicate the interactive modes pertaining to their new electric/acoustic environment. They are forced to move their eyes and minds in a non-linear way while exploring the effects of the printing age through the dynamic probes of the mosaic. By so doing, they train themselves to become active players of the electric and acoustic environment.

In *The Gutenberg Galaxy*, McLuhan recapitulates the probes/glosses at the very end of the book, in a sequence which can be perceived as an *imagistic* table of contents for the whole book. Readers could, in fact, work just on the probes/glosses listed at the end, juxtaposing them in order to trigger new speculations, and new understandings and knowledge. By so doing, readers are promoted to the role of co-creators. The aphoristic probes/glosses contained in the end section evoke all that is discussed in the book. The insightful silent reader can act as a storyteller and extend McLuhan's production of meaning and knowledge. In this sense, the probes/glosses can be perceived not only as idea boxes but also as imagist one-liners and contextual puns, in the sense that Pound meant his cantos to be read. What is first hidden in the clever musicality opens itself, upon reflection, to a concrete representation of an idea. Upon reflection, we find out that the probes are not being juxtaposed according to a linear subordination, but instead are aimed at triggering associations.

Here is an example of one of McLuhan's probes/glosses – or one-image poems – from *The Gutenberg Galaxy*. Once you read *through it*, you find yourself digging out an idea that explores the historical interface of orality and literacy:

*Civilization gives the barbarian or tribal man an eye for an ear
and is now at odds with the electric world.*

A typical McLuhan probe, it immediately renders the cyclic vision of human history, as expressed by McLuhan himself in his grand narrative on media. It offers a good example of how he retrieves the metaphorical structure of language and plays with it. The terms, *barbarian or tribal man, civilization, electric world,* immediately evoke three different social constructs; they imply three different relationships between the individual and the environment, also denoting a different sensorial order. One fell swoop is: the world *before* the invention of the phonetic alphabet; the world *after* the phonetic alphabet and the printing press; the world *after* the commercialization of electricity. The passage *from ear to eye* indicates the passage from the ancient acoustic mode of perception – inclusive and simultaneous – typical of tribal society, to a sequential and linear one pertaining to literate Western society, now obsolete or no longer adequate to (*at odds with*) the electric environment (which, through its re-tribalization, is rediscovering acoustic and tribal dynamics). This probe (as all others) can therefore be figured out in depth, and used as a way to access a more complex ground. Also, in the Gutenberg book, the juxtapositions of various probes enables one to reconfigure the galaxy the author is probing, digging out the network of analogies and links which, all together, reveal 'casual operations in history':

> Thus the galaxy or constellation of events upon which the present study concentrates is itself a mosaic of perpetually interacting forms that have undergone kaleidoscopic transformation – particularly in our own time.[9]

The juxtaposition of probes results in a progression of effects through its modernist montage; the title, *The Gutenberg Galaxy: The Making of Typographic Man,* offers its formal cause synthesis; it encapsulates McLuhan's operative project and poetics, his probing of various 'environments.'

Playing with Form

McLuhan continued to elaborate on the probe as the core element of his mosaic, as well as of his form of communication. As a storyteller, he loved puns and one-liners, another way to condense meaning and to turn his audiences on. Consistently, in some of his books, the probe is formally conceived as a pun. It is structured as a witty 'caption' to immediately convey the psychodynamics triggered by the interplay of a new medium being introduced into a given environment; it is meant to immediately engage, provoke, and plug his readers into the text. It is, for instance, the case of his most famous books, *The Gutenberg Galaxy* or *Understanding Media: The Extensions of Man*, or of a less well know but equally as interesting volume, *Take Today: The Executive as Dropout*, where puns and word games aim to induce in the reader a different attitude to learning, often touching the responsive chord of humour. Here are some examples of this (Joyce-like) playful attitude from *Understanding Media*: 'Telegraph: *the Social Hormon*'; 'The Telephone: *Sounding Brass or Tinkling Symbol?*'; 'The Phonograph: *The Toy that Shrank the National Chest*'; 'Movies: *The Reel World*'; 'Radio: *The Tribal Drum*'; 'Television: *The Timid Giant.*' Still others from *Take Today*: 'Postures and Impostures of Managers Past'; 'Tribal Community to Magnetic City: Irresistible Force By-Passes Immovable Objects'; 'Households to World Shopping Centres: The Real McCoy and Genuine Fakes'; 'Tribal Chiefs and Conglomerate Emperors.' These provocative titles can be read and enjoyed as more or less successful headings, but they can also be explored as aphorisms that describe cognitive, societal, and cultural changes, involving the new medium or the new environmental situation discussed in each chapter. They also bring together popular and more refined forms of cultural discourses, which are further explored and clarified in the chapters through a constant juxtaposition of various registers: from academic dissertations to anecdotic storytelling, from commercial-like one-liners to verbose quotations.[10] The juxtaposition of different registers therefore is a carefully chosen rhetorical strategy which leads to a polyphonic ensemble piece, at once including, addressing, and engaging heterogeneous audiences. It is not a casual pastiche. McLuhan was thus pursuing the search of the great fool. As Shakespeare taught us, you must be 'wise enough to play the fool' because 'This is a practice / As full of labour as a wise man's art.'[11] McLuhan forged his practice at the school of Athens and at Cambridge.

The paratactic juxtaposition of the various probes is developed through language, but also through drawings, images, headlines, and photographs; hence, the mosaic not only combines different registers, but also borrows from different communicative codes. Several among McLuhan's later volumes retrieve a cubistic montage which turns the reader on to a simultaneous awareness of several vanishing points; and yet, these books are designed as provocative artefacts in which ideas and

intuitions are offered through a witty terminology and through absolutist claims – after all, the 'mosaic is the mode of corporate or collective
image and commands deep participation.'[12] In other words, in these
books McLuhan's mosaic style of writing is either a satirical or a humorous rendering of the very change (from *point of view* to *tribal perspective*)
which he does not truly like. But here is the genius of McLuhan: his literate goal remains the same; the form he conceives and employs is aimed
at a renewing of the literate strategy he pursues. This is especially true
for the *acoustic* 'pocket-books' that the by then world-renowned Canadian media theoretician co-wrote, often in collaboration with celebrated
graphic artists, and which were published throughout the late 1960s and
early 1970s. *The Medium Is the Massage, War and Peace in the Global Village,
Counterblast,* and other volumes, have often been labelled as witty marketing ploys – weird artsy-fartsy products – reiterating ideas already stated
in McLuhan's earlier books. I think that this is a way to oversimplify the
genesis of these volumes. Certainly, these probing graphic-text interfaces
must be assessed in the light of the profitable marketing strategies McLuhan, the English professor, designed to disseminate his 'media guru's'
status worldwide. However, in a way, they are foretelling the graphic novel's potential of disguising serious intellectual considerations as 'pop-art'
explorations. Look closely at *War and Peace in the Global Village* and you
will find in it strategies of communication predicting a net of analogies
and cross-readings, as well as theories of art and of mass communication,
that offer the reader a chance to become aware of the new media environment displayed on any Web page today. How did he do it? By writing
about the strategies that will demand the same intense participation that
reading in general will put on readers of commercial computer screens
in a few short years. It is a percept that McLuhan addressed on various
occasions and explored as one of his most fundamental tenets, combining his passion for literature and his understanding of media effects. It
is a tenet he clearly expressed in the introduction to his sole academic
volume, *The Interior Landscape,* a collection of his literary criticism: 'The
effects of new media on our sensory lives are similar to the effects of new
poetry. They change not our thought but the structure of our world.'[13]
As every art critic now knows, interfacing new media of communication
with older forms of art through iconic juxtapositions or through an associative montage is also an act that contains its own heuristic function.

   In a similar way, the playful twist of a word can trigger not only humour
but also knowledge and understanding, as the Freudian slip clearly indicates. McLuhan never conceives the triggered twist for its own sake or as

'art for art sake,' but as a strategy to introduce a progression of effects leading to a form that renews one's general knowledge. For instance, the celebrated 'the medium is the message/massage/mass-age/mess-age' is a shifting pun that for McLuhan, as for Joyce, is not just a banal word game conceived to entertain readers. Instead, it is a multi-dimensional poetical attempt to reveal the interconnected pattern of forces acting inside the electric word of *Finnegans Wake.* As McLuhan often said, paraphrasing Eliot's idea: a poem works on you while you are distracted by its content. Therefore, *form is as important as content,* and readers are to be made aware of the structure (ground) containing the story (figure). Hence, the medium is the *message* (the form of communication has a lasting impact on content); the *massage* (individuals who are not aware of such a process are invariably numbed by media); the *mass-age* (mass society produces new media and new agencies to mould individuals); and the *mess-age* (those who cannot see through the form of a medium inevitably misread and make a mess of its mediation). Think, for instance, of the perennial question concerning how violence is supposedly transferred from films or TV to audience: it's an oversimplified correlation which is not conducive to a full understanding of the complex interplay among at least three main actors: audience, medium, and society. Violence does not pass from a medium to us as does a vitamin when we drink milk or fruit juice. Violence is a behavioural response to various environmental issues of which technology is one among many; violence relates to questions of identity, culture, education, and much more. Do you think that we will no longer have gun-shootings in our streets if we no longer show gangster movies? Emulation of borderline behaviours is a serious problem, but it is not simply by censoring movies shown on TV, on the Internet, or in theatres that we can solve it. Living in a more and more invasive digital mass age, it is mandatory for us to better understand the message of old and new media, as well as how they interface with each other. We have no choice; rather than fear our mediascape, we must engage with it. It is our rational and playful way of counterbalancing the otherwise phenomenally numbing massage we constantly receive; it is our way of being active 'digital citizens' and avoiding making a mess of what we could, instead, achieve through media. McLuhan proved that literature, being a function and not simply a subject, contributes to knowledge and understanding of evolving mediascapes, that is, of our own actualities. The truly active digital citizen cannot but be a literary literate.

It is true, though, that McLuhan's best-selling pocket books were conceived to attract diverse audiences by making use of what was at the time an avant-garde technique (derived from cubism, Dadaism, graphic novels, and the ubiquity of pop art). Reinterpreted in this light, they are a media-mosaic of various artistic languages, including advertising, because 'advertising is the greatest art form of the 20th century.'[14] But in all these mass-market paperbacks, the printed page preserves and retains its role as the interface between image and the word, overlapping and enlightening each other in ways that facilitate an understanding of new cultural patterns. For instance, take *War and Peace in the Global Village*, designed together with the much sought after book designer and artist Quentin Fiore: its word/image interface is conceived to offer 'an inventory of some of the current spastic situations that could be eliminated by more feedforward.'[15] In it, McLuhan and Fiore examine the inevitable clash between Eastern and Western cultures forced to meet on the global village's stage, and give shape to a new cultural hybridization and syncretism both linear and ideogrammatic. To render (but not 'narrate') the new cultural interfacing, it combines sensorial (or emotive) and cognitive dynamics. Each of the pages of *War and Peace in the Global Village* has a different outline, but together they form an asymmetric collage that readers are asked to read sometimes from left to right (as in Western literate culture), at other times from top to bottom (as in Eastern culture).

The authors of *War and Peace in the Global Village* are recreating their contemporary sensorial split between eye and ear by feeding-forward juxtapositions inherent to the culturally polyglot situation in the global village; they recreate inclusive and acoustic modes of perception by playing with the traditional outline, for instance, by forcing the reader to rotate the book itself in order to read it. At first it appears like a simple trick, which might annoy some readers, while amusing others; but it is nevertheless a trick which immediately conveys the *overturning* of previous sensorial situations while inducing a *tactile* and *participatory* (that is, an *interactive*) experience. What is particularly interesting in this book is the juxtaposition of different modes of perception and fruition, revealing how the acoustic post-literate games retrieve previous forms of orality and knowledge pertaining to cultural matrixes of the past. In most of its pages, in fact, the acoustic effect is obtained by dividing the printed text into vertical columns whose margins are decorated with images, annotations, and quotes from *Finnegans Wake*, suggesting the illuminated effect of ancient manuscripts (which, as I will later discuss, are themselves a sort of *schizophrenic form*, as they bring together dynamics pertaining to both the literate and the oral worlds). In *War and Peace in the Global Village* the columns are not embellished with hand-painted drawings but with photographs, illustrations, and excerpts from the text itself now used as post-literate marginalia (on both sides of the page) to *all at once* emphasize or enlighten concepts discussed in the main text. In other pages, the ratio between images and words is totally inverted: the latter blur and almost disappear, becoming minute but subtler aphorisms captioning overwhelming images. In such a composite mosaic, appropriate quotations from Joyce's *Finnegans Wake* are treated like leitmotivs or *insights* to connect the self-contained fragments and engage readers in the production of new meanings. These Joycean quotes provide the feed-forward element that the authors use to counterbalance 'current spastic situations.' The quotes from Joyce, which appear as aphoristic, playful, evocative, and complex linguistic boxes, become here a tool employed to encourage readers to recompose the textual fragments and read them simultaneously and in depth. They also alert us like a running commentary to ongoing cultural changes. In effect, it becomes apparent by the end of the book that the authors themselves are offering their readers an alternate thread out of the labyrinth.

Render Not Narrate

Looking through McLuhan's mosaic makes us perceive it as a hybrid which brings together old and new forms of knowledge and communication, develops around verbo-voco-visual (that is acoustic) units called probes, and has a discontinuous structure engaging readers in an active process as co-producers of meaning. As a form of writing, the mosaic interfaces literacy and orality and turns them both into a different perceptual experience. The mosaic embeds post-secondary orality: it merges the secondary orality of new electronic media with the orality of pristine forms of knowledge based on a language now mediated through a *literate* form. But contrary to linear writing, the mosaic is designed to preserve depth and participation, urging readers to take action and not to passively follow what is offered in print. Interfacing is, in fact, an idea to whose development McLuhan himself contributed in an original way. David Sobelman, an independent filmmaker and scholar, writer of the insightful documentary *McLuhan's Wake*, stresses in an early draft of his screenplay that there are four citations in the *Oxford English Dictionary* which identify McLuhan as their original user: *structuring*, *retribalization*, *interface*, and, of course, *mcluhanism*. In particular, Sobelman points out that McLuhan was the first to employ the term 'interface' in a specifically *mcluhanesque* context: 'Interface is the meeting of two structures, or cultures, or conflicting technologies and the way they change each other.'[16] *The way they change each* other is a key idea that in effect provides us with a background to McLuhan's own probe of the passage *from the eye to the ear* – that is, 'from linear to acoustic space' – and that also indicates how he forged his own mosaic technique of investigation. In the mosaic, McLuhan's literacy and orality meet and change each other. Consequently, his books would no longer be readable in a traditional way; as he often repeated,[17] more than for a final discovery, they would have to be experienced as continuous processes of discoveries. Unfortunately, released into the consumer environment, the depth of McLuhan's *modus operandi* was often blurred and perceived mostly as a series of clever or fuzzy one-liners (such as 'I have a small brain but I intend to use it' or 'I wouldn't have seen it if I hadn't believed it'), jokes, or slogans. Oversimplified interpretation of his 'messages' contributed to his presentation as a former artsy professor, now a media 'guru,' in love with progress, change, and technology. Most of his interpreters, those who shared and those who rejected his ideas alike, did not grasp the figure in the carpet: they saw each figure as a world in its own. They make me think of my student reading only some pages out of a novel: he would know a lot about … nothing ('The scientist rigorously defends his right to be ignorant of almost everything except his specialty').[18] It took two decades for the evolution of the World Wide Web to realize the potentialities of McLuhan's linguistic probes, as well as the complex structure and function of his mosaic. Today, his language can finally be assessed, in book form, on various Web sites and on YouTube, detached from the excessive emphasis, rivalries, and polemics which always accompanied the *phenomenon* of *McLuhan.*

Many are still puzzled by the paradox of asserting that the *media guru* or the *oracle* of the electric age should be retrieved as someone who experimented with and developed a new critical *discourse* and who developed a new form of *writing.* After all, it is McLuhan who did not hesitate to proclaim the end of literate *civilization,* and therefore *the end of the book!* And yet, the paradox can be easily overcome by reconsidering McLuhan's use of the terms 'literate/literacy' and 'book.' First of all, recall that McLuhan did not use words to *represent* the world in a mimetic way, but worked upon language in order to *render* the ongoing cultural and societal processes *through* it. He adopted an imagist approach to language, not a referential one. Terms such as *civiliztion* and *book* must therefore be read *through,* as semantic boxes containing a broader set of concepts. Following Pound's teaching, McLuhan used both terms to epitomize 'an emotional and an intellectual complex in an instant of time.' He used these terms to render modes of interaction and communication relating to a precise and complex environment that in his grand narrative, he defined as 'the mechanic or Gutenberg age.'

The term *civilization* immediately recalls the idea of a complex human construct characterized by given anthropological, social, and cultural patterns. If we take the above into consideration, then expressions such as *literate civilization* or *literate society* can be understood as verbal icons referring to a society dominated by a linear and cumulative approach to knowledge. The related environment is perceived in terms of *linear* and *visual space*, that is, an idea of space which is clearly measurable through sight, which traditional literate media encourage and embrace. Consistently, McLuhan uses the image of *the line* to symbolize the perceptive and organizational modes of such a *linear* or *literate* civilization, as opposed to the ancient oral society, rendered through the image of *the tribal circle*. The same image – a line – is used to define the ensuing models for almost all discoveries, inventions, and products of the literate age as they accumulated between the Renaissance and the late nineteenth century: the uniform lines of the printed page; the *equitone* line in literature; the linear perspective in the visual arts; the line of the assembling chains in manufacturing industries; the logic or linear reasoning of modern philosophy until Kant. In McLuhan's thought – as translated in his writings – *book* and *literacy/literate* are therefore *images* that immediately render the environment he was probing – an environment which the new electric media started to remodel from the middle of the nineteenth century, slowly inducing a sort of cultural schizophrenia, which McLuhan rendered through the expression 'from the eye to the ear.' This image immediately translates the passage from the mechanic to the electric cultural mode, that is, from *linear* (implying an atomistic visual approach to space) to *acoustic* (implying an oral space-time-oriented approach to duration). 'From eye to ear' is a one-liner which invites us to read in depth and grasp the complex implications of the passage from an old to a new *space-time sensibility* projecting us into an acoustic space we have to experience through our five senses.

McLuhan's Interactive Mosaic or Post-Secondary Orality

In the new global village, Gutenberg's *fragmented man* must reconvert himself into the *integral tribal man*; if not, his environmental perception will be numbed or *schizophrenic*, that is, it will be only *partial*, not *integral*.

The book, nevertheless, remains but as one among other means of communication. To counter-fight obsolescence, though, the written page
must be updated to new patterns, restoring a multi-sensorial – that is, no
longer visually biased – perception. As early as 1959, in a lecture offered
to the American Association for Higher Education, McLuhan anticipated
that the book must adjust to include different experiences, namely, that
'the future of the book is inclusive.'[19] On that occasion, he discussed the
various forms that the book had assumed in his time, pointing out that
'poésie concrète' inspired different uses of old printing techniques; he
set the book against the new electric ground formed by radio and television and suggested that in the near future, children and students would
learn more and more through apprenticeship and less and less through
study. He was right. Today we know that the new cultural and technological context (the new *verbomotor* electric culture) preserves literacy and
the book, but encourages them both to respond to their new electric
ground; literacy and the book are literate *figures* which must adjust to a
clear sensorial and environmental change, to a different *ground*. Ong,
himself a professor of English interested in cultural phenomena, set
out to convincingly prove that, in time of secondary orality, people are
inevitably also retrieving a different approach to knowledge which pre-
supposes 'a kind of corporate retrospection,' a renewed involvement in
the learning process.[20] After all, aren't we tempted to define ourselves
in terms of 'tribes'? For sure, commercials rely on that. Secondary orality interfaces writing and orality, juxtaposes inner and outer worlds. It
turns each of us into both a consumer and a producer of meaning: the
prosumer in us is the trendy specimen whose habits and characteristics are
now studied by media scholars and sociologists alike.

As a young professor meeting the new kids born in the post-radio years
and now experiencing TV, McLuhan was constantly reassessing the meaning and function of education. In his role as a professor, he questioned
the tools education should employ, and he interpreted the relation
between teacher and pupils in terms of a dynamic cognitive interplay:
learning by doing – apprenticeship – and not just learning by studying.
It is now quite an intelligible and a relevant idea, which we can easily
apply to later pedagogical tenets, as we learn from various approaches to
media education existing today. Also, we are all becoming familiar with
different typologies of new tools now at our disposal. These days, the
electronic or the digital book is the latest specimen on the evolutionary
technological chain of *book as an object*. As McLuhan clearly indicated in
his *Understanding Media*, in the electric age, analytical thought gives way

to analogical and syncretic thought, and the sequential line is replaced by the electromagnetic field.

The old medium stays around, but it is reshaped according to the new potentialities embedded by the new medium. As many of McLuhan's probes attest, the old medium becomes the content of a new medium, which adapts, changes, and evolves. In the early twentieth century, the Italian futurist poet and writer Filippo Tommaso Marinetti invented the expression *parole in libertà*, literally 'words in freedom.'[21] On Marinetti's futurist page, words were free to move and combine in a myriad of ways, resulting in a colourful montage of forms, dimensions, and sounds capturing the 'speed' and the 'accelerated pace' of the new environment; readers were invited to plug in and play through all their senses, not only through their eyes. The printed page was no longer a one-dimensional feast for the eyes; it became the interface for a more involving tactile experience. McLuhan's 'words in freedom' aim to achieve a similar type of experience, and his mosaic style of writing becomes an interactive tool that teaches you by un-doing your linear expectations, that is, by letting you experience his mosaic-montage process and refusing to let you study him and his texts in a linear way. Learning from previous avant-garde movements, McLuhan understood that the written page had to become the interface through which the new electric simultaneity would reveal itself, and that at a time when hypertexts were but a speculative possibility among a limited group of researchers. Bush's essay 'As We May Think' (1945), which is acknowledged by media scholars as a founding text in communication studies, was not popular yet, even though McLuhan might have known it. McLuhan worked with the language at his disposal, which he started to deconstruct and reassemble in a new creative, even artistic, modality. As already stated, he did not elaborate a linguistic theory, nor did he develop models for textual analysis similar to those later conceptualized by other schools of criticism. Instead, he experimented with language in the wake of new avant-garde interfaces – all experiments mediated through his solid humanistic tradition.

The paradox underpinning the elaboration of the mosaic style of writing is how to open the old medium – writing – to new media in a way that preserves the thought processes *of the old medium itself*. But it is, in turn, part of another paradox which is implicit in the very form of the electric media. *Acoustic* perception must, in fact, be expressed through a form which is inevitably (and here is the paradox) *visually* rendered and shaped. The electric age comes after the literate age; by necessity, according to McLuhan, it must take the literate age as its content. Individuals cannot cancel centuries of literacy – even if they think they can – because the orality induced by the new electric media is itself a *literate* secondary orality. Instead of asking the old question, Can Dick and Jane read? we now ask: are they media *literate?*

The new electric and electronic media are still dependent upon the written medium. As Ong reminds us: 'The electronic age is also an age of "secondary orality," the orality of telephones, radio and television, which depends on writing and print for its existence.'[22] Secondary orality is a sort of 'impure' and 'hybrid' orality, since both writing and printing stay as fundamental components of the new technological language. It is, in fact, a *parole* or spoken language determined by acoustic and tactile means. Secondary orality is so called because by its very nature or 'physiology' it is both spoken-as-written and/or written-as-spoken. It is the related interplay of speech and text, that is, the perceptive dynamics which take place between media and their users on the computer screen; or when text-messaging; or when activating applications through image and touch on i-phones. The acoustic aspect, as implied by McLuhan, means the remodelling of the environment by turning it from a visual bias to an oral bias even while using, at the same time, older media as fundamental components of the ongoing communicative process: old media integrate into new media and are re-elaborated into new combinations and hybrids. Old media don't die; they just fade into the background of new media. Hence, an old medium does not disappear; on the contrary, the new medium often enhances the old medium's subtler properties, which have so far been neglected because of standardized use.

This is another paradox which relates to McLuhan's well-known idea of the rear-view mirror effect. A new environment (meaning here the complex set of interactions which take place between media and individuals) not only enables us to fully see the previous environment, but it becomes itself the ground upon which the old medium is then turned into a renewed figure. The old environment is therefore retrieved and turned into an observable content. The reverse of this coin is, of course, that because of the rear-view mirror effect, we risk seeing the old ground, now behind us, more easily than the new figure, until that figure itself becomes the old ground. Imagine it this way, as McLuhan did in his perennial best-seller, *Understanding Media*: thought is the content of speech; speech is the content of written words; written words are the content of books; novels (sequential narratives) are the content of movies; movies are the content of television.

Now imagine the kind of change digital access will bring to analog content, causing a convergence that will mediate the total mediascape into the content of thought. That is no longer the world of secondary orality. Electric media retrieve both the alphabet and the printed word and include them in the newly convergent *post-secondary orality*: this is, in fact, our new evolving ground. Through the digital, we are shifting from secondary orality to post-secondary orality. What is now done in digital hypertexts, McLuhan had already started doing on the printed page. His discontinuous mosaic form of writing was what showed me, in 1996 when I first read *Gutenberg Galaxy*, the new potentialities inherent in the old linear medium of print. Released and freed from a too rigid structure imposed by the mechanics of print culture, words can retrieve ancient heuristic properties linked to ancient societal constructs and systems of knowledge. Today, we are on the brink of these new heuristic potentialities, which are emphasized and retrieved by new forms of media that seem to enhance participation in process more than privacy and detachment, albeit in vicarious ways.

McLuhan was not around when the Internet turned planet Earth into a connected globe. But he read Norbert Weiner on cybernetics and understood that the electrified command and control of the computer age would preserve the book nonetheless. He grasped what the new form would do to communication studies, and reconfigured its effects and how it would launch the electric tribal circle. Adopting and adapting strategies derived from modernist explorers, he transformed his printed pages into crafty radars detecting and revealing the electric simultaneity. The mosaic style of writing is a form of writing that is an open skill. It encourages deep participation, whereby readers are asked to fill in the gaps, so that both knowledge and ignorance play a role in the process. McLuhan's bold associations make resonate both what we know and what we do not know. It is the application of Bacon's broken knowledge to electric simultaneity, mediated, in turn, through modernist techniques. The mosaic rhetorical strategies are employed to convey the complexity of generating knowledge. If we do not play according to the rhetorician's intention, we behave like I.A. Richard's mathematicians and turn the implicit *paideia* into a trivial version of *Reader's Digest*.

A similar risk is always present when exploring the World Wide Web: we jump from a *fragment* to the next one, but if we do not make the interval *resonate*, we flatten our understanding and turn *knowledge* into *information*; we also tend to oversimplify complex issues, and neglect history or the nature of our stratified memories. We must look for the archetype in

McLuhan's communicative process if we want to preserve an independent critical attitude, something which is, in fact, the greatest challenge in a world saturated by hyper-reality and corporate simulacra. In the late 1950s, McLuhan suggested that in order to counterbalance the side effects of media already active outside the classroom and turning students into 'consumers,' the 'co-authors' of information and knowledge – teachers and scholars – should no longer be 'the source of data but of *insight*.'[23] Consistently, his probes do not translate data, but the dynamics underpinning the probing process, of which the mosaic is the interactive playground. While engaging with the mosaic, we learn by apprenticeship, by doing, that is, in an interactive mode.

Post-secondary orality is the world in which human beings are dematerialized and rematerialized, or, better, mediated through technological interactivity: touch screens popularize new ways of interfacing organic and inorganic components; digital design creates artificial landscapes we experience physically in 3D. In such an environment, to learn often means to also have fun. If we approach McLuhan's mosaic as a post-secondary orality device, we realize that, in fact, it is the precursor of today's interactive languages: through it we, too, can materialize and dematerialize ideas and environments. But, most importantly, through the mosaic we can also experience McLuhan's own persona, while at the same time playing with all his masks at once: the oracle, the guru, the modernist, and the techno-fan. Depending on the mask we focus upon, a probe will appear as either a *formula*, or an *interval*, or a *fragment*, or a *link* to his material body, to his complex *discourse*. But, if you think of it, each of these terms is nothing but a synonym for a *tessera*, a piece of the mosaic which acquires meaning when juxtaposed with all others. Let's now probe the mosaic through McLuhan's various masks. In the end, we will learn that it is the written body which preserves McLuhan in the present, tying all his discarnate versions to the solidity of his own evocative verbo-voco-visual words.

3 Thus Spoke the Oracle

Oracular Pronouncements

It is not difficult to visualize the mask of McLuhan *the Oracle*: we see a good discarnate version of it in the documentary *The Medium Is the Massage*.[1] Released in 1968 and based on the volume published the year before, we have a powerful series of images showing McLuhan the oracle in the process of translating his thoughts into speech. In an effort to translate his ideas orally, that is, not through a linear sequence but through verbal pronouncements, McLuhan is portrayed through close-ups, his face always at the centre of the scene. The overall effect is quite enchanting: he appears to be uttering uncanny formulas – oracular pronouncements – orchestrated to facilitate memorization. Alert audiences soon realize that those formulas are in the probes and puns we have already encountered in his writings. We also know that, through the years, many have tried to interpret them in various contexts. So much so, that even though they were first uttered by a capable elocutionist well aware of rhetorical strategies, in time those same words have in turn been twisted, oversimplified, over-celebrated. In the hands (or mouths) of either too skeptical or too faithful interpreters, they have often flipped into their reverse and become slogans: McLuhan's archetypes have become clichés. As with all oracular pronouncements, it is the listeners and not the oracle who produce and adapt meaning to their contingent needs. Why should it have been any different for the *oracle* of the University of Toronto Coach House?

It seems to me that of the various masks we have put on McLuhan, the oracle is the most suitable one. *Oracle* is a term which traces back to a form of communication related to oral societies, and the idea of clairvoyance which is traditionally associated with the oracle's powers is also strictly connected to the oracle's endowments as an observer and as a storyteller. Questioned by her/his own people about future events, the oracle stood between humans and gods, mediating between ignorance and knowledge. Speaking from the navel of the world, or from another cave in the Mediterranean city of Cumae, the most famous oracle of Delphi, or others less popular but equally intriguing, such as the Cumaean Sibyl, gave their responses in the form of obscure sentences, which the audience was compelled to interpret and translate into meaningful *prophecies*. The oracle's ambiguous responses were inscribed into the popular oral tradition, and linked to the history and vicissitudes of the community, but were also open to different, even opposing, interpretations. The oracle's response always followed his/her observation of a given environment: the flight of birds, the way the water flows, the way a leaf falls, are all *signs* that the oracle perceived and rendered orally through a narrative which is intentionally arcane: it must preserve the prestige and power traditionally connected to the mystery of reading the signs of fateful nature. To read and to know meant, in fact, power, and it still does. The oracle's pronouncements are therefore based on a rhetorical construction capable of embedding experience in an 'open' way, but often conveyed through formulas or riddles which, though arcane, are nevertheless easy to remember. The oracle's responses are built, not upon an analytical or linear construction, but upon an analogical and associative verbal assemblage of images, which must be revealed first intuitively, and then questioned and analysed for their possible meanings. The oracle's prophecies are therefore conceived as a poetic translation of natural signs, which often acquire a full meaning only when the events have in fact taken place. The listeners have a role to play: it is through their interpretation of the oracle's speech that words acquire meaning. As mediators of knowledge, the oracles urge their audience to enquire further, to take responsibility and connect to what is eventually 'revealed.' The warnings on the Temple of Delphi leave no doubt:

I warn you, whoever you are …
Oh, you who wish to probe the arcanes of nature, if you do not find within
    yourself that which you seek, neither shall you be able to find it outside.
If you ignore the excellencies of your own house, how do you intend to find
    other excellencies?
In you is hidden the treasure of treasures.
Oh, man, know thyself and thou shall know the Universe and the Gods!

Come to think of it, McLuhan's mosaic aims to do just that. It does not offer a final interpretation or final truth; instead, it engages its readers in a reading process conducive to experience and the production of meaning through a verbal construction which might sound arcane. But it is only different from what audiences would expect. And, just as has happened to the oracle's pronouncements, McLuhan's statements have become clearer through time: we have come to know ourselves and our electric environment better, and we have started to access the electric universe and gods.

The oracle belongs to a society which is predominantly oral and tribal. Marshall McLuhan belonged to a literate society which was rediscovering a new orality through electric media, while evolving into the post-literate environment we live in now. Through his oracle's mask, McLuhan retrieved, in fact, an ancient oral tradition which he employed to adjust literacy to the high-tech communicative potentialities. I do not think it is by chance that Walter J. Ong, who came to know McLuhan's work firsthand when they met at Saint Louis University and who attended classes on the Renaissance and rhetoric taught by the Canadian scholar, is the one who has postulated the interfacing of literacy and orality. In both his letters and books, Ong often acknowledged that McLuhan was in fact 'a superb teacher' who 'could stir people's minds.'[2] Through his teaching and conversations, McLuhan insisted that in the electric age a different approach to writing could contribute to restoring the balance between oral and visual perceptive modes, in turn restoring harmony between inner and outer worlds. It is in this direction that McLuhan's acoustic writing began to operate.

While McLuhan applied orality and its rhetoric to literacy through artistic modes, Ong contributed a scholarly investigation of their interface. In his classic *Orality and Literacy: The Technologizing of the Word* (1982), he overtly acknowledges the pioneering role of McLuhan's 'oracular pronouncements, too glib for some readers, but often deeply perceptive';[3] Ong discusses McLuhan's probes as 'gnomic' sayings, and suggests that McLuhan's investigations, even though they are based on literacy, re-enact oral interplay. To define McLuhan's probes as 'oracular pronouncements,' as he does, implies perceiving them as *uttered* or *outered* statements; in other words, Ong tells us that, by impersonating the oracle of the electric age, McLuhan probed the artificial nature of the new environment, and mediated its signs through what we can appreciate today as witty post-literate sayings. Ong insists on McLuhan's 'vast electric learning and his startling insights,' and on his 'oral-textual contrasts,' while he at the same time hints at the fact that literacy is 'infinitely adaptable': 'Literacy can be used to reconstruct for ourselves the pristine human consciousness which was not literate at all ... such reconstruction can bring a better understanding of what literacy itself has meant in shaping man's consciousness toward and in high-technology cultures.'[4] This is what the mosaic can do for us. Let us now discover how the oracle enters McLuhan's written body.

Interfacing Orality and Literacy

In *Orality and Literacy*, Ong defines some basic tenets pertaining to orality which can be summed up as follows: oral-based expressions are additive rather than subordinative; aggregative and not analytic; redundant or copious; conservative or traditionalist; directly related to the human lifework; agonistically toned; empathic; homeostatic (that is, preserving inner equilibrium); situational and not abstract. If we assess McLuhan's mosaic in the light of these characteristics, we realize that, in fact, it matches almost all of them: the mosaic is therefore a *literate oral* form of communication, that is, a post-literate form of writing which readjusts literacy *through* and *to* oral cognitive modes. I trust Ong when he says that 'the basic of orality of language is permanent,' so much so that while oral expression can exist without writing, writing cannot exist without orality.[5] Consistently, McLuhan's mosaic is a literate form which can be appreciated as an orally based expression translating McLuhan's oracular pronouncements, as well as his way of being in the world. We know that, especially in his later years, McLuhan resolved to dictate his ideas as they came to him; it is fascinating to notice that they came to him in the form of probes or puns or aphorisms, something that can be witnessed by watching his video interviews. Hence his language, be it uttered or written down, mirrored a frame of mind which he trained and consolidated through his humanistic roots: McLuhan experienced his own world while inhabiting an ancient oral tradition which he had put on since his years at Cambridge. That is the quintessential McLuhan we discover and retrieve through the mosaic. Orality is therefore a fundamental component of his post-literate oracular language: it is not just a way to dress his prose, but *his own way to function*, as a scholar and as an individual.

According to Ong, orally based thoughts and expressions are first of all 'additive rather than subordinative.'[6] Similarly, McLuhan's mosaic is built upon a series of additive juxtapositions (both/and, and/and)

and not upon subordinate clauses. The various comments on his probes are either quotations or statements, which are offered and delivered, not according to a subordinate logic, but as being *equally important*. The invitation to open his books and read/explore them from any page is a consequence of a paratactic construction based on equity and not on hierarchical or linear order. The mosaic is a direct syncretic and therefore additive form which immediately renders the simultaneity of perception, action, and reaction of living in the acoustic space of the electric environment. Subordinative forms of narrative are inevitably linked to visually based approaches. Linear progression is, in fact, structured to provide reinforcement around a central concept, embellished and complemented through ideas which are perceived as subordinate or accessorial to it, much like the by-side elements framing the vanishing point of a carefully conceived canvas.

In McLuhan's mosaic, new concepts add to the previous ones, forcing them all to realign in the light of the insight that the new fragment encapsulates. Altogether, they give shape to a complex ground, and the various probes and quotations are perceived as figures, all equally present and all equally important. The mosaic conceptualizes the difference between 'method' and 'knowledge broken.' A similar difference is found, for instance, when comparing a painting by Cimabue and a painting by Raphael, that is, when comparing late Middle Ages and Renaissance visual art: in the latter, perspective is what conveys a visual order to the scene, and the ideas of foreground and background translate into a subordinative rendering of the various elements whose narrative has been arranged by the painter. Observing a late Middle Ages canvas is a different experience: everything is offered as if standing on the same plane and simultaneously; proportions are not rendered realistically, but symbolically or emotionally, and to appreciate its narrative we have to complete the canvas through what we already know. We contribute to that very narrative ourselves; we convey order and importance to what we see and experience. As McLuhan would say, in a Renaissance painting, figures and ground separate; in a Middle Ages canvas, they collapse. Each painting strategy mirrors a different environmental setting: Renaissance society was, in fact, an accomplished literate society; the Middle Ages were instead an age of transition from the oral to the literate. A few centuries later, other works of art mirrored another shift, from the literate to the post-literate: from the late nineteenth century, post-Impressionism, Futurism, Vorticism, Cubism, Expressionism, and other avant-garde schools of painting returned to *additive* renderings, now complicated by the simultaneous re-conceptualization of evolving physical and emotional realities. They were re-entering orality.

A form which does not subordinate but adds is also 'aggregative rather than analytic'; as such, Ong teaches us that oral expressions depend on 'formulas to implement memory.'[7] This is a crucial passage in his analysis because he also discusses formulas in relation to the making of *commonplaces*; since both terms play a role in the way we have come to approach McLuhan's pronouncements, it is worth investigating how these terms relate to the interfacing of literacy and orality in his own form of communication.

Ong retrieves the evolution of commonplaces in relation to their original double meaning: *LOCI COMMUNES* (commonplaces) were in fact either 'seats of arguments considered as abstract headings in today's parlance' or 'collections of sayings (in effect formulas) on various topics ... that could be worked into one's own speech-making or writing.'[8] In a given society, commonplaces and formulas can therefore serve two different functions: originally, they bring the community together and constitute a shared knowledge which they condense so as to facilitate memorization; in time, their semantic depth flattens, and they remain as mere decorative elements of either speech or writing. What was originally conceived to preserve the unity of a group becomes, instead, a tool to captivate and persuade the audience: the rhetorician who best performs his/her speech wins consent. We consider, in fact, rhetoric to be *the art of persuasion*. *Craft* is perhaps a better definition, as rhetoric has rules that its disciples have to learn: *inventio, dispositio, elocutio, memoria,* and *actio* are the five classic parts of rhetoric one has to master to become a good orator. The idea of 'good orator' changes through time. In the ancient oral society, the good orator addressed all knowledge by mastering the liberal arts of the *trivium*. But in time, a split took place between grammarians and dialecticians, based on a different interpretation of how to pursue knowledge. Through *precepts* was the strategy of choice if you were a grammarian; through *concepts* if you were a dialectician. Hence, if you decided to be a grammarian, rhetoric would become your sister art in the exploration of the book of nature through language and its etymology; if you were to become a dialectician, rhetoric was the craft you needed to mesmerize your audience and disseminate your truth. Grammar and rhetoric combined led to broken knowledge (aphorisms); dialectic and rhetoric combined led to method (formulas). The split of the liberal arts of the *trivium* ends the spirit of the School of Athens and opens the gates to the School of Paris, to modernity: from then onward, *logos* is no longer both language and reason, but either one or the other. Soul and mind proceed separately, and, in Western society, method wins over aphorisms.[9]

The basis of all eloquent speech was, therefore, the act of *inventio*, that is, the discovery or finding of arguments, which you could improve through *dispositio* and *elocutio*; the former helped you to 'dispose' or arrange your arguments; the latter contributed to their formal and stylistic elaboration and made your elocution unique. Over time, though, *inventio* shifts from an original activity to a simpler operation of stock-taking: arguments and findings accumulate in sayings, which are then stored in the individual or collective *memoria*, or memory. Artfully retrieved and repeated in front of an audience through an *actio*, a public speech, the shared *formulas, sayings, commonplaces*, were finally perceived as reassuring manifestations of popular wisdom. This transition is typical not only of orally based societies, but also of the first chirographic renderings of speech, usually in a poetical form. In pristine forms of literacy, formulas – which an oral community perceives as the synthesis of complex experiences and which constitute an aggregative moment for the community – are turned into rhetorical devices enabling the community to memorize a collection of sayings, which are now part of the folklore and traditions of that very community. This is the case, for instance, of the Anglo-Saxon *kenning* in poetry, a rhetorical figure which encapsulates things and people in verbal expressions which become popular and stay in people's minds as a shared rhetorical alphabet.

Within the humanities, McLuhan perceived himself as a grammarian; doubtless, his probes constitute the synthesis of a broader set of speculations that they store and render available to the community at any time, provided that the community shares not only the same knowledge, but also a similar approach to it. So conceived, McLuhan's mosaic is in fact an analogical form juxtaposing discrete units and textual fragments which are tremendously aggregative. It is this characteristic that brings us into the picture as active readers, as a community which accepts the task of linking each condensed probe to a broader set of data (knowledge). If we perform our task successfully, we preserve and experience the various meaningful nuances the probe embeds (the medium is the *message/ massage/mass-age/mess-age*); if we do not, we continue to turn it into a formula; that is, we preserve only one of its many meanings. From probes to formulas, from archetype to clichés – this is particularly true if the probe is quoted outside of its original text, that is, if it is deprived of its simultaneous interplay with other probes or with their relevant ground.

We often hear McLuhan's probes repeated as all-fitting formulas. Such formulas as 'the medium is the message' are now part of a shared jargon people use worldwide. Doubtless, there is a positive element in this: we often speak *mcluhanese* at a global scale, even though we are not always aware of it; we have put on McLuhan's language to embellish our conversations and to consolidate our belonging to a world community, our 'global village.' We have gained some cohesion as a worldwide audience, but we have certainly lost track of the original source: Marshall McLuhan. We are passive, not active, users of McLuhan's language; we do not appreciate its potentialities and have flattened its original function. By so doing, we not only dismiss the mystery of his oracular pronouncements; we also miss the potentialities of his post-literate interface. Moreover, we tend to delegate others to interpret those pronouncements for us. Beside an oracle often stood a high priest who acted as an interface between the audience and the oracle. While the oracle's pronouncements mediate what is unknown (the future) and what is known (nature), leaving the audience acoustically suspended with a multitude of meanings, the high priest turns the circle into a line: he or she mediates the arcane and solves, that is, interprets, the riddles for us. From multiple choice to one-way understanding, from archetype to cliché – generally speaking, today's media analysts, the priests of the high-tech world, do not *employ* McLuhan's mosaic as a device: generally, they are still distracted by its content; they are not focusing on its form. McLuhan's books are more than packages for his 'slogans': they are interactive educational tools in which it is the interplay between form and content that conveys meaning. They are, so to speak, *processes* not *anthologies;* they are not just *collections of sayings.* Not understanding such a difference is a way to actually kill McLuhan, not just his oracular mask.

Performative Storytelling

McLuhan was not a moderate oracle; understatement was not his favourite rhetorical device. He loved to talk – his biographers tell us that he used to call friends in the middle of the night to share his ideas with them. Wordiness was to his written body what blood was to his physical body. While his grand media narrative can be reduced to a few tenets and to four simple laws, that same narrative is told again and again all through his books, while continuously probing both media and environmental situations. McLuhan's mosaic pinpoints *redundancy* or copiousness, another feature of oral forms of communication.[10] Repetition is therefore a strategy he consciously employed when performing his oracular pronouncements to develop intertextuality between lines, paragraphs, chapters, and, of course, the text, its outer context and readers. The ideas underpinning his explorations are presented several times in his texts through slightly changed statements in a way which recalls another rhetorical device typical of early forms of poetry, that is, *variation*. Through variation, in fact, the same idea was repeated throughout the text in order to accustom the readers to it. For example, in *Understanding Media*, the idea that TV is a 're-action medium' – that is, a *cold* and therefore involving medium[11] – is a core idea and is repeated again and again in the volume. The repetition is often carried out through loan-translations (a *copia* or a *calco*) positioned only a few pages apart, as in the case of the Mckworth head-camera: this experimental device monitoring the physical responses of TV viewers is introduced twice with almost identical words, to emphasize the involving character of TV as a medium.[12]

Of course, you can also say – as many critics have – that McLuhan did not polish or edit his books as he should have. But, in fact, he was pursuing his own writing strategy, which, in turn, mirrored his frame of mind, his way of thinking. Repeating the same concept in different parts of the same volume, juxtaposing it to new ideas, new associations, new glosses, keeps readers engaged. It sounds more like conversation than predication: don't you repeat things more than once when you want to make sure that your listener is in fact with you? Repetition also breeds familiarity and encourages readers to retrieve a series of thoughts which might have previously gone unnoticed; it is a way to trigger *new implications for old content*. It is a strategy that all storytellers know: the same plot is repeated before old and new audiences, thus creating a communal bond and a shared mythology. Each time, however, good storytellers either add or change some of the details, so as to keep interest alive and to encourage participation in a renewed process of discovery.

Redundancy and copiousness also relate to what Ong defines as the 'conservative or traditionalist' character of orality: you say over and over what you have experienced and what you know, in order to preserve it against time. The risk is that this 'inhibits intellectual experimentation' due to the ensuing establishment of a 'highly traditionalist or conservative set of mind.'[13] Prior to the written form, memorization was the only way to retain experience. In fact, the characteristics of orality examined so far aim to facilitate memorization; its being additive, aggregative, formulaic, and redundant contributes to preserving arguments and their related experiences. By translating these characteristics, McLuhan's mosaic also aims to retain what has been previously learned. In this sense, we can consider the mosaic as a form of writing which is *literally* conservative, as it preserves and retains knowledge through literate language. But being also post-literate, that is, being an oral-literate and not simply either an oral or a literate form of communication, McLuhan's mosaic does not necessarily mirror a conservative set of mind (the one which keeps the small tribe, or the little community, together); it does not inhibit intellectual experimentation, unless, of course, you turn probes into formulas, that is, unless you close the window, so to speak.[14] As a form, the mosaic preserves knowledge while triggering intellectual experimentation. Or, better, the mosaic triggers intellectual experimentation precisely because it preserves the complexity of knowledge through its broken language. It is the dislocation of a visual medium according to old and new oral/acoustic modes which enables the use of literacy to 'reconstruct for ourselves the pristine human consciousness which was not literate at all.'[15] McLuhan's post-literate mosaic uses several oral communicative features. However, it gives shape to more complex experiences which no longer belong to a group limited in time and space, but to the heterogeneous crowds who now inhabit the world of instantaneous communications. Intellectual experimentation is enhanced not inhibited. How readers approach the oracle's pronouncements, whether or not they read them as plain clichés or slogans, or use them as probes, depends on their skill in reading *through* them.

Words matter; language matters; language, so to speak, *weights*. In the mosaic, language does not translate theoretical speculations, but pragmatic and solid investigations, just as does an imagist poem: words are *things*; they are *actions*, not *abstractions*. Again (yes, I'm repeating things: are you with me?), McLuhan's retrieval of the *logos* is to be understood as the retrieval of ancient grammar. Knowledge is experienced not *taught*. Percepts counterbalance concepts. Metaphysics meets Physic. Logos retains its original complexity: logos as *logic*, and logos as *verbal*. McLuhan goes back to a tradition which is clearly pre-Platonic: it is Plato who replaces Homer's storytelling and opens the doors to literacy, and later to 'the School of Paris' (the school of dialecticians), as the new pillars of Western culture. In *Understanding Media*, McLuhan indicates Plato as the one who started to envisage a new educational system based on specialization.[16] McLuhan's storytelling aims instead not to preach reality but *to perform it*, that is, to bring it and his readers together through an active and engaging act of reading which is, in itself, a way of experiencing reality and knowledge; it is an act of reading which aims to learn the evolving grammar (the basic principles) of the 'depth-involving newness'[17] of the post-literate age. It is difficult to mediate what we constantly experience because we are too involved in it to actually grasp it. But the mosaic succeeds in rendering the simultaneity of the electric age; as a post-literate form, it is close 'to the human lifework' of its time, which is now characterized by 'the absence of elaborated analytic categories depending on writing to structure knowledge.'[18] The mosaic triggers actions; it performs a role and participates in the process of understanding. It is a direct rendering of the electric wholeness, a live show of the world in action. Whereas linearity encourages specialization, McLuhan's writing encourages *holism* and tries to convey wisdom and knowledge *as a whole*, and he asks his readers to play the same game. It is a strategy which does not seek to win consent, but which encourages confrontation and challenges; McLuhan's mosaic is therefore 'agonistically toned' because 'by keeping knowledge embedded in the human lifework, orality situates knowledge within a context of struggle.'[19] And it was a struggle which also transcended the mosaic and reached the oracle: his approach to knowledge was questioned, debated, and opposed as much as it was celebrated.

A performative storytelling is therefore a narrative which engages and challenges not only the teller, but also the audience. In oral societies, this idea well translates the mimetic approach to both language and environment. Orality is in fact 'empathic and participatory rather than objectively distanced.'[20] Writing is a medium that brings objectivity and makes us look at things from a distance. Speech is a medium that abridges distance between individuals and their environment. Literacy encourages detachment and rationality; orality encourages involvement and intuition. Anthropologists have shown us that oral societies do not share our idea of *private space*, nor our idea of the *self* or of *the individual*: they have not elaborated the idea of distance typical of literate Western societies. Oral societies do not experience a dichotomy between *inner* and *outer* world; their way to approach their environment is mimetic. Individuals inhabit a space together and share experiences within a choral context that they preserve and defend. In this sense, Ong defines oral societies as being 'homeostatic'[21] and 'situational rather than abstract.'[22] They live in the present; their communal bond is reinforced through storytelling, whose goal is to preserve the knowledge they have acquired through experience, by doing and not by theorizing. In our post-secondary orality societies, such an inclusive and mimetic way of living is artificially retrieved. We tend to live in the present, in the here and now ('Life is now' was the slogan of a popular wireless telephone company), and technology helps us in that. We juxtapose reality and its mediated rendering, sometimes blurring the two levels in an uncanny scenario, as when we watch TV on our mobile phone while travelling on buses or waiting in line to enter a public office. And we use language in paradoxical ways to express all that, often unconsciously. What is a *reality show*? What is now *real*? What is *fictional*? Do we think about these linguistic and conceptual paradoxes when we employ language this way? Or are we numbed by the homeostatic characteristics of our accelerated depth-involving newness? McLuhan loved paradoxes and played with them; but he did so consciously and with a probing intent. Playing with the mosaic trains us to both ask and answer these questions, but not because it tells us how to do that: we engage with situations, we experience them, we perform. We learn by doing.

As a performative storytelling, while re-enacting the movement, the mosaic trains us to work on its patterns. It takes us inside (as orality does) and keeps us detached (as literacy does). It is a dynamic form which brings together inner and outer landscapes, and recreates cognitive experiences leading to knowledge, not through distance, but through inclusion. It does it through literacy, which is here meant not to guide us, but to involve us and tune us into the electric *sensibility*; our idea of *being* – that is, direct participation in action and events – replaces the idea of *becoming* – which implies a traditional acquisition of knowledge based on a rational and progressive approach to experiences perceived through distance as other than oneself. It is through the retrieval of the whole *logos* that we regain control of the world in progress and perform an active role in the process: 'Before writing, logo was active and metamorphic rather than neutral: words and deeds were related, as were words and things. The logos of creation is of the same order: "Let there be light" IS the uttering or outering of light.'[23] The mosaic creates knowledge, not through notions, but through a constant challenge to its readers.

'*I warn you, whoever you are …*'

4 Let the Guru Resound

The Gurus' Guru

Both love and truth are in the eyes of the beholder. Many of McLuhan's former students keep saying that McLuhan *got the sixties*, by that implying that he was among the few who engaged with the countercultures of the time, while the academic world resented them. Fair enough. But McLuhan was not, as the same students also imply, in favour of those countercultures *tout court*. Neither was he against them. Those who considered McLuhan as *one of them*, be *they* Frye's anti-intellectuals or activists, were but interpreting his oracular pronouncements one way. McLuhan was both inside and outside his time; like Poe's mariner, he contemplated the 1960s maelstrom through the interplay of all the various figures in turn emerging from the water spirals. And, like Poe's mariner, he also had some fun in doing it. His playful detachment made him popular – that is, trustable – among very different audiences alike. Today, it is easier for us to realize that McLuhan's broader vision enabled him to guide others through the maze of the electric age. He helped to bring *some light*. This is what a guru does:

> *Guru*
> The syllable gu means shadows
> The syllable ru, he who disperses them,
> Because of the power to disperse darkness
> The guru is thus named. (*Advayataraka Upanishad* 14–18, verse 5)

A guru is therefore a teacher, someone who disperses the shadows of ignorance and enlightens his pupils. As a media guru, McLuhan enlightened many different pupils both inside and outside his classrooms; and, being a popular guru, he attracted all sorts of pilgrims, including those who were leaders and sages in their own temples.

Imagine that it is the late 1960s, in Toronto, and that you are crossing the St Michael campus, rushing to your next class or meeting. All of the sudden, you see John Lennon and Yoko Ono arriving at the Coach House and entering Marshall McLuhan's Centre for Culture and Technology. Then imagine that happening on a regular basis: a never-ending procession of celebrities from both the corporate or institutional world and the world of countercultures entering McLuhan's temple at the University of Toronto. McLuhan was more than just the *media guru*: he was the *gurus' guru*, discussing the future of communication and technology with other popular people, as diverse as Lord Beaverbrook, Keith Carradine, and Pierre Trudeau. McLuhan was a sought-after figure for both young rebels and representatives of the most traditional institutions: he was in demand among both those who believed in and defended the establishment, and those who wanted to turn it upside-down. In that, McLuhan-the-media-guru was unique: at a time of dramatic technological change, he was perceived as a lighthouse by all sorts of mariners lost in the new media maelstrom. It is as if both President Obama and Sarah Palin went to the same spin-doctor!

In the 1960s, when the three *M*s of the day were Marx, Mao, and Marcuse, McLuhan provided a fourth *M*; it was the only *M* who never fought for a specific political or cultural cause, even when brought close to either one or the other.[1] He explored across situations, engaging with whomever was interested in his ideas on communication. McLuhan probed not only people and ideas, but also new media as factors of change affecting the making of a new technological holism which was relevant among political, corporate, and cultural agencies alike. Through his language, he brought the opposites together: 'Computers are the LSD of the corporate word' was a perfect probe that he coined to epitomize what stood beyond that holism, something that he defined as the *depth-involving newness* of his time. How could you not be fascinated by his knowledge of what was going on in the world when all previous wisdom and authority were constantly questioned? Inevitably, in the 1960s his media guru mask prevailed and was soon translated into an icon, which crystallized McLuhan into the 'high priest of popcult and metaphysician of media.' This definition was offered as an introduction to a famous interview published by *Playboy* magazine in 1969, which consolidated McLuhan's fame worldwide, but which also led to the misunderstanding later recalled by

Northrop Frye. In that interview, McLuhan is cast as a pop guru enlightening different audiences on the new media metaphysic, discussing 'psychic communal integration made possible by the electronic media,' and reading the youth counterculture in terms of the new electric tribalism. Those of you who take time to carefully read that interview will immediately realize that McLuhan was, in fact, discussing a very complex set of social, cultural, anthropological, and technological issues; but they are all blurred by the overwhelming introductory captions. What I want to do instead in this chapter is to approach the mask of the media guru as the one bringing into the mosaic the fertile encounter between Eastern and Western cultural traditions.

The mosaic is in fact based on a renewed idea of time-space interplay which characterizes both traditional Eastern philosophies and Western scientific discoveries in the field of physics which, at the turn of the previous century, led to the technological developments that McLuhan himself was later experiencing and unveiling. Let's start by stating that McLuhan considered the meeting of Eastern and Western traditions as the inevitable consequence of the dynamics of the new media, leading to the sudden clash and juxtaposition of different cultural systems; but he also perceived that encounter as an opportunity for both cultures to enter into a fruitful dialogue, that is, to learn from each other. Together, they could work out and engage with the evolving *sensibility* of the global village, an environment which was now shared by all cultures alike and which McLuhan defined as the *fourth world* of instant communication embracing all the pre-existing worlds.[2]

We now approach the mosaic as the interface through which the dialogue between Western and Eastern cultural traditions is consciously enacted. It constitutes a new space through which lights disperse shadows and the media guru guides you out of environmental ignorance.

Redefining Space

McLuhan's idea of *depth-involving newness* is based on a renewed approach to space which he developed by juxtaposing Eastern philosophies, Western physics, and, as we will further explore in the following chapter, modernist experiments. It was a bold juxtaposition which immediately resonated with the countercultural holism of the 1960s and 1970s, when cross-investigations of apparently unrelated – if not opposing – fields of study were encouraged. Written in 1975, physicist Fritjof Capra's *The Tao of Physics: An Exploration of the Parallels between Modern Physics and Eastern Mysticism* is still an Evergreen best-seller and a classic of countercultural holism. Even though it was published at a time when McLuhan had already established his own writing technique based on his interdisciplinary approach, *The Tao of Physics* became a revealing subtext of his later productions, and especially of Marshall and Eric McLuhan's *Laws of Media*.

As we shall see, McLuhan's interest in Eastern cultures and quantum physics did not originate from a systematic study of both areas of knowledge; rather, it was often derived from indirect sources. Doubtless, he had a generalist (and very much criticized) approach to both domains; and yet this approach was based on a clever intuition conveyed through a conceptual and operative metaphor. McLuhan translated both Eastern literacy and philosophy, and the principles of quantum physics, into the idea of *field-approach* – *field* being both a basic concept of the latter, and a precise image mirroring the complexity of the former. McLuhan used this term to epitomize his way of probing the hidden pattern of forces always at work in any given environment. His field-approach dismissed the classic physics idea of space, and embraced the new quantum physics concept of space-time continuum (literally: 'The four-dimensional continuum of one temporal and three spatial coordinates in which any event or physical object is located'). It is, in fact, a more dynamic approach. through which all investigated situations are considered to be shifting, their state depending on the constant interaction between things and people, as well as environmental conditions. In such a vision, the linear concept of *distance* is replaced by the acoustic idea of *interval*, meaning the space of interaction through which both action and reaction (that is, interactive communication) are activated. This functional idea, bringing together quantum physics and Eastern cultures, was often developed through paradoxes which challenged logic and encouraged indeterminacy and relativity: 'The modern physicist is at home with oriental field theory'; 'The method of the twentieth century is to use not a single but multiple models for experimental explorations – the technique of suspended judgment.'[3] It is an idea which also reconfigures the role of the players (be it the Western scientist or the Eastern philosopher) because they are asked to choose their understanding of the paradox (be it the uncanny result of an experiment, or the ambiguous riddle of a koan) from among a network of meaningful alternatives which are *all possible at the same time*. In both domains, the *paradox* is therefore applied as a strategy to accommodate what, in appearance, is disconnected or unrelated but which, in fact, is not. As Heisenberg himself recalled, all the contradictions will later be understood, following the progress of discovery.[4]

Paradoxes are as central in McLuhan's mosaic as they are fundamental to his provocative probes.

McLuhan's cross-reading of different domains, and his holistic approach to a renewed idea of *field*, anticipate an attitude also later explored by literary critics. For instance, in her seminal work, *The Cosmic Web: Scientific Field Models and Literary Strategies in the Twentieth Century*, Katherine Hayles describes the isomorphic approach to the idea of field characterizing scientific and humanistic research alike from the turn of the previous century. She defines the characteristics of the new narrative in terms of 'its fluid dynamic nature, the inclusion of the observer, the absence of detachable parts, and the mutuality of component interactions.'[5] It is a definition which also applies well to McLuhan's mosaic, which is a narrative based on a juxtaposition of field models derived from various exemplary domains, from ads to avant-garde experiments, from haikus to aphorisms. In particular, to develop his own idea of space and translate it into a model encapsulating his own explorations, McLuhan made great use of literature and the arts to mediate between different cognitive (classic and atomic physics) and cultural (Western and Eastern philosophies) approaches.

To this end, observations on various ideas of space and the related psychodynamic implications are scattered throughout his works, and they are then elaborated into a systematic methodology in a volume that was conceived with artist Harley Parker and published in 1968: *Through the Vanishing Point: Space in Poetry and Painting*. The intent of this book is nothing less than the investigation of the history of humankind through the interplay of painting and poetry, in order to reveal how 'men have groped toward the arts in hope of increased sensory awareness.' It is an ambitious project pursued through the constant juxtaposition of an inner and an outer journey, through poetry and painting respectively: 'a journey inward' – through poetry – and 'a journey outward to the appearance of things' – through painting. Inner and outer landscapes are interfaced through the arts in order to trigger a renewed awareness.[6] Here, the inter-art study is meant not to simply investigate the effects of one art on the other one, but, instead, to speculate on how cultural and environmental experiences have affected the human *sensorium*, with clear effects on our *sensibility* (to be understood as the way in which individuals perceive things) which the arts have registered and rendered through time. The authors write to prove that 'all the arts might be considered to act as counter-environments or counter-gradients,' so much so, that they 'can serve to increase the level of awareness, at least until they become entirely environmental and unperceived.'[7]

The cross-reading of artistic situations and production is conceived as a training for readers on how to become active players and how to work out the hidden pattern of forces underpinning one's own visible environment in real time. It is a follow-up to Pound's idea of the artist as 'the antenna of the race,' now updated by McLuhan as the image of art as the new DEW (Distant Early Warning) line, a definition which relates to the establishment of a system of radar stations in Arctic Canada during the Cold War. As a new technology, radars replaced the previous barrage-balloons system employed as an anti-aircraft environment during the Second World War.[8] To render his idea of how art and literature should now be employed, McLuhan juxtaposes two technological metaphors, each implying a different approach to the way observation is carried out: the balloon system offers a top-bottom perspective; whereas, radar replaces it with full-scale observation. The former is visually based and, as in a Renaissance canvas, perception is oriented in relation to a given visual vanishing point; whereas the latter is acoustically based and, as in a painting of the Middle Ages, perception reveals objects altogether and simultaneously. These two metaphors develop from a different approach to space, which is, in fact, the crucial paradigm in defining what we imply by 'perception.' However, as McLuhan notes in *Through the Vanishing Point*, we are not always aware of space, nor of our relation to it, because we tend to perceive it as an invisible component of our own reality: 'To contemporary man space is a cliché, an unexamined assumption: it is environmental, and modern man is therefore unaware of it.'[9] It is another way of saying that *water is unknown to a fish until it discovers air.*

When discussing space, McLuhan confronts Ernst Gombrich's *Art and Illusion*,[10] and argues that space is not a container for people or things; rather, space is created by people and things. It is not *given*, as it is reconfigured each time in relation with the modes of interplay between individuals and things within a dynamic context which is constantly evolving; it is a concept that contemporary architecture has fully exploited, creating forms which mould new spatial geometries and suggest to us new ways of moving through space (think of Frank Gehry's Guggenheim Museum in Bilbao, or of Daniel Libeskind's New York Green Garden Tower). It is for this reason that the idea of space of tribal societies (acoustic space) differs from the idea of space of Renaissance man. Similarly, the idea of space of Renaissance man (visual space) differs from that of the individual living in the electric age. And yet, the idea of space of the individual living in the electric age somehow recalls that of tribal man, as 'the new electronic interdependence recreates the world in the image of a global village.'[11] As the Italian Futurist painter Umberto Boccioni declared, when entering the electric age individuals become 'primitives of an unknown culture.'[12]

Holistic Mosaic: Western Science, Eastern Philosophies

As McLuhan probes in *Through the Vanishing Point*, the different perception of spatial existence is reflected in different sensorial modes which the arts have registered over time. Spatial existence also reflects different societal matrixes and different cultural models, in turn characterized by different approaches to knowledge and different scientific paradigms. In McLuhan's mosaic, space becomes a structural tenet reflecting his perception of the fourth world. To better appreciate this idea, some of Capra's tenets in his *The Tao of Physics* can be recalled as investigative patterns, in turn bridging Western science and Eastern philosophies as conceptual hybrids opening our doors of perception. In fact, Capra's positive comparison of Western rational knowledge, Pythagorean 'mathematical mysticism,' and modern physics, on the one hand, and Taoism and Eastern mysticism, on the other hand, is another way to translate *countercultural holism*, that is, a way to look for connecting patterns rather than differences between apparently opposing and very different contexts. In Capra's volume, 'field' is a key concept used to merge apparently dichotomic approaches. The physicist does not read his materials through Newton's rational logic; rather, he anticipates Hayles's 'cosmic dance' and works out a complex patchwork of field connections. In this book, Capra himself challenges the traditional Western scientific discourse through a holistic approach to both nature and the human mind. His premises are to be found in the shocking epistemological revolution which physicists began in the late nineteenth century and which came to full maturity in the first decade of the twentieth century:

> ... Newtonian mechanics was for a long time considered to be the final theory for the description of all natural phenomena, until electric and magnetic phenomena, which had no place in Newton's theory, were discovered. The discovery of these phenomena showed that the model was incomplete, that it could be applied only to a limited group of phenomena, essentially the motion of solid bodies ... Today we know that the Newtonian model is valid only for objects consisting of large numbers of atoms, and only for velocities which are small compared to the speed of light ... This does not mean that Newton's model is 'wrong' or that quantum theory and relativity

theory are 'right.' All these models are *approximations* which are valid for a certain range of phenomena ... The Eastern mystics, too, are well aware of the fact that all verbal description of reality are inaccurate or incomplete.[13]

We can define Capra's approach to knowledge as at once *holistic* and *ecological*, because new scientific models integrate and interact with all previous ones. Earlier forms of scientific models are not simply replaced or made obsolete; rather, they are accepted with all their limitations – *by approximation.* Their understanding is therefore *extended* by the acceptance of their scientific and cognitive incompleteness or indeterminacy (as Heisenberg admitted, 'One had learned that the old concepts fit nature only inaccurately').[14] They are preserved even though new discoveries are considered more relevant, and there is an awareness that even the latter can only provide a better understanding, not of a given scientific principle, but of its approximation. This is a paradox and a crucial tenet that forces us to reconsider the very idea of scientific truth or law, which is no longer understood as dogmatic but as a 'work in progress.' As we shall see in Part Three, McLuhan himself challenged the idea of *scientific law* or *statement* in his posthumous volume *Laws of Media: The New Science*, a volume which contains several references to Capra's ideas. The subtitle refers to Vico's idea of 'New Science,' a philosophical interpretation which undermined the modern idea of science in Descartes and Newton. In his preface to the volume, Eric McLuhan recalls that, working on a new edition of *Understanding Media*, his father started by reviewing its most severe criticisms; he found that some of the most recurring criticisms 'seemed to form a chorus of that's all very well for you, but it's NOT scientific.'[15] Hence, *Laws of Media* stands as a paradoxical challenge to that accusation. For Capra, as well as for McLuhan, the *interval* between various levels of approximation is what triggers curiosity and encourages further testing and research. The process of discovery is therefore conceived as a continuous dialogue which also gives meaning to errors and indeterminacies; old models are part of, or contained in, new ones, and knowledge is a continuous networking of possibilities.

A fascinating account of this process of discovery is offered by Werner Heisenberg in his volume *Physics and Philosophy* when he discusses the historical development of the quantum theory. The volume is, in fact, a beautiful journey into the change of approach to knowledge that the new physicists took at the turn of the previous century, when their experiments somehow dismissed most of what was traditionally accepted by classical physics. The description of Planck revealing his conceptual shift to his son while taking a long walk in the Grunewald wood outside of Berlin constitutes a powerful image conveying the acceptance of conceptual limits and the entering of a new cognitive wilderness which, in fact, turns those limits into positive stimuli. Heisenberg recalls how these scientists (himself, Planck, Einstein, Rutherford, Bohr, and others) accepted contradictions and paradoxes as part of their process of discovering theories which, nevertheless, were substantially true. He offers many examples of how 'again and again one found that the attempt to describe atomic events in the traditional terms of physics led to contradictions.' Heisenberg admits that 'the strangest experience of those years was that the paradoxes of quantum theory did not disappear during this process of clarification; on the contrary they became even more marked and more exciting ... By this time many physicists were convinced that these apparent contradictions belonged to the intrinsic structure of atomic physics.'[16] This is an idea which, in literature, the modernist writer Ford Madox Ford adopted when stating that his new impressionist novels were based on 'suggestions not dictates.'[17] Consistently, all his main characters are uncertain in their actions; they doubt and hesitate, and aporias become a structural tenet of his narrative.

The idea of paradoxical interrelated patterns is common to Eastern philosophies as well, whose very nature is holistic and ecological. Not only are Eastern philosophers aware of the complexity of each experience, but they also acknowledge the importance of paradoxical aspects of reality – an act which linear thinking cannot convey precisely because paradoxes cannot be fully explained. Paradoxes must be processed through the technique of the suspended judgment. All related speculations are therefore translated through a system of signs (ideograms), each relating to a set of experiences. Eastern literacy developed through communicative techniques which enhanced an aggregative rather than analytical combination of those very signs; the Japanese *koans* and *haiku* are at once poetical renderings and ways to experience the world. They are boxes of knowledge to be memorized and investigated. This implies that reading a koan or a haiku is a very active experience. It is an event: meaning depends on the probing of the conceptual aggregation encapsulated in a few words. What the new physics and Eastern philosophies have in common, as Capra clearly points out, is the *acceptance of contradictions* as the ordinary way of thinking, and the ordinary language, when confronting paradoxical situations. In other words, they both acknowledge the *approximate nature of all statements*, that is, the relativity of all translation of factual and conceptual discoveries into ordinary language.

In fact, in an effort to contain the complexity of intellectual experiences underpinning new scientific or philosophical discoveries, both groups employ symbols to condense information: scientists to contain something for which 'they would need several pages of ordinary writing,'[18] Eastern philosophers to convey the complexity of the probing itself (their real experience) while offering content. Both these ways of rendering reality are at once abstract and compressed, but they are based on a meaningful correspondence to the facts and the ideas they stand for. Both are complex literate systems that engage readers in a participatory process which transcends the mere visual approach. The readers themselves are to provide the connections and retrieve not only what each symbol stands for, but also how that relates to all other juxtaposing symbols, that is, to their hidden patterns.

McLuhan's interest in Eastern culture and its forms of communication, as well as his interest in new scientific discoveries, were not born in the 1960s. These interests dated back a few decades and evolved from his discovery of modernist avant-garde experiments. It is important to recall that McLuhan's sources were often secondary sources, namely, experimental forms of writing pertaining to the Western world of the twentieth century avant-gardes and adopted to pursue engaging poetical projects. For modernist writers, the search for new forms was neither a naïve nor an inspired act, but a conscious act mirroring their new way of conceiving reality. Pound, Eliot, Joyce, and other great masters of modernism abandoned the Romantic idea of the work of art conceived as a *mechanism* and adopted a more modern one of presenting their work as an *organism*; each component, each fragment of the whole, was not only a part of it, but also a representation of the whole itself, a sort of metonymical rendering of the more complex reality. It is an idea clearly derived from the new sciences of their time, as it introduces a dynamic concept which also includes the observer as an active part of the organism itself: it is an idea which relates to the presentation of a process, or of a work in progress. The image of the organism therefore constitutes a much more appropriate model to refine new aesthetics, which were already working with the ideas of movement and interplay in order to suggest an elusive and not a descriptive approach to reality. Regarding Eastern arts or letters, the modernist discoveries were not based on anthropological or ethnological investigation into 'otherness' as a pursuit of a real understanding of a different *civilization*; these, too, originated from an intellectual exploration aiming at challenging previous representative canons. Generally speaking, the search into Eastern philosophies was not a search pursued to understand and appreciate diversity as such, but an ambiguous appropriation of communicative codes functional to one's own aesthetical quest. Following a similar path, McLuhan's mediated probing of the field approach and of the ideogram derives from the need to respond to the above mentioned cultural and cognitive challenges of his time. He collaborated with scientists, as well as with cultural anthropologists, but his interest was primarily guided by his will to explore and compare different forms, techniques, and technologies of communication, to probe actuality in the pursuit of his media *grand narrative.*

In McLuhan's mosaic, Western literacy acquires the potential and significance of opening the traditional linear structure; and, in so doing, it acquires characteristics also similar to those we found in oriental cultures, where the ideogram is conceived as a true *gestalt:*

> For the ideograph even more than the hieroglyph is a complex *Gestalt* involving all the senses at once. The ideogram affords none of the separation and specialization of sense, none of the breaking apart of sight and sound and meaning which is the key to the phonetic alphabet.[19]

Following Pound's experiments with language, McLuhan interpreted the ideogram as a complex form which preserves a harmony and a deep connection between signifier and meaning unknown to the phonetic alphabet, and which involves all the senses simultaneously. Even though it appears visually as a *sign*, the ideograph still preserves a mode of perception which is multi-sensorial, referring to a series of images in nature, combinations, situations, and actions which force the reader into active sensory and cognitive participation. The passage from orality to literacy in Eastern societies did not contribute to a sensorial change since it relied upon a non-phonetic form of writing which preserves and renders an acoustic environment with its multi-sensorial dynamics: '… non-phonetic writing does not isolate the senses. Tactility is not a sense but an interplay of all senses.'[20] The ideogram is therefore associated with the idea of acoustic or tactile space, an idea which will be further commented upon later in this chapter, but is here associated with the idea of *mimesis.* This concept is key to understanding why in McLuhan's writing the acoustic dimension is conceived as *tactile* – or *interactive* – to the point of the two terms (acoustic and tactile) being often used synonymously – a fact which detractors used as evidence of McLuhan's lack of precision and of his superficial treatment of things.

Such an idea of tactility is enhanced by Eastern literacy. Whereas the phoneme represents the extreme atomization of sound and, therefore, the extreme fragmentation of space and knowledge in micro units detached from a meaningful context, the ideogram is a complex and intricate unit which preserves a harmony between perception and conceptualization. Whereas the phonetic alphabet isolates the figure from the ground, the ideograph preserves the two in a syncretic way. Following the adoption of the phonetic alphabet, in the Western world,

> the letters ... came to be regarded as not only having no meaning but also as having no properties. The alphabet served as the formal cause of the dialectic (logic and philosophy) and of visual (geometrical) space.[21]

Western literacy encouraged an imbalance between the eye and the ear and contributed to the theorization of visual space; both situations were unnatural and led to abstract perceptions and dissociated sensibilities:

> Schizophrenia may be a necessary consequence of literacy.[22]

> Visual space is the only form of space that is purely mental: it has no basis in experience because it is formed of abstract figures minus a ground, and because it is entirely the side-effect of technology.[23]

Visual space is therefore presented as an artificial space created through the consolidation of Western literacy, in relation to a technology that spreads and extends words but, at the same time, modifies their power of being capable of containing the whole world. Literacy is a form of expression which separates *percept* – that is, the mimetic and immediate perception – and *concept* – that is, the cognitive process of reasoning which enables us to objectify our experience by detaching from what we perceive and observe. In sensorial and cognitive terms, the process results in a separation between *inner* and *outer* worlds, between the inner self and the broader set of external situations. The *self* also becomes a clear concept through the adoption of the phonetic alphabet and the spread of literacy because this medium encourages a form of introspection unknown in oral and tribal cultures and puts the individual, not the group, at the core of the community.

As discussed all through *The Gutenberg Galaxy*, it is precisely through the adoption of the phonetic alphabet that a clear difference between Western and Eastern *sensibilities* arose. From this point onwards, the former was taught through new pedagogical models that promoted one sense (sight) at the expense of others; whereas, the latter preserved a sensorial balance enabling an immediate identification between the individual and the environment. In time, the different approaches to literacy inevitably mirrored different models of social organization, wherein human relationships were regulated either according to *roles* and *holistic knowledge* (East), or according to *specialization* and *specialist knowledge* (West): '... the numerous specializations and separations of function inherent in industry and applied knowledge simply were not accessible to the Chinese.'[24] Contrary to Western literate societies, Eastern societies tended to be participatory and inclusive, preserving cognitive modes also typical of oral societies.[25] In Eastern participatory and inclusive societies (as well as in oral societies), cohesion also derives from the immediate, mimetic identification between *those who* observe and perceive, and *what* is observed and perceived. Such reciprocal interplay annuls the individual self because perception is based on an inclusive and synesthetic act. In Western societies, 'typography tended to alter language from a means of perception and exploration to a portable commodity.'[26] Perception thus relies upon the prevalence of sight over other senses and results in a mediated translation, not of what people experience, but of what they see. *Perception* becomes, in fact, *perspective* and is based on a clear-cut distance between the observed landscape or situation and those who observe. *Points of views, angles of visions,* are all expressions which reveal how 'typography cracked the voices of silence'[27] and gave men an eye for an ear.

Touch-A Touch-A Touch the Guru

In the Western world, what evolved was the idea of an empty space separating ground and figures on the basis of linear parameters. In visual space, people and objects are situated depending on *continuity, sequence,* or *proportions,* and empty space is elaborated in terms of *visual distance.* And yet, such an idea of continuity is, in fact, an abstraction because the idea of *empty space,* of *vacuum,* did not exist until the development of Euclidean geometry, according to which each object creates its own space. This idea was not fully conceptualized among Eastern cultures, where literacy had a different structure and space was never perceived through distance but rather through interplay and inclusion. This implies that our view of space is never other than the view of the observer, and that it is the observer who determines that view because of his/

her own observation. Such an idea also pertains to quantum theory, as acknowledged by Heisenberg: '... what happens depends on our way of observing it or on the fact that we observe it.'[28]

Similar to oral culture, in Eastern cultures the idea of space did not extend to the same idea of vacuum as in Western cultures. Things and individuals were perceived, not according to the idea of continuity (linear concept), but instead according to the idea of *simultaneity* (acoustic concept), in which all is present at the same time. McLuhan returns to such an idea when presenting his laws of media. In discussing it, Eric and Marshall McLuhan quote from Capra and his cross-cultural (and countercultural) holism, pointing out how

> the East bypassed hardware and absolute concepts in favour of precepts, that is a 'direct, non-intellectual experience of reality.' 'The most important characteristic of the Eastern world view – one could almost say the essence of it – is the awareness of the unity and mutual interrelation of all things and events, the experience of all phenomena in the world as manifestations of a basic oneness. All things are seen as interdependent and inseparable parts of this cosmic whole; as different manifestations of the same ultimate reality' (*The Tao of Physics*, 174). The East, which never had a phonetic alphabet, never had a Euclid and never developed absolute concepts of space and time.[29]

In Eastern cultures, space and distance between objects were not understood as clearly defined and delimited concepts. Instead, they constitute the harmonic interval through which interplay occurs. It is, therefore, an approach to space which enables all identification with one's own environment. In other words, it is *a point of contact* with that which is perceived as *us* – and which then *becomes us* – and not something *other than us*: 'The Chinese uses the intervals between things as the primary means of getting "in touch" with situations.'[30]

The idea of *tactility* (to be *in touch*) mirrors here the idea of acoustic space, implying the simultaneous interplay of all senses *to feel, be,* and *become* what we experience. In *Laws of Media*, Eric and Marshall McLuhan quote Jacques Lusseyran to discuss tactility and the way blindness enhances it: touching objects which you cannot see makes you 'tune in on them'; you become part of what you touch, which, in turn, becomes your own extension.[31] You do not live *in front of things*, but *with them*; you inhabit an acoustic space in which perception is not distorted by the abstraction of one of the senses (i.e., sight) and leads to a total identification with the environment. *Contact* takes place through various elements which are all present at the same time in a harmonic and simultaneous relation: 'Tactile space is the space of the resonant interval, as acoustic space is the sphere of simultaneous relations. They are as invisible as osmic or kinetic space (smell or stress).'[32]

In *Laws of Media*, McLuhan borrows the term *resonant interval* from Werner Heisenberg, who used it to convey such an idea of *touch*;[33] it is an idea already encapsulated in Albert Einstein's observation that 'there is no empty space, that is, there is no space without field.'[34] The tactile identification which McLuhan elaborates through the interaction of paradigms of oral and oriental cultures is, therefore, consistent with the re-creation, in a contemporary age, of an environment remodelled by the medium of electricity, in line with what was being explored by the new quantum and atomic physics. Electricity is, in fact, a tactile medium as it reintroduces to the Western world a multi-sensorial mode of perception which renders the interaction between the individual and the environment integral once more. It is precisely this type of perception, re-enacted by the electrically conceived oral, acoustic, and tactile environment, which McLuhan tries to re-create in his writing, as the latter is conceived in a way to help readers to readjust to the new electric sensibility: the mosaic embeds the psychic communal encounter with electronic media. Its form is articulated according to spatial models borrowed from Eastern artistic experiences, which McLuhan, borrowing from the early studies on the brain of Julian Jaynes and Robert J. Trotter,[35] metaphorically translated as being *right-brain hemisphere* cultures encouraging parataxis instead of connectives; discontinuity is not only a rhetorical device, but a performative strategy to activate readers' interplay with their environment, in turn encouraging mimesis and participation in the learning process. It is a model also in tune with the electric scenario, a similitude which McLuhan renders by quoting from another book pertaining to the Eastern tradition, Okakura Kazuko's *The Book of Tea*: 'The Present is the moving Infinity, the legitimate sphere of the Relative. Relativity seeks Adjustment; adjustment is Art. The art of life lies in a constant readjustment to our surroundings.'[36] Role playing defines Eastern traditions, whereas specialization defines Western ones. A flexible paradigm defines a culture dominated by the right-brain hemisphere; a more rigid paradigm defines a culture dominated by the left-brain hemisphere. In McLuhan's writing, paratactic association and discontinuous juxtaposition open spaces that readers are invited to probe, since they are not empty spaces; nor are they errors of syntax. These spaces are resonant intervals to be used as suggestions, as moments of deep interplay with the text and with the context, that is, with the ground to which everything in the text constantly relates. It is a form of juxtaposition that should also be read according to oriental cultural models: the potentialities of suggestion are encouraged; as readers, we are invited to enter the interval and to 'fill up the full measure of [our] aesthetic emotion.'[37] In the mosaic, space between probes, quotations, and comments is the space of interaction, of contact between author and reader, the space of active participation. Acoustic space puts us in touch with the real essence of the media guru; it allows us to perceive him well beyond his masked surface. We are not engaged with a linear fragmented vacuum, as many dialecticians explained, but with a meaningful interval which readers are invited to let resonate: let the guru resound; get in touch with him through his written corpus. Explore the unsaid connections through his network of analogies, which are enacted by the juxtaposition of figures and ground, that is, of probes, texts, and subtexts, and also by your own subjectivity and knowledge. It is role playing – in the Eastern sense of the word – which, in the contemporary Western age, modernist experiments began to investigate and to elaborate, as in the case of the acoustic writing of the imagist poets; in their poems, 'the words stop and the meaning goes on.'[38]

McLuhan's fascination with these modernist experiments lies precisely in the fact that they encourage a dialogue between linear and acoustic worlds and, by doing so, help to reveal the short- and long-term side effects of the impact of the fourth world on already-existing environments. In *Through the Vanishing Point*, McLuhan discusses Pound's 'one image poem'[39] as a form capable of overcoming the visual limits imposed by Western literacy through the elaboration of the associative model offered by the aggregative structure of oriental ideograms, and their paratactic combination in koans and haikus. In his analysis, McLuhan associates these forms with the idea of interplay, as well as with the idea of a complex system, two concepts which modernist writers had translated and unified into new participatory or tactile forms. In this way, modernist experiments may be regarded as useful models for mastering and merging Eastern and scientific heuristics in order to heighten sensorial perception. McLuhan uses these experiments as counter-environments which expand the level of awareness through their broken knowledge conceived to make individuals *experience* and *participate* in the process of discovery so as to let the meaningful intervals resound.

5 A Conscious Modernist Craftsman

A Pioneer of (New) Modernist Studies

In the 1980s, as an undergraduate at the University of Bologna specializing in modernist studies, I had no idea of the existence of a volume called *The Interior Landscape: The Literary Criticism of Marshall McLuhan*. Originally published in 1969, that volume had in fact been translated into my first language, Italian, in 1983 but had not made it into university curricula, with perhaps a very few exceptions. McLuhan was renowned worldwide as the media guru, or the media oracle, but certainly not as a professor of English literature; in addition, in the 1980s his star was no longer shining as it had during the two previous decades, no matter if his aperçus had by then entered our international jargon. When I finally managed to read McLuhan's literary criticism, I had already entered a PhD program, and I was almost ten years older; by the middle 1990s, modernist studies were something different from what I had been taught originally; new scholars had opened the field up to new interdisciplinary perspectives and had, so to speak, broken the vessels of previous interpretations. Comparing McLuhan's early investigations of modernism with those of later critics reveals that the Canadian thinker anticipated lines of interpretation which only blossomed in the last decade of the previous century, that is, almost three decades after McLuhan's book was published. To have read *The Interior Landscape* at an earlier stage in my educational career would have helped me better understand literature not only as a subject but also *as a function*, because in that book McLuhan turns the modernist literary masterpieces into cognitive tools to better understand new environmental processes. He does so through a careful analysis of their fragmented forms, as well as of their unusual and refined use of language. The investigation of language and the play-ful creation of neologisms capable of translating the societal dynamic processes are what McLuhan mostly admired in Joyce and in the other modernists. Etymology plays a major role in McLuhan's media explora-tions; it stands at the core of his own laws of media. And etymology plays a major role as well in conveying a renewed energy to McLuhan's mosaic, combining the right words (*les mots justs*, to borrow from Ford Madox Ford and Gustave Flaubert) in a fragmented structure whose goal is to make us see, to make us hear, and, above all, *to make us feel* (to borrow from Joseph Conrad): in other words, to make us experience and better understand our environment. Below the surface of McLuhan's modern-ist mask lies a conscious craftsman who deliberately chose to explore actuality through language and who played with words to elaborate a probing form to awaken his audiences.

By casting modernism in the light of broader cultural and theoretical approaches, McLuhan anticipated future trends of modernist studies. In the early 1990s, Marjorie Perloff commented on the dichotomic lines of research dominating that area of studies at a time when McLuhan was already developing a different strategy of observation:

> Surely no literary term has raised more controversy and misunderstand-ing than the modest little word *modernism* ... Once the site of all that was radical, exciting, and above all new ... by the early 1970s modernism found itself under attack as a retrograde, elitist movement – at best the final phase of the great Romantic revolution and, at worst, the aestheticist reaction for-mation to an alienated social life that had close links to fascism ...[1]

To investigate the way in which modernist studies have evolved would offer an interesting perspective on how our attitude and approach to literary criticism have also evolved; it would contribute as well to trac-ing the changing mentalities of the different decades of the twentieth century. Some critics have tried, in fact, to do this. In 1992, Kevin J.H. Dettmar offered one of the first attempts to historicize modernist stud-ies, suggesting three possible stages: the first, 'characterised by outrage,' sees a strong reaction against most modernist productions in real time; the second, until the late 1960s / early 1970s, characterized by 'an insti-tutionally approved way of reading the Modernists,' aims at controlling the manner in which modernist texts should be read, therefore 'domes-ticating' them; and the third, characterized by the attempt 'to rediscover just what it was that once seemed so new in the Modernists,' is the one that Dettmar calls 'postmodern criticism,' still to be fully written at the time, but already defined as eclectic and oriented towards the acceptance of open and not absolute interpretative paradigms.[2] Today we know that such a third phase has led to different and even opposing interpretations of modernism and modernist art, often – and not surprisingly so – depending on the critics' politics, agendas, and backgrounds. For sure, in the 1960s, McLuhan was ahead of his time when writing about Joyce, Pound, Lewis, and other modernist masters; not following the domesticated line of interpretation, he pioneered new interdisciplinary approaches.

Generally speaking, recent approaches to modernism have in common the idea that modernist writers were not looking at actuality from unreachable ivory towers but were instead fully inhabiting their own time; they were not academics, but as practitioners of their crafts, they were explorers of different cultural and artistic situations. Critics now agree that their aesthetics are, in fact, deeply imbued with the spirit of their time, as well as with its dynamics. They were not developed simply to seclude (or protect) artists from their society; on the contrary, they were elaborated as a response to the cultural and political phantasmagorias of those very realities.

Modernist art – and especially art produced in the first two decades of the twentieth century – was originally understood as *art for art's sake*, or as art defending a privileged status quo, consciously detached from the then forming mass society, the result of an elitist rebellion performed by either snobbish or hungry young men and women living in an ideal intellectual limbo. It is true that most modernist poetics – and for sure those discussed in relation to McLuhan's poetic – still appear to be detached from the mass of new readers, being too arcane to reach a broader audience, especially in their final renderings. It is also true that many modernist writers wrote against the most materialist aspects of mass society, often understood as a society trivializing a certain idea of art. As Pound wrote in his *Hugh Selwyn Mauberley*: 'The age demanded an image / Of its accelerated grimace / ... The "age demanded" chiefly a mould in plaster / Made with no loss of time.'[3] And yet, it is also undeniable that those very poetics derived from that society and were deeply influenced by its new environmental, technological, and cultural dynamics.

I think it is more appropriate to define modernist poetics as elitist in their rendering, but not in their underpinning strategies (and perhaps not even in their broader goal, as they meant to awaken society). Those strategies were based, in fact, on a renewed approach, even to the most popular cultural forms of their time. Inevitably, if we continue to read modernist art and narrative only through ideology, then we might decide that those provocative experiments and achievements were not only elitist but also conservative; however, this is an approach which, though it has some points, risks blinding us to other, more articulated perspectives.[4]

Philip Marchand was among the first to point out that Marshall McLuhan's approach to modernism was, in fact, an original one which anticipated later discussions. In particular, Marchand recalls the role that modernist poetics played in helping McLuhan to start to understand the importance of sensorial perception in the rendering of one's own time:

> These writers and teachers also gave McLuhan the first hints of what later became a key element of his ideas: the notion that human perception varied greatly according to which senses were predominant in the perceiver. The poets of interest to McLuhan, for example, emphasised the role of sound in their poetry ... More significant was Eliot's well-known advocacy of the 'auditory imagination.'[5]

Marchand points out not only the intellectual legacy, but also the solid humanist roots of modernist research. He recalls that McLuhan approached the modernist masters as new grammarians because his twentieth-century time sensibility was also based on the return of grammar. If the Middle Ages emphasized dialectic, the Renaissance encouraged a return to grammar and rhetoric, which were then banished again in the seventeenth century following Descartes's *méditations*; in the twentieth century, the works of modernist writers and the New Criticism encouraged a return of grammar. Grammar was the world of integral awareness, the world of perceptive synaesthesia which centuries of literacy had, so to speak, put on hold and which new media were now retrieving: from the ear to the eye, from the eye to the ear.[6] It is in fact in *The Interior Landscape* that McLuhan clearly acknowledges the deep impact that modernist writers had on his study of media; they taught him how to mediate the sensorial implications of new technologies through new forms apt for detecting and revealing the new spirit of their time. By so doing, he suggested a fascinating approach to modernism which, unfortunately, is still neglected.

Universal Quest, Fragmented Rendering

In many essays collected in *The Interior Landscape*, McLuhan points out the close links existing between the modernist experiments and the new technological and cultural environment of the time. In these essays, he combines his activity as a literary critic with his intellectual explorations of new media. He points out how the modernists bore witness not only to the making of a new age, but also to the long-term effects of that process on the collective and individual psyche. These essays continue the explorations of media we found in McLuhan's other books, and they give clear and even more explicit acknowledgment of the role played by the modernist masters in the development of his own rhetorical devices and poetics as a media explorer. My point is that McLuhan employed a modernist strategy from the very beginning. With this premise, I consider *The Mechanical Bride* as McLuhan's most modernist work, while his later books establish his most original mosaic. *The Mechanical Bride* brings together formal experimentation, the cross-hybridization of high and popular art forms, and the denunciation of all those hidden agencies which were redesigning culture, power, and, therefore, society by taking advantage of a numbed and accommodating audience. What he denounces in his preface is, in fact, comparable to T.S. Eliot's denunciation of a waste land now dominated by young carbuncular individuals 'on whom assurance sits as a silk hat on a Bradford millionaire,' or to Pound's vision of his society as one where 'Caliban casts out Ariel' and a 'tawdry cheapness / shall reign throughout our days.' In his later books, McLuhan dismisses such an overt judgment of a consumerist society, thereby choosing to refuse to act on the basis of an intellectual bias, something which most modernist poetics have often been accused of. After *The Mechanical Bride,* McLuhan moved from the particular to the general (that is, to the universal) and, as a modernist, shifted from the vision of John Dos Passos to that of James Joyce.

The works of the American Dos Passos and the Irish Joyce are in fact compared in *The Interior Landscape,* where McLuhan juxtaposes the universality of the latter to the political (therefore historically contextualized) commitment of the former. Although McLuhan acknowledges Dos Passos's merits and relevance as a writer, he sees his works as undermined by the writer's explicit ideological agenda, something which situates those works inside a specific time and place. In the essay comparing the works of these two modernist writers, McLuhan recalls how they both bring light to the status of modern man inhabiting the new metropolis, now turned into a robot-like individual by the joint action of industrial organization and mass communication; but he points out that it is Joyce who offers a universal, rather than a partial or biased, vision of the new condition. Joyce's Dublin stands as a mythical place, and his Ulysses is a character epitomizing a universal quest; Dos Passos's New York, instead, stands as an actual place, and his fragmented characters are trapped into a too clearly defined situation, so much so that their experiences are doomed to become obsolete.[7] This essay should be a must among students of modernism; it should be listed in all syllabuses as a mandatory reading; the whole book should, in fact, be a classic on modernism. In particular, the Dos Passos–Joyce essay would help to exemplify a delicate and controversial issue pertaining to that field of study, that is, the uncanny relationship between 'objectivity' and 'subjectivity.' What McLuhan praises against Dos Passos's ideological rendering is, in fact, Joyce's rhetorical strategy. Joyce's form translates personal temperament into universal epiphanies. He is a master of etymology and knows how to turn his subjective observations of life into an objective rendering; Dos Passos turns the objective renderings derived from avant-garde art into a prose which brings to the forefront his subjective approach. If Dos Passos is interested in 'American know-how' and registers 'a personal reaction to society,' Joyce's storytelling is translated through what Eliot defined as a 'mythical method'; it is a narrative fully inscribed into a solid tradition, which makes Joyce's work representative of a universal human condition. His epiphanies bring to light fragments of truth intelligible to us, in spite of time and space and notwithstanding the complex textual architecture. In *The Mechanical Bride*, McLuhan starts as Dos Passos and evolves towards Joyce: in spite of a clear-cut introduction which offers a key for interpreting the following chapters as a reaction to a world shaped by advertising agencies, McLuhan does not write to merely 'query ideas.' He says so openly, warning his readers.[8] While discussing the folklore of industrial man through a vivisection of American consumerism, McLuhan aims to explore a more universal landscape because he wants to offer his readers 'a grip' for 'taking hold of it.' He does not want to fix a point of view on a situation; he wants to encourage a mobile point of view on evolving processes.

The ideas of subjectivity (of perception) and objectivity (of rendering) are therefore crucial for many modernist aesthetics, as the latter aim at rendering a reality which can no longer be understood only in Romantic terms. T.E. Hulme's philosophy praising the dry hardness of classicism, his idea of a geometrical art opposing all Romantic vital and soft art, offered a theoretical construct to many of the so-called modernist impersonal poetics.[9] Inevitably, these poetics are based on a conceptual paradox: they aim to convey the universality of all experiences, while knowing full well that it is almost an impossible task and that they can only succeed in part. Hence, while the new poets and writers are asked to investigate language and tradition, they are forced to select among their experiences only *moments of being, impressions, objective correlatives,* and *epiphanies* capable of conveying truth and reality through approximations. Just like Heisenberg's modern physicists, they acknowledge the incompleteness or indeterminacy of their quest, while pursuing it. And just like the new scientists, they realize that such incompleteness is a consequence of the fact that all observations are, in fact, relative, as they cannot fully transcend the subjective element. What the German physicist wrote when discussing the rendering of scientific experiments, also works well for a discussion of many modernist experiments:

> ... the transition from the 'possible' to the 'actual' takes place during the act of observation. If we want to describe what happens in an atomic event, we have to realize that the word 'happens' can apply only to the observation, not to the state of affairs between two observations ... This again emphasizes a subjective element in the description of atomic events, since the measuring device has been constructed by the observer, and we have to remember that what we observe is not nature in itself but *nature exposed to our method of questioning.*[10]

Here, Heisenberg imposes the idea of subjectivity over something which is supposed to be totally objective, that is, scientific observation. The modernist writers and poets often portray themselves as new scientific observers, in turn vivisecting their own society through their impersonal poetics. They question the absolute Romantic ideal vision of humanity and the centrality of the author: they do not trust the poet as the sole medium; and they look for models to provide a parallel capable of conveying a shared universality (Joyce and myth, Pound and epic). As suggested, the new poetry is no longer conceived simply as a mechanism but instead as an organism, each of its parts affecting and somehow containing the whole. Most new aesthetics are often expressed through metaphors pertaining to both the world of hard sciences (Eliot's vision of the poet as a catalyser; Pound's metaphor of 'the rose in the still dust,' referring to the rose pattern formed in iron filings by a magnetic field of forces) and to other cultural traditions, mostly deriving from oral-based societies (Pound's ideogrammatic method; the idea of primitivism underpinning several artistic and literary formal explorations). Most metaphors translating modernist poetics acknowledge at once the attempt to foster objectivity in observation and the paradox of the subject being part of all such processes: life therefore is perceived as an impression, or as a luminous halo, or as a semi-transparent envelop through which we are challenged to look. Even more, objectivity itself is based precisely *on the acknowledgment of the ways the subject might interfere, change, or condition the act of observation*. What complicates the analysis even further is the fact that most modernist poetics were not always born from a writer's neutral approach to society, but were, in fact, inscribed inside a more entangled participation in the historical and political events of the time (for instance, Pound's *Guide to Kulchur*, written at the time of Pound's flirtation with the Italian fascist regime, is ambiguously presented as a series of notes for a *totalitarian treatise*).

Subjectivity and objectivity are also components of McLuhan's media investigations, especially as far as their rendering is concerned. As the discussion of McLuhan as a media guru has shown, he borrowed the idea of a marriage between poetry, the arts, and sciences as a basic tenet for his own media explorations and understanding. He always maintained that he had no point of view on the situations he was investigating, and always underlined his detachment as an explorer (the modernists would have spoken of 'aloofness'). He often repeated that his was a *mobile* point of view because this is what the act of probing literally implies. Finding himself inside the new media maelstrom, McLuhan was still assessing the action of the vortex, which he was seeking to understand: 'If you have a point of view, it means that you have already mastered the situation. You are not with the situation, you have already abstracted it, and angled it.'[11] He was sharing his explorations with his own readers and was also co-opting them in the process of discovery by adopting and adapting modernist inclusive poetics. In his volumes on media, he constantly refers to modernist techniques when he needs to discuss the depth-involving newness of the time: already in *The Gutenberg Galaxy*, the experiments with language of Gertrude Stein, e.e. cummings, Ezra Pound, and T.S. Eliot are mentioned as 'carefully devised strategies to get the passive visual reader into a participant, oral action.'[12]

By blurring inner and outer realities, the modernist experiments rendered on the printed page the depth-involving newness *both* of the electric environment *and* of its probing; that is, they aimed to render at once both the observed object and the act of observing. It was experimental writing conceived at exactly the same time that new experimental fields in the sciences, for instance, in medicine, were conceived; arts, literature, and the hard sciences were therefore developing new models to assess their subjects at a time of change. Such an isomorphism could only signify a major change in the time sensibility, as McLuhan notices in *The Gutenberg Galaxy*: 'It was notably Claude Bernard's approach to experimental medicine in the later nineteenth century that reconquered the heterogeneous dimensions of the *milieu interieur* at exactly the same time that Rimbaud and Baudelaire shifted poetry to the *paysage interieur*.'[13] Between the nineteenth and twentieth centuries, inner and outer landscapes blurred and visual limits had to be renegotiated through new approaches to both domains. In 1908, Filippo Tommaso Marinetti spoke of the electric or wireless imagination to exemplify the change of time sensibility; a few years later, Guglielmo Marconi's experiments with wireless communication had a strong impact far beyond the technology itself: they led to the creation of the first wireless commodity, the radio. Not only did radio lead to break-through developments of other media, but it also enhanced imagination and holistic *visions*: demand for content transcended the technology itself, and people started to perceive themselves as immaterial beings, simultaneously inhabiting different ages and lands, their lives being mythical and real *at the same time*.

To Make You Feel: Probing through Language

In the 1930s, while at Cambridge, McLuhan learned more about the shift from Victorian to modernist mentality. In particular, he began to appreciate the complexity of the modernist research, which he perceived, in fact, as a struggle to develop a form capable of preserving the integrity of the process of observation. Being themselves inside the whirlpool, literary and artistic experiments were questioning the whirl. Modernist writers took to translating movement and uncertainties through their hallucinatory and fragmented renderings of their sporadic epiphanies. It was thus inevitable that modernist narratives or poetry did not comfort the reader, did not confirm traditional values, did not encourage accepted ideas, and did not progress in linear and reassuring ways. On the contrary, they deconstructed all commonplaces to show 'the community in action.' They unveiled and rendered the chaos, the disorder, the aporias, which inevitably accompanied change and shocked readers. Through their work, they provoked, attacked, and, by so doing, stimulated critical thinking.

Just as in a cubistic canvas, the vanishing point in modernist narratives is outside the work. Readers are challenged and engaged as co-authors; novels and poems mirror processes of change, and all are related to coeval uncertainties. They do not offer solutions, nor do they foretell what such changes will produce; they are narratives conceived *in medias res* – in the middle of things – returning a dynamic, not a static, portrait of the time. The reassuring omniscient narrator no longer exists. Writers now bear witness to a change in progress by playing with their narrations, and with their readers, by constantly challenging them. Technically speaking, modernist works are strongly participatory, as they are based on the same mobile point of view which McLuhan adopted for his own explorations; as readers, we, too, have to adopt it, as our way to share both the probing and the discoveries. It is also our way of participating in the process and experiencing the function of the work of art. As revealed by Joseph Conrad in his famous Preface to *The Nigger of the Narcissus*, the goal of the new modernist narrative is 'to make you see, to make you hear, and above all *to make you feel.*' That turns reading into a cognitive process that is not based on the acceptance of the author's vision, his or her point of view; instead, it encourages our active participation as readers, as we cannot but adjust and respond to an uncanny mobile formal structure if we want to make it resound. As readers, it is our own 'moment of being.' We are elevated to the authorial level of co-explorers and co-producers of meaning. It is this idea that McLuhan not only adopted but also tried to popularize through his public appearances and through his books: his modernist mask embeds that idea into his mosaic.

As suggested by Conrad, the *vision* to which modernist writers aspire does not coincide with the mere visual spectrum; instead, it is a complex one which is connected to a global dimension capable of overcoming all representational traditions based on a *spatial abstraction,* on a *dissociated sensibility* which only relies on sight. It is a non-Euclidean vision; it is both tribal and oral, oriental and inclusive, and can be obtained through a renewed syntax which retrieves multi-sensorial modes of perception or, as Marchand recalls, Eliot's 'auditory imagination.' 'Write for the ears,' 'The words you will see are not the words you will hear,' and 'Read me with your ears' are the primary instructions that modernist writers offered to their readers, suggesting a different approach not only to their works, but also to their times. Experiencing modernist art means, therefore, experiencing change and being on the alert.

McLuhan adopted the modernist idea of art as warning signal. It is, in fact, the central idea that leads us to conceive literature not as a subject but as a function. His experiments with form, which shape his own operative project, stand in the wake of experimental writers who had put on the world of electric media, cross-pollinating the civilization of the eye

(Western world) and the civilization of the ear (Eastern world), reconfiguring the world in the image of a tribal village. Their work translated
the new cultural situation through acoustic forms, which also retrieve
previous oral traditions pertaining to older forms of society now given
a new vitality. It was the awakening of the tribal hero, Finn, that Joyce
set out to turn into an emblematic myth of our universal history. The
retrieval of an ancient science such as etymology – fully inscribed in the
realm of grammar – pervades several modernist poetics, and provides
the background for the actual process of understanding; words become
not just *verba* (words) but also *res* (things); they connect past and present
traditions and acquire new meanings when applied to actuality. As Eric
and Marshall McLuhan wrote in *Laws of Media*: 'The need of poet, musi-
cian, and artist for ever-new means of probing and exploring experience
sends them back again and again to the rag-and-bone shop of abandoned
cliché.'[14] It is in the hands of the new modernist grammarians that the
cliché returns to its archetype.

McLuhan the modernist loved to play with language, with genres, with
codes, that is, with various forms of communication. Language is in fact
what contains change through literary tradition; through language you
shore your ruins, as Eliot wrote in *The Waste Land*. Modernism started
with a renewed approach to language, with the will to break the linearity
of the literary productions of the time. Proto-modernist writers such as
Joseph Conrad and Ford Madox Ford opposed naturalism through their
literary impressionism. As recalled by Ford in his memoir *Joseph Conrad:
A Personal Remembrance* (1924), Conrad could spend hours if not days
discussing how to render a certain feeling, a certain experience, and certain impressions. Certainly, as a Pole who spoke English as his third language, you could assume that his interest was motivated by the fact that
he was learning a new language; it was much more than that. Conrad,
as well as Ford and many others, was experimenting with language while
searching for a new form *to make us feel through his word*. Conrad and Ford
continued the work of Flaubert, of the Russian masters, of Henry James;
through their experiments, they engaged a dialogue that bridged different literary traditions in the pursuit of new knowledge. McLuhan knew
their works almost by heart. It is through those works that he started to
probe his own times: they helped him to adjust to his own world, to move
from subject to function.

The modernist mask therefore shows us McLuhan investigating language in the wake of both symbolist poets and proto-modernist and
modernist writers. He, too, acknowledged the important role played by

the French *poètes maudits,* and was fascinated by their breaking of linearity, which he saw as a consequence of their interest in new forms of communication. Titles like 'Joyce, Mallarmé and the Press' and 'Wyndham Lewis: His Theory of Art and Communication' prove the immediate connection between the professor of English and the media scholar. By reading those writers, McLuhan understood how, in the twentieth century, form was not just a frame to contain words but a fundamental component of the narrative process. Modernist writers taught McLuhan that writing could no longer be representational because new discoveries in many different domains (physics, medicine, communications, social sciences, etc.) were challenging both traditional knowledge and traditional canons. Victorian narratives were obsolesced and had to be replaced by experimental forms, more elusive and in progress. But the modernists also taught McLuhan that such elusiveness was counterbalanced by the solidity of language rediscovered through the study of etymology. Words were no longer perceived as abstractions but as containers of multiple meanings, constantly reassembled and hybridized with other semiological codes, from music to painting, from theatre to cinema.[15] You find words and sounds on Picasso's canvases, music on Joyce's pages, cinematic close-ups in Fitzgerald's descriptions: Modernist productions are no longer 'mono-sensorial,' but 'multi-sensorial' – that is, multi-media – renderings.

McLuhan himself considers words as 'complex systems of metaphors and symbols' through which 'the entire world can be evoked and retrieved at any instant.'[16] It is precisely this intrinsic power of words that the new modernist poetics are evoking. Inevitably, the writer, as well as the artist, is no longer portrayed as an inspired and gifted individual, but instead as a conscious craftsman. As a craftsman, the new writer must know how to mould language and must always be aware of his tools (rhetoric, grammar, etymology) in order to control their effects. McLuhan was a good apprentice and learned the tricks of the trade from Ezra Pound – *il miglior fabbro,* 'the better craftsman,' as per Eliot's dedication in *The Waste Land* – from T.S. Eliot, Ford Madox Ford, James Joyce, Wyndham Lewis, and all those craftsmen that he encountered through them.

As with other modernist writers, McLuhan no longer wanted *to narrate* reality; he, too, wanted *to render* it; he, too, wanted 'to show the community in action,' to convey action itself (both inner and outer) in all its dynamism. His probing of old and new media is disseminated the same way other modernist writers had successfully done it; their comments are the constant leitmotif of his media storytelling. In his *Laws of Media,* he still recalls the English imagist school of Pound and Aldington, and praises its attention to 'the exact word'; he describes Pound and Eliot as 'the Cicero and Quintilian of our time' for their incessant work upon language, and for their 'modern artistic enterprise [of] the ancient modes of rhetoric and grammar.'[17] The search for the exact word, his search for a new form, is therefore inscribed inside the humanistic traditions which McLuhan the modernist never ceased to explore.

Yes, it would have made a huge difference to me if I had met McLuhan when I first discovered modernism; I would have approached those refined poems and novels not only as solid cross-roads of different cultural and literary traditions, but also as experiments throwing light on new media processes and their related societal dynamics. As I mentioned earlier, McLuhan literally *put the modernists on*, so much so that I think his books on media are based on those experiments. As a media theorist, McLuhan did not only limit his interest to modernist 'messages' (most writers did, in fact, discuss media and new forms of communication, as well as the then forming mass society); instead, he used their language, their formal discoveries, and their artistic achievements as ceaseless acts with which to engage actuality and its related cultural processes.

For McLuhan, to study modernist poetics was, indeed, a way to take part in the process of understanding the type of societal and technological change whose long-term effects he was experiencing, as an individual and as a professor. In his introduction to the Italian edition of *The Interior Landscape*, critic Amleto Lorenzini has well captured the essence of McLuhan's modernist lesson:

> McLuhan tells us that literary criticism should not be academic, but should learn from Pound; it should be clearly polemical, brave enough to tell what must be told. That's why, McLuhan also tells us, academics have ignored Pound's criticism or, whenever they acknowledged it, they were against it: Pound's criticism, capable to illuminate two masters like Yeats and Eliot, constitutes, in fact, the ground of his Cantos – which is the greatest poem of our century, still the most misinterpreted one.
>
> McLuhan applies the lesson he learnt from the great masters of literature to the study of mass media; not to the messages they convey, but to their language, to their process in order to codify their functioning and to avoid becoming their slave.[18]

Through modernism, McLuhan developed an approach to media aimed at understanding the hidden ground of patterns underpinning each medium, but also the confluence of different media inside a society where technological progress was racing fast-forward. He aimed to unveil media languages and processes, thereby contributing to the stimulation of people's awareness (to prevent them from becoming cultural 'slaves'). The medium is the message, and literature is our warning signal, helping us to detect the grammar of a change in the environment. This was, in fact, what McLuhan proved was possible.

6 The Hyper-Language of the Media 'Fan'

Media Fan or Grammarian of Media?

Many critics assumed that Marshall McLuhan was a fan of technology because he discussed new media all through his books. If you think of it, it is a vey naïve idea, which I will discuss further in Part Two of this volume. Let me say right now that it is also a false idea: McLuhan was not a media geek; he was not lost in technological space. Or, better, since he *was* lost in technological space, he started to question the related maelstrom, just as Poe's mariner, being lost in stormy waters, started to question the liquid whirlpool. It's a matter of survival, as you well understand. Hence, the mask of the media or techno fan is a deceiving one as it turns McLuhan into the champion of what, instead, he was simply probing: new technologies, new media. The mosaic has often been read as the objective correlative of McLuhan's passion for media, thereby translating his curiosity into a confused elaboration of data overload intelligible only to the media-geeks tribe. Unfortunately, through time, that tribe itself has contributed to the consolidation of this interpretation. Instead, I argue that more than a media fan, McLuhan was a grammarian of media, as what he did was to explore the new media environment in order to find its patterns. The mosaic is, in fact, not a hypertext embedding the media fan, but a new hyper-language which discusses new technologies through the humanities.

It is true that McLuhan did anticipate future developments of information and communication technologies with uncanny precision. He did not envision the production of the BlackBerries, iPods, or iPhones, but he imagined their technological effects and anticipated the environmental side effects of the digital and interactive technologies which we now manage on a daily basis. John Moss, in his introduction to a collection of essays dedicated to a reappraisal of Marshall McLuhan, has in fact pointed out this futuristic aspect of McLuhan's media investigations:

> Labour Day evening, 2001; the CBC is rebroadcasting a mosaic of interviews from 'This Hour Has Seven Days,' originally televised in 1966 ... And there is Marshall McLuhan, introduced by Patrick Watson with the warning that only ten percent of the interview makes sense, even to McLuhan; make of it what you will, the Americans love him. And then McLuhan speaks about things we now take for granted, and does so with clarity and wit; he does not have the terminology or the technology, but he envisions the World Wide Web with uncanny precision. He describes the present with prophetic acumen, a futurist positioned by history to anticipate the past. His genius is confirmed not by how much his ideas now surprise but by how little. It is like Newton and gravity.[1]

Moss is certainly right about how McLuhan's ideas on new media offer little surprise to us today: in truth, those very ideas might even sound obvious to younger generations who were born into and always lived in a world dominated by electric, electronic, and digital media. In his witty and paradoxical style, McLuhan himself was the first to remind his audiences that he had carefully predicted only what had already happened! But, with the paradox comes the serious revelation derived from the humanistic philosophical traditions: the effect always precedes the formal cause, so much so, that the future can only be an invention of the past.[2] The idea of McLuhan as the oracle of futurist forms and processes of communication is in fact crucial if we want to understand the reception of his ideas and, consequently, his fortune or misfortune as a media thinker. Blair Francis Stone, in an insightful Ph D dissertation dedicated to McLuhan and his humanist tradition, has rightly underlined that the twist from a more traditional to a 'futuristic' approach to media studies is what characterizes a book like *Understanding Media*, especially the chapter entitled 'Hybrid Energy – Les Liaisons Dangereuses': 'For it is here that McLuhan departs from the role of historian and begins to play the role of scientist, or prophet, a function not always equally appreciated by everyone'[3] – a prophetic scientist or a scientific prophet who, in the common judgment, popularized media and supported them: a media fan.

Forget that. Return to Poe's mariner and remember that, as a *scientist* and as a *prophet*, McLuhan acted as someone committed to finding the hidden cause of what was already visible: what triggers the mechanism of the vortex? Where does the dynamic process of the maelstrom origi-nate? How does it all evolve? Thus, continues Stone, 'it is enough simply to recognise that the basis of McLuhan's predectiveness is his theoreti-cal construct.'[4] This theoretical construct is rooted in the humanistic tradition, a fact which is often acknowledged only superficially by those enthusiastic critics who consider McLuhan as a patron saint of whatever is new in the field of the information and communication technologies. Such a situation invites us to reconsider a technological metaphor that is often applied to McLuhan's own form of communication; as a matter of fact, the mosaic is too readily defined as a hypertext *ante litteram*. By doing this, we translate what is perhaps a more complex form into what we immediately understand and associate today with interactivity and multimedia communications. Isn't such a comparison more a cliché that limits a real understanding of the way in which the mosaic interfaces with readers, knowledge, and actuality?

Hypertexting the Mosaic

In fact, it is not that wrong to read the potentialities of McLuhan's mosa-ic through the heuristic process of hypertext, especially since the newest theories on digital hypertext have convincingly discussed it as a form which enables and even fosters a convergence between technology and contemporary critical theory. To return to the previously recalled hyper-text theories which George Landow has been examining since 1982,[5] we can in fact acknowledge that

> ... we must abandon conceptual systems founded on ideas of centre, mar-
> gin, hierarchy, and linearity and replace them by ones of multilinearity,
> nodes, links, and networks ... Almost all parties to this paradigm shift,
> which marks a revolution in human thought, see electronic writing as a
> direct response to the strengths and weaknesses of the printed book, one of
> the major landmarks in the history of human thought.[6]

What is particularly interesting is that both critical theories and hypertext theories converge in conceptualizing and designing structures based on discontinuity which turn readers into authors, that is, into *creative read-ers*. Hypertext 'blurs boundaries between reader and writer'; it encour-ages 'reading-as-writing.'[7] Landow often refers to Barthes's famous *S/Z* and to his idea of a 'plural text,' built on the intertextuality embedded and triggered by a series of textual *lexia* (namely, 'blocks of signification' or 'units of meaning'). Similarly, in *Literary Machines*, T.H. Nelson theorizes hypertext as an interactive system based on a discontinuous form, focused on the user's freedom:

> By hypertext I mean non-sequential writing – text that branches and allows choices to the reader, best read at an interactive screen. As popularly conceived, this is a series of text chunks connected by links which offer the reader different pathways.[8]

Of course, there are many other studies on the hypertext, and their list would be too long to be mentioned here. But, generally speaking, all definitions seem to converge on the idea that, in practice, hypertext is an updated version of Bush's *memex* – a neologism combining the ideas of memory and index – a device conceptualized as early as 1945.[9] However, if it had been presented to King Thamus as a gift to improve our memory or thought, quite certainly the *memex* would have prompted the same judgment that he pronounced when Theuth introduced the invention of writing to him. This episode, originally recalled by Plato in his *Phaedrus*, is by now a classic in communication studies, and it is often quoted to epitomize the way people tend to look at the pointing finger and not at the moon beyond it. As you might remember, Theuth, a famous god and inventor of Naucratis, in Egypt, showed several of his inventions to the god Thamus, 'the king of the whole country of Egypt'; while so doing, he enumerated the advantages that each of them would bring to their people. When he came to literacy, 'the letters,' Theuth praised that invention as capable of enhancing people's memory and therefore wit. Thamus surprised him by replying that, instead, writing was nothing but a means to trigger forgetfulness to the detriment of real wisdom or knowledge. Since 'the parent or inventor of an art is not always the best judge of the utility or inutility of his own inventions to the users of them,' Thamus showed Theuth the full moon beyond his finger. From that moment, Thamus warned Theuth, people would instead become more and more ignorant, relying on writing to bring things to their remembrance through external signs. People would lose the capability of looking through things, to participate in the process of learning; they would have 'the show of wisdom without the reality.' If my parallel stands, then the *memex* is to memory as writing is to orality. The point now is to decide if McLuhan's probes relate more to writing and memex, or to memory and orality. My idea is that, being verbo-voco-visual 'tools,' the probes' *substance* is closer to the latter pair, even though their *function* might recall the one offered by 'links' in hyper-texts.

We can certainly read the mosaic as a hypertext if we work out the parallel at a general level, focusing, for instance, on our mode of frui-tion. Each probe in the text (be it a quotation, a provocative question, an image, an aphorism) could be conceived as a *window* opening on a series of more complex ideas that readers decide to disregard or explore. Read-ers must therefore decide which paths to take in the exploration, wheth-er to open one window/page after the other, or move backward and forward across them, or whether to navigate the hypterxt following the menu, or to proceed freely through it. Readers create their interactive reading patterns. Intertextuality, which is a clear feature of hypertexts and of McLuhan's mosaic, takes us inside and outside both structures at once, suggesting hyperlinks to various inner and outer landscapes. The condensed probes of McLuhan's mosaic seem a particularly apt form also for hypertext, as brevity is what makes electric communication more efficacious.

However, even though the metaphor works at a primary level, it becomes less valid the moment we further explore the complex-ity of McLuhan's intention and the experience that he aims to induce through his mosaic. It is an experience based on a tactile idea of inter-facing, in turn connected to what he considered to be the multi-sen-sorial situation re-enacted by electric media. As Sobelman noticed, McLuhan developed the idea of interface in relation to cultural proc-esses, interface being the meeting of structures, or cultures, or conflict-ing technologies and the way they change each other. In other words, the term interface, which is currently used in information and com-munication technologies, is associated by the Canadian thinker with a hybrid, the meeting of two or more media or cultural situations/proc-esses inside a given environment; as well as, to the new structural forms which originate from such a hybridization. Consistently, when trans-lated into an operative device to convey such hybridization, the idea of interface also relates to the idea of juxtaposition, which we find at the core of almost all modernist avant-garde experiments. McLuhan's mosaic interfaces glosses, images, and quotations in a form which fur-ther explores the way these juxtapositions change one another, in turn producing cognitive potentialities. There is also another level of inter-facing or juxtaposition in McLuhan's mosaic, more sophisticated and even intriguing. As I will discuss, it is based on a theoretical construct which not only assures the survival of literacy itself while adapting it to an electric world which tends to make it more and more obsolete; it also seems to preserve some inner characteristics of language and an idea of knowledge which new electric, electronic, or digital forms of communication do not necessarily share or support.

De-hypertexting the Mosaic

It is a brilliant essay by Michael A. Moos which offers the ground for new interpretations of McLuhan's mosaic, as the North American critic suggests that, more than a hypertext, the mosaic appears in fact as a *hyper-language*.[10] In his 'The Hypertext Heuristic: McLuhan Probes Tested (A Case for Edible Spaceships),' Moos traces the origins of the hypertext heuristic, as well as the connections between that heuristic and new literary theories developed in the late twentieth century, as previously mentioned. Bush's idea of the *memex*, Nelson's concept of hypertext, Barthes's *lexia*, Foucault's textual strategies, and Landow's convergence of critical theory and technology are discussed here. While so doing, Moos detects an interesting 'aporia' which is crucial to our discussion of the humanistic substance of McLuhan's 'electric' mosaic:

> On one hand, the idea that with hypertext one now has a means of testing postmodern theory remains precisely that ... until one actually has the specimen in question: either an adequate hypertext interface or at least a writing sample that embodies the requisite tropes of interactivity. It is the opposite of the position the software pirate often finds himself in: we have the manual but not the actual program it refers to.
>   On the other hand, to the extent that the Web instantiates hypertext, it must be noted that this is a distributed hypertext. The original problems ..., those of compression and selection across a wide field of available data have not been solved ... For the solitary user, the Web exists as a relatively untapped pool of hyperpotential, awaiting the powerful thrust of browsers and the torqued search engines of an organising intelligence.[11]

It is an idea which also connects to McLuhan's idea of *organizd ignorance*, an overload of information which we still do not know how to master except by trusting a more or less recognizable intelligence which organizes it for us. Organized ignorance is conducive to a conservative attitude towards knowledge, which ends by blocking progress. McLuhan insists that previous knowledge is what tends to be preserved 'when you look at new things for new keys. It is knowledge that creates real ignorance, just as wealth creates poverty.' Organized ignorance is presented 'as a way of bypassing the problem of knowledge as confusion and as block to discovery.'[12] Again, this idea relates to Thamus's interpretation of a new technology as a threat to traditional wisdom, something which encourages *recollection* instead of *memory* (which, in an oral society – and in some ways also in a post-oral society – is understood as the key to knowledge and wisdom) and creates addiction to external devices or matrixes. And where there are devices and matrixes, there are engineers and masterminds: someone is there to design a ground for the user to use, a system of preconceived signs and codes inside which each user – be it a literary theorist or anyone else – can search for an individual path. In other words, there is always an organizing intelligence to organize ignorance, which might then appear as the visible result of a hidden pattern of forces of which users are not always aware.

It is a situation which induces speculation on the languages of the Web-extended hypertext, on the concept of authorship – of real freedom of movement and association for the user – and of active/passive citizenship. What looks like an independent act of association and composition could, instead, be revealed as being a sterile collage of different codes and media, previously selected and limited by the designer. If we do not fully possess the technological language or the matrix, our action as writers could be turned into a sterile act masked as a powerful and creative one. We get the illusion that we are truly participating in a process, but we are not really interfacing at a deeper and meaningful level (we are just *users* not *producers* or even *prosumers*). In particular, in the case of written texts, the direct transposition on screen could translate into a lesser intensity in the communicative process due to the accelerated pace of the new medium. The new texts which, each time, are reconfigured by means of users' juxtaposition and selection acquire a dimension which is more and more *virtual, volatile,* and *ethereal;* they risk being immediately erased, leaving the screen to newer selections and juxtapositions. Hence, the screen becomes a highly technological interface where we can visualize new data and forms, which, nevertheless, might only have an ephemeral life. As beautiful and coloured butterflies, they attract users but do not stay, vanishing rapidly.

To respond to the above mentioned aporia, Moos introduces some interesting considerations on McLuhan's mosaic and proposes to invert the process of hypertext construction. Instead of using the screen as an interface, we can use McLuhan's pages as the interface on which we can plug other media, thereby verifying how the heuristic underpinning of the electronic (or now digital) hypertexts could eventually be applied to McLuhan's form of writing. The goal is to test the explorative potentialities offered by the mosaic: 'He shows how you can take the low-tech interface of the page and reverse engineer it so it can handle other inputs, so that you can, in effect, plug other media into it.'[13] In this hypothesis, McLuhan's glosses are considered as *adapter cables* which activate interfacing, juxtaposing different media on what stays as a 'text-based operating system.' The form *book* is renewed through the contact with 'the diverse and discontinuous life forms,' at the same time revealing a new exploratory technique:

> The structure of McLuhan's analysis can answer what critical theory looks and feels like in hypertext, what it is like to think critically in a hypertextual mode. McLuhan not only considers the multilayered prose a 'serious art form,' but a necessary mutation if cultural criticism is to keep pace with the increasing complexity of the objects it purports to describe.[14]

After all, it is the human brain, with its ability to associate simultaneous and inclusive events, and to keep images and situations in mind and retrieve them in renewed contexts, that has offered the ideal model for hypertext. By combining the new studies of the bicameral brain structure with his humanistic knowledge, McLuhan could thus elaborate his mosaic as an inclusive and simultaneous form of writing which 'optimizes language on the page with better compression techniques, enlarged memory storage, and enhanced program logic,'[15] thereby overcoming linearity and opening the phonetic form to new potentialities. It is for this reason that the mosaic can be retrieved as the objective correlative of a new cultural and critical discourse, more in tune with the electric environment than other later discourses.

The mosaic is therefore based on an idea of interface which McLuhan had already started to conceptualize in his Introduction to *The Bias of Communication*, H.A. Innis's most celebrated volume, when commenting not only on his colleague's ideas but also on his language. In particular, interface is presented as a structural component of Innis's investigative methodology as McLuhan underlines how Innis places his 'insights in a mosaic structure of seemingly unrelated and disproportioned sentences and aphorisms'; he also notices how Innis's writing generates 'insights by the method of interface.' McLuhan points out the lack of connectives in favour of a paratactic technique which turns Innis's written page into an interface reflecting 'the natural form of conversation or dialogue rather than of written discourse.'[16] The emphasis placed here on language and orality confirms that, in dealing with communication (as in the case of Innis's innovative 'discourse'), McLuhan's interest was mainly for the dynamics and the related processes of interaction. Consistently, as he developed his own form of communication, McLuhan focused on the cross-hybridization of different media involving different relational attitudes. In this way, he tried to convey a tactile quality to his written page, that is, a quality engaging readers to participate intensively in the communicative process; he hoped to *turn them on*, to stimulate them to *get in touch* with the communicative situation in order to participate fully in the act of learning, exploring, exchanging. In particular, in the previously mentioned chapter of *Understanding Media*, McLuhan tells us that 'of all the great hybrid unions that breed furious release of energy and change, there is none to surpass the meeting of literate and oral cultures.'[17] In that paragraph, he is discussing the environmental and societal effects of hybrid unions, but the idea translates well also to all related hybrid forms of communication, even more so, because the new hybrid energy derived from the cross-pollination of different media is what encourages new epiphanies precisely because of the new form that it creates, characterized by an 'extraordinary intensity':

> The hybrid or the meeting of two media is a moment of truth and revelation from which new form is born. For the parallel between two media holds us on the frontiers between forms that snap us out of the Narcissus-narcosis. The moment of the meeting of media is a moment of freedom and release from the ordinary trance and numbness imposed by them on our senses.[18]

The form of McLuhan's mosaic, then, is born out of the meeting of orality and literacy, and the resulting extraordinary intensity snaps us out of the Narcissus-narcosis imposed on our senses by the mechanicity of literacy. This form certainly anticipates later forms of communication, such as hypertext; and, as previously said, it certainly shares similar tenets to hypertext itself in structure (i.e., the analogical combination of probes and textual fragments) and in modes of fruition (i.e., the possibility to freely move backward and forward inside the text). But, as a form, it is meaningfully different because it is rooted in the ancient liberal art of grammar. This is something that today hypertext does not necessarily imply. What this grounding implies is an approach to knowledge based on 'the art of exposition and interpretation of phenomena,' rather than a compartmentalized take on concepts and ideas then assembled in hyper-textual modes.[19]

McLuhan's mosaic is primarily a tool enhancing our capability to learn and apprehend through the interplay of ancient wisdom and cognitive stimulation; it is not simply a way to convey simultaneity and dress knowledge in a format employing different media models in order to offer a more *lively*, *real*, and *immediate* experience. It is not, so to speak, the embodiment of the media fan, but rather of the media grammarian. The mosaic relies on the witty power of puns and words to perceive analogies between apparently unrelated things. It opens *windows* to unpack all the *compressed* learning: quoting Bacon and his nineteenth-century commentators, Moos rightly recalls the great concept of *portability of thought* based on 'an internal mobility of language through which thought itself advances.'[20] Such a concept is also assessed in relation to McLuhan's study of H.A. Innis's language, where McLuhan defines each of Innis's sentences as a compressed monograph: 'He includes a small library on each page, and often incorporates a small library of references on the same page in addition.'[21] Consequently, reading becomes an active process not simply because it enables us to understand what is written in the book and to participate in the creation of meaning, but mostly because it encourages us to continue exploring, and if we fully engage in that form it will further foster knowledge. As Moos insightfully suggests, McLuhan's writing (as well as Innis's) does not anticipate hypertext as a database that we can access, but as 'a mode of thinking that reaches back into your own "headset" and accesses you.' The mosaic taps 'into the reader, to access and activate his inner storehouse':

> The effect is to enable those very functions computer hypertext regards as a constitutive yet still strives to define, namely, integration of the reader into the writing process and real-time access to the archive … Thus Innis 'expects the reader to make discovery after discovery that he himself had missed.'[22]

The act of reading the mosaic, then, is envisaged as an experience which enhances the process of construction of knowledge, as well as a process of *actualization* of a knowledge elaborated through time and space. It is that very process of actualization which awakens readers from the Narcissus-narcosis. The mosaic, as the form which embeds and allows such an experience, is a cold medium or a truly tactile one because it forces the reader to compensate for what is not obvious in the text but which is, nevertheless, present and compressed in a probe or in a pun. The *portability of thought* so translated is what makes the mosaic a hyper-*language* more than a hyper-*text*. After all, language is an oral/acoustic concept and text is a linear one, with all it implies in terms of sensorial awareness and active participation.

Electrifying Hybrid

As previously discussed, the hybridization of literacy with other media is fundamental to its own survival; what is fascinating to note is this hybridization is not only preserved by McLuhan, but he also re-energizes it. He turns his mosaic into a probe while relying on ancient educational dicta. If you appreciate that, then you cannot but be *electrified* by the energizing force of the mosaic. And as an electrifying hybrid, McLuhan's mosaic could be defined as the LSD of post-secondary-orality readers: it triggers inner trips which, in fact, enlighten on cultural and media processes; also, it forces us to *enquire farther*, to explore old and new knowledge, old and new books, ideas, visions. To hazard a parallel which, I'm sure, will irritate most fans of hypertext, the mosaic retrieves an encyclopedic learning, while hypertext relies more on a *Reader's Digest* approach to knowledge. This is not a way to bless one form and blast another, but simply a way to point out that they express a different type of authorship, imply a different type of audience, and, even though they share similar reading techniques, they nevertheless induce a different form of participation and involvement. The way we tend to read hypertext is perhaps more comparable to zapping, whereby we can still acquire a sense of *progressing* in mapping actuality or a given field of investigation. If we apply the same zapping technique to McLuhan's mosaic, we can certainly have fun, but we do not have the same sense of *accumulating* knowledge. In order to fully appreciate what is hidden in McLuhan's verbo-voco-visual language, we have to act as an interface ourselves. We are the effective terminal of the communicative process.

An even bolder parallel would be between the way data are electronically moved and the way McLuhan's probes move inside the readers' heads. A message sent through the World Wide Web is decomposed into small units and bits which move independently across the various 'channels' of the net, and once at their destination, they are recomposed on the receiver's screen and form a readable message. In a similar way, McLuhan's mosaic is received as a discontinuous and fragmented form whose smaller units or bits of a deeper train of thought continue to move inside the reader's brain; in time, they combine with new ones until they enlighten each other and spark knowledge. It is an effect linked to the above mentioned concept of 'portability of thought' and which, at the same time, recalls the one suggested by T.S. Eliot in discussing the real use or meaning of poetry: while diverting attention through content, the poem works upon readers through form. Readers and writing are therefore juxtaposed in a dynamic interplay, which could be understood as a crucial element capable of overcoming the finiteness of the printed page, of books, because discontinuous writing acquires new meaning with each act of reading, depending on the reader. The pages of the electronic hypertext are virtually unlimited because they can be constantly updated and enriched by posting new data, or new juxtapositions enhanced by readers themselves; however, that does not necessarily imply that what was there before stays forever *visible* or settles in the readers' minds. The continuous renovation of hypertext is, in fact, more a matter of the quantity of posted data, than of permanency or stability of knowledge. With McLuhan, in spite of the clear limit imposed by the printed-page format, his mosaic renews at each reading, not because new data are added, but because what he writes resounds in a different way in the readers' minds; as effective terminal of the communication process, readers bring their renovating selves into each act of reading.

The investigation operating on the old medium (writing) is what helps to overcome the limits of the new one, as the former enables the retention of the intensity of the communication, the *train of thought*, that the electric media, which encourage speed and fast communication, do not always preserve and encourage. Even though based on literacy, the low-tech interface of McLuhan's mosaic stands as a powerful technology for re-enacting knowledge while preserving a tactile approach to memory. Through its verbo-voco-visuality, the mosaic brings us in touch simultaneously with both tradition and actuality, and engages us in a continuous actualization of our probing and learning experience. The media fan is, in fact, a tricky if not a false mask, which vanishes inside McLuhan's written corpus if you only take time to enter or access it.

PART TWO

Modernist Ascendancies

7 McLuhan and Media Studies

Labelling the Media Theorist

In an essay written for a new volume on modernism,[1] I suggested the advantages of cross-reading media studies and literary studies in order to better understand certain aspects of cultural phenomena pertaining to the early twentieth century. In that essay, I offered an overall approach to some modernist poetics in the light of the study of the new communication technologies of the time (telegraph, telephone, radio, as well as the new journalism and the press approached as objective correlatives of electricity and of electric media). I adopted an interdisciplinary approach inspired by Marshall McLuhan's understanding of both literature and society. The underpinning intention in my essay was to convince colleagues that not only was McLuhan's literary criticism quite good and still neglected, but that the Canadian thinker had also fully explored the pivotal role both literature and the arts have to play within a high-tech society. Remember: *from subject to function.* I wanted to discuss how, in McLuhan's hands, the humanities had regained a gnoseological function outside of their most traditional domain, something which is particularly needed at a time of information overload. As well, I wanted to demonstrate that McLuhan had not only *read* and *understood* Pound or Joyce, but also, most importantly, he had turned their aesthetic achievements into effective tools to explore and grasp the *implications of [their] action and of new knowledge in [their] own time.* I hope I struck a chord there.

In the following chapters, my goal is somewhat similar, as I hope to convince not only literary scholars, but also media theorists, of the literary origins of McLuhan's ideas on media, that is, of the literary origins of media studies *as per McLuhan*. This does not simply mean recalling McLuhan's training as a professor of English, or his love of literature and the arts; instead, it implies a deeper understanding of the role that literature played in the making of McLuhan as a 'media oracle/guru/ modernist/fan' (your choice, of course, but if you stay with one mask, you will miss the whole persona). In particular, it implies a different take on avant-garde literature: to understand it as a tool conducive to the development of a new way to approach and perceive both the history and the actuality of McLuhan's media studies.

To someone from outside, as I am, media studies, as both a field of research and a discipline, still appears to be a work in progress. As recently as 2003, in the very useful volume *A Companion to Media Studies*, editor Angharad N. Valdivia defines it as

> the dynamic interdiscipline of Media Studies … Media Studies is a relatively new interdiscipline, roughly dating back to the 1920s as a set of studies and the fifties as a 'formal discipline' … The contemporary situation is such that as an interdisciplinary field, Media Studies has no easy boundaries or parameters. It draws on some of the more established disciplines both in the humanities and the social sciences such as history, political science, sociology, psychology, anthropology, linguistics, and literature. Media Studies also has great overlaps with newer disciplines and interdisciplines such as cultural studies, popular culture studies, film studies, American studies, journalism, communication, speech communication, education, and ethnomusicology, to name a few.[2]

To many, the above might sound like an evolving epistemological chaos. To others, it might appear as the final accomplishment of cross-hybridization inside the humanities. Somehow, it seems very much in tune with some of the dynamics pertaining to our own global village today, at least in terms of overlapping of previous boundaries, cross-fertilization and contamination of cultural phenomena, as well as – why not – marketing of new approaches to old issues. And yet, such a blurred situation needs to be translated into university curricula, syllabuses, and all that makes media studies a popular but also a recognizable field of investigation, production, and expertise within higher educational systems. Bravely enough, some scholars have in fact started to canonize texts in media studies, trying to provide a historical view or some kind of order to the magma. The works of Marshall McLuhan are often quoted among the reference sources, accompanied, in turn, by praise or criticism.

As stated in the Prologue, this book is not about what McLuhan said, and I will not venture into an analysis of the fortune of his media investigations by providing a gallery of the most recent takes on his work. However, I will make a single exception and quote from the volume *Canonic Texts in Media Research*, also published in 2003, as a good example of the way in which McLuhan is often read: his literary roots are fully acknowledged but not investigated as a staple of his media theories, and even though Joshua Meyrowitz's essay on McLuhan certainly is the most articulated one written in recent years, it nevertheless is introduced and simplified by the editors through the specific approach of technological determinism. In general, what the above mentioned volume does offer is a good and an interesting (I imagine that some critics would instead use the word *arguable*) overview of the texts and the schools that have *created* media studies in the twentieth century: the Columbia School, the Frankfurt School, the Chicago School, British Cultural Studies (or the School of Birmingham), and, of course, the Toronto School. What interests me in this study, however, is the way in which the editors introduce the work of Marshall McLuhan since it enables me to tackle the most famous interpretation of McLuhan's approach to media studies – technological determinism – and to try to deconstruct it in and through literary terms.

In their introduction to the section dedicated to the Toronto School, the editors of *Canonic Texts in Media Research* recall that

> Marshall McLuhan entered media studies through a side door and stormed onto center stage. A scholar trained in English literature, he shifted from an initial interest in media content to put all his weight on form (of which his Cambridge mentors might approve) and on technology. By 'the medium is the message,' the best known of his aphorisms, he meant that the dominant medium of each age *uniquely* constrains the ways in which our brains process information, which, in turn, shapes our personality and our social system.[3]

I will later engage with the idea that McLuhan entered media studies 'through a side door.' Although in principle I agree with this statement, which recalls McLuhan's humanistic background as a starting point of his media studies, what bothers me here is the word *uniquely* in the sentence discussing the famous aphorism. If not otherwise commented upon, it inevitably reinforces the idea of McLuhan's technological determinism. In principle, I resist this association, as I have discussed elsewhere.[4] What I want to add here is that, in the particular case of McLuhan, that label does not convince me for several reasons: it reduces the complexity of his works to a linear interpretative cliché; it appears as a strategy developed by critics in response to the lack of a direct political engagement in McLuhan's media analysis, so that his *neutral* works can be used for different causes (not a negative strategy *per se*, but one which might encourage misinterpretations); it implicitly creates a persistent bias of seeing McLuhan as a media or techno-fan, convinced of the goodness of technological progress. Instead, I think that McLuhan was more an *artsy-fan* or even an *artsy-geek*, not at all in love with technology but a skeptic. He employed his literary studies as a counter-environment to better focus on both the functions and the side effects of a too much celebrated technological progress.

Evolutionary Grammarian

Come to think of it, the very idea of technological determinism draws upon a mechanical vision of the world based on a clear and direct relation between cause and effect; that is, it draws on an assumed linear progression of knowledge and understanding. For a man who was developing a new field approach to knowledge based on simultaneity and inclusiveness, a man familiar with the works of Heisenberg and who appreciated his principle of indeterminacy, technological determinism appears as a definition that is too reductive. Certainly, McLuhan based his grand narrative of media on the analysis of the impact of the so-called dominant medium – generally a technology of communication – as a leading factor which conditions both individuals and society; and yet, if we carefully read his explorations, that simply cannot be considered as the factor *uniquely* shaping both our personalities and our social system. The fact that he considered communication in terms of *transformation* and not *transportation* could be interpreted as encouraging a deterministic approach to technology; however, McLuhan himself often repeated that it is *the environment* that changes people, *not the technology*.[5] Technology is one of the factors (a figure) which constitute the environment (the ground), the environment being a dynamic setting for interrelated processes.

The case of the printing press – the medium which dominates McLuhan's observations in *The Gutenberg Galaxy* – is, in fact, quite an interesting one with which to assess the idea of a dominant medium and therefore question how technological determinism works. For instance, the same applied technology, the printing press, led to different effects in the Eastern and in the Western worlds due to their different societal constructs; that is, it led to the existence of different environmental set-tings, each employing a different approach to literacy. In China, paper was invented and used earlier than in the Western world, and, similarly, the first mobile type were created in China in the eleventh century. But the nature of the Chinese alphabet characters conditioned the recep-tion of such a technology, and it never became a 'dominant' medium as it did in the Western world, where a small number of letters of the phonetic alphabet could be easily combined into clear-cut words suited to the printing press. The complexity of the thousands of ideograms and symbols in Chinese, whose combination required a different strategy and interplay, did not contribute to making the printing press a popular technology for quite some time. A different type of alphabet and a dif-ferent type of societal construct created a different environment, in turn affecting the development of a new technology (the printing press).

The idea of a dominant medium is therefore *relative* and *not universal*; it depends on the society in which a given technology is used, as well as on which other technologies are already in use, something which *per se* undermines the idea of technological determinism *tout court*. In addi-tion, even when a medium becomes dominant inside a given society, that medium is not necessarily what *uniquely* constrains us as individuals and as a group. A technology, even when it is the dominating one, acts in synergy with a series of factors which, in turn, condition its reception and affect its permanence as a dominant medium. It seems to me that, more than a linear cause/effect approach, McLuhan used the techno-logical variable to discuss what might be termed as the *grey or hybrid zones*, that is, the areas of passage from one given model of society to another. His idea of interface is in fact associated with the idea of 'hybrid energy' released by the meeting of two or more old/new media. (Remember? 'The moment of the meeting of media is a moment of freedom and release from the ordinary trance and numbness imposed by them on our senses.')[6] In particular, he investigated the moments in history when two or more dominant media overlapped and inevitably changed each other. He also used art and literature to work out such grey or hybrid zones by showing how, through their work, artists and writers had often anticipated the complexity of change in relation to the wide spectrum of potential side effects associated with a new technology operating inside a given environment. Again, his was not a linear approach, but a field approach to situations, that is, an approach which is characterized by the ideas of networking, complexity, variables, and accidents or chance. His explorations were 'a mosaic of perpetually interacting forms that have undergone kaleidoscopic transformation – particularly in our own time.'[7]

As I have discussed when introducing the mosaic, McLuhan's field approach was translated into probes which were conceived to condense the complexity of observation into a brief statement which is, in fact, based on a broken knowledge. However, probes can be (and often have been) read, not as *portable thought or knowledge*, but as linear statements and, therefore, as absolute statements.[8] If we read a probe as an isolated figure, we can certainly translate McLuhan's thought in terms of cause/effect and therefore apply a deterministic bias to it. Again, much depends on our approach to the text, as well as on our approach to knowledge. Even when discussing what he defined as 'The Gutenberg Galaxy,' McLuhan did not pursue a direct and logical discussion of the effect of print on humankind; his 'absolutist statements' are in fact probing aphorisms. He discusses *the processes* which led from orality to literacy, the way such processes affected thoughts, politics, and imagination through time, and the interesting in-between zones bringing together different models of society. He approaches the latter consistently as complex environments which in part integrate and in part overlap, until one becomes more successful, consolidates, and is fully visible – a fact which does not imply that the other necessarily disappears, as it can instead adjust or adapt to the new one.[9] Technological *evolution* is perhaps a better word than mere *determinism*; even though it is a process of selection (which, in the case of technologies, combines natural and artificial factors), evolution also accommodates various possibilities, from *adaptation* to *co-evolution*, from *co-operation* to *speciation*. These are terms which suggest a broader interplay and networking than mere 'determinism.'

At the core of *The Gutenberg Galaxy* there is, then, the intention to probe evolving environmental situations, starting with a new and complex paradigm of investigation: technology. But technology itself is here understood, not as a *thing* or as an *object*, but as a *process* deriving from and presenting *all at once* various communicative, social, and political variables pervading the human domains. Technology so understood becomes a dynamic concept which does not exist in a vacuum but pertains to society at large, depending on time-and-space factors. The concept of technological grey or hybrid zones therefore constitutes a counter-environment to the idea of technological determinism, as it encourages the idea of the cross-reading of technological discoveries and cultural matrixes. For instance, when discussing the passage from orality to literacy (in *The Gutenberg Galaxy*, as well as in all his later books), McLuhan focuses on the role played by manuscripts to accommodate an old medium (language, speech) in the new one (literacy), in turn, translating the development of different forms of society (pre-literate/literate, Middle Ages / Renaissance). McLuhan's observations are based not only on the object *per se*, but also on the services it engendered as an innovative form of communication and knowledge. The manuscript is therefore presented as an example of a communicative tool merging two environments: a written text (literacy) was read aloud (orality) in monasteries or at courts, to educate or entertain people. And yet, the manuscript also created a more intimate approach to reading, as individuals could also be introduced to the pleasure of intimate readings, to a private interaction with this medium. The printing press made this possibility (private reading) available on a larger scale, accelerating a process which had already started in the Western world. Through time, the interplay of this technology with other environmental situations is what brought long-term effects on both individuals and groups. Literacy became a powerful instrument inside religious and secular institutions alike; as Innis wrote in his *Empire and Communication*, means of transports and new infrastructures contributed to the spread of literate empires through either space or time; in modern times, in commerce and war alike, literacy was a crucial element. It's a complex network of forces, not just a medium, which shapes, through time, personalities and social systems, mentalities and sensibilities. Always remember that, as a grammarian, McLuhan used language and words as 'complex systems of metaphors,' that is, as an evocation of experiences and processes. To forget that leads to a flattened understanding. As he wrote in *The Gutenberg Galaxy*: 'The oral polyphony of the prose of Nashe offends against lineal literary decorum.'[10]

McLuhan's investigations appear to be even less deterministic when applied to the electric era, presented as a passage in progress in which he himself was living at the time, conscious of the fact that individuals were now crossing another grey zone: new environmental patterns (post-orality, electric age) were approached through old and more familiar ones (literacy, mechanical age). In his works, McLuhan introduces the new perceptive modes brought by the new technologies which were quickly becoming the 'dominant' media of his time, but he does not explain them in terms of cause and effect only. On the contrary, he often points out that he was simply probing the effects, which, he insisted, always precede the cause.[11] It is both a provocative thought and one which undermines the idea of technological determinism. If the dominant medium (a given technology) was what 'uniquely constrains the ways in which our brains process information' and then determines our personalities and social systems, we could easily foresee in a clear linear way what comes next (we know the cause and anticipate the effects). Instead, the technological variable assists in introducing new environmental situations. We can only understand these by probing a complex network of forces which we perceive first in terms of effects (what is immediately visible) and, only later, in terms of their hidden pattern. The oracle of the electric age offered his own explorations, his own intuitions, through a form which was often interpreted as ultimate or absolutist, that is, through clear-cut, provocative concepts. He wrote and spoke as a grammarian, but was read and interpreted as a dialectician: from archetypes to clichés, that is, to commonplaces understood as 'collections of sayings (in effect formulas) on various topics.' As in the case of the oracle's audience, the process of interpretation is no longer in the hands of the seer. As McLuhan himself stated in Woody Allen's movie *Annie Hall*, it is the audience that must choose a side and decide if his 'whole fallacy is wrong'; and, rightly so, in that movie his pun was addressed to the character of a young professor at Columbia who is trying to impress a young lady with a linear interpretation of McLuhan's acoustic probes. Can you square a circle?

A Political Thomist

To define McLuhan's media studies in terms of technological determinism could also be interpreted as a way to classify someone who never associated media research with political thinking in an explicit way, at a time when politicization was generally assumed. Not only 'love' but also 'ideology' was in the air in the 1960s and 1970s. From the beginning, media studies were associated with a broader take on society in relation to political agendas or interpretations. The media industry was at the core of the different approaches, be it to investigate the new social systems in terms of audience attitude and behaviours, mass impression, propaganda, or societal bonds. Ideology was often at play, and media studies were a way not only to assess the making of the new world societies, but also to position or support in political discourses across the political spectrum. As we saw, McLuhan himself was tempted to take sides when he began to apply 'the method of art analysis to the critical evaluation of society.' In his preface to *The Mechanical Bride*, he introduced a moral approach to his explorations, as he sets out to reveal the way in which various agencies 'manipulate, exploit, control' old and new audiences. The confession is encapsulated in a few initial pages, but thereafter he never returns to the topic in such an explicit way, as many critics acknowledge. In all his later volumes, and especially in those which made him famous worldwide (*The Gutenberg Galaxy* and *Understanding Media*), McLuhan simply ventured into the new media world with no clear party bias as an intellectual. His approach to media was as neutral as possible, as objective as possible: from Dos Passos's political commitment to Joyce's universalism. His strategy of exploration took into account the humanistic tradition, not to *win consent*, but to invite his readers to *enquire*, as Bacon said, *farther*. Biographers and critics agree that McLuhan never discussed his political ideas nor his religious beliefs in front of an audience or in his works. The only exception is perhaps to be found in an essay written in 1934 when he was a young student at the University of Manitoba, of which Philip Marchand has offered an account.[12] Later in his career, when pressured to comment on political issues or on political thinkers, McLuhan twisted his comments more to communicative issues than to ideological ones. For instance, he mentions Karl Marx, not to discuss if he was right or wrong, but to compare two modes of observation: 'Marx was looking in the rear-view mirror of Adam Smith and Ricardo. I'm looking in the rear-view mirror of Joyce, Carroll, the Symbolists, Adolph Hildebrand. They related the sensory life of metamorphosis and transformation in contact with new technology.'[13] As on many other occasions, he avoids discussing political or economic issues in detail, using instead his literary roots to counterbalance all possible implications and shifting his focus to the environmental analysis. Needless to say, the so-called 'engaged critics' never forgave him.

Despite biographers' acknowledgment that in private McLuhan's ideas were close to those expressed by conservatives, in recent years some North American scholars have attempted a sort of methodological reconciliation between Marxist thinking and McLuhan's. For instance, in his seminal book *Method Is the Message*, Paul Grosswiler suggests some similarities between McLuhan's explorations and Marx's dialectic; in particular, Grosswiler has presented 'some points of convergence between McLuhan and the Frankfurt School,'[14] something which, as we will later see, Umberto Eco also postulated when reviewing the Italian edition of *The Mechanical Bride*. Grosswiler positions both experiences inside a type of intellectual continuum which brings together authors as diverse as McLuhan, Marx, Adorno, Walter Benjamin, and Mark Horkheimer, as well as the new generation of postmodern critics in the wake of Jean Baudrillard. Among the many merits of Grosswiler's volume is the working out of the 'serendipitous collision of McLuhan and Marxism,'[15] as that opens up new and refreshing critical discourses that our time perspective now allows. However, Grosswiler insists that in his last volumes, McLuhan's approach to Marx appears to be more articulated than what was normally understood, and that McLuhan's judgment on Marx's political thought is never entirely negative. But if there is not an assessment of Marx's *ideology* in McLuhan's writing – in *Take Today: The Executive as Dropout*, McLuhan does not discuss Marxism as an ideology, but as a *historical* product of a series of dynamics of which technology is one – it is not so important to speculate on McLuhan's *political* take on Marxism; it seems more interesting to focus the investigation on possible points of convergence of their 'visions' of environmental processes so as to work out more refined patterns of 'causal operation in history.' Marshall McLuhan did not go political in public; as a result, he remains a challenging battleground for all those who want to win him for one cause or the other *post mortem*. We continue to put the masks we love best on him. And, after all, this is also what explains why he still is a fascinating figure.

When I first approached McLuhan's writings, I myself was not comfortable with the lack of a clear and open political discourse in his media observations. It simply did not seem right precisely because of the complexity of the historical background in which he was living, and also because of the tremendous role media had been playing in conditioning both public debates and the agendas of various establishments worldwide. I also thought that McLuhan's neutrality could damage his own fortune among media scholars and a general audience alike, not only because everybody might try to claim him as the champion of very different causes simultaneously, but also because it might foster the accusation of nihilism, with negative consequences for his own studies on media and for media studies at large. What is the point if you do not demonstrate how to use media to foster a cause, settle societal processes, or encourage active participation of audiences and citizens? I myself got trapped into various McLuhan masks and lost sight of his whole persona. Taking a step back and assessing McLuhan's works as a media scholar through the literary variable has helped me reconcile with his 'apolitical' thought and to realize that he was taking another road, maybe a much more needed one – so much so that, at present, I think that *McLuhan was, instead, very political, but he never was ideologically so.* I'm retrieving here the Greek origin of the word 'politics': 'politiké,' meaning 'pertaining to the city,' and combining the terms *polis* – city – and *tèchné* – art. Originally, to be political meant embracing the art of taking care of the public sphere, a social commitment of encouraging participation and pursuing the public good.

McLuhan was a Thomistic Catholic; he knew St Thomas Aquinas's *Summa Theologica* very well. St Thomas pursued his faith, and his search for truth led him to various traditions: Roman, Greek, Muslim, and Jewish philosophers are all part of his network of references. Aquinas was never ideologically biased because he considered himself on a mission transcending human materiality. McLuhan followed a similar approach when venturing into media studies. Contrary to most intellectuals of the time, he did not pursue media studies as an area encouraging ideological speculations on public uses of media (and especially of the newest medium of his time, television). Rather, his definition of media is based on their intrinsic operational aspects, their *function*, and not on the relationship between medium and power (be it political, consumerist, or sociological). I am convinced that this neutral approach has contributed to the reading of McLuhan's works in terms of technological determinism. The way I see it, to think of technology primarily in terms of operative processes, of function and functionality, is not necessarily an apolitical or an ahistorical operation. It is, instead, a preliminary and fundamental step towards assessing both its potentialities and limits for then employing the acquired knowledge to achieve public good. It is, therefore, an epistemological approach preparing the ground for a deeper understanding of the possible short- and long-term usages associated with a given medium.

Understanding the characteristics of new and old technologies and their mutual interplay may also lead to speculations about the related psychodynamics involving individuals and groups sharing the environment reshaped through those very technologies. In this context, to probe means to work out hypotheses which can be either proven or disproven, especially if one acts, not as a technological determinist, but as an explorer of environments. It is a way *to be with it*, to be with the situation you are exploring with no *a priori* bias. You do not impose an abstraction on the situation you are probing; nor do you impose a preconceived notion or a point of view or an ideology on it. What you do instead is an interchange, as your point of view is modified by the interplay with environmental dynamics. Remember? 'If you have a point of view, it means that you have already mastered the situation ... You have already abstracted it, and angled it.'[16] When dealing with new technologies, you must be prepared to accept the approximation of your viewpoint, its incompleteness and indeterminacy. As a media theorist, McLuhan accepted such an approximation and used language to probe a network of possible side effects, to be later experienced, tested, exploited, or rejected. By so doing, he established a strategy which might prove useful to envisage a set of technological and cultural possibilities inside a society. To assess them by analysing which ones were in fact adopted or refused, as well as by whom, how, when, and for what purposes, might become another way to add a dimension of insight to the whole process.

To fully understand the nature of technology also puts one in a better position to evaluate the invisible aspects linking dominant media and political, cultural, and sociological agendas. First, learn the structure and operational mechanisms of the medium (meaning that you do not take sides pro or against, but rather acknowledge its existence and functions), then set it against its social and political context and decide how to employ your knowledge. 'When technology extends *one* of our senses, a new translation of culture occurs as swiftly as the new technology is interiorized.'[17] We need to master both that shift and that translation. It is a process comparable to learning a new language: you need to learn some basic principles (sounds, vocabulary, grammar) in order to master it at your pleasure and in your own original way. The development of new media modifies our environmental *langage* in terms of new potentialities as well as new limits; each time, we have to agree on the *langue* translating the new set of communicative tools and mould our own *parole*, as individuals, as well as groups:

> Nobody yet knows the language inherent in the new technological culture; we are all deaf-blind mutes in terms of the new situation. Our most impressive words and thoughts betray us by referring to the previously existent, not to the present.[18]

This very statement is more consistent with the idea of *indeterminacy* than with the idea of *determinism*. We know that new media will affect society, but we do not know how, when, and for how long that will happen. As in all evolutionary processes, we know that our predictions might be either confirmed or disproven, the variables being innumerable. And if this is true for the natural world, it is even truer for the hybrid and artificial worlds which human beings continue to forge, the human factor always being the most unpredictable of all variables, especially when acting in a more and more complex technological setting.

While remaining on a neutral ground and avoiding explicit political judgment, McLuhan nevertheless played with the political variables by relating them to the new media language and function. He elaborated provocative and playful statements which make more sense today than when they were uttered. We are looking at them through the rear-view mirror and can historicize them in the light of our experience with some of the media which McLuhan approached as a pioneer. Just one example will help to better understand what I mean. Imagine that it is 1954, the year of Joe McCarthy's official defeat but still a time when a lot of people were seriously working to keep the Western bloc *safe* and the Red Scare *under control.* How would you *then* react when reading what McLuhan wrote that very year in his first version of *Counterblast*, namely: 'We can win China and India for the West only by giving them the new media. Russia will not give these to them. Television prevents communism because it is post-Marx just as the book is pre-Marx.'[19] And how do you react *now*?

The idea of McLuhan's objective detachment as a media explorer still puzzles critics, and even more so if his works are not interpreted in terms of technological determinism. McLuhan lived through at least four complex decades which changed the world (he witnessed a world war, the Cold War years, the 1960s and the 1970s with all what those years implied). Could it really be possible that he did not have his own political agenda as a media phenomenon, as well as a media theorist? Was it really possible to stay neutral and detached given those political, cultural, and social revolutions and counter-revolutions? Consider this well: nearly all the modernist writers whom McLuhan took as his masters had in effect been engaged with the politics of their time, and often in a very direct if not disturbing way. So why cannot we deduce that McLuhan had an agenda of his own? After all, he was a converted Catholic, and he wrote about religion and religious issues in relation to social issues in private letters, as well as in several essays now collected in his posthumous *The Medium and the Light* (1999). He considered God a *constant presence* which resonated within him. As a converted atheist (that is, as someone who has followed the reverse path, from inborn Catholicism to rational secularism), I would welcome an investigation of the religious subtext of McLuhan's literary and media writing, as well as its impact on his world vision. Certainly, it would not be an easy quest, though, due to McLuhan's sophisticated understanding of theological issues and the complexity of his network of analogies.

In particular, McLuhan admired the work of thinkers who, even though they were writing from inside the Church, still had a controversial relation with it, precisely for their intellectual challenge to dogmatic issues. Apart from St Thomas Aquinas, McLuhan appreciated the writing of Pierre Teilhard de Chardin and his attempt to combine theology and evolutionism, that is, religious and scientific thought; consistently, he also was a great connoisseur of Jacques Maritain's philosophical thought, clearly rooted in St Thomas Aquinas. And, most importantly, McLuhan understood media as processes long *before others*. All these elements could work well to introduce not only the idea of McLuhan as the chief evangelist of the electric (and TV) age, but also the idea of an electric (and TV) evangelism underpinning his various probings. Cronenberg's representation of McLuhan as Doctor O'Blivion in *Videodrome* hints at that, through a powerful though deceiving rendering of the media guru mask, as we will see in the final section of this book.

Yes, if I bring religion into the picture, I do have some doubts about McLuhan's neutrality, because he was a truly political Thomist; however, I cannot find any explicit *political* (nor *religious*) commitment or judgment in McLuhan's work after those two early pages introducing his *Mechanical Bride*. What I do constantly find instead are endless references to all sorts of books – sociological, historical, economical, anthropological ones – with a clear preference for literary texts. William Shakespeare opens *The Gutenberg Galaxy,* and Alexander Pope ends it. Also, all these writers do not stand as clever decorations to a text discussing the impact of new technologies on the making of either the mechanical or the electric age; rather, they stand as key sources for understanding the complex processes underpinning cultural and technological passages. If thinking of McLuhan as a technological determinist counters our puzzlement about his non-ideological commitment, thinking of him as a humanist retrieves the heuristic potentialities of literature. To me, it offers a broader understanding of both the messenger and the message.

A Classic Modernist

Finally, to define McLuhan in terms of technological determinism also permanently casts him as an enthusiast of media or techno-fan; while it might imply political neutrality, it does not imply technological neutrality. Most critics seem, in fact, to assume that, being a technological determinist, McLuhan was in favour of technological progress. He was not, but the assumption is that if you discuss something again and again, you are in favour of it. We have obsessions and we have passions. New technologies were one of McLuhan's obsessions, but they were not one of his passions. On the contrary, he often repeated that he did not favour change, especially technological change. He was not on good terms even with those daily commodities and technologies which have consolidated the North American dream; he did not even drive. His interest in technology was a consequence of his interest in literature (especially of modernist literature), that is, of his curiosity as an intellectual who had consciously chosen to explore what there was outside a safer ivory tower. Those who interpret such an interest and such a curiosity as enthusiastic responses to technological change are seeing McLuhan through their own eyes: no matter whether they read it as a positive or as a negative thing, it never was a fact.

McLuhan's encounter with new forms of communication started with Mallarmé and the symbolist poets, and continued with Joyce and the other modernist writers. He was fascinated by their attempts to elaborate words to render their own reality so as to match the new spirit of their time, a spirit inscribed inside an unprecedented and overwhelming technological change. New scientific discoveries were unveiling exciting possibilities, and they were blasting most established certainties. New applied technologies were triggering other ways of being together, offering a wider audience the possibility to be at the centre of the communicative process as both senders and receivers, as never before. In other words, the world was moving on, and the avant-garde writers and artists were trying to master what they perceived as a lasting schizophrenic situation, an uncanny *dissociation of sensibility*, as Eliot put it: change was quicker than its acknowledgment (at the individual level as well as at the environmental level), not to speak of all the possible reactions or adaptations to it. When McLuhan discovered the works that the modernist masters had written a couple of decades earlier, his own actuality was already a different one; he had his own epiphany while at Cambridge, where he started to connect the former to the latter in order to explore the ensuing perceptual schizophrenia (which we might read as reflecting the grey zone in which mechanical and electric media interfaced). Those literary works became not just 'the object' of his studies on media; they became operative models defining his future investigations as a professor of English and as media scholar.

It has been said many times that McLuhan's pronouncements sound clearer today than when they were first stated, each time in relation to new interpretations of his works. A similar statement is often made when dealing with the works of the great modernist masters, whose complex works are constantly juxtaposed to new critical epiphanies in various fields of research. Through time, all clear-cut interpretations of the former and the latter are questioned and turned upside down, each time triggering debates, controversies, and new understandings. As John Nerone writes, 'We will be reading McLuhan ... long after diligent scholars have disproven or complexified all of his factual conjectures.'[20] I agree. But why is it? I think that it is possible to say that McLuhan's works, like the modernist works, are by now twentieth-century *classics* of *media studies literature*, the way Italo Calvino defines classics:

> The classics are books which exercise a particular influence, both when they imprint themselves on our imagination as unforgettable, and when they hide in the layers of memory disguised as the individual's or the collective unconscious ... A classic is a work which relegates the noise of the present to a background hum, which at the same time the classic cannot exist without. A classic is a work which persists as background noise even when a present that is totally incompatible with it holds sway.[21]

In other words: 'A classic is a book which has never exhausted all it has to say to its readers.'[22] Marshall McLuhan's works continue to talk to various audiences through time and space no matter how scholars, critics, or curious readers interpret or dismiss them. Also in this sense, McLuhan's works, just like other modernist works, are *open works*, both in terms of authorial design (form) and reader's response (reception). They break previous canons and encourage formal explorations, in turn combining different codes, genres, styles. They no longer offer a unique and absolute vision of the world they portray; they accept uncertainty into their epistemological approach. Precisely because of the formal complexity, each act of reading can lead to new truths and new epiphanies that will be challenged again and again, as they progress with new knowledge through time. McLuhan's nonsensical language is instead full of *diverse meanings*, as various interpretations of his messages through time continue to affirm. But if we focus on the architecture which shapes those messages, we soon realize that the most important and lasting effect of reading his books is in the continual challenge he poses to our rational thinking through his non-linear form. The medium, once again, is the message, and it offers us a way to keep awake and engage in a critical exploration of our own cultures and technology. This is the original contribution that McLuhan's literary roots can bring to media studies.

8 From Literature to Media Studies

Conscious Planning

McLuhan did not enter media studies 'through a side door'; he entered media studies from the main gate, and that did not happen by chance. His letters reveal, in fact, that he 'stormed onto center stage' out of a carefully designed plan, which started to be conceived while at Cambridge University and which was later developed when he took his first job as a university English professor. McLuhan chose to become a media scholar *consciously*, learning through literary readings and academic practice how to turn his humanistic knowledge into a newly conceived device to better understand the technological and media complexity of his own time. In the process, he did not betray his first passion – literature; on the contrary, he based everything on it, with literature becoming the background against which to develop his own unique operative model. Once again, McLuhan acted in the wake of the modernist writers: he was not an *inspired* or an *illuminated* guru; he was instead a conscious *fabbro*, the better craftsman as T.S. Eliot wrote of Pound, a maker of meaning who knew his tools well, as far as those tools went. That's why he was also a good teacher.

Everything got started at Cambridge University, and it is there we must return to fully grasp the literary origins of McLuhan's media studies.[1] In England, he rediscovered literature and the humanistic tradition, while discovering himself as a man and as a scholar. Once back in North America, he was well equipped to read his reality in the light of those discoveries. From the late 1940s, he started to employ literature to discuss, through the rear-view mirror of history, various phases of humanity. To read his works on old and new media means to constantly engage with a long list of literary and philosophical figures, embracing, among others, Shakespeare, Blake, Vico, Bacon, Cicero, Plato, and Thomas Aquinas. It is against this vast and solid sacred wood of literature that the great modernist writers stand as giants, enlightening the passage from the mechanical to the electric age. As McLuhan discusses in all his works, writers such as Eliot, Joyce, and Pound explored their present and unveiled the processes underpinning the making of a new mass society. Forget the ivory tower: the modernists wanted to take over the control tower, as did McLuhan a few years later.

While at Cambridge, the study of contemporary English literature allowed McLuhan to understand and work out the probing potentialities of innovative poetic strategies; it changed once and forever not only his approach to literature and the arts, but also his understanding of the responsibilities of a teacher as a man of letters now inhabiting an evolving technological world. In this sense, Cambridge was a shock. There he was challenged to use literature as a radar to detect and adjust to the new cultural and social transformations. And it was at Cambridge that he came to realize how the modernist avant-garde experiments constituted relevant analogical mirrors to better see the technological and cultural processes reflected in his times. How ironic it is to fully acknowledge the impact of Cambridge University on the would-be pioneer of media studies, knowing that such a discipline is not even endorsed as a subject or as a qualification for admission by that very same university. Perhaps returning media studies to McLuhan's original humanistic approach would help its reconsideration at Cambridge.

Already during his first year in England, McLuhan came to understand what he wanted to become and how he could achieve it. The letters he wrote to his family from Cambridge bear witness to his self-discovery as a Canadian, but also as a man of letters engaged with his own time:

> ... Wow! I never felt so helplessly futile and ignorant before. I have an exact knowledge of nothing. When I really get a grip on English I shall be in a position to understand other arts more readily. My mind is a ferment these days – boiling with new ideas and experiences. I must keep it so for years yet, if I am to be worth anything as an educator. Believe me I would vastly prefer dairy-and-orchard culture to this intense mental culture. The latter is not easy and its results are less certain.[2]

And again:

> The mere formal educator cannot transform the radical modes of life of

which he is usually only too natural a product. My life in Canada will be a continuous discontent. My task as a teacher will be to shake others from their complacency – how is it possible to contemplate the product of English life (i.e. literature) without criticising our own sterility.[3]

Once he got 'a grip on English' – and, in particular, the new literature then taught at Cambridge University – literature became the tool he employed to awaken from Newton's sleep, first, his North American students, then his international audience. Cambridge offered, in fact, a unique setting for McLuhan's formation, since that university was among the first – if not the first – to include contemporary ferment into its curricula.

Practical Mystics

Even though the role played by the modernist writers in cleansing *the doors of perception* constitutes the crucial element in the development of McLuhan's media investigations, it did not come at once, nor impromptu. It was the result of a progressive understanding of both literature and the arts, the final step of a process which took McLuhan along a path in a different habitat than the one he had experienced while at the University of Manitoba. In England, he soon discovered one of the 'products of English [literary] life' who became his first literary hero: G.K. Chesterton, whose work had a major impact on McLuhan's boiling mind. Even though he cannot be counted as an innovative modernist writer, Chesterton remains, in fact, among McLuhan's favourite intellectuals, both as a writer and as an individual. His love of paradoxes, his verbal playfulness and sense of humour, as well as his ability to be a master of popular detective stories, were three powerful elements which made Chesterton a point of reference for McLuhan as a professor of English, and as a media theorist. Similarly, Chesterton's Catholicism had a lasting impact on young McLuhan's approach to religion.[4]

Not only did Chesterton's ideas contribute to McLuhan's conversion to Catholicism (Chesterton's *Orthodoxy*, as well as his *St Thomas Aquinas: The Dumb Ox*, provided some solid ground for combining Christian theology and an intellectual reassessment of Aristotle's tradition inside Christianity),[5] but they also helped the younger intellectual to establish a network of literary and philosophical correspondences which stood forever in McLuhan's interior landscape. Already while studying and reading Chesterton's works, McLuhan started to concentrate not only on what was in those texts (*meaning*), but also on their rhetoric (the *lan-*

guage they employed to shape meaning), that is, on how it was framed and conveyed. It is on Chesterton, the 'Practical Mystic,' that McLuhan wrote his first academic essay.[6] Contemplate that title for a moment: it is a probe in itself! It is a Thomistic rendering of Chesterton's approach to knowledge, his way of bringing together secular and religious values without compromising the integrity of either. Chesterton is, in fact, the author who, in his Father Brown stories, turns the priest into a detective who follows an *intuitive* rather than a *deductive* methodology all through his investigations, contrary to what his more famous colleague Sherlock Holmes used to do. Percept versus concept: a grammarian and a dialectician, the former reasoning intuitively, the latter logically (after all, Sir Arthur Conan Doyle was not only a writer but also a physician, that is, a man of science). In *The Secret of Father Brown*, the leading character explains his method as such:

> You see, I had murdered them all myself ... I had planned out each of the crimes very carefully. [...] I had thought out exactly how a thing like that could be done, and in what style or state of mind a man could really do it. And when I was quite sure that I felt exactly like the murderer myself, of course I knew who he was.[7]

Father Brown *puts the other on* to understand a situation; he performs a mimetic act which leads him to the final revelation, which therefore derives from a calibrated mixture of physical and metaphysical elements. Sherlock Holmes, on the other hand, believes that 'detection is, or ought to be, an exact science and should be treated in the same cold and unemotional manner ... Some facts should be suppressed, or, at least, a just sense of proportion should be observed in treating them. The only point in the case which deserved mention was the curious analytical reasoning from effects to causes, by which I succeeded in unraveling it.'[8] As a writer, an intellectual, and a converted Catholic, Chesterton was the champion of the tradition which McLuhan himself also championed.

In his essay 'G.K. Chesterton: A Practical Mystic,' McLuhan carefully discusses the author's rhetorical devices and language, focusing on their precision and complexity. McLuhan elaborates sentences which emphasize the effort to be *literal* while combining precision and humour, at the same time amusing and challenging the reader: 'In short he [Chesterton] is *original* in the only possible sense, because he considers everything in relation to its *origins*'; 'It is plain that he is literally a *radical* because he goes to the *roots* of things.'[9] The etymological precision is conveyed here through a formal construction which anticipates McLuhan's later verbal puns as operative strategies, which can be approached as a playful paradox exploring reality. Chesterton is the master of paradoxes, of clever rhetorical sentences, as McLuhan himself points out in his introduction to Hugh Kenner's book *Paradox in Chesterton* (1948). Chesterton turned popular sayings, proverbs, and allegories inside out, transforming them into puns challenging all complacent acceptance of conventional wisdom. His style consciously differed from other writers of his time, especially Oscar Wilde. Wilde's puns and aphorisms, in fact, reflected a different way to be an artist, and a different philosophy of life, which Chesterton discussed in his famous book *Heretics*. The practical mystic couldn't but perceive the dandy's creed as 'very powerful and very desolate ... It is the carpe diem religion; but the carpe diem religion is not the religion of happy people, but of very unhappy people. Great joy does not gather the rosebuds while it may; its eyes are fixed on the immortal rose which Dante saw.'[10] Chesterton's explorations of language related to a different approach to his own actuality, practical as well as aesthetical, engaged with social and economical issues while pursuing the immortal rose. His lesson, which combines a formal search with a social commitment, stayed with McLuhan, the professor of English and a practical mystic himself.

As a literary man, Chesterton was a master of rhetoric, a writer of detective stories, and an admirer of the fiction of Edgar Allan Poe, another of McLuhan's literary heroes. Poe's 'Philosophy of Composition' offers a set of speculations introducing a methodology which McLuhan came to associate with the making of the modern spirit. As he later wrote to Harold Adams Innis, 'Retracing becomes in modern historical scholarship the technique of reconstruction. The technique which Edgar Allan Poe first put to work in his detective stories.'[11] It is precisely the inductive method of Poe's and Chesterton's detective stories which McLuhan was then applying to his own critical observation of the new folklore of the industrial man; moving from some visible representations of his society, his *Mechanical Bride* traces their hidden formal cause. Acting as a perceptive detective observing the present through his humanistic roots, McLuhan wants to unmask what lies underneath the surface of things: 'Where visual symbols have been employed in an effort to paralyze the mind, they are used here as a means of energizing it.'[12] The technique of the detective story is unfolded through a paradoxical approach to reality which turns reassuring visual imagery, sayings, and allegories inside out in order to counterbalance – by unveiling – all numbing processes at work inside his own society.

The rhetorical strategy developed first by Poe and later by Chesterton is used by McLuhan as a conscious device to reveal and give shape to actuality, following a process which could be interpreted also in philosophical terms, as it is meant to address what the author conceived as the underpinning *formal cause*. As in Aristotle's philosophy – later referenced by St Thomas Aquinas himself, another of McLuhan's life-long sources – formal cause relates to *ideas* existing in the thing itself, effects which are *embodied in the matter*, which can only be fully appreciated through deep contemplation or probing. Applied to the probing of an environment, the formal cause is what embeds the effect of the thing in one's own time. McLuhan acquired such an awareness of formal cause through his philosophical and literary investigations, including his study of Chesterton's literary and philosophical writings.[13] After having written a few literary essays testing his new literary and cultural approach, he was ready to write *The Mechanical Bride*, his first attempt to provide a counter-environment and bring to light the hidden forces constructing the new media environments. As a young scholar in the humanities, he hoped to interest and to alert, that is, he hoped to 'shake others from their complacency' and elicit critical responses and active participation. This is what he would try to do from then onwards. His was neither a blind love for media, nor was it a way to test and consolidate a theory (technological determinism); it was his way to employ the devices he knew best (literature, rhetorical strategies, poetics, humanistic knowledge) towards the understanding of his own world. *The Mechanical Bride* is the first result following from McLuhan's understanding of literature as 'a *function* ... inseparable from communal existence.'[14]

During his years at Cambridge, McLuhan could therefore explore the literary offering in the light of the university's well-established humanistic tradition, which, and this is the crucial point, had also started to question the idea of the English canon by including new modernist writers in its university curricula. Among others, I.A. Richards and F.R. Leavis were developing new ways to explore literary texts, changing the approach to literature and starting a new school of critical theory, which McLuhan will later help promote in the United States and Canada.[15] To open university curricula to the works of T.S. Eliot and other contemporary writers also constituted the beginning of a new way to read and interpret modernist experiments; the modernist masters were read not only for their poetic achievements, but also for their new ideas on art and society.

The first important impact, then, was to work out patterns connecting what was new with what was old inside the text. No matter the various modernist blasts against the past, no matter the modernist motto 'make it new,' what the new critics started to acknowledge through their way of reading the text was the fact that there was a broader republic of letters embracing various traditions alike and that each new work was there to contain and actualize them. For McLuhan's *mind in ferment*, Cambridge was the perfect setting to acquire a solid humanistic background while encouraging a lively curiosity for contemporary literary experiments. Since that time in the 1930s, the continuous juxtaposition of literary productions pertaining to different times and traditions became a clear tenet of McLuhan's methodology as both a literary critic and as a media explorer. His investigation of mass culture in *The Mechanical Bride*, in fact, shifts the analysis to a different form of 'text' – the sum of messages conveyed inside the mass-media culture – but preserves the same focus and methodology: the analysis of pop imagery, metaphors, settings, and themes is the thread of McLuhan's parodic and satirical close-reading of his own societal architecture, his own life and times. Coming back from Cambridge, he was well equipped to enter the world of mass culture.

From Renaissance to Modernism

McLuhan completed his PhD dissertation in the United States, while teaching at the University of Madison, Wisconsin. In 1943, due to war-time, he could not return to Cambridge to defend it. However, the origins of his research project and the elaboration of his explorative methodology clearly have roots in his university years at Cambridge. He chose a subject, 'The Place of Thomas Nashe in the Learning of His Time,' which was consistent with his culture and religious searching at the time, associating the pursuit of knowledge with the understanding of human behaviours and societal matrixes. By his own admission, his reading of Chesterton's works 'opened [his] eyes to European culture and encouraged [him] to know it more closely.'[16] His dissertation was a way to combine such a search with a more personal one; it therefore became a journey into knowledge which, in time, provided him with a solid ground for all his later explorations, both in public and in his private domains.

In 'The Place of Thomas Nashe in the Learning of His Time,' McLuhan employs a comparative methodology to discuss the development of the liberal arts of the *trivium*: rhetoric, grammar, and dialectic are investigated across centuries, from pre-Socratic authors up to the English Renaissance, when the *querelle* between Nashe and Harvey mirrors the clash of two different ideas of 'knowledge' and 'learning' (something which McLuhan saw as the final battle inexorably dividing the complex nature of 'logos' into two separate units, logic and word, the former winning over the latter from the Renaissance onward). As previously discussed, it is a work that would help McLuhan to investigate and to build a rich literary and philosophical background, which he will use as a reservoir for his own media analysis, providing intellectual humus, exempla, references, and complex reasoning.[17] Most importantly, however, it is a work which ends with a brief and quite surprising reference to the work of James Joyce, introduced as 'a successful devotee of the rhetoric of the second sophists.'[18] This is a surprising and bold statement which establishes an interpretation of Joyce broader than the one that, at the time, portrayed him as one of the most interesting though controversial modernist figures. McLuhan considers Joyce as a well-read and conscious writer, not simply a modernist but a humanist – in fact, as a second sophist, who has a scholarly understanding of previous literary traditions and who contributes to the renewal of his own period. He is not the *mere formal educator* who cannot 'transform the radical modes of life of which he is usually only too natural a product.' He is a man of integral awareness.

Joyce is the artist capable of grasping all implications of knowledge throughout historical time. In those very few lines written to close his doctoral dissertation, McLuhan introduces a concept which he will later retrieve when defining his own mosaic as *applied Joyce*. The Irish master is among the writers who oppose specialization and stand for a holistic approach to learning and culture. Even though Joyce is a modernist, he is also a classicist because his idea of learning is universal and inclusive. Following the teachings of Bacon, Vico, and other philosophers, Joyce is able to show the complexity of human actions and productions in history. Joyce's humanism is also shared by Pound, Ford, Eliot, and Lewis; they are *humanists* addressing their own times, investigating the underpinning processes of change. Acting as *docti grammatici*, they invite their readers to experience the involving newness through a renewed act of reading and participating in their own works.

Through his study of modernism, the English Renaissance, and the ancient liberal arts, McLuhan was in a position to confront and borrow from different literary and artistic traditions. Consciously choosing to pursue the modernist lesson was the first step towards the development of his new approach to media studies. The modernist achievements showed him that media were in fact man-made artefacts; as such, they were now part of the contemporary aesthetic, pervading language through newly conceived metaphors and modifying the way individuals inhabit and perceive their environment. It took a few years for McLuhan to fully come to terms with this epiphany, and to translate it into an investigative practice as a media theorist. First, he had to write his PhD dissertation; that is, he had to learn and consolidate his humanistic knowledge, from the classic to the contemporary age. Then, he had to experience teaching in North American universities, to face the new world and language of the younger generation living inside the evolving consumerist society that the modernist writers had only started to figure out. His meetings with both Ezra Pound and Wyndham Lewis helped him to better accomplish this passage from literature to media, as each of these writers developed a theory of communication in relation to his own theories of art. As well, McLuhan's meeting with Pound turned out to be another crucial passage in his formation, as it led to his discovery of another, more neglected proto-modernist writer, Ford Madox Ford, an author whose works had a tremendous impact on McLuhan's then developing intellectual project.

The four modernist writers whom I discuss in the following chapters, Ford Madox Ford, James Joyce, Ezra Pound, and Wyndham Lewis, stand as literary milestones in the making of McLuhan as a media theorist; they offered him operative models to conceptualize his own methodology of explorations. Needleless to say, they were not the only modernists whose work had an impact on him, but it seems to me that they developed some epistemological tenets which, in time, were adopted by McLuhan as progressive pillars crucial to the development of his own approach to media studies. Ford Madox Ford, considered by most critics as a 'proto' modernist writer for his original understanding of both tradition and innovation, is the writer who not only theorized the need of a 'new form,' but also started to conceptualize and develop new rhetorical techniques to 'render his own time in the terms of his own time.' Ford's declared goal was to encourage a 'critical attitude' in his readers in order to fight all accepted ideas promoted by the joint action of political agencies, new forms of communications, and complacent writers and critics.

James Joyce is the writer who further explored form and language to connect to his times and sensibility; he turned linearity into an acoustic mode and retrieved etymology to vivisect society. His playful and uncanny experiments gave life to a verbo-voco-visual landscape whose investigation would teach us how to participate in the process of grasping *implications of new knowledge*. To apply Joyce's model meant to work out an operative model through which to probe old and new environments.

Ezra Pound is the engaged intellectual who connects arts and society in even newer ways; he acted as the propaganda agent to disseminate the operative model among intellectuals and new audiences through a witty combination of literature/art and popular forms of communication, which is nevertheless ambiguously indebted to actuality and to new political settings. Pound was also a cultural gate opener to McLuhan, a teacher acting outside of the classroom, introducing him to other masters and to an eclectic and bold approach to knowledge and culture.

Wyndham Lewis is the writer who investigated the perturbing side effects related to new communicative processes and media through a redundant prose combining philosophical speculations, politics, artistic credos, and literary criticism. The master of satire and parodic portraits, he was the *enemy*, the *outcast* inside the modernist community. His theories of art and of communication blasted all time-philosophies *à la Bergson* and blessed the retrieval of the spatial paradigm to counterattack the 'world of the Unconscious or automatic in the sense.'[19] His works are among the first to conceptualize the idea of the global village, as well as the idea of tactility, two concepts which later became tenets of McLuhan's theories on media.

To juxtapose McLuhan's works with these four writers will confirm that his achievements came as the result of a constant and conscious *progression d'effet*, as steps taken while pursuing his commitment to become a good educator, and not a mere formal one. Each of these writers stands as a landmark for McLuhan's own progress as a man of letters and as a media scholar; they represent different intellectual epiphanies, each taking a turn to guide the Canadian critic through his *intense mental culture*.

T.S. Eliot is the great excluded from my tetrad of McLuhan's modernist masters; and yet, he stays as a constant leitmotif, his name being repeated throughout most of my chapters in this book. Certainly, I am convinced that McLuhan's most famous probe – *the medium is the message* – can be read as a response to and an adaptation of T.S. Eliot's ideas as expressed in *The Use of Poetry and the Use of Criticism*. However, after having poured over McLuhan's letters, it seems to me that, at some point and for some reasons which are not entirely manifested, McLuhan quoted less and less from T.S. Eliot and more and more from other modernist writers as if pursuing a different path as a media explorer.

As one of his letters reveals, McLuhan's encounter with T.S. Eliot took place in 1934, and it was almost like love at first sight.[20] Eliot is immediately approached as a kindred spirit, praised as an observer of reality, as well as an 'extremely careful and conscientious artist in words and metre and rhyme,' a master of rhetoric, two elements which will also pervade McLuhan's own investigative project as a man of letters. Yet, after this explicit enthusiasm for the work of T.S. Eliot, a few years later McLuhan seems to be more interested in the other men of 1914, Joyce, Pound, and Lewis. Even more puzzling, in a letter written to Ezra Pound, he ventures so far, as we shall see, to question Eliot's ambiguous suppression of all reference to Ford Madox Ford in his own works, as if it were revealing of an intentional attempt to deny the older writer's role in the development of twentieth-century letters. Again, in *The Interior Landscape*, T.S. Eliot's works are discussed only in essays dedicated to other modernist writers, as McLuhan's essay 'Mr Eliot's Historical Decorum' (1949) is not among those selected for the volume. In particular, Eliot's poetic is mentioned in connection with Bergson's philosophy ('... Bergson, Eliot, and theosophy, in which the emotions are used as the principal windows of the soul')[21] and as the antithesis to the poetics of Pound and Lewis, as if suggesting two opposing approaches to the new cultural and artistic patterns. Clearly, in this volume as well as in others, McLuhan does not take sides against Eliot – whose value and merit are never diminished – but he seems to concentrate mostly on Joyce, Pound, and Lewis. It took almost ten more years for McLuhan to return to Eliot, when his essay 'Pound, Eliot, and the Rhetoric of *The Waste Land*' was published late in 1978.[22]

In spite of differences in their respective poetics, all the above mentioned figures – including Eliot – were not only creative writers, but also intellectuals and critics whose literary explorations constituted a way to further investigate the role of the humanities in a consumerist world. Generally speaking, none of them was in favour of the new mass society, and all feared the consequences of the new environment on the very ideas of art and the artist. Inevitably, they experimented with form and questioned literary canons while pursuing their aesthetical quests, and they took sides within the political scene of their time. In particular, Ford Madox Ford, T.S. Eliot, Ezra Pound, and Wyndham Lewis were all conservatives and openly so, even though each of them in a different way (Joyce's position is assumed to have been a more progressive one).[23] Eliot combined politics, religion, and aesthetics in a single vision and stood for 'Anglo-Catholicism in religion, royalism in politics, and classicism in literature.' Ford Madox Ford defined himself as 'an old fashioned Tory,' even though in his editorials written in pre-war London and in post-war Paris, he was never too tender towards what he defined as 'the Conservatives of the day,' denouncing the loss of values in conjunction with their exploitation of the new mass society. Ezra Pound admired Benito Mussolini and broadcast for Italian Fascist Radio. In the early 1930s, Wyndham Lewis – who portrayed himself as the Old Lion of the Right – published a pro-Hitler pamphlet, and a few years later recanted with another pamphlet denouncing the 'Hitler cult.' It is therefore impossible not to take into account the political dimension when dealing with these four authors, especially Pound and Lewis. When discussing their works, we are compelled to juxtapose aesthetics and ethics; we know that if we do not, we are consciously avoiding a challenge. Yet there are no references to the political engagement of these writers in McLuhan's works, at least no direct and clear references. In 1949, when Ezra Pound received the Bellingen Prize, McLuhan supported the decision, as did the group of Southern Agrarians (such as Tate, Brookes, and Penn Warren), therefore opposing the Liberals (such as Bennett and Howe), who instead condemned the choice and considered Pound an intellectual who had betrayed his country and had associated himself with a fascist regime. McLuhan defended Pound on the basis of his literary merits only and did not publicly comment on the political *querelle*.

I am not sure if he was consciously avoiding a challenge, but it is an attitude which did not increase McLuhan's fame among modernist scholars. However, McLuhan was by then envisaging his own mission; he was in pursuit of a universal quest and was not ready to compromise it with historical materiality. He approached the modernist writers as grammarians of the electric age opposing the dialecticians still adopting a mechanical and specialist approach to knowledge and situations. He considered their works, not in the light of each writer's biography or personality, but only for how they represented experimental attempts to map change. He read those works through practical criticism – through the approach he had learned to make his own; he understood the importance of form as a cognitive component of his explorations. He then became interested in the relation between those formal experiments and the new media networking culture. He often commented on the lack of attention that, so far, critics had paid to the latter, contrary to what had happened in the literary and artistic domains. 'It is strange that the popular press as an art form has often attracted the enthusiastic attention of poets and aesthetes while rousing the gloomiest apprehension in the academic mind,' he wrote in his famous essay 'Joyce, Mallarmé and the Press.'[24] He taught us that it was precisely the new forms of communications that, from the turn of the twentieth century, were offering cognitive models to social architecture: the press, the telephone, and radio were all helping to implement rhetorical devices capable of turning the printed page into a multi-sensorial medium, and translating the complexity into the electric age. As a consequence, if we agree that 'every medium of communication is a unique art form which gives salience to one set of human possibilities at the expense of another set,'[25] McLuhan taught us to apply 'the method of art analysis to the critical evaluation of society' as the strategy to pursue for the sake of understanding.

On a Mission

Shortly after having published his first book, McLuhan set forth to actualize such a strategy. Appointed chairman of the Ford Foundation Seminar on Culture and Communication, during 1953–5 he promoted and edited the review *Explorations*, which contributed to the establishment of not just media studies but also cultural studies, as its declaration of intent clearly reveals:

> [*Explorations*] is designed, not as a permanent reference journal that embalms truth for posterity, but as a publication that explores and searches and questions. We envisage a series that will cut across the humanities and social sciences by treating them as a continuum. We believe anthropology and communication are approaches, not bodies of data, within each of the four winds of the humanities, the physical, the biological and the social sciences intermingle to form a science of man.

If we consider that only a few years later, C.P. Snow was still conceptualizing a cultural divide in his well-known book *The Two Cultures and the Scientific Revolution* (1959), it is clear that McLuhan was suggesting quite a different approach to knowledge. Juxtaposing these two intellectuals (Snow and McLuhan) is somehow a way to replicate the Harvey/ Nashe *querelle*, even though the two thinkers never engaged in a direct argument. Snow's polarization of perspectives clashes with McLuhan's trans-disciplinary one, the former being based on clear-cut and reassuring *specializations*, the second on a more provocative *generalism*. The way interdisciplinary studies have evolved in the second half of the twentieth century seems to confirm that Snow's approach constituted the final attempt to preserve a dying order, something belonging to an age (the mechanical age) now replaced by the new age of electricity with its new forms of communication, and a renewed approach to knowledge.[26] After Gutenberg came Marconi, and the world shrank into a global village where everything collided and mingled. New modes of explorations had to be envisaged, and, for sure, McLuhan was a well-equipped pioneer ready to do just that. As his friend and life-long collaborator Ted Carpenter, wrote:

> Marshall possessed what Lévi-Strauss called 'the dithyrambic gift of synthesis, the almost monstrous faculty to perceive as similar what other men have conceived as different.' He treated academic boundaries as barriers; professionalism as constipation; ignorance as an asset. His approach resembled Operations Research, a Second World War programme in which biologists and psychologists worked on problems ordinarily assigned to engineers and physicists. He loved to apply one discipline's insights to another discipline's data ... The magic of joining opposites delighted him. Every cliché became an inverted cliché. In the country of the blind, he said, the one-eyed man is a hunted criminal.[27]

McLuhan's 'dithyrambic gift of synthesis' was not an inborn gift; it was worked on through his years of education as a man of letters, his continuous readings, and his encounters with some of the most intriguing literary figures of his time, who helped him to elaborate his own original way to approach actuality as a new art form, as a new man-made environment. McLuhan's letters clearly reveal how he was convinced of the importance of developing new strategies of investigation capable of fully exploiting all potentialities embedded in literature. McLuhan was on a mission and was ready to overthrow his time 'debased scholasticism ... with the maximum amount of noise.'[28] It sounds like a declaration of war to a dying order, to a crumbling educational establishment; he was out to recruit his own troops to reconnect the study of literature to communal existence. He was conscious of both his aims and projects and of the related risks, as he candidly confessed to Wyndham Lewis:

> As for my aims and projects. Sensing, these past years, a kind of indeterminacy in my life and milieu, yet having a strong need to work towards making more and more of my studies, and the life around me, intelligible, – of raising the particulars to the level of intelligibility, I have cultivated a sort of 'negative capability,' trying to achieve a readiness to act in some unforesee-

able way when that way should define itself. That is the present position. There is some sort of work in me. I shall impinge in some sort of way, but whether academic or not I am unable to see. But what complete isolation governs the maturing of any thought in this country![29]

Nobody better than Wyndham Lewis could appreciate McLuhan's lament on the 'complete isolation' governing 'the maturing of any thought,' Lewis being the enemy *par excellence*, contrarian to all accepted ideas and always committed to challenging both the establishment and *the demon of progress* (here to be understood as a passive acceptance of all that came with the machine age). Similarly, McLuhan seems here to be questioning his own way of being an academic at a time of cultural change, something which he pursued all through his professorial life: he constantly wrote about the changing role of education, about the need to develop new pedagogical approaches to mass society. *City as Classroom: Understanding Language and Media*, co-written with his son Eric and with Kathryn Hutchon in 1977, comes out of a search he had pursued for four decades. He was aware of the necessity to open up old curricula to ongoing societal dynamics. The titles of the courses he proposed when negotiating his new position at Assumption College are quite revealing of his intention and of his would-be probing process. 'Culture and Environment,' for instance, is proposed as a course analysing the present scene through a cross-reading of 'advertisements, newspapers, best-sellers, detective fictions, movies,' a strategy which stands at the basis of *The Mechanical Bride*, the volume he was already writing at the time.[30]

A few years later, in a letter to Harold Adams Innis, McLuhan speculated about the possibility to 'organize an entire school of studies' in the field of communication. In this letter, McLuhan insists on the solid links between modernist avant-garde experiments and the study of new forms and technologies of communication:

> But it was most of all the aesthetic discoveries of the symbolists since Rimbaud and Mallarmé (developed in English by Joyce, Eliot, Pound, Lewis and Yeats) which have served to recreate in contemporary consciousness an awareness of the *potencies* of language such as the Western world has not experienced in 1800 years.
>
> Mallarmé saw the modern press as a magical institution born of technology ... Its very technological form was bound to be *efficacious* far beyond any informative purpose. Politics were becoming musical, jazzy, magical.[31]

This was his way of pointing to 'the political.' It was different than taking sides within the political spectrum, than choosing among ideologies. He connected both figure and ground when exploring technology; it was his way of unveiling processes and environmental dynamics, of which political discourse was one of the figures. Not to be aware of that made all discussion on ideology useless or, worse, biased and a function of the hidden pattern of forces then at work. In the above quote, the real meaning or function of all technological form ('to be *efficacious* far beyond any informative purpose') already implies a complex set of concepts defined later on through the famous motto *the medium is the message*. What is in this letter will be retrieved in almost all his later essays, works, interviews, and lectures.

Ford, Joyce, Pound, and Lewis offer some interesting viewpoints from which to observe the development of McLuhan's poetics. They act as symbolic torchbearers leading to the making of McLuhan's unique form of writing, not only as a literary scholar but also as a media scholar. As in the case of the modernist formal experiments and achievements, the formal architecture of McLuhan's investigation is to be understood as a major element of the cognitive process, one that reveals the complexity behind the literary origins of his media studies.

9 Ford Madox Ford: 'Not Mere Chat'

Literature Matters

Dear Pound,

My epistolary socks have sagged lately. You know, going through [Ford Madox] Ford, and trying to read all that he says I must, has given me quite a feeling of inadequacy and irrelevance. That will pass by the time I have finished the next 200 volumes. But the sense of only now reading things I should have known all along has sapped me. And to write to yourself, who have for forty-five years taken for granted all this learning, perception and art, well it seemed sheer impertinence. (Marshall McLuhan, letter to Ezra Pound, Sunday, 7 Nov. 1948)

Ford Madox Ford was as a guardian divinity of 'Belles Lettres,' one of those writers who contribute to the spiritual well-being of all those who are in love with creative writing, modernist scholars or aficionados of literature alike. This declaration stems not so much from the refined pleasure I have always derived from reading his proto-modernist works; instead, it is based on Ford's incessant and strenuous defence of the social and political values of both literature and the arts. By defending the role of all arts – and of literature *in primis* – inside a growing consumerist society, Ford seems to give hope to all the existing Don Quixotes who are devoted to 'Belles Lettres' for either professional or passionate reasons.

When cultural trends lead us to question the real meaning and impact of what we do today as literary critics or as 'artsy aficionados' acting in a world in which progress, as well as success and welfare, are clearly associated with other departments of life, Ford's visionary statements contribute plenty of good reasons to go on. Statements such as 'Only from the arts can any safety for the future of the state be found'[1] and 'The public of today has to go to the imaginative writer for its knowledge of life, for its civilisation'[2] comfort us. Ford reassures (and even worries) us by repeating as a constant leitmotiv all through his writing that literature stands as 'the only civilising agency that is at work today as in other dark ages' because you cannot have 'a business community of any honesty unless you have a literature to set and maintain a high standard.'[3] No matter if these hyperbolic and absolute assertions, these *emotive utterances*, are perceived by the majority of people as mere illusions. And it matters even less if *some mathematicians* find these utterances *to be false*, to us – who accept the fact that 'in the poetic approach ... logic comes in, if at all, in subordination, as servant to our emotional response'[4] – they resonate as true.

Literature matters, and literature is a very serious business.

Still.

Certainly, literature mattered to Marshall McLuhan, professor of English, who always linked his media analysis and his own probing of the evolving mass society to his literary studies. Yes: media studies, as per McLuhan, have solid literary roots.

To date, critics have neglected the role played by Ford Madox Ford in shaping the way in which Marshall McLuhan employed the arts and literature as analogical mirrors casting light on ongoing cultural, technological, and social processes. This neglect is nothing new: for many decades, Ford was a little-known writer, especially in comparison to the popularity achieved by other modernist writers. For some time, Ford was considered as *a writers' writer* whose literary tenets, unknown to the public, influenced the development of later poetics. His works and the role he played at the turn of the previous century as a proto-modernist writer helped trigger the debate on literature and the necessity to open the form to new societal realities. But his contributions went unnoticed until the last decades of the twentieth century, when the studies of Malcolm Bradbury, Frank MacShane, Sondra J. Stang, and especially Max Saunders brought him back to the foreground.[5]

Today, we know and appreciate Ford's impressionist tenets, conceived to render his time in the spirit of his time, turning the writer into a new type of social historian different from Zola's naturalist writer and poles apart from Wilde's poetical principles.[6] Ford's project was to renew English letters and realign them with the good literature of the time, which, in his own view, was coming from France as a counterbalance to Zola, namely, the *imaginative* literature of Flaubert, Maupassant, and the symbolist poets. To pursue his dream of an international Republic of Letters, Ford edited two literary reviews (*The English Review*, in London from December 1908 to February 1910, and *the transatlantic review*, in Paris throughout 1924). As Douglas Goldring recalled, they 'were to perform a glorious and much needed service to English letters, by setting up and maintaining a standard of literary values, of real writing … They were, above all, to start a Movement and to found in the French sense, a school.'[7] And, in order to start such a Movement, Ford fought late-Victorian Intelligentsia – 'The quite natural tendency of Intelligentsia is to make of literature as unconsumable a thing as may be, so that … they may cement their authority over an unlettered world.'[8] He scouted for talented among new young writers, would-be internationally renowned masters of literature, including D.H. Lawrence, Ezra Pound, W.H. Hudson, Wyndham Lewis, Jean Rhys, and Ernest Hemingway. In the promo that he wrote and circulated at the end of 1923 to launch his forthcoming *transatlantic review*, Ford wrote of the dual goal he pursued as an editor:

> The major one, the purely literary, conducing to the minor, the disinterestedly social. The first is that of widening the field in which the younger writers of the day can find publication, the second that of introducing into international politics a note more genial than that which almost universally prevails. The first conduces to the second in that the best ambassadors, the only non secret diplomatists between nations are the books and the arts of nations.[9]

In spite of Ford's commitment and his persistent generosity towards younger writers, most of his young protégés revolted against Ford over time, often denouncing his excessive paternalism, as well as his ambiguous take towards tradition.[10] Ford never embraced the most extreme avant-garde credos against the past and – in contrast with most radical modernist *isms* – he based his poetics on a constant dialogue among literary and artistic traditions. This is an attitude which can be easily compared to both Eliot's and Pound's later idea of a *best tradition* to be preserved as inscribed in 'the sacred wood' (Ford's International Republic) of Letters. There was one 'protégé,' Ezra Pound, who always acknowledged his debt towards Ford Madox Ford's teaching and always defended Ford's role as a writer and a thinker.[11] It is through Ezra Pound that the young Marshall McLuhan encountered Ford Madox Ford's works and ideas.

An Imaginative Writer

In 1948, McLuhan wrote in a letter to Pound, 'Can you or Mrs. Pound tell me why T.S. Eliot carefully suppresses all references to Ford or his writing? There must be some explanation. My interest in the matter is not at the gossip level. It seems to me to be necessary for an understanding of 20th century letters.'[12] In the letter, McLuhan emphasizes Ford's learning and quotes Goldring's book *South Lodge: Reminiscences of Violet Hunt, Ford Madox Ford and the English Review Circle.* Even though Goldring's book is quoted as a homage to Pound himself (as its author praises the influence of Pound on 'the birth of the later Yeats'),[13] it is important to realize that McLuhan had already read it at the time. This is one of the few testimonies of Ford's role as an editor and a writer written almost in real time (in 1942, three years after Ford had passed away), a role which provided McLuhan with the opportunity to learn about his vision of the writer as a new type of *scientific observer.* As a scientific (not a naturalist) observer, the new writer must investigate his own time and render it with no party bias (in this way, Ford's ideal writer is also a social historian). Literature is the key to such a rendering, especially the type of literature that Ford named *imaginative* as opposed to the merely *factual,* as well as to the merely *fictive.*[14] What Ford envisaged (already in his 1909–10 editorials) is a new idea of 'realism,' as in Flaubert and Maupassant, mirroring a new type of writer:

> It will be observed that this elevates the novelist of this school to the rank of a scientific observer. His business is to lay before the readers the results not of his moral theories, not of his socially constructed ideas, not even of his generous impulses, nor even of his imagination, but simply the results of his observation of life.[15]

Similarly:

> The more modern novelists – or, at any rate, those of the school to which Mr Ford Madox Ford belongs – write with two purposes: they try to produce work according to the canons that they have derived from light vouchsafed them. Within those limits they try to render – not to write about their times without *parti pris.*[16]

Both these statements could be used as grounds for McLuhan's later pun on his role as a scholar in communication: 'I'm not an explainer, I'm an explorer': the task of any scientific observer is in fact that of showing the community in action, not judging it.

As we shall see, direct references to Ford's work are not easily found in McLuhan's writings. Yet starting from Ezra Pound's fundamental mediation, it is possible to assert that the Canadian scholar was well aware of Ford's literary impressionism; and it is possible to speculate about Ford's impact on McLuhan's approach to literature and the role it could play as a probe to explore societal matrixes. In his memoirs, essays, and critical writings, Ford teaches us that literature is, in fact, quite a serious business and not just another form to entertain, amuse, or even manipulate people. Literature is the perfect figure to understand the complexity of the ground from which it emanates. Even though he was criticized for historical inaccuracies,[17] Ford's idea of the novelist as a scientific observer whose task is not to judge society, but instead to signal the ongoing cultural, political, and societal processes, anticipates McLuhan's call to face societal change. Also, by developing a series of rhetorical strategies based on a carefully conceived *progression d'effet*, Ford writes, not to pontificate to his readers, but to encourage their participation in the process of understanding. His goal is to awaken a blurring critical attitude (which McLuhan will later define as the Narcissus narcosis, the collective hypnosis that his probes intended to challenge).

In Ford's view, imaginative readers must make themselves grasp the juxtaposition of situations that the author develops in his novels. The reader has to become an active producer of knowledge through a renewed act of reading, and by grasping hidden implications; thereby is her or his awakening encouraged. Ford used to repeat, 'Nothing was more true than the words of Flaubert, when he said that, if France had read his *Education Sentimentale*, it would have been spared the horrors of the Franco-Prussian War.'[18] The clue here is to understand *how* to read, something which, in turn, mirrors a new way of writing, a new form. Certainly, Ford elaborated his form, not to accommodate his readers to his own views, but to induce their active response and, by so doing, to start a process leading to epiphanies.

Hence, to appreciate the impact of Ford on McLuhan's writing is not simply a pedantic academic exercise. On the contrary, it becomes a useful link for further understanding and clarifying the literary origins of McLuhan's media and communication studies, both in terms of the operative project (to explore and investigate his own times) and the form through which it is enacted (that is, the 'mosaic,' built to provoke and not to comfort his readers). It is a way to retrieve the role played by the humanities not only in relation to the process of understanding the ways in which our high-tech society developed; it is also a way to assert the importance of tracing a constant *fil rouge* connecting literature to the world, text to context, figure to ground.

Things, Not Words

Paraphrasing McLuhan on Eliot, we might ask: why does Marshall McLuhan suppress any reference to Ford or his writing? Is it an intentional or an unconscious omission? In fact, Ford's name is missing from the long list of writers, artists, and thinkers whose quotes are continually found in McLuhan's most popular works. However, I have found two exceptions: a brief reference in an essay entitled 'Coleridge as Artist,' in which Ford's novels are associated – *en passant* – with those of Henry James and Joseph Conrad for their 'confessional and digressive' element; and the recalling of Ford's reading of Sinclair Lewis's *Babbit* as 'the American *Madame Bovary*.'[19]

It is only in McLuhan's letters to Pound and to his friend Felix Giovanelli, that is, in his private conversations, that we find open references to Ford. And yet, for Ford's alert readers, this lack of direct references in McLuhan's major books is somehow compensated for by the constant presence of several 'indirect' references: McLuhan's pages resound with expressions which echo in the scholar's ear and form a sort of Fordian *progression d'effet*. For instance, when in *Understanding Media* we read the comment 'Flaubert, the French novelist of the nineteenth century, felt that the Franco Prussian War could have been avoided if people had heeded his *Sentimental Education*,' we cannot but juxtapose both this quote and its allusive use to Ford's original note.[20] It is not a matter of plagiarism, since that very quote has certainly been repeated by many other critics and writers. Yet, the persistent impression is that McLuhan has appropriated Ford's lesson, his ideas on art and literature, his language and technique, in such a strong and lasting way that it has become almost an unconscious platform pervading his own language, and technique, as well as his *modus operandi* as a media explorer.

After what McLuhan himself confessed in his preface to his *The Interior Landscape*, I do not think that it is too much to state that the process of elaboration of Ford's theories into his own writings derives from McLuhan's direct investigation of Ford's works, and from his study of other modernist writers who knew Ford and who adopted and further developed his original impressionist tenets, namely, first and foremost

Pound. It is a process which is never acknowledged overtly, but which tends to emerge sometimes in unexpected ways, and which is translated as 'little' epiphanies. For instance, Father Lawrence Dewan, who was one of McLuhan's assistants in the 1950s, recalls the importance that McLuhan gave to the search for *le mot juste* – the right word. He uses an expression that McLuhan himself used and which reflects one of Ford's most famous impressionist tenets (in turned based on his study of Flaubert's new style as carried on during his collaboration with Joseph Conrad). The expression was used by Ford to emphasize the important role played by form in the creation of content. It is another (*ante litteram*) way to say that 'the medium is the message': to select and to juxtapose words is a conscious act that the writer performs to cast a form capable of driving the reader towards impromptu epiphanies, irrespective of the plot or content.[21] Ford's most famous novel, *The Good Soldier*, embodies the major technical devices which Ford elaborated to make us see, hear, and feel: the *juxtaposition of situations*; *progression d'effet*; *time shift*, and, of course, the perennial *search for the right word, le mot juste*.

Omissions and indirect testimonies cannot be considered as factual evidence for the purpose of this book. For this reason, it is safer to investigate the few direct references to Ford Madox Ford which we can find in McLuhan's letters. To conclude this chapter, I will also suggest a reading of Ford's historical romance – *The Fifth Queen* – in the light of McLuhan's investigation of old and new media. The intention is to show that McLuhan's appraisal of Ford was based as well on the clear understanding that, in his novels, the English writer had grasped the implications of various environmental changes triggered by new technologies, be it in the late Renaissance (as in *The Fifth Queen*), or in Edwardian society (as in *The Good Soldier*). McLuhan sees these two historical moments as conducive to the passage from the oral to the mechanical age and from the mechanical age to the electric age, respectively.

It is important to stress that McLuhan read Ford through Ezra Pound's critical mediations. In June 1946, together with Hugh Kenner, McLuhan visited Ezra Pound at St Elisabeth's Hospital for the Criminally Insane. In the course of an encounter which 'fired McLuhan intellectually,'[22] Pound introduced his two young visitors to Ford's work. Later, in August, McLuhan writes to Pound informing him of his reading 'for the first time' of Ford's *Some Do Not, A Man Could Stand Up, Last Post*, and *The Good Soldier*, recently released by Penguin Books. In his letter, McLuhan comments that 'these books repay the reading certainly, and I'll get them read by others.'[23] A few weeks later, McLuhan writes about Ford to his friend Felix Giovanelli in a letter which is crucial to our understanding of McLuhan's immediate and deep grasp of Ford's poetic and rhetorical strategies:

> Let me say that you will get much pleasure and enlightenment from Ford Madox Ford's *Return to Yesterday*. Light on Pound, Lewis, et al. … Ford deals with *res non verba*. His anecdotes always point to social, political, economic aesthetic axes and dynamics within a situation. His *March of Literature* (1939) is the best book on comparative lit. I've ever come across.[24]

And again, a few days later in another letter to Giovanelli, he continues:

> Ford and Pound talked and talked about everything from 1908–1922 when Pound went to Italy. They agreed on everything except Cicero and Mommsen … Ford's memoirs are not mere chat. The chat is a series of epiphanies of carefully considered social and literary structures and their inter penetration.[25]

These brief passages show that McLuhan had clearly understood three major aspects of Ford's poetics, three aspects which later will pervade his own as well. The first, Ford Madox Ford deals with *res* (things – that is, facts and actuality – with clear reference to a concrete use of language, which implies a careful process of selection of *le mot juste*) and not with *verba* (here to be understood as abstractions or redundant and soft words); that is, Ford uses language in a new way, conveying to language a natural and concrete quality, as other modernist poetics will later do (i.e., Pound's imagism).[26] The second, Ford considers literature and storytelling not as a mere *divertissement*, nor as a preaching strategy, but as an active component of his observation of his own time ('His anecdotes always point to social, political, economic aesthetic axes and dynamics *within* a situation'). The third, Ford adopts a comparative and broad approach (he talks 'about everything,' he is not a specialist but a *generalist*) to develop his observations, thus turning literature into a tool to approach various aspects of an ever growing complex society.

Thus, as a young man passionate about literature and as a professor of English, McLuhan anticipated what most modernist critics fully acknowledged only some decades later. As a matter of fact, in his letters to Giovanelli, he implicitly traces some crucial tenets of Ford's literary impressionism which later critics will define as the will to *render* and not to *narrate*. The intention is to embrace at once social, political, economic, and aesthetic phenomena through a renewed approach to literature; to develop a renewed form of storytelling based on anecdotes that appear simple and naïve at first glance, but that are, instead, carefully conceived; and not to moralize but to show one's own times in the terms of one's own existence. In addition, McLuhan points out the important role which Ford played as a proto-modernist writer (as mentioned before, Ford was a renowned 'talent scout,' helping several would-be famous writers to get published). The reference to the intense and continuous dialogue which took place between Ford and Pound during 1908–22 is not only a fact, but also stands in McLuhan's letter as an appropriate metaphor to epitomize the handover of artistic principles between two authors who, even though belonging to different cultural backgrounds and eras, nevertheless shared a similar approach to literature at a time of social and cultural change. Consistently, through his conversations and correspondence with Ezra Pound, McLuhan further developed his ideas on the role of a man of letters inside a growing consumerist and technological society – that is, his declared goal to detect and explore change.

If we compare the poetics of these three men of letters – Ford, Pound, and McLuhan – it is easy to realize that they all have a similar understanding of the role of the artist in society. Ford Madox Ford considers the imaginative writer as a new type of scientific observer – a modernist social historian – who, in the true spirit of the time, wants to help his readers acquire and preserve an independent train of thought and to not succumb to accepted ideas. Ezra Pound, a former young protégé of Ford, presents the artist as the antenna of the race monitoring and alerting readers to the ongoing change;[27] and McLuhan, who read Ford through Pound and who well understood Pound's prose, presents the artist as the individual of integral awareness, in 'any field, scientific and humanistic,' who perceives the implications of 'new knowledge in his time.' In each of these cases, the artist is seen as the dynamic counterenvironment to the spreading of the Narcissus narcosis.

Comparing Strategies

Ford, Pound, and McLuhan consider literature as a heuristic experience preserving free thinking at a time of rapid cultural change. According to McLuhan, this was even more pertinent when he started his own media investigations in the early 1940s, when new technologies of communications were reconfiguring the interplay between individuals and their own environment at an accelerated pace. Times of action and times of reaction speeded up, and the space for reflection, for processing, for rational thinking was inevitably being reduced. McLuhan responded by applying the 'method of art analysis to the critical evaluation of society,' a strategy, as we shall see when discussing Lewis's influence on McLuhan, aimed at arresting the information overload in order to create a counter-force to change. It is a way to promote aesthetic and societal awareness also among non-artists:

> It's always been the artist who perceives the alterations in man caused by a new medium, who recognises that the future is the present, and uses his work to prepare the ground for it ... But the ability to perceive media-induced extensions of man, once the province of the artist, is now being expanded as the new environment of electric information makes possible a new degree of perception and critical awareness by non artists.[28]

As a non-artist, McLuhan approaches the new reality by borrowing the artist's strategies, and considering the new man-made environment as a unique 'artefact' for which all previous strategies of analysis are obsolete. Through his books, and through his new form of writing, McLuhan pursued his explorations while testing out new epistemological tenets.

A similar strategy of exploration had already been advanced by Ford Madox Ford, not only through the development of his 'impressionist' new form, but also through editorship of his literary reviews, *The English Review* and *the transatlantic review*. In his editorials, Ford denounces the increasing dominance of what he calls *accepted ideas*. He sees these as a side effect of the new era of mass communications that is characterizing the passage from the nineteenth to the twentieth century, when new technological developments changed the way news was distributed, and started the process which we now define as 'information overload':

> For it was the struggle with the Boers that made the fortune of the more frivolous Press ... It should be remembered that the South African War was the first vital struggle that this nation [England] has been engaged in since the telegraphic Press was really organised. Before that time, though this tendency was gradually dying, the public was accustomed to accept with equanimity news that was a day or two old – to accept it with equanimity and to ponder over it for some small length of time. But nowadays, even in more remote country districts, the Englishman is overwhelmed every morning

with a white spray of facts - facts more or less new, more or less important, more or less voracious.

The overload of information induced by the telegraphic press, and later by the wireless radio, is presented by Ford as a constant, continuous, and even voracious flow of data which blurs categories and classifications, and contributes to a superficial approach to both facts and the analysis of facts. For instance, in his editorials for *The English Review*, later collected in a volume bearing the revealing title of *The Critical Attitude*, Ford encourages his readers to rebel against what he calls 'the half-penny Press,' to resist all brainwashing, and to regain a true critical attitude or free will. He laments that 'the days of most rapid travelling are the days of most frequent misunderstandings between the races of mankind,' mostly because 'accepted ideas' – spread through new processes of communication – are replacing individual and original thinking:

> The fact is that what humanity desires passionately and almost before other things is a creed. It craves for accepted ideas; it longs more for a mind at rest ... The tendency of the great public is more and more to leave all public matters in the hands of a comparatively few specialists.[29]

In his first volume – *The Mechanical Bride* – McLuhan follows a similar analysis and writes to counter the accepted ideas and the numbing processes induced by the *Reader's Digest* mentality, or by the *Book of the Hour*.

As previously discussed, in his later volumes McLuhan will never repeat such a clear-cut criticism of cultural phenomena. He will no longer *explain* what he sees; rather, he will only *render* his explorations with no party bias. As he pointed out: 'I try to avoid value judgements ... I neither approve nor disapprove. I merely try to understand ... I'm an observer in these matters, not a participant ... My personal point of view is irrelevant.'[30] It is an attitude which Ford himself had already encouraged when acting not as an opinion-maker but as an impressionist writer:

> ... the only thing of value is the concrete fact; the concrete fact is only of value as an 'illustration' of a state of mind, a characteristic in an individual. The fact should be stated first. The 'moral' may or may not be drawn in so many words. Theoretically it ought not to be, because the first duty of an artist is not to comment and precisely, not to moralise.[31]

In this way, there begins to appear a network of correspondences between two intellectuals who belonged to different cultural settings and
to different professions: Ford Madox Ford, an imaginative writer seeking
suggestions and *not dictates*,[32] who observed the passage from an old to a
new world order and who tried to render it through his fictional works,
as well as his literary criticism, with the goal of preserving and encouraging a critical attitude in his readers; and Marshall McLuhan, a professor
of English and a literary scholar sharing the same goal, becoming an
explorer of new media-induced environments and dynamics, acting on
the basis of his humanistic training, and creating a new way to approach
actuality. As a writer, Ford Madox Ford denounced the malaise of his time
in an allegorical way, through his fictional and anecdotic storytelling,
enlightening what lies behind the opalescent surface of things; whereas
McLuhan used fiction, anecdotes, and the storytelling of Ford and other
writers as his own life-long subtext, as analogical mirrors to speculate on
the world in progress and to develop a new strategy that rendered not
only what he saw, but also the very process of observation in which he
engaged. Even though Ford and McLuhan experimented with different
genres and areas of study, they both were engaged intellectuals trying to
read 'the language of the outer world and relate it to the inner world,'[33]
and they were both innovators in their own field, as they developed a *new
form* to render and mould their operative project. Their own new forms
became not just a way to embellish their observations, but an important
part of their cognitive process.

Rendering Change

The poetics of both Ford and McLuhan originate from their desire to be
witnesses of complex cultural ages, which were also ages of passage from
one societal matrix to a new one, characterized by an expansion in technologies of communication. During the transition from the nineteenth
to the twentieth century, Ford witnessed the phenomenon of a new journalism parallel to the establishment of a new transnational mass society.
A few decades later, McLuhan witnessed another crucial moment leading to the consolidation of that same mass society, since the post–Second
Word War years were those in which mass media triumphed and become
the powerful leading factor in all sociological, anthropological, and cultural changes. Looking at the same phenomenon from two different
but contingent moments in history (Ford died in 1939, just as McLuhan
started his career as a university professor), Ford and McLuhan become

witnesses to the shrinking of the world on a vast scale, as well as to a standardized approach to actuality (increasingly mediated through new media and a new media infrastructure).

The global village which McLuhan theorizes was already intuited by Ford Madox Ford, who presented his version of it in the volume *A History of Our Own Time* as follows:

> Be that as it may, it is, premising that we peoples whose shores nearly enclose an inland sea are already all one people – it is with that as its *chose donnée* that this book will set out ... We are, that is to say, at one in every thing save the barrier that we still maintain at our frontiers; and those barriers are purely artificial and, by all logic, absurd. An exposé of how we all now resemble one another – of the present day standardisation of the Western World – I do not need here to make. Anyone can make it for himself ... It is sufficient here to point out that, with the enormous increase of means of communication, not merely by locomotion but with ear and eye, and with the establishment in all our relationships of nearly standardised and practically secularised system of universal primary instruction, the minds of us all are being very truth standardised; and with a very little more attention to education in modern languages there is no reason why a native of Levallois-Perret should not feel as at home in Hoboken as in the other suburb of his birth ... So that we are all, whether as a nation or individuals, much of a muchness whether in blood or civilisation. And we are all made up of about the same matter and our civilisations are all of much the same blend ... But the material point to observe is that these purely artificial and pseudo-scientific, pseudo-historic dividings up of humanity are nowadays as absurd as were the custom-barriers that small Germany potentates used to set up at every few miles of main road through Low Germany. And they grow more absurd everyday.[34]

It is unlikely that McLuhan ever read Ford's statement because even though his manuscript originates approximately in 1930, it was not published until 1988 (and was in the Cornell University Library since 1973). Yet, his reference to a cultural assimilation which overcomes geographical borders still preserved by the various nation-states, his discussion on the fundamental role played by 'increase of means of communication' understood as achieved 'not merely by locomotion but *with ear and eye,* and the inevitability of the process of standardization of the Western world: these are all concepts which also form the basis of McLuhan's idea of the global village. 'After three thousand years of explosion by means of fragmentary and mechanical technologies, the Western world is imploding ... As electrically contracted, the globe is no more than a village.'[35] And again: 'The new electronic interdependence recreates the world in the image of a global village.'[36] Other considerations reflecting those stated by Ford concerning the adoption of a 'nearly standardised and practically secularised system of universal primary instruction' also emerge out of McLuhan's production. In particular, as I will expand on later, in his essay 'An Ancient Quarrel in Modern America,'[37] McLuhan traces the various phases which have led to the passage, in the modern age, from a cultural and educational tradition based on the ancient idea of encyclopedic learning to a hyperspecialized one, based on the separation between heart and mind. The ensuing dissociation of sensibility was still perceived in the contemporary age to be to the detriment of wit and a critical attitude. A similar comment is to be found in Ford's *The March of Literature* – a volume McLuhan read and praised – when he discusses the decadence of institutions such as Balliol College at Oxford, now dedicated to preserving a distorted idea of education based on notions of training and no longer on learning.[38]

Finally, it is important to further stress that the poetics of Ford and McLuhan may be compared not only in terms of their underpinning operative project (to awaken their readers/audience and provoke critical thinking), but also in terms of their interest in developing a new form to embed and actualize that very project. It is a form clearly synthesized by McLuhan when he affirms that 'Ford deals with *res non verba.*'

At the start of the twentieth century, Ford was among the first to write about the impotence of Victorian rhetorical canons to fully convey the complexity of his changing times. Together with Joseph Conrad, he worked out new tenets renewing the approach to language and cross-breading other artistic domains, especially music and painting. In their novels, the two writers developed and experimented with new techniques whose names immediately convey their interest for discontinuous and non-linear structures: *time shift, juxtaposition of situations.* In particular, Ford's search for the right word opened up the printed line through the retrieval of the heuristic power of words. In his works, words become polysemic containers of complex experiences. When reading Ford's fiction, a reader is engaged in a progression of effect which leads to the final epiphany only if all juxtapositions and all verbal suggestions are carefully assembled in the reader's mind. His storytelling unfolds as if he were talking to us. He moves back and forth, and is often uncertain and full of doubts, unreliable even, as his prose is continually interrupted, as if he were following an associative train of thoughts, as in oral communication.

McLuhan later developed a similar strategy. As he pointed out, Ford's sentences are not mere chat and his anecdotes are small epiphanies of 'carefully considered social and literary structures and their inter-penetration.' As we saw earlier, for McLuhan words are also more than a series of letters; they are 'complex system of metaphors and symbols' through which 'the entire world can be evoked and retrieved at any instant.' For him, too, the world cannot be narrated but must be rendered to his readers in a direct way. McLuhan's mosaic, just like Ford's *new form* – his impressionist novels – is a complex and broken form of writing based on the juxtaposition of verbal probes acting just like Ford's *impressions*, juxtaposed in order to involve the reader in a progression of effects leading to epiphanies, to knowledge and understanding. Both Ford's and McLuhan's forms of writing develop, not through distance or linear rendering, but in *medias res* and through a direct mimesis, because the world cannot be narrated: the world – and our own experience of it – *IS*.

Ford's *The Fifth Queen*: Probing the Making of the Gutenberg Galaxy

It still surprises me that the works of Marshall McLuhan have never before been linked to those of Ford Madox Ford, at least not in a systematic way as they should have. I did try, in fact, to suggest that connection about ten years ago at a Ford Madox Ford conference in Münster, Westfalen, Germany. On that occasion, I approached Ford's historical romance *The Fifth Queen* (1906–8) in the light of McLuhan's media theories; I still remember the perplexed glance among my colleagues in literary studies. It was both an odd and a funny experience. A decade later, after the blooming of new interdisciplinary studies, I think it is worth retrieving that approach to show how the interplay of media and literature can in fact enlighten the cultural grey or hybrid zones, that is, the interfacing passage from one form of society to the next. I will therefore now elaborate on that essay, which was nevertheless published by the benevolent organizers of the symposium in a volume dedicated to Ford Madox Ford's 'individual talent.'[39]

Ford's trilogy can in fact be read as a literary work that supports one of McLuhan's fundamental assertions, namely, that each new medium, each new technology, participates in a series of chain reactions which, unavoidably, have a deep impact on the environment, as well as on the interplay between that environment and the individuals who inhabit it. Ford's *The Fifth Queen*, which tells the story of Katharine Howard, King Henry VIII's fifth wife, can be approached as a peculiar analogical mirror which facilitates an in-depth investigation of that historical period. No doubt, the first half of the sixteenth century was a critical moment in the history of England, as well as of the Western world. As a matter of fact, that historical period is commonly taken as a decisive passage from the late Middle Ages to the newly forming Renaissance society, that is, to modernity.

McLuhan considers this passage as the crucial one for the final establishment of what he calls the literate society, the book age, or the Gutenberg Galaxy. It is important to recall here that according to McLuhan, the interplay of a new technology with other societal agents ends in a modified environment and triggers a series of side effects which are not immediately perceived by the individuals. Only over time does it become possible to focus the complex set of cultural dynamics following the impact of a new medium. As we saw earlier, McLuhan called this a backward process of understanding. Hence, as in a rear-view mirror, *The Fifth Queen* helps the reader to focus the implications related to the passage from the Middle Ages (the old environment) to Renaissance society (the new environment).

McLuhan considers a new technology as an agent participating in a complex series of anthropological changes whose *subliminal fluxes and re-fluxes* (to borrow from Ford himself) are registered by the arts through time. *The Fifth Queen* seems to have been written precisely to enlighten our grasp of the making of the Gutenberg Age; it is tempting to imagine that McLuhan might, in fact, have employed it to better focus his own understanding, even though there is no published evidence of such a use. The printing press, invented by Gutenberg in the fifteenth century, was the new emerging technology whose effects were becoming more visible at the time of Henry VIII, in England, a century later. McLuhan writes in *The Gutenberg Galaxy*, and in *Understanding Media*, that the invention of the printing press speeds up the consolidation of the so-called literate society, thereby giving men 'an eye for an ear.' In the Western world, this process had started following the invention of the phonetic alphabet, itself a technology which had contributed to turn the ancient tribal society first into a chirographic society, a sort of hybrid society in which orality and literacy coexisted, and then into a typographic society. From a psycho-social perceptive view, the invention of the phonetic alphabet started to unbalance a previously harmonic and multi-sensorial perception of the environment, and slowly favoured the eye over all other senses. In the fifteenth century, the invention of the printing press contributed to the consolidation of this process. The new medium of the printing press clearly marked a new age, McLuhan's so-called mechanical age. It contributed to the transformation of the integral man of the oral society into Gutenberg's fragmented, literary man. As McLuhan writes: 'It would appear that to see one mother's tongue dignified with the precise technology of print released a new vision of unity and power ... The sentiment of spatial and territorial nationalism that accompanies literacy is also reinforced by the printing press, which provides not only the sentiment, but also the centralised bureaucratic instruments of uniform control over wide territories.'[40]

As a result, the concepts of nationalism, state, individualism, order, and hierarchy became even stronger, and the ancient harmony emanating from communal values gave way, in time, to Machiavelli and his bold theories: '... Machiavelli stands at the gate of the Modern age, divorcing technique from social purpose.'[41] The new technology, the printing press, seems to bring a new idea of space itself: space can now be divided, ordered, and dominated by a new logic built upon the opposition of centre and margins. Also, the idea of privacy is born, and men start to divide outer from inner space. As we saw earlier, in the visual arts, this change was underlined by the development of the technique of perspective, that is, a new way of observing and rendering the landscape: everything is positioned according to a pre-set vanishing point which facilitates giving each object its proper order. The concepts of uniformity, order, and repeatability which accompany the printing press characterize the modern or mechanical age, which is also well known for being the age of specialists. It is important to point out that the specialist mentality, which marks this period, complements the fragmentation of the ancient encyclopedic learning. This process continued in subsequent centuries, leading to what Ford termed the 'standardised and practically secularised system of universal primary instruction,' a definition which, as said, would have pleased Marshall McLuhan.

What McLuhan and media studies teach us, Ford renders in his trilogy. He succeeds in grasping the essence of that historical moment, which McLuhan theorized about five decades later. More precisely, Ford uses his literary craft to enlighten the passage from an Old to a New order. This is so evident that, in order to render its true spirit, he does not hesitate to twist history, and change historical facts and evidence, as has been suggested.[42] Therefore, we refer to Ford's trilogy as a historical *romance*, aware that Ford's idea of realism, shaped by his literary impressionism, is much more elusive than traditionally understood. It is not an accident that *The Fifth Queen* is dedicated to Joseph Conrad, the author with whom Ford strenuously discussed new techniques to apply to a new form for the novel.

In the trilogy, Ford uses characterization as a narrative device to convey all the hidden tensions which underlie the passage from the Old to the New order. Each of the three main characters represents one of the major attitudes towards change at the time. Katharine Howard, the Catholic, is the tenacious and truthful defender of the Old Faith; Cromwell, Lord Privy Seal, is the ferocious champion of the New Order, promoting new alliances with the German and Lutheran princes; whereas King Henry is presented as a man still contemplating a choice. The king embraces all the doubts and uncertainties linked to that historical moment. Ford presents Henry VIII as constantly oscillating from one pole to the other, as he is attracted, in turn, by Cromwell's self-assurance and Katharine's innocence. As the King's daughter, Lady Mary, a Catholic, tells Katharine, the King is made out of doubts. Katharine herself, who for a while tried to resist this reality and thought she could lead the King, and England, back to the Old Faith, ends by defining him as 'a weathercock that I should never blow ... to a firm quarter.'[43]

As Ford suggests, the fight between Katharine and Cromwell is much more complex than would appear at first glance. This struggle is slowly revealed not only through the repeated conversations between them, but also through a series of entangled sub-plots which wittily provide a carefully conceived *progression d'effet*, culminating in the final epiphany. The religious quarrel opposing Katharine and Cromwell is, in fact, concealing the fight between two different philosophical and theological traditions. This fight dates back a few centuries, but during the Renaissance period, it became a crucial one, as it is subtly linked to the making of modern society itself. I am referring here to the well-known quarrel opposing the grammarians, the defenders of the Old Learning and the dialecticians, the champions of the New Order. The grammarians were the defenders of the ancient *paideia*, the encyclopedic and humanistic tradition which, in the Middle Ages, was preserved through the practice of the *translatio studii*, consolidated by Augustine and the Fathers of the Church, and commonly referred to as Patristic. The dialecticians, on the other hand, stood for the new principles of the Scholastic as expressed in the Middle Ages by the famous School of Paris. In Renaissance England, this quarrel had among its famous protagonists Thomas Nashe, a grammarian, and Gabriel Harvey, a dialectician. It is their quarrel which McLuhan discusses in his PhD dissertation, as well as in several parts of *The Gutenberg Galaxy*.

Katharine, who is 'well read in the learned tongue,' can quote from the works of the classical authors, knows the philosophical works of the Fathers of the Church, and tells Cromwell that she supports 'the Old Faith in the Old Way.'[44] She shares the Patristic method, which preserves the world as a harmonious continuum, as a net of analogies which one must investigate through allegorical exegesis. By contrast, Cromwell is the champion of the 'print-made split between head and heart,' that is, of the 'trauma which affects Europe from Machiavelli till the present.'[45] Also, Cromwell is presented as a 'setter up of walls,'[46] a definition which immediately renders the new idea of space fragmentation that McLuhan associates with the Gutenberg Age, and that led to a new perception of both outer and inner space. Ford underlines this fragmentation through a peculiar setting of dark rooms lost inside huge palaces where people spy through doors ajar. These delimited spaces are mostly perceived through a reduced, narrowed visual perspective, either through a fissure or a hole. The very act of spying can, in turn, be read as a subtle metaphor of the passage leading from an open society to an increasingly closed one – an individualistic society built upon the idea of nationalism and progressing to a new logic which reconfigures space according to the ideas of the relations of the centre to the margin. By contrast, Katharine is often represented as standing in the open air, seated on a balcony, walking in a garden; even the Royal Palace, after Cromwell's death and Katharine's marriage to the King, seems to be brought to a new life.

In his trilogy, Ford seems implicitly to have caught another important element of the making of the new modern society, something which also constitutes a central tenet of McLuhan's ideas, namely, that the printing press accelerated the passage from the ear to the eye, unbalancing a previously harmonic way of perceiving one's environment. According to McLuhan, the sensory balance which characterizes the oral tribe and is preserved in the Middle Ages, even though the spread of a literate culture is starting to undo it, is finally overcome by the invention of the printing press. That technology accelerates a passage in progress: acoustic space is turned into visual space, and Renaissance society is progressively turned into a visual society, a society where the eye becomes the alpha and omega of all perception. Thus the split between head and heart that Cicero foresaw, and that McLuhan underlines in his works, is finally accomplished. In turn, Ford seems to have also grasped this in his way. It is evident that the word *eye* recurs often on almost every page of his trilogy. The colour, the attitude, the movement of eyes are all elements Ford uses in order to present his characters – elements that, in most cases, replace a more traditional and detailed description of the characters themselves. It is from the eyes that most words are spoken: 'Show me your eyes,'[47] the King asks Katharine when they first meet, and Cromwell walks beside Katharine 'with his eyes on her face';[48] Gardiner's eyes are 'agate-blue … sombre, threatening, suspicious';[49] Magister Udal alerts Katharine to Cromwell, presenting him as 'Circumspectatrix cum oculis emisitiis!' … 'A spie with eyes that peer about and stick out';[50] 'My eyes are your Highness,'[51] Lady Mary says sarcastically to the King, her father; Cromwell's eyes are 'sagacious,' the King's eyes can be 'crafty,' and Katharine's can be 'cold,' depending on the moment and the situation. The same can be said of all characters, including the so-called minor ones, from Hal Poins to Katharine's maids of chamber and servants. In this way, Ford continually presents his characters through a single physical detail, a single component of the human body, namely, *the eye*. Through this metonymical use of language, he seems to underline the making of what McLuhan would later define as Gutenberg's fragmented and visual man.

The beginning of the trilogy could be easily defined as a true masterpiece of literary strategy as, in a few pages, Ford manages to convey the true essence of his book. Wittily, he chooses to open the trilogy with a peculiar setting: a print-shop. It is in the print-shop that the reader is introduced to many apparently minor characters who, however, will later play key roles in the unravelling of the plot. Not surprisingly, John Badge, the printer, representing the New Order, calls Lord Cromwell 'God's engine,' and is immediately opposed by his father, who instead defends the Old Order and sees Cromwell simply as 'a brewer's drunken son.' This opposition of father and son dramatically reinforces the idea of a passage towards a new form of society in which ancient and noble values give way to new, individualistic, and mechanical ones. At the printer's shop, arriving at the same time, is Magister Udal, 'the Lady Mary's pedagogue,' who had also taught the learned tongue to Katharine Howard before her arrival at court – a man who, 'Being of the Old Faith,' hates 'those Lutherans – or those men of the New Learning – that it pleased his master [Lord Cromwell] to employ.'[52]

From the very beginning, then, Ford relates belonging to one or the other of the religious parties with a clearly identifiable cultural and exegetical tradition. In fact, the New Learning mentioned by Magister Udal inevitably points the reader to the quarrel between grammarians and dialecticians, which also bears social and political implications. To learn that Magister Udal, despite being well-read in the encyclopedic tradition, and being Lady Mary's Catholic's pedagogue, is also a Cromwell's man ('his master') should make the reader a bit suspicious. This circumspection is reinforced by the fact that the printer, whom Ford presents as an 'artificer' and whose art is opposed to the 'Magister's learning,' sharply names the Magister a 'Latin mouth-mincer.' It is a witty image which Ford uses to emphasize how the Latin spoken by Magister Udal is a 'learned' tongue, a refined form of Latin that, as proved by Walter J. Ong in his *Orality and Literacy*, became institutionalized precisely when the vulgar tongues started to consolidate during the passage from the Middle Ages to the modern age.

A newly codified version of Latin, submitted to written rules and paradigms, is a language that, despite being the learned tongue spoken by the new man of learning, is less and less associated with an ancient idea of knowledge, and more and more connected with a new idea of power. In the Renaissance period, in fact, Latin is the language of international bureaucracy, the language used to write treaties, to establish connections, to execute secret plots. It is a language that is no longer simply related to knowledge, but to the very idea of power itself. It is Cicely Rocheford, one of Katharine's maids, who clearly enlightens the reader. Answering Katharine, who still defends the old values and believes in ancient traditions and rules, Cicely underlines how learning nowadays is a mere instrument, a tool men use to reach individual purposes, and repeats hotly: 'This is no place for virtues learned from learned books. This is an ill world where only evil men flourish.'[53] Inevitably, Magister Udal will, in the end, serve Cromwell first, and the King later. His task is that of translating their letters into the 'learned tongue,' that is, translating letters which are of political relevance and, once delivered, could change the history of England. Such is the case of the letter of submission that King Henry VIII, urged by his fifth Queen, plans to write to the Pope in Rome, a letter which is written and rewritten many times but never sent. Somehow the Magister himself, despite his learning, embodies the final strengthening of the new, individualistic, and literate Gutenberg society. No wonder he is despised by Lady Mary the Catholic, who, unlike him, is firm in her faith.

In the print-shop the reader also meets the Poins siblings, Hal and Margot, who, once they arrive at court, will, in turn, repeat the opposition between Old and New order, as Hal will serve Cromwell, and Margot, Katharine. In the print-shop, you hear the names of 'Sieur Machiavelli' and Lord Cromwell; of Lord Edmund Howard and Thomas Culpepper, respectively father and cousin of Katharine; and also, the name of Anne of Cleves, the fourth wife of King Henry VIII, who has just arrived in England from Germany. The new marriage has been arranged by the Lord Privy Seal, who showed the King an unfaithful portrait of the Queen, resulting in Henry's disappointment with her true aspect and habits. Ford seems here to underline, emblematically, the paradox of following a blind trust in the eye, and to signal the relevant risks; if people look *at* things rather than *through* them, they will lose the integral perception of the things and situations themselves. On the contrary, it is through the speech she delivers during an elaborate masque at court, that Katharine conquers the King's attention and love: the opposition of visual (love and commitment through a portrait) versus acoustic (love and commitment through words) again reinforces the forthcoming split between head and heart. Letters from Germany always arrive at the print-shop, and Germany is the very place where the Lutheran protest began. Finally, the print-shop is located beside Cromwell's palace, separated by a wall which Cromwell has forcibly erected encroaching on the Badges' garden. Again, the setting up of walls returns the reader to that logic of centre and margins which characterizes the making of the modern state.

As previously suggested, the barriers which Cromwell imposes do in the end affect both inner and outer space, and therefore mirror the new idea of *privacy*. Lord Cromwell is the Lord *Privy Seal*, a title that, in itself, well encapsulates this new idea. Opposite to this attitude, Ford depicts Katharine's sociability and lively entourage, which makes the reader associate her with a communal idea of society. This is a form of society that Cromwell's politics is slowly destroying, although it seems to be temporarily restored after his death:

> In the shadow of the high walls, and some in the moonlight, the serving-men held their parliament ... And some said it was marvellous that there they could sit or stand and talk of such things – for a year or so ago all the Court was spies, so that the haymen mistrusted them that forked down the straw, and the meat-servers them with the wine. But now each man could talk as he would, and it made greatly for fellowship when a man could sit against a wall, unbutton in the warm nights, and say what he listed.[54]

But this is only the final act of a dying order, as Ford suggests through a subtle presentation of the hidden tensions among servants themselves; it is too late to halt a change which has already permeated the social strata.

To show the final accomplishment of this change to his readers, towards the end of his trilogy, Ford returns to the same print-shop, using the same setting to render the way Katharine Howard, the Fifth Queen, is undone by the conspirators of the New Order. Ford shows his readers a new and linear situation where there is no more outstanding opposition but only well-established biases. The younger printer can now dominate all the space: 'His old father was by that time dead ... so that the house-place was clear. And of all old furnishing none remained. There were presses all round the wall, and lockers for men to sit upon.'[55] And new men like Lascelles, who acts according to Cromwell's (or 'Sieur Machiavelli's') logic, firmly seated in the print-shop of John Badge the Younger, will finally defeat Katharine and the Old Order she stands for.

Marshall McLuhan wrote that in the process leading from orality to literacy, 'the rich interplay of all the senses that characterised the tribal society is sacrificed.'[56] Similarly, Katharine, who stands for the Old Order, must be defeated and sacrificed. She understands the inevitability of what comes through change, and Ford conveys all her understanding in a last, dramatic monologue which can be taken as the testament of a dying age:

> And so, now I am cast for death, and I'm very glad of it. For, if I had not so ensured and made it fated, I might later have wavered ... I came to you [the King] for that you might give this realm again to God. Now I see you will not – for not ever will you do it if it must abate you a jot of your sovereignty, and you never will do it without that abatement. So it is in vain that I have sinned ... for this world is no place for me who am mazed by too much reading in old books ... So now I go![57]

Katharine is brought to death, and, with her, both the Old Order and the Old Learning die too. The new individualistic society is finally born, and the Middle Ages give way to modernity, something which will completely reconfigure man's outer and inner space. The Western World will soon move towards what William Blake defined as 'the single vision and Newton's sleep,' a new reality whose effects various men of letters, and various conscious craftsmen and artists, tried to probe and counterbalance through their works. As McLuhan understood, Ford's chat 'is a series of epiphanies of carefully considered social and literary structures and their inter-penetration,' because 'it's always been the artist who perceived the alteration in man caused by a new medium.'[58] In the rear-view mirror offered by Ford's *The Fifth Queen*, we can learn something about the complex implications pertaining to the newly fermenting Gutenberg Age, and better understand the real ground upon which a new technology finally becomes set.

See? Literature matters! It is a function inseparable from communal existence: it makes us see, hear, and feel. It keeps us awake. Now, go and get a copy of Ford's *The Fifth Queen*. Read it, then think: 'Does the interiorization of media such as "letters" alter the ratio among our senses and change mental processes?'[59]

10 James Joyce: Vivisecting Society

Applied Joyce

In 1951, Marshall McLuhan published his first book, *The Mechanical Bride: Folklore of Industrial Man*. On the cover, the word 'Illustrated' promised something different from other more traditional academic publications. Readers would not be deceived: the book consisted of forty-nine essays, in which McLuhan discussed different *mythologies* pertaining to the new mass culture (the 'Front Page' of the *New York Times*; the 'Ballet Luce'; 'The Market Research'; 'Superman'; 'Tarzan'; 'The Great Books,' and many more) through a montage of icons, puns, and more serious comments and quotations. A year later, he wrote to his mother commenting on his first literary achievement:

> [*The Mechanical Bride*] is really a new form of science fiction, with ads and comics cast as characters. Since my object is to show the community in action rather than prove anything, it can indeed be regarded as a new kind of novel.[1]

The professor of English did not see his volume as a scholarly enterprise, but as a work of fiction to the point that he also defined its genre: science fiction. I like to think that he was right: *The Mechanical Bride* was a new kind of novel; but it was so new that nobody took it as such. Even today, we quote it as a prototypical investigation anticipating later works in the field of either semiotic or cultural or media studies. Approached as the antecedent of volumes such as Roland Barthes's *Mythologies* (1957), *The Mechanical Bride* still stands as an original and successful attempt to unveil hidden patterns of the then forming mass culture. However, why not to trust McLuhan and accept the idea that, at the time, he saw it as a new kind of novel? Remember that in his introduction to that book, he overtly tells us that he is probing how to apply the method of art analysis to the critical evaluation of society. In other words, McLuhan tells us that he is consciously experimenting with a new form capable of translating his own observations of the world in progress. And what is a novel if not the rendering of the writer's perception of reality?

McLuhan had a plot – his own actuality, with ads and comics cast as characters – and was now elaborating it into the most appropriate form. Joyce offered him a good model. The final result was a grotesque and satirical portrait of the 'Folklore of Industrial Man,' vivisected and reassembled on McLuhan's printed pages in a progression of effect leading to the exhibition of his own community in action. From 'Horse Opera' to 'Soap Opera,' North America was now crossing the ultimate frontier of mass consumerism: the celluloid West was mesmerizing the American imagination, customizing dreams for collective hygiene and optimism. It was *really* a new form of science fiction in which human beings are portrayed as servo-mechanisms of an artificial landscape they no longer master. The world of collective 'Soap Opera' is, in fact, not so perfect; suffering is intense and prolonged. Individuals are numbed and dominated by collective psycho-pathologies which make them look like sleepwalkers in a screenplay written by others. McLuhan's science-fictional landscape in *The Mechanical Bride* is the perfect introduction to the landscape readers will later explore in the avant-garde science fiction of a writer like J.G. Ballard, or of a film director like David Cronenberg. After all, as the letter to his mother reveals, McLuhan was conscious of being up to something *new*, something that he had started to pursue while trying to 'make more and more of [his] studies, and the life around him, intelligible.'[2] Consciously or unconsciously, later writers and thinkers would move along in his own wake, in a continuous cross-pollination among literature, the arts, and media and communications studies – just as McLuhan had moved in the wake of Joyce's *Finnegans Wake*, 'a dream of world history ... couched in a new language, a comic mixture of all the tongues of Europe.'[3]

From the late 1930s, McLuhan was back in North America, where he started his teaching career at the University of Wisconsin. His biographers inform us that, at the time, he was a charming and determined young professor of English, a specialist in the English Renaissance, but passionate about modernist writers. In particular, in those years, McLuhan transformed his admiration for the works of James Joyce into a more serious investigation of a rhetorical model which mirrored the Irish writer's time and which could be adapted to grasp the implications of the future media oracle's actions and of new knowledge in his own time as well. As suggested by Philip Marchand, Joyce was the 'supreme nut to be cracked,' one which McLuhan set off to master: he read a few pages every day, guided by Robinson and Campbell's *Skeleton Key to Finnegans Wake*, and ... cracked it.[4] The way I see it, Joyce was not so important for the development of McLuhan's ideas on media; instead, he was fundamental for the elaboration of McLuhan's own poetics, and especially for the elaboration of his own form of writing. The fact that McLuhan himself defined his own investigative method as 'applied Joyce' confirms this idea. As a 'successful devotee of the rhetoric of the second sophists,'[5] Joyce taught McLuhan how to bring past and present together through language; in Joyce's works, analogy replaces logic, and words are elaborated following their evocative power, not their traditional syntax. In *Finnegans Wake*, the old science of etymology is retrieved to create surprising verbo-vocal-visual chains of meaning that resonated through McLuhan's scholarly background. Both Joyce's mythical method and his playful linguistic explorations helped McLuhan to look through the opalescent surface of things and move towards understanding.

Through Joyce, then, McLuhan learned crucial rhetorical strategies to translate his own *auditory imagination* into an operative model to explore the electric maelstrom. While Joycean influences and quotations can be found throughout McLuhan's works, it is in *The Mechanical Bride* that McLuhan first *applies* Joyce. The Irish writer showed him how to bridge literary criticism, media studies, and cultural studies in an original narrative. McLuhan's 'new kind of novel' further explores Joyce's combinatory use of language by including ads and comics, which, in fact, were the new language of the time: a language spoken by McLuhan's university students, but of which they had not necessarily mastered the grammar. As a professor of English, as a Thomist and as a grammarian, McLuhan set off to fill in that gap.

Orphan Annie, Li'l Abner, Bogart Hero, Cokes and Cheesecake, Tarzan, Superman, and the Book of the Hour are some of the *characters* McLuhan cast against a landscape that they inhabit together with industrial man. McLuhan elaborates these immaterial figures into an architecture which, as said, emanates from Joycean aesthetic but then evolves into a more articulated formal pastiche. *The Mechanical Bride* also echoes a series of other more traditional literary genres which McLuhan knew and appreciated: while reading the book, you think of Poe's or Chesterton's detective stories ('The Drowned Man,' 'Crime Does Not Pay'); of Swift's satirical and grotesque narratives ('Galluputians,' 'Heading for Failure'); of Carroll's allegorical and paradoxical plots ('The Poor Rich,' 'Magic That Changes Moods'). These models have also been assimilated by McLuhan and turned into formal subtexts of his *Mechanical Bride*: by that I mean that the formal structure of each of the forty-nine essays in the book is modulated according to carefully envisaged literary models, assembled and juxtaposed to pursue a precise goal for which Joyce is the supreme master. Their cumulative effect is our reward: it is the final epiphany which frees us from our 'public helplessness.' It's our own *Readers Wake.*

McLuhan started to work on this book in the 1940s, while reading *Finnegans Wake*, meeting Ezra Pound and Wyndham Lewis, and trying to determine how to be a professor of English outside of the academic ivory tower. When his first book was released, not many got it, both inside and outside the universities. McLuhan became truly popular only later on, and, certainly, he did not become famous as a writer of *a new kind of novel*. At the time, the effect of such a broken technique on the standard format normally reserved for critical and academic essays can be compared to the disruptive impact that, at the beginning of the twentieth century, the modernist formal discoveries and achievements had on late Victorian literary tradition. Just like the modernist writers and contrary to the eminent Victorians, McLuhan had no prepackaged truth for his readers, his book's goal being to show a dynamic world *in progress*. And, like in other modernist writers' works, the writing process was itself part of the show.

Come to think of it, the book came out at the right moment: McLuhan presented the folklore of industrial man precisely when the passage from the modern to the contemporary age, which he dates back to the late eighteenth century with the discovery of electricity, was becoming a mass phenomenon, that is, when it was becoming a visible figure. The rapid development of the new mass media would, first of all, help speed up communications between nations and cultures, turning literate society into a post-literate society where traditional geographic and cultural boundaries conflate, and where space and time paradigms are quickly subverted.[6] The same passage that James Joyce had subtly perceived and rendered in his works, McLuhan was now in the position to deconstruct and reveal for the masses.

Here comes Joyce again, the writer who 'exhibits a complex clairvoyance in these matters. His Leopold Bloom of *Ulysses*, a man of many ideas and many devices, is a freelance ad salesman.'[7] Here comes everybody. Here comes the Industrial Man. Here comes the Sage of Waldorf Towers. Here comes Superman. Here comes Blondie. Here comes the Mechanical Bride.

Starting with *The Mechanical Bride*, Joyce's *Ulysses* and *Finnegans Wake* are applied by McLuhan as a warning signal alerting us to the shift of sensibility taking place inside the electric mediascape:

> The west shall shake the East awake
> While you have the night for morn

Here comes the global village. Here comes his messenger. Here comes his message. Read with you ears; you will crack that nut.

Sci-Fi Phantasmagoria

Following Joyce's example, then, in *The Mechanical Bride* McLuhan started to recompose, through his 'illustrated' language, the landscape in which the above-mentioned shift was taking place. As such, he progressed towards the revealing of that hidden environment he would further explore in his later books on media. Prior to Roland Barthes and Umberto Eco,[8] McLuhan perceived the complex pattern of forces affecting human consciousness in a new mass society and gave an early account of several signs or *myths/mythologies* belonging to what could be defined as the new folklore. Not only that, but he turned those same signs and myths into satirical weapons to reveal hidden social, anthropological, and cultural implications. As Umberto Eco wrote in his review of the Italian edition of *The Mechanical Bride*, 'Paradoxically, this book makes us think of Adorno speaking in comics. You have a different philosophical and argumentative apparatus, but the same indignation. The difference is that McLuhan invites you to read and understand these phenomena from "the inside," so to master them.'[9] Here comes Poe's sailor again. Here comes the modernist lesson again: reality is an elusive and ambiguously conceived idea which writers are called upon to unmask. And here comes McLuhan the modernist again, setting fragments against the ruins of his consumerist society. It was the first and last time in his whole life that he would do so, as he wrote to Jonathan Miller a few years later, when the latter was writing what became a controversial essay on McLuhan the media-guru.[10]

McLuhan's innovation in *The Mechanical Bride* lies in the fact that he neither uses the traditional essay format, nor does he write within a previously defined literary genre. He himself tells his mother that his achievement is something 'new.' He starts from the idea that his environment is an artefact self-made by humans, a complex *effect* deriving from different overlapping experiences (and processes) which can be better perceived through an artistic approach. According to McLuhan, the artistic perception offers a more objective possibility of observation of both *ground* and *figure*, especially of the former, as it enables us to work out what stands below the visible surface: 'A whirling phantasmagoria can be grasped only when arrested for contemplation.'[11] Thus, the artistic perception facilitates a special estrangement, a probing aloofness that McLuhan often turns into satirical or humorous juxtapositions to identify the distortions and problems of a system still in progress. As McLuhan provocatively wrote, the result can be compared to a new form of science fiction whose landscape has more than an affinity with later science-fiction landscapes. As previously suggested, the landscape in such works of J.G. Ballard as *The Atrocity Exhibition* or *Crash* comes to mind: human and mechanical shapes melt and overlap in situations that are at once grotesque and apocalyptic, and that, if not unveiled, end by seriously numbing all critical attitude and perception.

The new wave of science fiction of which J.G. Ballard was a renowned champion began a few years after *The Mechanical Bride* was released, in the early 1960s; it was another response to the new consumerist and highly technological world. Ballard's novels – as well as, a few years later, Cronenberg's movies – remain in the present, thereby negating traditional tenets of science fiction: there is no futuristic location, no timeshift; there are no monsters, nor aliens. Apparently normal men and women interact, following a sort of dream-like logic which, nevertheless, the writer employs to discuss uneasy themes. These themes, taken together, pose a series of unresolved questions which are already disseminated through the pages of *The Mechanical Bride*: the technological extension of the human body; the psychology of human beings living in a hyper-consumerist amoral landscape; the blurring of the inner and the outer self; and the subversion of traditional sexual biases.

Ballard – and other writers and artists in his wake – was a science-fiction explorer or innovator, as he consciously positioned himself at the border of the mainstream; he preferred to employ science fiction as a disrupting probe to investigate the dark side of his own contemporary world. He was not interested in the future, nor in distant worlds: his interests were the twentieth century and its related psychopathologies – psychopathologies that he perceived as more or less conscious effects of an environment constantly reshaped by a complex combination of scientific discoveries and media-induced psychodynamics. As a consequence, individuals were modifying their way of being, their way of perceiving themselves, their inner and outer selves, their bodies and their minds; their reactions to technological and cultural change reconfigured both the environment (if by environment we mean the dynamic interactions among individuals, social factors, and technology) and their perception of that environment. In Ballard's experimental works, inner and outer landscapes overlap and merge in quite familiar, yet disturbing, settings which force the reader to face what Cronenberg will later define as *the psychology of the future* – something which, paradoxically, is deeply linked to our present. Cronenberg's film adaptation of Ballard's novel *Crash* caused strong controversies among international audiences, but was awarded the Jury's Special Award for 'its audacity and innovation' at the 1996 Cannes Film Festival. The artist sniffs out environmental change before others.

Ballard and Cronenberg have often compared themselves to neutral explorers, borderline observers, not content with safe and pre-established formulas; as explorers rather than explainers, they use their art to show and reveal extreme situations and possibilities which often defy all given rules and shared moralities. Consistently, their analyses do not simply begin from a moral bias; they do not move from the definition of a given order which is then violated. Instead, as I will further discuss in Part Three, these two artists intend to explore an environment which is technologically progressing rapidly, and which is characterized by fetishist and consumerist trends, as well as the potentialities and extreme effects (both positive and negative) that these trends may have on individuals and, therefore, on society. The human body and technology are components of a wider context within which apparently pathological dynamics develop, at once affecting human physicality and cognitive parameters. Individuals shape tools which, in turn, shape individuals (as per one of the most celebrated probes by McLuhan: 'We become what we behold. We shape our tools and then our tools shape us').[12] This, too, is not a mere determinist tenet; rather, it is a complex phenomenon that not only combines organic and inorganic, but also implies the development of more or less conscious cognitive acts. Similarly, for Marshall McLuhan:

Any invention or technology is an extension or self-amputation of our physical bodies ... Man becomes, as it were, the sex organs of the machine world, as the bee of the plant world, enabling it to fecundate and to evolve ever new forms. The machine world reciprocates man's love by expediting his wishes and desires, namely, in providing him with wealth. One of the merits of motivation research has been the revelation of man's sex relation to the motorcar.[13]

McLuhan's quote would work beautifully as an introduction to Ballard's and Cronenberg's *Crash*, a novel and a movie exploring the interior landscape postulated by the new wave of science fiction. Such a concept was explicitly and boldly theorized in *Understanding Media*; but McLuhan had already started to investigate the uneasy connection between sex and technology in his first published book. Already, in *The Mechanical Bride*, cars and other technologies are juxtaposed with gender-changing roles inside his society.[14] In 'Husband's Choice,' he asks his readers if the car is what rushed us 'into some sort of polygamy,' or if the car has taken up 'the burden of sex' inside a world which he sees as increasingly emasculated. Sex is here used, in investigating the folklore of industrial man, as a crucial paradigm for detecting the way individuals do or do not comply with collective behavioural patterns. The Galluputians are the statisticians who tell you whether you are in line with others or not; and if you are not, you start to worry. What Ballard and Cronenberg will later do, instead, is to insinuate the idea that sexual 'perversions' are in fact symptoms of individual awakening: in the new science fiction genre, a psychopathology, that is, a different behavioural pattern, is a possible response to the Narcissus Narcosis.

The Galluputians we find in *The Mechanical Bride* are among the most fascinating characters of McLuhan's science fiction; they seem like little inhabitants of a bigger reality that they try to reduce through polls and forecasts. They vivisect what they see, but their vivisection is not as fertile as Joyce's: they do not know how to cross-pollinate the fragments they extrapolate, which, in their hands, cannot but remain as lifeless relics of a society which is not thinking anymore. Galluputians fascinate 'the Lilliputian mind'; they tell it where to fit and, by so doing, help it to be an outstanding mind (if you are not a Lilliputian, you get the pun: your OUTstanding mind stands OUT. From what, it is your goal to determine). Galluputians are therefore grotesque characters, as are all the other characters in McLuhan's new science fiction. Just like ads and comics, the men and women we encounter in *The Mechanical Bride* are no longer 'humans' but fictional replicas of themselves: the woman in a mirror, the men of distinction, the Bogart Hero, are in fact masks playing a role for which the ads or comics provide an artificial setting juxtaposed with the natural one in uncanny ways. The overall effect is somehow paradoxical and surreal, as reality blurs into an overwhelming *depth-involving newness*. It is an effect that Ballard himself retrieves in his works and overtly discusses in the preface to his novel *Crash*, when he comments about our 'all-voracious present':

> We have annexed the future into the present, as merely one of those mani-
> fold alternatives open to us. Options multiply around us, and we live in an
> almost infantile world where any demand, any possibility, whether for life-
> style, travel, sexual roles and identities, can be satisfied instantly. In addition,
> I feel that the balance between fiction and reality has changed significantly
> in the past decades. Increasingly their roles are reversed. We live in a world
> ruled by fictions of every kind ... We live inside an enormous novel. It is now
> less and less necessary for the writer to invent fictional content of his novel.
> The fiction is already there. The writer's task is to invent reality.[15]

In *The Mechanical Bride*, McLuhan maps the enormous North American novel of the time. He offers a portrait of that shifting landscape, where past and present are merged, 'devoured by the all-voracious present.' This is an all-voracious present (a *depth-involving newness*) which confuses reality and fiction, and whose numbing mechanisms McLuhan probes and reverses in his book by displacing its signs through a provocative formal montage; it is an all-voracious present which Jean Baudrillard will later define in terms of *hyperreality*. According to Baudrillard, reality and fiction overlap in our Western consumer society, but also, in fact, in our global village; our perception of both paradigms, as well as their interface, leads to the creation of a series of communal simulacra and simulations. The result is a sort of alienating and alienated technology- and media-shaped hyperreality, which neutralizes all subjectivity, and fits both the individual's body and mind into one or other trendy simulacrum. Hyperreality is therefore characterized by hyper-representations (simulations) of shared models (simulacra). The balance between fiction and reality is in fact changed: ours is the time of *reality shows*. This Western consumerist hyperreality constitutes the setting for most of Ballard's novels and certainly for McLuhan's new kind of novel, *The Mechanical Bride*. Both writers vivisect society and offer a surrealist representation of reality, creating an atrocity exhibition which mirrors a truly grotesque humanity. Nevertheless, compared to Ballard, McLuhan's exhibition appears to be more amusing, though still alarming. It contains a quality embedded in most of McLuhan's writing, inspired by

Joyce's linguistic model, in which sharp puns and paradoxes expand the potentialities of the grotesque and, in the end, lend a playful tone to the vivisection of an otherwise nightmarish society.

The new Frankensteins presented in McLuhan's new type of science fiction are both ourselves and the manipulators of the psyche, who work to 'get inside the collective public mind. To get inside in order to manipulate, exploit, control.'[16] The 'social body' is in danger, and human beings must counterbalance the attack of 'many thousands of the best-trained individual minds' who want to generate 'heat not light.'[17] Given the danger, it is necessary to counterattack. Following the example of the mariner in Poe's 'A Descent into the Maelstrom,' which McLuhan quotes in his preface to the book, in a mass society individuals must retrieve their personalities, not by resenting or fearing the environment, but by critically observing and penetrating it. They should no longer be paralysed by *looking at it*, but should learn how to *look through it* in order to finally grasp its hidden mechanism. McLuhan sets out to vivisect the given collective mind, by amplifying single aspects of it in order to let the ground, that is, the invisible net of mechanisms aimed at the manipulation of people's consciousness, emerge by contrast. Science fiction is a good genre for that endeavour, precisely because it subverts the established order. In a human world, science fiction creates robots and thinking machines; in a dehumanized world, science fiction stirs 'a more human state of mind.' Comic strips, ads, and images from the popular press are McLuhan's science fictional characters; they are, in fact, metonymical representations of a complex and ominous reality. Despite an initial moral bias, his intention is not simply to judge society but rather to dig into a dynamic reality with a mobile point of view which leads him to shift from one fragment to the other.

Grotesque Vivisection

As previously suggested, the idea of 'vivisecting' society (also a *topos* in the science-fiction genre) has an illustrious antecedent in James Joyce. McLuhan's analysis of Joyce's idea of vivisection occurs in an essay where he comments on Joyce's aesthetics, noting that Joyce has developed a new artistic form combining ancient rhetorical strategies with the new possibilities of expression offered by the new mass media. McLuhan quotes a famous passage from Joyce's *Stephen Hero* in which the writer states: 'The modern spirit is vivisective. Vivisection itself is the most modern process one can conceive.' In *The Mechanical Bride*, in addition to

Poe's aesthetic, McLuhan recalls precisely this Joycean aesthetic, so that the very same term, *vivisection* – as well as other terms discussed by McLuhan when commenting on the above passage in *Stephen Hero*, such as *community in action, reconstruction, detection* – can also be used as key words in examining McLuhan's first book.

Following Stephen's idea of 'modern spirit,' in *The Mechanical Bride* McLuhan observes a community in action and tries to work out the setting. To this end, McLuhan uses the technique of vivisection to combine different forms of serious art with popular art, as well as with new forms of mass communication ('Much popular art would seem to be a mere repetition of the environmental effects created by new technologies');[18] then to break standardized repetition through a vivisective technique which, on the one hand, is capable of dismantling the whole and, on the other, of amplifying, by contrast, single parts of it, thereby helping to recreate the whole itself in order to see it under a revealing light. In other words, vivisection might help to deconstruct the given patterns and lead to epiphany; this is itself another tenet of Joyce's aesthetic.

McLuhan's collage in *The Mechanical Bride* is what makes this his most modernist book: the technique of juxtaposition was a favourite modernist tenet, each time associated with a more specific terminology. *Collage, juxtaposition of situations, grotesque, montage* are words coined by various avant-gardes to render their aesthetic visions. All these terms work very well for *The Mechanical Bride* as modes shaping McLuhan's vivisective approach that turns ads and people alike into spare parts of a machine-like collectivity. The chapter which gives the book its title puts vivisection itself 'on a pedestal,' together with the beautiful legs that the Gotham Hosiery Company presents to its customers; they stand for the 'ultimate model' conceived to replace your old one. Legs, busts, lips, hips, are all spare parts of a human body which is of interest only through these replaceable consumerist parts, not as a whole. It is their grotesque assemblage which matters to McLuhan: epiphany comes through a distorted vision, through the grotesque recreation of reality, just as on an Expressionist canvas. His own collage, or montage, or grotesque juxtaposition progresses in an original book critics did not know how to read. No omniscient narrator was there to guide them. They had to dive into a curious narrative and engage with a verbal and a visual challenge. This is precisely the kind of interaction most modernist works of fiction require. Certainly, it is what Joyce's works require. To read a work like *Finnegans Wake*, the reader must revise a logical approach and be prepared to work out each neologism and pun in order to grasp the various implications in the polysemous linguistic structure. Therefore, what Joyce defines as our *abcedmindedness*, an expression which can be read as 'absent-minded' (inattentive or careless), or as 'ABC-minded' (alphabetically biased), is constantly challenged by both Joyce's and McLuhan's new forms of writing.

McLuhan thus turns the new mass media, brands, and comics into significant signs belonging to an articulated world in progress, signs that people overlook as they read the ads – signs already established as a ground, as a comprehensive wrapping, a sort of mental and physical space which is taken for granted. McLuhan operates his dislocating 'verbo-voco-visual' technique on such a ground and uses bold associations of contrasting signs as enlightening paradoxes. As I have often repeated in this chapter, this proto-semiotic vivisection is easily rendered through, and inevitably leads to, a grotesque effect. Scanning and juxtaposing images belonging to an evolving mass society creates a distorted amplification of different icons which are condensed into what could be described as a disturbing, yet ironic, expressionist-like mosaic. This is a new form of critical writing that, through an intentional disharmony, forces the reader to reconsider what was previously perceived as a uniform and harmonic ground. It is precisely through the grotesque element that popular art and 'serious' art meet and cross-fertilize one another. On this topic, McLuhan himself quotes from Ruskin's *Modern Painters*, suggesting that his definition of grotesque also offers a formula for 'vivisection':

> A fine grotesque is the expression, in a moment, by a series of symbols thrown together in bold and fearless connection of truths which it would have taken a long time to express in any other verbal way, and of which the connection is left for the beholder to work out for himself. [19]

McLuhan emphasizes that James Joyce succeeds in rendering his grotesque vivisection in his two epoch-making works, *Ulysses* and *Finnegans Wake*. In *Ulysses*, the character of Leopold Bloom and the city of Dublin metonymically stand for a universal community, which is increasingly characterized and shaped by the new mass media; technically, the novel can be approached as an immense newspaper, itself a grotesque and parodic amplification of the mock-heroic Homeric epic of an everyday man living an everyday life, and symbolically representing all men. In *Finnegans Wake*, the grotesque element pervades the peculiar linguistic construction which brings together different aesthetics belonging to both classic and popular traditions, and explores the new intriguing possibilities that the new forms of mass communication had been offering to modern artists for almost a century. As Joyce writes in *Finnegans Wake*, 'The war is in words and the wood is the world': it is precisely through deconstruction of traditional syntax and the hybridization of language, form, and artistic codes that both the artist and the critic can find new meanings and new epiphanies rendering the true spirit of their time. In his essays on Joyce collected in *The Interior Landscape*, McLuhan shows how Joyce clearly went on to experiment with language and artistic forms, expanding on the symbolist poets' achievements; similarly, McLuhan developed a new 'media poetics'[20] by following Joycean strategies.

Newspaperwise Attack

Despite his legendary erudition (or maybe because of it), Joyce did not resent the new media; on the contrary, he perceived them as possible epistemological tools and, combining his knowledge with the possibilities offered by these new forms of communication, turned 'the superficial cross-section of the popular press'[21] into a powerful probing model. As an artist, Joyce was ready to face the new cultural implications of his time. Not surprisingly, McLuhan considers the artist, and therefore also Joyce, as 'the man of integral awareness' who 'grasps implications of new knowledge' and turns them into a new aesthetic and sensory experience. In doing this, the artist anticipates both critics and academics. The modern newspaper offered a new aesthetic model to modern artists like Joyce. On the pages of the newspapers, different and heterogeneous events, news, and images overlap and are brought simultaneously together *here and now*, the page of the newspaper naturally turns into a sort of cathartic space presenting the whole human experience through an objective, estranging technique bypassing all previously established aesthetic canons. Both Joyce and McLuhan looked at the French symbolist movement as a pivotal moment in the development of a modern aesthetic. According to McLuhan, Stéphane Mallarmé is 'the fabulous artificer, the modern Dedalus,' of the new aesthetic as it began to be shaped at the turn of the century; he was the first to grasp all 'the aesthetic consequences and possibilities of the popular arts in industrial man': 'Mallarmé sees this impersonal art of juxtaposition as revolutionary and democratic also in the sense that it *enables each reader to be an artist.*'[22] The 'impersonal art,' which Mallarmé rendered through the reportage-like technique that was subsequently developed by Joyce, became more and more an aesthetic need, a new epiphany deeply rooted in the grotesque and paradoxical estrangement that the new form of mass communications had contributed to revealing to the artist. As McLuhan wrote: 'With its dateline June 16, 1904, *Ulysses* is, newspaperwise, an abridgment of all space in a brief segment of time, as the *Wake* is a condensation of all time in the brief space of "Howth castle and environs."'[23]

'You never thought of a page of news as a symbolist landscape?' 'Why is a page of news a problem in orchestration?' These are the kind of questions that McLuhan addresses in his first book, *The Mechanical Bride*, insisting on the structure and form of all new cultural situations. The *divertissement*, enabling aloofness and detached observation, once more makes the reader think of Poe's mariner in 'A Descent into the Maelstrom.' As you might recall, in his preface, McLuhan underlines how the mariner manages to survive the most dramatic moment of his dreadful adventure thanks to his capacity to use humour as a part of his survival strategy.[24] Humour is a leitmotiv in *The Mechanical Bride*, although, in the end, the tone of the book appears both satirical and humorous: indeed, the comic and parodic amplification of the new mass mythologies ends up becoming a clear statement set against the social and cultural forces of the time. Nevertheless, more than a moral or cynical satire, McLuhan's can be perceived mostly as a Menippean satire, which is devoted to intentionally attacking the reader in order to wake him/her up. Menippean satire was, in fact, conceived as an attack, not on a single individual, but instead on general attitudes defining categories such as bigotry, pedantry, or others; it developed inside the classical grammarian tradition, delivered in a prose form employing a fragmented narrative. Once more, a direct influence of Joyce on McLuhan's writing is revealed, as parody and Menippean satire are both elements evident in the works of the Irish writer, wittily displayed through his peculiar and sophisticated use of language.[25]

The new form of writing elaborated by master Joyce and adopted by his apprentice McLuhan can therefore be summed up as a *verbo-voco-visual* structure capable of increasing the probing potentialities of each linguistic sign, turning each line into a warning on mass-media sensibilities. Joyce is admired not only as an explorer and an experimenter; he is admired because he could be both, thanks to his intellect and learning. In the early 1920s, Joyce retrieves the aphoristic *dictum* and succeeds in combining the learned tradition with mass media. His retrieval of etymology gave him a solid knowledge and precision:

When Joyce quipped to a critic, 'Some of my puns are trivial and some are

quadrivial,' he was being, as always, precise. When my critics imagine I am
being vaguely metaphorical, I, too, am trying to be literal and precise.[26]

McLuhan, too, acted as an erudite grammarian because grammar 'concerns the interpretation of written texts and the ground patterns in
words, etymology.'[27] He pursued a careful study of the ancient doctrine
of the logos, or doctrine of names, through a direct study of the original
texts (even though most in translations), as well as through the retrieval
of the Thomistic tradition of the Middle Ages, of Bacon's and Vico's lessons in the modern age, and of James Joyce in his own time. After Joyce,
McLuhan investigated language looking for a literal and precise form
capable of taking advantage of the intrinsic metaphorical value of words,
that is, their evocative power. The constant attention to the polysemous
references of words, linked to a new interest in etymology and, therefore, in grammar, is another fundamental tenet of McLuhan's prose
which derives from his understanding of Joyce. Words are rediscovered,
perceived as metaphors, or *technologies of explicitness*, evocative of the
whole human experience, and their probing potentiality is renewed in
every sentence, in every verbal association. If so understood, words can
be employed as counter-environments reassessing the balance between
figures and ground.

Therefore, the intrinsic epistemological value that pervades both
Joyce's and McLuhan's aesthetic clearly emerges: in both authors, the
search for a new form capable of enlightening while exploring the world
in progress is constantly addressed through the retrieval of an ancient
epistemological tradition preserved all through the Middle Ages by the
Patristic School through the *translatio studii*. A dissertation on 'The Place
of James Joyce in the Learning of His Time' would confirm that he was
a solid *doctor grammaticus*; in fact, that dissertation has been already written under different titles. A dissertation on 'The Place of McLuhan in
the Learning of His Time' is still a work in progress. Why not start from
The Mechanical Bride as a new kind of novel; that is, why not to take his
prose seriously as applied Joyce? Because, if you thought that Joyce or
Salvador Dali had a monopoly on surrealist savagery, *The Mechanical Bride*
can make them look like Disneyland. You know, one must talk with two
voices to be understood today. But we still have our freedom to listen. So
what is that rising noise? A new sex machine or a collective yawn? Or is it
everybody coming? Marshall McLuhan: what were you doing?

11 Ezra Pound: Pursuing Persuasion, Translating Cultures

Epical News

Your Cantos, I now judge, to be the first and only serious use of the great technical possibilities of the cinematograph. Am I right in thinking of them as a montage of *personae* and sculptured images? Flash-backs providing perceptions of simultaneities? ...

I've been pondering your remark that Cantos 1–40 are a detective story. Should be glad of further clues from you ... Are the entire Cantos such a reconstruction at once of a continuing crime and of the collateral life that might have been and might still be?[1]

In his letters to Ezra Pound, Marshall McLuhan not only pays homage to *the better craftsman*, but – more often – he discusses Pound's rhetorical strategies as both a poet and a critic. McLuhan, a young professor of English, was quite intrigued by the writing technique which Pound had been developing since his earlier experiments, which had been published by Ford Madox Ford in *The English Review*. Without any doubt whatsoever, he openly acknowledges Pound's influence as a master of form and operative methods. Hugh Kenner concurred and even designated the modernist period and its post-war coda as *The Pound Era*.[2] Pound's idea that his *Cantos* are in part conceived as 'a detective story' quite certainly offered McLuhan, who appreciated the cognitive potentialities of the genre, much to think about; and, in fact, his book review of Kenner's *The Poetry of Ezra Pound* pays homage to the achievements of Pound the poet, and to Kenner's enterprise for offering an exegetical system to his innovative verses.[3] But approaching the media maelstrom,

McLuhan became particularly interested in Pound's non-fictional prose or cultural pamphlets, especially his *Guide to Kulchur*, which stands as a possible epistemological model for McLuhan's *The Mechanical Bride*, together with Wyndham Lewis's theories on art and communication.

In the 1940s, McLuhan was developing his own understanding of mass society; to meet Pound and to have the possibility of discussing Pound's prose, and much more, directly with him was a real *passage* in establishing that literature is, in fact, a function and not a subject. A young professor now at St Michael's College, University of Toronto, he started to correspond with Pound while he was still working on his first book, which originally had been envisioned as 'two books on popular culture.'[4] All the while, McLuhan was also experimenting with form and language as a literary critic and as an intellectual engaged with his own times. As underlined by the editors of McLuhan's *Letters*, McLuhan 'was most receptive to Pound's esoteric knowledge of literature, while more or less disregarding his heated prejudices and recondite theories. McLuhan's letters to Pound soon echo the elliptical mode and anti-establishment tone of Pound's letters to McLuhan ... – though not Pound's verbal eccentricities ..., not the cantankerousness ... which McLuhan ignores in his relatively conventional, and respectful, replies.'[5] It is another way to underline that McLuhan's truer interest was focused on modernist formal experiments, far from their political or ideological aspects. In his letters, the younger intellectual practised his would-be writing style, engaging directly with one of his favourite masters, echoing his prose, and testing how to preserve its functionality freed from its ideology.

Hugh Kenner, with whom McLuhan first visited Pound, defined the poet's cantankerousness as 'epigrammatic snarl,'[6] a definition which immediately conveys a powerful image of Pound's solitary, resentful status at St Elisabeths Hospital for the Criminally Insane. His well-known personal history makes us aware that it is somehow difficult to separate Pound's works from his political thinking, especially if we consider that he was a master of rhetoric, as well as a connoisseur of the new forms of communication. Certainly, we can trace Pound's obsession concerning usury and capitalist society back to his works preceding the First World War, therefore accepting his *bona fide* views on later related societal developments. Yet, it is difficult to imagine that Pound was not aware of the impact of radio transmissions on a mass society, especially if that very medium of communication was wittily employed by a totalitarian regime to win consent or create consensus.[7]

In Pound's works – both his poetry and prose – form is embedded in meaning through the force of his own intellectual and ideological engagement. He was never neutral; he was committed to showing society its own self-destruction, its own *accelerated grimace*, a mask for the *modern stage* which has banished the beauty of an ancient *Attic grace*. If Joyce succeeds in translating his observation of society into a universal quest for everyman, Pound's works start to shift that universal into a more recognizable consumerist setting. Wyndham Lewis will complete the process by bringing the focus specifically on the hollow men of the twentieth century, no longer Eliot's zombies crossing over London Bridge, but soulless automata who have bargained away their personality in more or less conscious ways.

In the inter-war period, Pound developed a form which mediated between myth (Joyce) and history (Lewis), overtly engaging with his own society. Rightly, Fredric Jameson speaks of Joycean universal mythography and of the Poundian epic. The idea of epic in Pound does not simply relate to his own rhetorical method, but mostly to the dramaturgic function of his writing: his poems, as well as his prose, aim to elaborate common knowledge and tradition into a larger narrative in order to convey a sense of unity to a fragmented society. Pound's epic does not retrieve or update ancient myths; rather, it narrates modern and contemporary mythologies – no longer Odysseus, but Malatesta, Jefferson, and Mussolini are the controversial heroes whose deeds are now told. Pound addresses his educational pamphlets (*The ABC of Reading, Guide to Kulchur*) to modern and contemporary audiences, and, through them, he pursues persuasion as a strategy to alert his readers to, or even master, change. He develops a method which, even though it is based on encyclopedic learning, also exploits mass media and other popular forms of communication and entertainment; after all, 'literature is NEWS that stay NEW,' and the poet has his feet well planted in the matter of his own time.

From Old to New Learning

McLuhan carefully investigated Pound's prose, retaining his method but dismissing the explicit political intention. All through McLuhan's first few years in Toronto, Pound was a constant point of reference to assess modernist achievements, as many of the professor's letters to his friends and family reveal.[8] Intellectual ratio, analogies, and a certain attention to rhythm are all tenets of Pound's imagistic or epigrammatic poetry and prose which McLuhan much appreciated. McLuhan himself developed his own version of Pound's *ideogrammatic* or *epigrammatic* style in

The Mechanical Bride, even preserving in the preface some of the moral judgment to which Pound himself would certainly have subscribed. In this regard, McLuhan's first book on popular culture could be read not only as a new form of science fiction, as previously discussed, but also as a new form of a popular epic, acknowledging and investigating the existence of media-heroes, and written with the intent of awakening (if not educating) a mass audience. If you juxtapose the two books, you find that there are several elements in *Guide to Kulchur* which can be discussed in relation to McLuhan's *The Mechanical Bride*, all of them relating to the 'medium' or 'form' used to approach the epic of the time. First of all, the deterioration of the idea of *knowledge* or *learning*, which Pound relates to some materialistic aspects of his own time and which, in turn, McLuhan associates with the prevalence of the *Reader's Digest* logic (Bacon's *methods*) over a truly encyclopedic vision (Bacon's *aphorisms*). Pound's paratactic architecture, juxtaposing different words, drawings, fragments of musical scores, and Chinese characters, is then similar to the montage of puns, ads, images, and comments in *The Mechanical Bride*. Pound's use of quotations as strophic units to assemble a composite montage, which shapes Pound's meta-discourse with his readers, also anticipates McLuhan's intention to bring his own readers into the revolving picture and turn them into alerted explorers. However, while we can find a series of formal correspondences between Pound's and McLuhan's works, we do not necessarily find the same underpinning intent. As already said, McLuhan's mosaic aimed to explore the community in action; Pound, at the time writing from Italy during the fascist era, was pursuing an additional ideological purpose. He wrote about that explicitly in his *Guide to Kulchur*, as we shall later see in this chapter.

In his *Guide to Kulchur*, Pound calls his method *ideogrammatic*, using a term which condenses his imagistic idea of how to engage with a three-dimensional reality and render it on the flat surface of printed pages through words.[9] It is not an easy task, and it does not lead to an easy prose. On the contrary, Pound's ideogrammatic prose is a synthesis of different cultural experiences and more traditional knowledge (ancient philosophy or poetry) constantly juxtaposed on the printed page to form a series of composite pronouncements; the final orchestration recalls the multi-sensorial effects of new forms of communication, blurring space and time categories. Most experiences are, in fact, not narrated *ex novo* but conveyed through quotations in the attempt to create an original musical discourse through a reassemblage of previous fragments of learning; Pound went back 'again and again to the rag-and-bone shop of abandoned cliché.' Pound's ideogrammatic method is therefore built upon a concatenation of old verbal and visual *tessere*, which acquire a new iconic value because of their conceptual juxtaposition; the overall haiku-like effect complicates both perception and interpretation. Quotations combine verses of the *best tradition*, which Pound loved so much (especially Dante and the *dolce stil nuovo*), fragments of ancient and contemporary history and philosophy, as well as daily conversations captured as intermittent signals revealing common people's habits and thoughts. The new society that Pound was observing enters the poetical landscape not as a decorative, but as a structural, element acting in a historical continuum.

'Make It New.' With this motto, Pound declared war on both the Victorian and Edwardian ages; poetry was not meant to emote or enchant, but rather to stimulate ideas, historical perspective, and understanding of social, cultural, and political processes. Form is *techné*; form is instrumental to knowledge; form plays a role in enlightening men and history. Pound's poetry and prose engage their actuality through the simultaneous combination of various time and space traditions.[10] Was he not the *miglior fabbro*? To juxtapose Pound's *Cantos* with his prose books – such as *The ABC of Reading* (1934) and *Guide to Kulchur* (1938) – is a must to fully comprehend his poetics, as the latter works complete his search for a style and are part of the same operative project. Once again, McLuhan understood this before others: 'In *Guide to Kulchur* I have found all the helps with the Cantos that anybody needs, including full light on your remark to me in Washington that 1–40 are a sort of detective story.'[11] And, not surprisingly, he wrote to his friend Felix Giovanelli that *Guide to Kulchur* is 'the Cantos in prose. And harder to read.'[12]

Following a technique employed in his poetry, as well as in *Guide to Kulchur*, Pound uses quotations to investigate and render his times and his ideas concerning, in this particular case, the *kulchur* of the new mass age. The use of quotations or (verbo-vocal-visual) fragments of discourses is in fact a *leitmotiv* in most modernist poetics; as Eliot clearly points out in the closing of *The Waste Land*, they are often shored against the time's ruins in an attempt to offer a solid epistemological barrier against coeval chaos. Such a use opens up a series of new questions which writers and readers are now called to face: the authority of tradition; the question of originality of authorial voices and their artistic creations; the need to adjust one's aesthetics to new societal matrixes; and the difficult relation between the artist and history. These are issues that reading Pound's work still brings into the foreground. The use of quotations in

Pound's *Cantos* remains, in fact, one of the most debated rhetorical strategies among all modernist productions. The *Cantos* are a summa of the twentieth century and, inevitably, a summa of all what was there before; quotations are therefore boxes of knowledge, history, and experiences constantly juxtaposed to form the most complex ideogram ever imagined, which still engages old and new readers in a never-ending intellectual and emotional investigation.[13]

In *Guide to Kulchur*, too, quotations do not all *look the same*, but take different shapes and are harmonized in different ways into the final textual architecture. Pound juxtaposes summaries of philosophical texts, including a whole chapter on 'DIGEST OF THE ANALECTS, that is, of the Philosophic Conversation'; a few *verbatim* quotes carefully separated from the main text, complete with bibliographical references; and anonymous quotations disseminated through the text which the reader can recognize because they are presented in a different type or outline. At times, quotations are not so easy to recognize: as in the *Cantos*, sometimes they are blurred inside the text and remain in the reader's ear as a series of echoes and repetitions – semantic *déjà-vus* – whose origin is nevertheless lost. At other times, they are clearly pointed out by means of inverted commas, but there is no reference offered either inside the text or in a footnote. In such a prose, quotations become part of the new text, acknowledged as other people's words, but most readers have no clue who these other people are. Pound could have read those sentences in books, or he could have grasped them while strolling around a city: they constitute a sort of subtext of anonymous voices – a noisy crowd – to whom the writer ascribes authority. In other cases, the quotations are non-verbal icons, an ideogram or a series of ideograms, or musical scores. Altogether, these quotations constitute traces of a knowledge which is no longer based on a linear and ordered sequence, but on a mosaic of bits and pieces which are juxtaposed following the writer's reasoning; the page landscape is, in fact, discontinuous, acoustic, and musical.

McLuhan was particularly interested in Pound's formal experiments. He discussed Pound's paratactic strategies in several of his letters to Felix Giovanelli, insisting that Pound's prose was 'precise,' that it should be read 'very slowly.' He also insisted on the importance of trying to read all of what Pound mentions and quotes to fully understand his 'analogical ratio,' as well as his 'musical ratio.' McLuhan was quite fascinated by Pound's use and assemblage of quotations, and he poured over Pound's rhetorical strategy to the point of clearly distinguishing between Pound's and Eliot's rhetoric. Through their works, both poets had investigated forms of communication of their own times, suggesting strategies to cope with and understand mass culture; as true heirs of the symbolist poets, Pound and Eliot had further explored their discoveries.[14] However, Pound's prose and poetry are more vigorous than Eliot's, the tone being less elegant and flexuous, which is to say that Pound's rhetoric is less appealing than Eliot's. But it is equally effective. It is a quality that McLuhan recognizes when, commenting upon Pound's letters, he discusses how extraordinary Pound's prose is: the letters show Pound 'in action'; his sentences are shining antennas detecting old and new talents; he is always supportive of old and new friends, including Joyce, Eliot, and Lewis. Pound was both vigorous and generous as a man of letters, ahead of his time and even ahead of previous ages. It's a paradox which McLuhan uses to emphasize how essential Pound's prose was, so similar to the rough and harsh lines of Elizabethan prose, to the point that you could even imagine he was a master for Elizabethans, too.[15] In his criticism on Pound, McLuhan underlines the role of Pound as 'an influence': he is the writer who brought to England the Yankee's *know-how* and turned it into a happy marriage of business, technology, American pedagogy, and the muses. McLuhan considers Eliot's *The Waste Land*, the later Yeats, and Joyce's works, as well as the *Cantos*, as children of such a marriage; prophetically, in 1950 he wrote that it would take many years for us to fully understand and appreciate Pound's era. We are still working on it.

As 'the better craftsman,' Pound was a master of rhetoric for McLuhan, too. It is possible to argue that McLuhan was also particularly intrigued by Pound's textual use of quotations because of its being in line with new forms of communication now employed by people inhabiting the global village. In volumes such as *Guide to Kulchur* or *ABC of Reading*, the continuous flow of textual fragments – be they words, ideograms, or musical scores – epitomizes the electric *melopoeia*, the musical ratio of the electric age, in turn based on continuous flows of scattered bits of information which immediately become our own. *Guide to Kulchur* is intentionally conceived as a mosaic of voices we perceive simultaneously:

> There is no ownership in most of my statements and I can not interrupt every sentence or paragraph to attribute authorship to each pair of words, especially as there is seldom an a priori claim even to the phrase or half the phrase.[16]

Quotations are no longer delivered as authorial voices, but as a part of a polyphonic discourse including all voices at once. Pound does not see this as a negative condition; he does not interpret it as the loss of identity or of historicity (as Lewis, instead will do) because he is not interested in dates or chronology *per se*, but more in what might be defined as a historical grand narrative or process:

> Run your eye along the margin of history and you will observe great waves, sweeping movements and triumphs which fall when their ideology petrifies … Ideas petrify … Knowledge is or may be necessary to understanding, but it weighs as nothing against understanding, and there is not the least use or need of retaining it in the form of dead catalogues once you understand the process.[17]

If accompanied by dates, names, or chronologies, quotations petrify and turn into verbal fossils, death elements detached from all historical dynamics; in other words, they become sterile pieces of knowledge, useless samples of ideas which the progress of history has already made obsolete.

Instead, if quotations become parts of a new discourse, if they are blurred into new voices, they live again and acquire a renewed set of epistemological possibilities, therefore contributing to a real process of understanding.[18] It is a new approach to the historical sense which might raise different responses, especially in relation to the provocative idea of a 'dead catalogue.' And yet, what is interesting to notice in the above quote is the idea that to understand the process is more important than to memorize knowledge. It is a statement which also sounds like an implicit condemnation of a mere accumulation of learning, typical of too specialized educational systems. And it is a statement which works well also as an introduction to Marshall McLuhan's poetics, whose mosaic is structured upon complex fragments – his probes – conceived as cognitive weapons to counterattack accepted ideas. And what are, in such a context, accepted ideas if not another form of 'dead catalogues' petrifying not only thought but also people? You are reassured by shared clichés and content yourself with looking through the rear-view mirror of history and knowledge. Just like Pound's prose, McLuhan's mosaic attacks previous knowledge by employing that same previous knowledge in a different way: old learning is broken, and the resulting fragments become cognitive units of a new discourse whose progression leads to new learning. It's the awakening of the Mechanical Brides, his Guide to the Kulchur of Industrial Man.

The idea of New Learning also pervades Pound's *Guide to Kulchur*, it is in fact the term Pound uses to define his final educational goal, conveyed here through a typical avant-garde technique which turns apparently unrelated textual fragments into a learning process. The idea of New Learning is, in part, ironical and, in part, ambiguous, as it defines what seems to be new in the domain of culture, but also retrieves Renaissance and modern philosophical speculations. Pound's idea of New Learning, in fact, aims to translate the culture of his own consumerist time by playing with Bacon's (and also Vico's) idea of New Learning, which, in turn, was rooted in ancient educational dicta embedded in and delivered through a clearly theorized form (broken knowledge). Nothing could be more appealing for Marshall McLuhan, the professor of English and a devoted grammarian: Ezra Pound's prose showed him how to use mass media to employ *kulchur* to claborate *culture*. From Baedeker to Encyclopaedia; from Cliché to Archetype.

(Ideo)Grammatic Baedeker

It is easy to imagine the fascination of an idea such as New Learning for McLuhan embarked on his own search for a new form. His doctoral thesis, 'The Place of Thomas Nashe in the Learning of His Time,' had brought him to examine the ancient *paideia* and to investigate the role played by form in shaping and communicating thought through time. More specifically, McLuhan acknowledged that Bacon's broken knowledge, demanding deep participation, constitutes the basis for a real advancement of learning, the *new* learning. This same idea also pervades the structure of *Guide to Kulchur*, which was conceived in the late 1930s, at a time when the process of popularization of more traditional encyclopedic learning started. A certain idea of mass education was implicit in the increasing pedagogical use of mass media, which began to act as societal counter-forces to more traditional school systems, especially in North America. Inevitably, education was at the core of many intellectual and public discourses combining culture, politics, and the public sphere, so much so that new school programs, syllabuses, and educational priorities started to be envisaged for the citizens of the twentieth century, the new age. In other geographical realities, where TV became a mass commodity later than in North America, and where television was often in the hands of a public rather than a corporate agency, the contrast between education and mass media was originally not so strong; instead, the new medium was often conceived as a means to foster national values and traditions, including education, rather than as a means to homogenize thought to consumerist models. Such was the case, for instance, in Italy, where the first popular TV shows to be broadcast were a very entertaining quiz-show ('Lascia o Raddoppia' [Take It or Leave It]) and such educational programs as 'It's Never Too Late' and 'Television, the Good Teacher': in the 1950s and 1960s, TV became a virtual classroom uniting Italians from north to south, teaching them how to speak and write their national language, as well as how to 'feel' Italian through the sharing of national history, culture, folklore, and knowledge. Only in the 1980s, with the advent of private networks, did Italy begin to experience so-called 'commercial television.' From *Culture* to *Kulchur* was then, too, the new issue on my home front; today we are still bearing witness to the long-term consequences of that passage. Thirty years ago, we welcomed the new networks as agents liberating us from the decades of intellectual monopoly of our '*mamma TV*' ('mum TV,' that is, our national television, RAI TV); but we forgot that, today, *tyrants* have other ways to rule, and that they often act disguised as market researchers. As a crowd, we were gently shepherded in the 'ways of utility and comfort.' Paraphrasing both Ford Madox Ford and Marshall McLuhan – and, of course, Gustave Flaubert – I have to say that if Italians had read *The Mechanical Bride*, they might have been spared the horrors of Mr Berlusconi's (still the owner of the most popular Italian commercial TV channels) new politics and 'videocracy.'[19]

In 1946, McLuhan was already at the vanguard of this discussion. He wrote about old and new learning and about education in his famous essay 'An Ancient Quarrel in Modern America,'[20] later republished in *The Interior Landscape*. What he feared was the insistence on dialectic to the detriment of grammar as a main educational tenet in American schools, meaning by that the dismissal of an encyclopedic learning in favour of a too specialized and fragmented approach to knowledge. McLuhan saw this debate, which was splitting American academia into two main factions, as a reflection of the ancient dispute between Socrates and the sophists or, at a later period, between grammarians and dialecticians or logicians. It was McLuhan's opinion that only an integrated approach among the various areas of learning could educate and preserve people's critical attitude. The same idea is discussed in *The Mechanical Bride*, where chapters on 'Education,' 'Book of the Hours,' 'Plain Talk,' or 'The Great Book' deconstruct the *Reader's Digest* philosophy of selling predigested notions that are often detached from their original context.

The paradox, then, was that after the educational change, even though

the number of readers increased, the number of those who could truly engage with the complexity of their age decreased. The modernist
works provided a faithful, complex mirror of this situation, as both their
mythical and epical methods rely on the sharing of some traditional
learning for their full comprehension: modernist works appear as 'too
refined' to those readers whose education is based on accepted ideas
and not on broken knowledge. Counter to the new *kulchural* context,
the polysemic broken structure of many avant-garde experimental writings was perceived as elitist and arcane, when not judged as anti-masses
in ideological readings tout court. The new learning of the time relied
increasingly on the oversimplified language of advertising, based not on
aphorisms, but on slogans best fitted to the mode of quick communication produced by the new journalism, radio, pop magazines, and, later,
TV and digital media. It is the reverse of the process which symbolist
poets, and modernist writers such as Joyce and Pound, had pursued and
encouraged. They had tried to employ the new language of mass culture in a structural way, not only to render the spirit of their time, but
also to alert readers to the hidden pattern of forces working under the
opalescent surface of consumerist society. Pound's New Learning must
therefore reckon with an even newer reality in which culture has already
been turned into *kulchur* and has become one among the many goods
used to conquer or maintain consent. Not surprisingly, in our times the
idea of education, and also the broader one of culture, is at the centre
of new debates, often in relation to its ambiguous connection to forms
of political and media power. The term *kulchur*, which Pound uses to
epitomize the function of his guide, is therefore quite a revealing and
a provocative one; it expresses his understanding of the ongoing cultural processes, but ironically it also indicates the will of the poet to fully
explore and exploit both its limits and potentialities. It was a very good
model for McLuhan, too.

In particular, *Guide to Kulchur* stands as a sort of threshold book between old and new forms of learning, embedding the passage from an
old to a new way of understanding education. As McLuhan himself later
pointed out, whereas once education was perceived as a counter-environment to societal forces, it was now more and more part of the same cultural landscape. Pound's target readers are those inhabiting the consumer
society, which we would call today the mass audience of our global village.
The poet tries, ironically and even ambiguously, to educate by opposing
more traditional institutions and academies, which were encouraging an
over-specialized approach to knowledge. As he writes in his opening:

This book is not written for the over-fed. It is written for men who have or have not been able to afford a university education or for young men, whether or not threatened with universities, who want to know more at the age of fifty than I know today, and whom I might conceivably aid to that object.[21]

The volume is therefore structured as a refined cultural Baedeker embracing different realities, encompassing China, Europe, and America, and discussing such heterogeneous themes as Western and Eastern philosophy, literature, and music. Pound acts as a new pedagogue who wants to teach a broad audience in a non-conventional way. He is a pedagogue who, nevertheless, is 'fully aware of the dangers inherent in attempting such utility to them';[22] but also, he is a well-read teacher who knows how to handle both tradition and innovation. That is to say, he is a witty orator who knows how to convince, and how to use his tools to persuade. Pound was developing his own agenda as an engaged intellectual, unlike McLuhan in later years.

The term *New Learning* also reflects an idea of knowledge customized specifically for consumers inhabiting the evolving mass society. If the *Cantos* are the poetic exploration of the 'great technical possibilities of the cinematograph' and of popular genres (including the detective story), *Guide to Kulchur* is the ambiguous response to a mass society increasingly dominated by mass media. As such, it suggests strategies to understand, engage with, and even impact the new sensibility of his times. Thus, it is easy to see why McLuhan honed in on Pound's rhetorical strategies just as he, himself, was about to develop his own style as a new teacher facing the *kulchur* of the electric age. As a matter of fact, McLuhan's letters to Pound seem like a workshop where he discusses literature and the arts, but also a place to work out his own sensibility and the need to understand both cultural processes and the way to address them:

Basic modes of cognition on this continent are not linguistic but technological. Artistic experience comes to the young only via that channel. Must work with that *at first*. Present procedure is to slap an alien culture *over* the actual one. The real one is killed and the alien one is worn as a party mask. You and Eisenstein have shown me how to make use of the Chinese ideogram to elicit natural modes of American sensibility. But I've just begun. Feeling my way.[23]

As the quotation above clearly reveals, Pound helped McLuhan to better understand the potentialities of cultural interfacing, that is, the potentialities of that 'hybrid energy' that he will later and overtly discuss in the chapter on 'Hybrid Energy' in his *Understanding Media*. 'Les Liaisons Dangereuses' is the perfect subtitle to that chapter, because the overlapping of situations can lead to 'civil wars' now fought through media 'fission' or 'fusion.' Again: 'Today the tyrant rules not by club or fist, but disguised as a market researcher, he shepherds his flocks in the ways of utility and comfort.'[24] As Pound's *Guide to Kulchur* implicitly demonstrates, the trivialization of educational processes passes through new forms of communication, which also imply new possibilities for mass thought control. The word *Kulchur* is juxtaposed to the word *Culture*, to paradoxically point out that today's learning is increasingly a question of kitsch and received idea – Ong's commonplaces and clichés. Such a trendy, but ephemeral, *educational kit* is well suited to the interests of different political and economical forces. In this work, as well as in *The ABC of Reading*, Pound speculates on the side effects of this idea of *kulchur* on individuals and offers a vision of the patterns connecting mass society, public discourses, public spheres, art, and technology that is somehow similar to those provided by critics on the opposite side of the political spectrum, including, among others, those of the Frankfurt School.

Today, historical perspective helps us to see that, beginning in 1920s, intellectuals on both sides of the political spectrum began by sharing a similar, skeptical attitude towards the idea of progress induced through new forms of communication. Similarly, the ideas of *freedom* and of *modernity*, which often accompanied the promotion of new technologies and new cultural habits, were deconstructed by both right- and left-wing thinkers and artists, often presented in all their complexity as ideas propagated by cultural agencies affecting free will, critical attitudes, and knowledge. Right-wing or left-wing intellectuals and coalitions differed, not in the unveiling of the ongoing cultural and sociological processes, but in their responses to them. During the 1920s to late 1930s, these ideologies were tested and unfortunately imposed both in the Eastern and Western European realities by experimenting with the potentialities then offered by new media, radio and cinema *in primis*. Hitler, Mussolini, Franco, and Stalin ruled with clubs and fists, as well as with market researchers. Within this context, Ezra Pound took sides, as did many others; a few decades later, when living in an expanding consumerist society during the Cold War, McLuhan did not. Even in his private letters to Pound, he never touched on political or ideological issues; he referred only to cultural and literary matters. In particular, Pound's ideas of *kulchur/culture* as a situation pertaining to the way knowledge and education are conceived inside the information society, underpins

McLuhan's narrative in *The Mechanical Bride*, as well as the narratives in several of the volumes that McLuhan wrote in the 1960s and early 1970s. *From Cliché to Archetype* (1970) is a clear example of the way he questioned the making of commonplaces in contemporary society, the way language embeds and mirrors specific cultural processes which, in turn, are strongly related to a broader and more complex societal dynamic. As previously suggested, here McLuhan aimed to move backwards, from *kulchur* to *culture*.

At the same time, Pound's ideogrammatic prose showed McLuhan a technique he could use to implement a new discourse combining literature, art, and popular forms of communication in order to bring together inner and outer landscapes (integral awareness). As will later be the case in McLuhan's mosaic, Pound's form of writing in *Guide to Kulchur* is disconcerting for many readers due to the bold process of association of heterogeneous materials, which might seem to result in nonsensical prose; the 'nonsensical' juxtaposition, which is accepted as a fundamental process in his poetry, is perceived as odd in his criticism and prose books. But this was, in fact, Pound's language, his way to look through his own times. Pound transcended the linearity of the printed page even in his private correspondence. He juxtaposes different forms, whose overall effect gives volume and movement to the flattened surface. The different forms are combined not only to create a truly avant-garde artistic or playful effect, but also to design a new form of writing able to immediately render the new inclusive spirit of the times.

Pound creates iconic pages aiming to convey the new 'acoustic space' that the new research in the fields of both physics and applied technologies of long-distance communication was exploring.[25] As we now know, simultaneity is what characterizes such a space, as well as inclusion, lack of hierarchical perspective (centre vs. margin logic), and the relativity of vanishing points. It is a space which can be translated only through discontinuity, by forever reconsidering all previous canons no longer in tune with the new sensibility. It is an extremely complex concept which Pound tries to mediate to his readers because he is aware of the cognitive dichotomy existing between a traditional form of communication and his own new form. To explain the formal novelty of his work, he nevertheless employs an analogy which immediately reveals the ambiguous interplay of formal epistemological investigation and popular forms of communication – as well as his intention to work out new rhetorical models that are also performative of the new 'sensibility':

The hurried reader may say I write this in cipher and that my statement merely skips from one point to another without connection or sequence. The statement is nevertheless complete. All the elements are there, and the nastiest addict of crossword puzzles shd. be able to solve this or see this.[26]

Pound compares his new form to crosswords – a verbal game featured in most popular magazines, as well as newspapers – suggesting that his ideogrammatic method also mirrors what he ironically sees as being the new *forma mentis* of most hurried readers. His analogy relates to a popular form which is also interactive and often perceived as a way to train or test the player's wit, memory, and knowledge. The world is moving fast and so are educational processes; *kulchur* is the product of such an acceleration. Pound goes on to suggest that his method can lead to new epiphanies precisely because of the principle of juxtaposition: in the scheme of crossword puzzles, the various terms overlap in a way which makes each of them a part of the other, thereby revealing unexpected conjunctions and similarities (semantic, playful, phonetic). Similarly, in the ideogrammatic method, the uncanny association of different concepts reveals unexpected epiphanies and new learning:

> At last a reviewer in a popular paper (or at least one with immense circulation) has had the decency to admit that I occasionally cause the reader 'suddenly to see' or that I snap out a remark ... 'that reveals the whole subject from a new angle.'
>
> That being the point of writing. That being the reason for presenting first one facet then another – I mean to say the purpose of the writing is to reveal the subject. The ideogrammatic method consists of presenting one facet and then another until at some point one gets off the dead and desensitised surface of the reader's mind, onto a part that will register.[27]

Pound is ironically explicit about what he is pursuing, about the technique he is employing. What he is, in fact, doing in this volume – something that McLuhan acknowledges in his letters as a main feature of all Pound's works – is translating one cultural situation into the other, his own *culture* guiding him and his readers to the new *kulchur*: hybrid energy, les liaisons dangereuses. This is precisely what McLuhan will do later in *The Mechanical Bride*, where he juxtaposes the new pop culture and the ancient humanist tradition; the meeting of two different cultural situations enhances mutual understanding and designs new creative aperçus on society. As he will later recall, the act of translation (be it linguistic or cultural) is a powerful and creative act having a great potential. It is a lesson he learned from *il miglior fabbro* himself:

The main advantage in translation is the creative effort it fosters, as Ezra Pound spent his life in telling and illustrating. And culture that is engaged in translating itself from one radical mode such as the auditory, into another mode like the visual, is bound to be in a creative ferment, as was classical Greece or the Renaissance. But our own time is an even more massive instance of such ferment, and just because of such translation.[28]

As a cultural translator, Pound had investigated the Chinese form of writing as a medium for his own poetry; his one-image poems are phonetic renderings which rely on ideogrammatic techniques to convey multiple perceptions all at once. Both structure and language are reconceptualized so as to overcome the limits of Western literacy. McLuhan recalls Pound's cultural translations and experiments in several of his later books, and especially in *Through the Vanishing Point* when discussing the different idea of space in the Western and Eastern traditions:

> 'The apparition of these faces in the crowd;
> Petals on a wet, black bough.'
> Ezra Pound

Earl Miner quotes Pound's accounts of the origin of his 'hokku-like sentence':

'Three years ago [1911] in Paris I got out of a metro train at La Concorde, and saw suddenly a beautiful face and another and another ... and tried all day for words for what that had meant for me ... And that evening ... I found suddenly the expression ... not in speech, but in sudden splotches of colour. It was just that – a pattern, if by pattern you mean something with a repeat in it. But it was a word, the beginning of a new language in colour.'

Pound observes further:

'The Japanese have the same sense of exploration. They have understood the beauty of this kind [i.e., 'imagistic' as opposed to 'lyric' writing] ... The Japanese have evolved the form of the hokku.

> The fallen blossom flies back to its branch:
> A butterfly.

That is the substance of a very well-known hokku ...
The one image poem is a form of super-position; that is to say one idea set

on top of another. I found it useful for getting out of the impasse left by my metro emotion.'[29]

The new form is a matter of super-position of ideas which are all present at once in the poet's mind and which cannot but be translated through analogies and parataxis. What McLuhan's recollection emphasizes is precisely the creativity deriving from cultural cross-pollination in unexpected and therefore surprising ways. Today, we call this serendipity, something which his mosaic aims to encourage.

Totalitarian Craft?

McLuhan called himself an explorer who was consciously adopting a mobile point of view on the new media and societal situations he was investigating, whereas Pound was named by Eliot *il miglior fabbro*, a conscious craftsman who, as we know and as he wrote, had a clear intent which he pursued through his art. Pound was not a neutral media theorist; he used media as a model to develop a style, and as a propaganda tool for his ideas on art and society. In *Guide to Kulchur*, he is quite explicit about his goal as he openly declares that his intent is to contribute to the education of contemporary men. In the light of such a statement, we must ask ourselves if the use of quotations in *Guide to Kulchur* is simply a strategy to disseminate and popularize knowledge of cultural and historical processes, or if there is something more that we should be aware of. In other words, in addition to the *poetical* use of quotations, is there an *ideological* use of quotations in *Guide to Kulchur*, especially if we consider that it was conceived in Italy in the 1930s?[30] We could, in fact, reverse the pattern and read *Guide to Kulchur* not only as an attack on, but also as an exploitation of, the *Reader's Digest* philosophy, written by an author pursuing an agenda and taking advantage of established educational agencies through an uncanny combination of ancient knowledge and mass-media communicative strategies. Such a reversal does not work for McLuhan's *The Mechanical Bride*.

What complicates any interpretation of *Guide to Kulchur* is the context of its writing. When writing it, Pound had openly taken sides in favour of Gesell's economic view and Mussolini's fascism, combining his aesthetic search with his ethical and societal vision. A few years later, during the period 1940–3, he broadcast for Italian fascist radio, exalting the leadership of Mussolini while defending his own economic creeds.[31] An uncanny sentence written by Pound in the initial pages of *Guide to*

Kulchur seems to suggest a precise correspondence between his artistic search and the will to educate his readers not only to *kulchur* but also to his own creeds. He defines his book as a *totalitarian treatise*:

> I suggest that finer and future critics of art will be able to tell from the quality of a painting the degree of tolerance or intolerance of usury extant in the age and milieu that produce it. That perhaps is the first clue the reader has had that these are notes for a totalitarian treatise and that I am in fact considering the New Learning or the New Paideuma ... not simply abridging extant encyclopaedias or condensing two dozen more detailed volumes.[32]

The intention is revealed: the rhetorician is acting in a conscious way, directly engaging his readers. The adjective *totalitarian* acquires quite a sinister nuance if we set it against fascist Italy. We could assume that Pound uses his new form and new learning as a strategy of persuasion, which can also be interpreted as a refined form of propaganda of a totalitarian (absolutist) ideology, in part his own (Pound's economic theories against usury) and in part corporate (inscribed in a new societal order that, at the time, Pound unfortunately found in the totalitarian vision of the fascist regime). To juxtapose figure (Pound's works of the 1930s) and ground (the related historical, political, and cultural setting) also means to speculate upon the complex relation between ideologies, on the one hand, and literary and artistic forms, on the other, especially regarding the idea of propaganda. The use of broken quotations can be inscribed inside a more or less explicit ideological discourse, which therefore conveys a different and uncanny interpretation to Pound's idea of knowledge as dead catalogues, as discussed before. His 'anonymous' grand historical narrative, in fact, appears as an ideogrammatic form of propaganda, which begins with an accurate selection of the voices to employ, and which blurs well-learned traditions (the authorial voice which gives credibility to the statement); the goal is to develop a form which aims at creating consent through strategies also borrowed from new forms of (mass) communication (the authorial voice becomes *vox populi* and turns into a cliché or a corporate slogan having a great cohesive strength). As Morawski clearly indicated:

> Quotations accumulate in art when the boundaries between it and other forms of social conscious become muddied ... Ideologies incessantly invoke their past and deliberately emphasize this lifetime. Without it ideology

would be hollow. In any case it looks for antecedents in even earlier ideologies if it wants to win over adherents.[33]

What is common in all ages was even more so in the 1930s, when quotations retrieving corporate values were turned into slogans, which then became the language also spoken by almost all governments, whether of free countries or those ruled by totalitarian regimes. Circulated inside a mass society, as well as inside a totalitarian one, slogans are offered as shared truths, parts of a cultural heritage, used to either comfort or homogenize people and, in time, acquiring an unquestioned authority.

Pound's text stands as an uncanny threshold where artistic and literary explorations cross into sociological and media domains in a way previously unknown, now inscribed in a newly progressing mass society. In the second half of the twentieth century, the correspondence between art, power, and subliminal forms of mass control through media became even more complex and ambiguous; as a response, most media studies became political. McLuhan did not follow suit, at least not overtly. He continuously warned of the risk of extending our consciousness to the computer world, alerting people to the mounting unperceived strategies of thought homologation and hypnosis. He wrote that 'only the dedicated artist seems to have the power for encountering the present actuality.'[34] However, what happens when the antennas of the race themselves use their artistic knowledge to persuade? For a brief moment, McLuhan took a risk by writing *The Mechanical Bride*, because he was somehow taking a side. But then he shifted his focus and became not a media ideologue but a media theorist or 'scientist.' Why? Because McLuhan decided to develop his own original form of exploration, one that would lead each of us to understanding the immediate, as well as the long-term, effects of evolving mediascapes. He showed us the moon beyond the finger, the water in which a fish swims, the reflecting phenomenon in which both the mirror and the individual are actors. He invited us to join him and become explorers ourselves. The medium is the user. He was forever grateful to Pound's formal lesson, but he was far removed from his cantankerous agendas.

12 Wyndham Lewis: Blasting Time, Blessing Space

A Proto-postmodernist

Ezra Pound's New Learning introduces the question of new forms of (subliminal) mass control; the works of Wyndham Lewis introduce a sharp critique of consumerist society, combined with a deep understanding of the impact of new forms of communication and technological industrialization on societal matrixes. They provide us with an opportunity to discuss the origin of concepts which will later be found in Marshall McLuhan's works on media – including such ideas as the global village, the artist as a satirist pointing to unseen aspects of society, and primitivism or the new tribalism – as well as the impact of Vorticism on McLuhan's mosaic. Although McLuhan read Lewis's works in the 1930s, together with those of the other modernist writers, and even though he met Lewis before Pound, in McLuhan's evolutionary process as a media theorist, Lewis's influence comes later.

If modernism can be summed up as 'The Pound Era,' then postmodernism could already be envisaged in most of Lewis's works. The fact that Lewis died in 1957 does theoretically disqualify him as a true postmodernist, but his literary and philosophical themes reveal a *proto-postmodernist*, an oxymoronic and a paradoxical definition which might have pleased him. He was, in fact, the master of different causes and counter-causes, the enemy par excellence of whatever was at stake, yet always with some credibility. Wyndham Lewis himself is a paradox but not an inconsistency. Lewis – as an individual, as an artist, and as a writer – seems to prove one of McLuhan's Laws of Media: whatever is pushed to its extreme flips into its reverse. Wyndham Lewis always had a fierce (if not violent) approach to whatever he did, wrote, or painted, always pushing it to its extreme. He flipped into many reversals, and he forces his critics and readers to cope with an evident difficulty of stabilizing their object and subject of observation, another tenet typical of postmodernism. Wyndham Lewis was 'at the same time the exemplary practitioner of one of the most powerful of all modernist styles and an aggressive ideological critic and an adversary of modernism itself in all its forms.'[1] He was too many things at once: a post-impressionist and an expressionist; an admirer of classicist rigours and an exploiter of Romantic wordiness; a man aware of history while theorizing the a-historicity of his own time ... and much more.

In 1979, Fredric Jameson brought Lewis back to the critics' attention with a controversial volume, acknowledging that he had been 'among the most richly inventive of modern British writers,' whose works merited 'unapologetic rediscovery and [could] sustain enthusiastic reading as well as the closest critical scrutiny.'[2] Since then, Lewis has received much-needed renewed attention, especially from critics such as Paul Edwards, C.J. Fox, Alan Munton, Andrzej Gasiorek, and Brett Neilson; nevertheless, there is still a lot of room left to situate him against the background of the twentieth century. Lewis is an artist who bore witness to the making of that century, cutting across crucial decades and perceiving most of it – and all before his death in the mid-1950s. The intent of this brief chapter is to place Lewis and his works within McLuhan's progress as a media explorer. It is just a tiny drop in a vast sea which, hopefully, will be navigated later. Whoever takes on this venture must know from the beginning that it will be a troubled journey into difficult questions – including racism and sexism – which have characterized the history of our previous century. As Jameson warned, 'The polemic hostility to feminism, the uglier misogynist fantasies embodied in his narratives, the obsessive phobia against homosexuals, the most extreme restatements of grotesque traditional sexist myths and attitudes – such features, released by Lewis' peculiar sexual politics ... are not likely to endear him to the contemporary reader.'[3] And neither does his 'brief flirtation with Nazism,' nor the elements of anti-Semitism that could be detected in his works. But all this, too, was the twentieth century; wasn't it? As McLuhan noticed: 'Lewis pleases nobody because he is like an intruder at a feast who quietly explains that dinner must be temporarily abandoned since the food has been poisoned and the guests must be detached from their dinners by a stomach pump.'[4]

Technically, Lewis was not a British, but a Canadian, writer, born on his father's yacht off the coast of Nova Scotia. It was precisely because of his

Canadian citizenship that McLuhan could meet the old lion of the right who was in North America when the Second World War was declared and could not return to England, the country where he had grown as an individual and as an artist and where he had established himself. Typical of Lewis, while in Canada he put on a mask and considered himself, together with his wife, Froanna, a *prisoner*. McLuhan met him in 1943, when Lewis lived in Toronto and taught in Windsor, where he lectured at what was at the time Assumption College.[5] Lewis's Canadian experience is controversially recalled in his semi-autobiographical (and *proto-postmodernist*) novel *Self Condemned* (1954), a novel which McLuhan quotes in the opening of his own *Counterblast*, a pamphlet written in the same year and conceived in Lewis's vorticist style to discuss 'Media Log.' Momaco, Lewis's fictionalized Toronto, is selected as the setting for what Lewis perceived as the ultimate unfortunate and mortal condition of a hyper-industrialized and culturally numbed mass society. His protagonist, René Harding, is born twice in the novel, as his name reveals, and each of his choices bears witness to his own trajectory as an individual living our modern times. As we shall see, René is in fact born first as a Nietzschean superman who challenges society and its established rules, then as a new kind of contemporary *everyman* inhabiting North American cities. After a rebellion against his professorial life in England and an escape to Canada, because he has to go 'somewhere out of sight of what is going to happen,' René will end his career as a university professor at an American university. He will adjust to the world-consumerist culture which Lewis often attacked in his philosophical prose, *The Art of Being Ruled* and *Time and Western Man*, in his fictional works, as well as in his memoirs, *Filibuster in Barbary*, *America I Presume*, and others. In such a consumerist world, human beings lose their personality and are forced to conform to commonly accepted ideas. They are portrayed by Lewis as empty masks or straw men. As early as 1914, he wrote: 'Men have a loathsome deformity called self; affliction got through indiscriminate rubbing against their fellows: social excrescence. Their being regulated by exigencies of this affliction. Only one operation can cure it: the suicide's knife.'[6] In reacting to such a numbness-inducing form of corporatism – for which new media were deemed to be in part responsible – the artist becomes the enemy of all accepted ideas; he becomes a self-displaced human being, a permanent 'transient' who counterattacks *kulchur* through ruthless satire.

Lewis had already started to dynamite straw men in 1914 and 1915, in the two issues of his avant-garde little magazine, *Blast*. It was the beginning, and he never stopped. In his inter-war productions, Lewis engaged with his time as if trying to affect and orient change, but in his later works, published after the Second World War, he seems to have lost all hope, even though he continues to denounce and attack the straw men's society. McLuhan met Lewis when he was already a bitter *enemy*, aware that to resist or direct change was no longer possible, if it ever was. As his post–Second World War fiction shows, all he could do was to continue to satirize the end of the individual and denounce the triumph of the corporate. In 1943, Lewis was a *self-displaced man*, a version of the enemy already in line with the postmodernist spirit of a 'deliberate refusal to resolve contradictions.'[7] Thus, while in Toronto, Lewis embodied not only the late modernist artist, but also the new postmodernist one. He was an outcast, a self-displaced individual bearing witness to the making of a mass society which he despised but borrowed from; he was also an *adjustee*, who tried to negotiate through irony, parody, and sarcasm 'the contradictions between [his] self-reflexivity and its historical grounding.'[8] As McLuhan wrote in *Counterblast*, 'In 1954 Wyndham Lewis blasted Toronto in the novel SELF CONDEMNED. His René (reborn) seeking his true spiritual self selects Toronto, Momaco: (Mom & Co) as a colonial cyclotron in which to annihilate his human ego. He succeeds.' On the contrary, as McLuhan would discover, Lewis did not annihilate himself; he preserved his *loathsome deformity*.

From Time to Space

After their first meeting, McLuhan engaged in a correspondence with Lewis that was mostly focused on his attempts to secure Lewis lectures and commissions for portrait paintings in St Louis, where McLuhan was teaching at the time. Generally speaking, this correspondence sheds light neither on McLuhan's intellectual take on Lewis nor on his works (as was the case of his correspondence with Pound), but it shows McLuhan's great admiration for Lewis as a portrait painter. Away from his mission as a Lewis promoter, McLuhan writes his letters in a style which resembles Lewis's own histrionic tone. He also seems to share some of Lewis's ideas on both Canada and the new role of the intellectual in the mass age, of which Lewis had written in *Time and Western Man* when discussing advertising. In the 1930s, in his letters to his family written from Cambridge, McLuhan had condemned Canadian sterility; in the 1940s, in his letters to Lewis, he further expands his criticism, writing passages like: 'Oh the mental vacuum that is Canada ... There is terrible social cowardice, and all action here seems so furtive that one can only conclude that some unacknowledged guilt is behind it all.'[9] McLuhan's statement recalls comparable comments which Lewis made in his essays on Canada.[10] Similarly, in other letters to Lewis, McLuhan expresses unsparingly ironical remarks on colleagues and other intellectuals such as Maritain,[11] as well as his discontent related to his life as a professor, as when he comments on the 'campaign of attrition against' him at St Louis University following the arrival of a new department head. He is sharing his own *blasts* with *the enemy* himself.[12] As with Pound, McLuhan mimics the style of his favourite modernist masters as if trying *to tune in* or *put them on*. It is, in fact, as if he is studying and testing their style, while searching for his own. After all, McLuhan openly admitted to Lewis that the writer 'had been, for years before [he] met [him], a major resource in [his] life.'[13]

More central to the understanding of the development of McLuhan as a media theorist are the letters that he wrote to Lewis in the early 1950s, when they resumed their correspondence after a few-year break following an impromptu outburst of Lewis against his Canadian friend. As the editors of McLuhan's letters recall, in February 1945 Lewis wrote a brief letter to McLuhan harshly rejecting his friendship for no clear reasons; the correspondence between the two men resumed in 1953.[14] In particular, in his later letters, McLuhan comments positively on some of Lewis's most recent publications, such as *Rude Assignment, Rotting Hill, The Writer and the Absolute*, and *The Human Age*. He also informs Lewis that he has written an essay discussing his theory of art and communication '*mainly in your own words.*'[15] McLuhan's essay was in fact a witty assemblage of Lewis's quotations taken from his various works (*The Lion and the Fox, America and Cosmic Man, Wyndham Lewis the Artist*) and introducing ideas on the role of the artist in a shifting technological society.

The essay bore the title 'Wyndham Lewis: His Theory of Art and Communication'; it was originally printed in *Shenandoah* in 1953, then reprinted in *The Interior Landscape*. It remains a crucial passage for fully appreciating not only McLuhan's approach to Lewis's work, but also the former's view on media in the light of the latter's ideas on art. McLuhan points out that Lewis 'took America as the laboratory in which was being produced the new ahistoric man,'[16] juxtaposing the role that the artist, on the one hand, and the modern scientist, on the other, plays inside such a new laboratory. While the former monitors society and enlightens on 'a particular aspect of existence,' the latter 'has developed formulas for the control of the material world and then applied this to the control of the human mind. He invades the human mind and society with his patterned information. That is the key to the nature of the new mass media.'[17] It is a statement which recalls McLuhan's denunciation in his preface to *The Mechanical Bride*, a book that McLuhan wrote following Lewis's lesson, as he clearly acknowledges in his correspondence: 'As for my book. It owes much to you of course.'[18] It was a debt which McLuhan had already confessed to Ezra Pound shortly before the volume was released.[19] As recalled in McLuhan's *Letters*, 'Part III of Lewis's *The Doom of Youth* (1932) contains a "Gallery of Exhibits" made up of newspaper headlines and extracts, with comments by Lewis ... that prefigures McLuhan's treatment of advertisements and other examples of popular culture in *The Mechanical Bride*. Lewis discusses advertising – "The spirit of advertisement and boost lives and has its feverish being in a world of hyperbolic suggestions" – in Book I, Chapter II of *Time and Western Man* (1928).'[20] It is an important reference; and yet McLuhan's debt to Lewis in *The Mechanical Bride* does not simply concern his treatment of popular culture and ads, but it also relates to McLuhan's understanding of Lewis's original aesthetic, which the writer theorized in *Time and Western Man* in terms of a new *spatial philosophy*. It is a 'philosophy of the eye' which 'attaches itself to that concrete and radiant reality of the optic sense'[21] but which is not conceived as a return to previous mechanical approaches to space; instead, it is conceived in an effort to retrieve a lost sensory balance induced by an excessive emphasis on time. Lewis blamed Bergsonism as the main cause for corporate hypnosis. By privileging *intensity* over *extension*, Bergson's time philosophy relied exclusively on the *sensa* world which Lewis defines as the 'world of the Unconscious or automatic in the sense':

> It is our contention here that *it is because of the subjective disunity due to the separation, or separate treatment, of the senses, principally of sight and of touch, that the external disunity has been achieved.* It is but another case of the *morcellement* of the *one* personality, in this case into a tactile-observer on the one hand and a visual-observer on the other, giving different renderings of the same thing ...

> So what we seek to stimulate, and what we give the critical outline of, is a philosophy that will be as much a *spatial philosophy*, as Bergson's is a *time-philosophy* ... The interpretation of the ancient problems of space and time that consists in amalgamating them into space-time is for us, then, no solution. For, to start with, space-time is no more real, but if anything a little less

real, in our view, than Space and Time separately. The wedding of these two abstractions results, we believe … in the ascendancy of Time … over Space: and of the two, if we have any preference, it is for Space; for Space keeps still, at least is not (ideally) occupied in incessantly slipping away, melting into the next thing, and repudiating its integrity.[22]

Time philosophy is the consequence of an abstracted sensory imbalance against which Lewis retrieves space as a matter-of-fact concept also embedding the empirical, historical, and social dimensions. As noted by critic Brett Neilson: "Since *Time and Western Man,* Lewis extended his notion of space so as to explore the implications following the multiplications of transnational fluxes, as well as the relationships between local and global. Lewis's analysis of space-time relations, of technological processes and of intercultural exchanges, theorised globalisation as a trend leading to cultural and social homogenization.' In *Time and Western Man,* he writes about a '"mercurial spreading-out in time," of an "overriding of place," of the annihilation of space which threaten to establish a "oneness," that is, a global uniqueness.'[23] To counterbalance such 'mercurial spreading-out in time' is the task of the artist, whose work must provide 'the experience of arrest' inducing consciousness.

Lewis was a constant case study for McLuhan, and a case study that he often discussed with Canadian writer Sheila Watson, who had written a doctoral dissertation entitled 'Wyndham Lewis: Post Expressionist' under McLuhan's supervision. As their correspondence reveals, discussing and assessing Lewis's poetics, his operative project, and his original form was a way to explore how to translate the new audile/tactile sensibility of their own time.[24] In particular, McLuhan's understanding of Lewis's vorticist aesthetic emphasizes precisely this counterbalancing of space over time:

> But it is important for an understanding of his vortex view of art and civilization to notice his insistence that the world of Space as opposed to the world of memory and history is the world of a 'pure Present.' 'The world of the "pure Present" of the Classical Ages is obviously the world that is born and dies every moment' … That is, the moment of art is not a moment of time's covenant. And art emotion is specifically that experience of arrest in which we pause before a particular thing or experience.[25]

Lewis's *vortex* is not conceived as a *flux,* but as a dynamic, progressive, moving image related to time but also containing a stable point, the spatial element from which its energy spirals originate. In Lewis's aesthetic metaphor, the stable point represents an original viewpoint from which the observer can finally embrace both dynamism and its causes. The epiphany follows the perception of something which is arrested briefly while progressing: the ensuing snapshot will inevitably emphasize the grotesque of a situation, which such an imposed pause alters and distorts. But it is precisely the distorted perspective which brings new light to the whole process and interrupts the otherwise reassuring and hypnotic flux.

Experiencing Arrest

Vorticist art retrieves extension over intensity and recreates the ground that reassesses all figures. It is a strategy that also offers McLuhan a model for his critical evaluation of society at a time when, as he theorized, our planet has been turned into a man-made artefact by media and technological discoveries and applications. It can therefore also become a way to arrest and reassess the overwhelming flow of information. McLuhan attempts this in his *Mechanical Bride*, as he clearly states in the preface: his strategy is to arrest the numbing flux by pausing before a series of specific mass icons and mass experiences that represent the 'Folklore of Industrial Man.' The pieces are no longer offered as reassuring components of a harmonious and homogeneous ground; instead, they have become grotesque masks distorting reality and returning it to hypocrisies and ambiguities. Following Lewis's aesthetic, McLuhan's *Mechanical Bride* becomes a troublesome mosaic, more than simply a new type of science fiction or a contemporary epic. As previously suggested in the chapters on Joyce and Pound, *The Mechanical Bride* becomes, in fact, a grotesque satire of mass media actuality. It wants 'the public to observe the drama which is intended to operate upon it unconsciously.'[26] From Lewis, McLuhan has learned how to reinterpret reality, combining so-called high and low forms of communication through a vigorous use of satire which should not only contribute to the preservation of the individual's self, but also counterbalance the overriding of various time philosophies prevailing in the literary and artistic domains.

The technique to experience the arrest is something McLuhan also relates to Edgar Allan Poe's detective stories. In *Counterblast*, Poe is defined by McLuhan as 'a press man and ... a science fictioner' whose technique is introduced as a derivative of the new technological culture;[27] as such, it is therefore possible to counter-use that rhetorical strategy to reverse the numbing process enacted by the masterminds, the market researchers, of the new mass age. Not by chance is Poe's 'A Descent into the Maelstrom' quoted in McLuhan's preface to his first book. In that short story, the mariner saves himself because he *stops* to observe the movement; his vision is therefore the consequence of a *conscious moment of arrest* which makes him see through the vortex flux. The mariner is inside the situation; he does not try to avoid it. And yet, as an insider, he *stops* and *plays with* it. Only later will he re-enter the vortex flux (time), but in the wake of a new environmental (spatial) consciousness. His epiphany follows his voluntary suspension from time through space, which also proves to be amusing in spite of the extremely dangerous situation. Or, precisely, because of that.

Amusement is also a key word inside a consumerist society: entertainment is, in fact, both an industry and a strategy to win consent and to 'keep everybody in the helpless state engendered by prolonged mental rutting ... '[28] McLuhan also discusses amusement in *The Mechanical Bride*, where he develops a use of the comic element which resembles more the one suggested by Lewis than the one theorized by Bergson.[29] He decides to use both humour and verbal playfulness as key strategies in his mosaic. As he clearly points out in his essay on Lewis, the French philosopher and the Canadian-born writer developed two opposing ideas of *laughter* and of the *comic*, as if suggesting the impossibility of a reconciliation between their different philosophies of life, time, and space. Whereas Bergson sees the roots of the comic in the fact that it 'does not exist outside the pale of what is strictly HUMAN,'[30] for Lewis 'the root of the comic is to be sought in the sensation resulting from the observations of a *thing* behaving like a person.'[31] Consistently, not only the root but also the aim of laughter differs in Bergson's and in Lewis's visions.[32] Contrary to what Bergson theorized, for Lewis the comic is not a strategy to enact social punishment employed by a community to exorcize and rectify a series of attitudes perceived to be in contrast with the *élan vital,* which, in Bergson's theory, stands for life itself. For Lewis, the comic does not restore a lost order or social harmony; quite the opposite, laughter has a *satanic* implication used to unmask the vacuum of *élan vital* itself, which Lewis sees as something inscribed inside an empty world dominated by a vulgarized science which 'makes us *strangers* to ourselves ... It instils a principle of impersonality in the heart of our life that is anti-vital.'[33] According to Lewis, the 'evolution of our machines' has deprived human beings of their personality, of their humanity; they are, in fact, things which try to behave like people. Thus, humans appear as empty puppets, zombies. Laughter is what comes out of such a sad situation, an epiphanic outburst which does not consolidate but compromises societal cohesion: 'No man has ever continued to live who has observed himself in that manner for longer than a flash. Such consciousness must be of the nature of a thunderbolt. Laughter is only summerlightening. But it occasionally takes on the dangerous form of absolute revelation.'[34] The tragic element of Lewis's grotesque humanity consists in the fact that, after the laughter, after the revelation, it is no longer possible to return to the previous condition: madness or submission is the only possible solution. Hence, McLuhan sees Lewis as 'a mystic or visionary of the comic, moving toward the pole of intelligibility instead of that of feeling.'[35] Lewis's grotesque laughter is as uncanny as it is revelatory; it is a type of amusement which has no moral pretence but which captures new environmental processes precisely through a defamiliarization of well-established behaviours.

In *The Mechanical Bride*, McLuhan develops a similar attitude to laughter and amusement: 'Many who are accustomed to the note of moral indignation will mistake this amusement for mere indifference. But the time for anger and protest is in the early stages of a new process. The present stage is extremely advanced. Moreover, it is full, not only of destructiveness but also of promises of rich new developments to which moral indignation is a very poor guide.'[36] In this book, amusement derives from a satirical mosaic-like rendering of defamiliarized mass icons which behave like people but which are in fact puppets controlled by 'the best-trained individual minds' of their times. Such a rendering owes much to Lewis, especially if we read its cumulative final effect as a grotesque expressionist landscape recreating satanic versions of our reality. Uncanny details are amplified, and reality is recreated by subsequent visions which arrest time and turn it into 'pure Present': such a grotesque *extension* of reality arrests it, halts its *intensity*, and makes us readers 'see' inside the flux because, for a few moments, space wins over time. McLuhan's *Mechanical Bride* consists of a series of decontextualized visual blasts, which are juxtaposed in an expressionist collage that reveals aspects of the folklore of the industrial man that individuals cannot see because they are too much in love with or dependent upon that very lore. It's McLuhan's mode of alerting the straw men of his times.

Counterblastings

McLuhan considered Lewis's works instrumental to his explorations of communication in culture and technology. Lewis's spatial philosophy, which considers art as 'that experience of arrest in which we pause before a particular thing,' offers McLuhan a conceptual form of writing which is designed, not as a flow, but as a mosaic, that is, as a juxtaposition of pauses or intervals in turn blasting the numbing acceptance of actuality. McLuhan links Lewis's work explicitly to his media studies, as he writes in the letter announcing his new role as the chairman of a Ford Foundation project dedicated to the study of culture and communication;[37] he tells Lewis that his books are 'indispensable' to achieving that study, because his research group is split over time and space, including both 'vertical and horizontal doctrinaires.'[38] It is a letter which bears witness not only to McLuhan's shift to media studies, but also to his own original approach. It confirms that he did not enter media studies through a side door, since as a professor of literature he had always been working on and with writers whose aesthetics were in fact deeply pervaded by new media. Ford, Joyce, Pound, and Lewis were constantly engaging with their societal and cultural processes to the point that their works of art can be used as modern tools of illumination (both in content and through structure). As a modernist scholar, McLuhan always considered Lewis's productions as counter-environments determined to detect and express cultural and technological change. McLuhan found, in the case of Wyndham Lewis, a number of ideas which would later prove to be crucial tenets of his own media analysis. For instance, Lewis provided McLuhan with a metaphor for the new depth-involving newness: the global village.

. It was in fact Lewis who, as early as 1929, wrote that 'the Earth has become ONE place instead of a romantic tribal patch work of places.'[39] In Lewis's analysis, such a place is mutually modelled by new media, new social actors, a new idea of art, industrialism, and politics; these are in fact understood as forces which determine culture and condition society (*The Art of Being Ruled*, 1926; *Time and Western Man*, 1927). In Lewis's writing, such an idea translates both a new environmental situation and a political take on his actuality: on the one hand, to think of the Earth as ONE place is a way to translate the shrinking imposed by new media on the environment;[40] on the other hand, it translates Lewis's idea of a 'new kind of universalism.' He was convinced that 'the machine age has made nonsense of nationalism.'[41] Thus, Lewis overcomes both the Joycean mythography and the Poundian epic: history and actuality are in fact the foundational paradigms for understanding his works. Lewis's artist must live in his own time fully; he must awaken in the *here and now*, avoiding escape into an emotional flow which only serves to preserve a sentimental approach to situations. Consistently, history and actuality play a major role in all his novels, and especially in his *Self Condemned,* whose main character, René Harding, is a professor of history who can no longer teach this subject because he no longer conforms to the institutionalized (or homogenized) epistemic approach encouraged by his home university.[42] After the writing of his controversial volume *The Secret History of World War II,* René Harding leaves England for Canada. North America is, in fact, the continent of the new civilization which Lewis opposed to the old one of Europe, a juxtaposition which enabled Lewis to enlighten both positive and negative aspects of such a civilization.[43]

America was portrayed as the cradle for the evolving Cosmic Man, a continent that Lewis could fully appreciate during his forced stay in the United States and Canada: 'Thus, even during the war, Lewis was eagerly taking cognizance of those characteristics of life on the American continent which most impressed him, the cosmic and the crude. Eventually he was to suggest a link between them.'[44] The global village and its related world primitivism (or better yet savagery) are the two elements which Lewis theorized and which were also later translated into McLuhan's terminology. The two intellectuals looked at their own times from the same outpost, but wearing two different uniforms. Lewis was *the enemy,* a satirist possessing a loathsome deformity and acting in terms of his temperament and personality; McLuhan became the *media explorer,* acting instead as a detached humanist observer interested in the new mediascape. Lewis threw his blasts to provoke his readers and induce reaction over societal and political issues; McLuhan's counterblasts were conceived to warn us, with no party bias, about the evolving environmental conditions and their side effects on both people and situations.

Even though he was among the first – if not the first – to theorize it, Wyndham Lewis did not particularly like the new global village (until he started to associate it to a renewed idea of internationalism, that is until his forced stay in North America). He feared the over-emphasis on the corporate, which he considered detrimental to free thinking; but what he feared most, in fact, was the annihilation of space in favour of time, a situation which led him to perceive the environment as inscribed inside a 'world of direct sensation,' no longer a 'world of distinct objects.' Thus, the *cosmic* aspect was also inexorably associated to the *crude* one, which Lewis defined in terms of a societal degeneration towards a newly conceived form of barbarism: 'Our civilization, with the impetus given it by machines, is turning from the settled to the restless ideal – from "civilization" to "savagery."'[45] To the *savagery* of the industrialized word, Lewis opposes the noble primitivism of ancient North African tribes, even though his understanding of those cultures was never based on a rigorous anthropological interest.

In *Filibusters in Barbary*, Lewis describes the slums of Casablanca, which he saw as being the most westernized city of North Africa, and asserts that 'capitalism and Barbary breed the same forms.'[46] And yet, he considers the situation of North American city slums more critical (in particular, he insists on the Chicago area), as it mirrors the passage from civilization to savagery and not vice-versa.[47] The new North American barbarism is therefore the product of a society now dominated by merchants, executives acting inside the corporate world of the machine age who appear as cultural inheritors of T.S. Eliot's new barbarians '... on whom assurance sits / As a silk hat on a Bradford millionaire.'[48] Lewis's original and brief fascination with progress and new technologies, or better his fascination with the promise of progress they seemed to encourage, was now superseded by his historical take on them. Lewis tells us that the aesthetic potential of machines has been replaced by the long-term effects of industrialization, which is no longer seen as bringing welfare, but rather degeneration and aberration. Lewis's admiration for the primitive world of North African Berber tribes is the admiration for a world in which 'industrialism has not put its squalid foot.'[49] Contrary to Lewis, McLuhan's idea of the global *village* leads to a discussion of retribalization as a social *dynamic*, not as a social *organization*. He does not discuss the idea of the primitive as a critique of mass society; instead, he privileges a discussion of the different forms of communication, characterizing oral societies as being in contrast with literate ones. The global village, as an electronic village, is an image which is immediately associated with tribalism and the primitive as the extreme consequence of a hyper-industrialized environment. As McLuhan wrote in his 1954 version of *Counterblast*: 'By surpassing writing, we have regained our WHOLE-NESS, not on a national or cultural but cosmic plane. We have evoked super-civilized sub-primitive man.'

As recalled earlier, in the 1960s McLuhan dropped all direct criticism of the media world, became the *explorer* not the *explainer*; as such, he explored satire as a possible rhetorical device, but fully embraced humor as his favorite one. He did not wear the mask of the enemy, like Lewis, but as we saw opted for other masks. He was the media oracle, the media guru, the modernist, the grammarian of media, and humour was a more appropriate strategy for pursuing his operative project. The humorous tone, freed from a moral bias which satire often preserves, helps to unmask hypocrisies. Sardonic or mocking laughter leads to irony; a satirical or sarcastic tone often sounds judgmental and makes you take sides pro or con situations. Generally speaking, McLuhan became a pop icon, therefore engaging with a less troublesome role than Lewis's 'the enemy.' From Lewis, he retained the verbal playfulness, as well as drawing on the most bombastic vorticist artistic experiments. McLuhan wrote two editions of *Counterblast*, the first dated 1954 (originally handmade and only recently published in book form), the second, designed and published together with Harley Parker and dated 1969. The first was written by a professor of English who found himself on the threshold of progressing mediascapes and who found models in avant-garde achievements; the second was elaborated by a media theorist collaborating with a celebrated artist of the time. Juxtaposing these two editions of *Counterblast* offers a way to map the evolution of McLuhan's poetics, in response to Lewis's (editor of the vorticist little magazine *Blast*, 1914–15) and in relation to his own progress as a media theorist. *Counterblast* (1954) is a pamphlet written in Lewis's vorticist style; McLuhan combines Lewis's works of 1914 (*Blast*), 1948 (*America and Cosmic Man*), and 1954 (*Self Condemned*) to work out his own approach to media studies: 'I have coming out a new version of BLAST which takes *Self Condemned* (1914–1954) as a focal point. As theme for Blast for forty years later I have taken in place of abstract art and industrial culture, the new media of communication and their power of metamorphosis.'[50] That passage is followed by a discussion of his idea of acoustic space. And yet, in his first short pamphlet, McLuhan still writes as a satirist in Lewis's wake, his blasts aiming at arresting the flux and grasping the genesis and direction of the related movement:

> In AMERICA AND COSMIC MAN Lewis saw North America as a benign rock crusher in which all remnants of European nationalism and individualism were happily reduced to cosmic baby powder. The new media are blowing a lot of this baby powder around the pendant cradle of the New Man today. The dust gets in our eyes.
>
> Counterblast 1954 blows aside this dust for a few moments and offers a view of the cradle, the bough, and the direction of the winds of the new media in these latitudes.[51]

Fifteen years later, in the new edition of *Counterblast*, he replaced the final sentence with some remarks presenting his new approach as a media theorist: his focus is no longer on the final goal, but mostly on the technique he intends to adopt to make the observation possible:

> The term COUNTERBLAST does not imply any attempt to erode or explode BLAST. Rather it indicates the need for a counter-environment as a means to perceive the dominant one. Today we live invested with an electric information environment that is quite as imperceptible to us as water is to a fish. At the beginning of his work, Pavlov found that the conditioning of his dogs depended on a previous conditioning. He placed one environment within another one. Such is COUNTERBLAST.[52]

Through time, McLuhan's counterblasts can therefore be defined not only in terms of an operative project ('to blow aside the dust for a few moments'), but also in terms of a formal strategy to pursue in order to achieve such a goal ('to place an environment within another one'). Hence, McLuhan was no longer 'fearing' the new environment, but was playfully probing it; he was, in fact, applying the method of art analysis to assess his mediascape, taking advantage of the perceptive energy released through montage and juxtaposition.

Consistently, McLuhan's mosaic places an environment inside another through its paratactic elaboration, which merges literacy and orality and offers a newly conceived ecological approach to a series of media and environmental issues. It's a hybrid energy which combines spatial and time philosophies to blow aside the dust that new tyrants continue to throw into our eyes.

PART THREE

Applied McLuhan

13 Literature and Media: A Round Trip

Engaging with or Applying McLuhan?

Sir Peter Medawar was right: 'we all tell stories,' and our stories 'differ in the purpose we expect them to fulfil, and in the kinds of evaluations to which they are exposed.'[1] McLuhan's 'stories' on media were told with the intention of exploring environmental processes and were exposed to various kinds of evaluations by mathematicians and poets alike. Today, the beginner who wants to approach McLuhan's works can rely upon a long bibliography of critical studies introducing both the man and his ideas on media. But I challenge you to find works which truly *apply* McLuhan's method of art analysis to the critical evaluation of society. Neither literary critics nor media scholars have systematically *applied* McLuhan to their own observations. McLuhan's ideas are often used as tenets to start new investigations, or as models to test and compare. But that is not 'applied McLuhan'; that is 'engaging with McLuhan.' For some reasons, his 'Laws of Media' have not been successful as an investigative approach and as an operative strategy for the observation of our reality and its media. Coming from the humanities, it still surprises me. I am puzzled by critics who remain skeptical about *Laws of Media: The New Science*, co-written with his son Eric and published posthumously, eight years after McLuhan had passed away. It's a great 'McLuhan book,' and, most importantly, it brings together ideas that McLuhan had been investigating and applying since the 1970s. As McLuhan often repeated, his 'Laws of Media' are a navigational tool for approaching all mediascapes. From my 'literary' point of view, it is important to emphasize that the essence of that book, and therefore of McLuhan's 'Laws of Media,' is consistent with McLuhan's humanistic roots; the *tetrad*, the operative model Marshall and Eric elaborated during their collaboration, which is presented and tested in the book, combines literacy and orality, knowledge and art, turns us readers into explorers, and encourages a mode of exploration which is participative and based on the human medium *par excellence*, that is, language. McLuhan's tetrad enhances *storytelling!* It's McLuhan's 'New Science,' which, as we will see, is nothing but the retrieval of the original idea of the *logos*: the tetrad considers words as boxes of knowledge; it amplifies their metaphorical value through a continuous juxtaposition of old and new meanings, usages, and understanding. No other previously conceived theory is implied; each observer – anyone – can participate in the exploration on the basis of his or her knowledge and experience:

> More of the foundation of this New Science consists of proper and systematic procedure. We propose no underlying theory to attack or defend, but rather a heuristic device, a set of four questions, which we call a tetrad. They can be asked (and the answer checked) by anyone, anywhere, at any time, about any human artefact. The tetrad was found by asking, 'What general, verifiable (that is, testable) statements can be made about all media?' We were surprised to find only four, here posed as questions:
> What does it enhance or intensify?
> What does it render obsolete or displace?
> What does it retrieve that was previously obsolesced?
> What does it produce or become when pressed to an extreme?[2]

The tetrad offers us a given set of four questions which anyone can ask; but as far as how to answer each question … that's up to us. The answers can be checked, that is, compared and juxtaposed, but there could be more than just one answer to each question because each of us is a unique individual: we observe and think in different ways because we have different backgrounds, knowledge, biographies, biology, histories, and, most importantly, languages. We look at our own world not only through our eyes but also through our own language: we experience our realities in different ways depending on the language we master. Why do Italians call 'natura morta' (literally: dead nature) what the British or North Americans call 'still life'? McLuhan's simple four questions on media lead to a bigger set of answers. But: what kind of *law* is it that takes into consideration such an unpredictable number of variables?

Inevitably, McLuhan's *laws* of media have not only puzzled but also irritated many critics; they still do. A few months ago, I was at a symposium in Milan, organized by sociologists and media scholars to celebrate McLuhan's centenary; I was the only one with a literary background (and, quite interestingly, the only woman present as a speaker), invited to comment on the literary origins of media studies in McLuhan's work. In my brief talk and in the following discussion, I mentioned several times McLuhan's tetrad as a good strategy to become active (and tolerant) explorers and to overcome the Narcissus narcosis: you look at a medium, observe it and observe through it, and then compare the results of your own observations with those of other explorers; by so doing, you actively contribute to working out the hidden pattern of forces characterizing a given environment. It's another way to say, with McLuhan, that the medium is not only the message but also ... the user! On that occasion, most of my colleagues confirmed their skepticism on the potentialities of McLuhan's laws of media. In particular, one of them told me that the tetrad was a trivial model (well, he used a harsher term) and that it was nonsensical to just stop at four questions; he himself had found at least seventeen questions which can be asked for each medium! He did not list them, though, and ended by saying that the tetrad is but a game we can play for a couple of hours before it tires us.

Sir Medawar was right, just like Richards was right when stating that 'scientific truth or statement' and 'poetical truth or pseudo-statement' require different attitudes in the listener. And a game tires when you do not know how to play it well. To my literary ears and to my artsy attitude, the tetrad is a good tool not only for approaching reality, but also for approaching fictional and imaginative renderings of reality. In addition, it is a good pedagogical tool, as it trains us to be active players: it forces us to take responsibility and to participate in a process of discovery; it encourages us to compare and juxtapose our findings. It stimulates us *to listen to other points of view*. It connects situations, experiences, traditions. It contributes to revealing a bigger ground, while probing some of its figures.

Think of it. Its potentialities are all already embedded in the provocative title of Marshall and Eric McLuhan's book: *Laws of Media: The New Science*. It sounds like an ambiguous paradox if we recall that McLuhan always claimed he did not have a clear-cut point of view on anything. But a paradox 'makes you see' precisely because it juxtaposes previous knowledge in an unexpected way. In the book, Eric McLuhan's introduction contributes to revealing the paradox and the amusing challenges it postulates: he tells us that, searching for a good definition of what constitutes a scientific statement, his father 'found an answer in Sir Karl

Popper's Objective Knowledge – that it was something stated in such a manner that it could be disproved.'[3] As Ted Carpenter would confirm a few years later, 'To Marshall, scientific laws, too, worked equally well in reverse.'[4] The paradox makes me accept the use of the term 'laws' in the title as being consistent with McLuhan's idea that he was an *explorer* and not an *explainer*. I playfully embrace his own mobile point of view on the very idea of 'law' as a point of departure for my own understanding of his tetrad, as well as for my own way of applying McLuhan to my field of study.

There is a reason why Eric and Marshall McLuhan discovered and tested four and not three or, even, seventeen questions. They were acting inside the tradition of the *translatio studii*; they were employing words to investigate the *rerum natura*:

> The tetrad is exegesis on four levels, showing not the mythic, but the logos-structure of each artefact, and giving its four parts as metaphor or word.
> The laws of media in tetrad form belong properly to rhetoric and grammar, not philosophy. Our concern is etymology and exegesis.
> This is to place the modern study of technology and artefacts on a humanistic and linguistic basis for the first time.[5]

McLuhan's observations are in the wake of Giambattista Vico, the author of *La Scienza Nuova* (The New Science), and of Sir Francis Bacon, two grammarians whose explorations had overcome the epistemological model postulated by coeval modern dialecticians. To the logic of the triad (thesis, antithesis, synthesis), McLuhan too prefers the rhetoric of the tetrad, which relates to the four levels of interpretation of texts as per the patristic doctrine: the literal sense (the story); the allegorical interpretation; the moral interpretation; the mystical or anagogical interpretation (eschatology).

Bacon's and Vico's names are both mentioned in *Laws of Media*, together with the names of Joyce and other modernist writers: 'Such men are not isolate eccentrics but links in a continuous tradition that extends from the present work back to the schools of manifold interpretation of the preliterate poets, including Homer and Hesiod.'[6] Consistently, as an exegetical tool, the tetrad leads to the creation of new verbo-voco-visual mosaics which translate various levels of understanding. The tetrad shows us that communication is not simply the passage of data from one point to the next one; communication is a process which transforms all its actors: senders, receivers, data, and the environment which contains them all. Communication is what creates a network of correspondences which are all valid at the same time:

> There is no 'right way' to 'read' a tetrad, as the parts are simultaneous. But when 'read' either left-right or top-bottom (Enhance is to Retrieve as Reverse is to Obsolesce, etc.), or the reverse, the proportions and metaphor – or word – structure should appear.[7]

The tetrad operates like a verbal equation which helps us to map the complexity of a ground through the interplay of its various figures; it combines physics and metaphysics because language can contain both reality and all human artefacts and artifices. By retrieving the metaphorical structure of words, McLuhan invites us to perceive each term as an *arché*, an archetype embedding experience. In *From Cliché to Archetype*, he wrote that the essence of an archetype is its awareness of retrieved knowledge. As such, the archetype is extremely cohesive; it attracts other archetypes.[8] The archetype becomes therefore something more than just a literary concept: it can be employed as a key to read and explore the world. Consistently, the tetrad is modulated upon the search for the archetypes, a cognitive journey which we can share through language and its metaphorical uses.

As an operative model, the tetrad recalls one of the most common rhetorical figures, the metaphor; in turn, the metaphor has some affinity with the traditional idea of scientific law. For Aristotle and the Baroque poets, the metaphor was a way to bring together what appears, at first glance, very different. It creates correspondences and links between things and processes. In a similar way, the scientist's innovative process lies in his or her capability to detect relations and patterns previously unknown or neglected.[9] Both the poet and the scientist use their imagination to elaborate new ideas, new connections, and therefore new visions and theories. The metaphor is the rhetorical figure which translates such imagination and opens new possibilities for knowledge and understanding. It is a rhetorical figure which also stands at the basis of McLuhan's idea of media as 'translators' of human experiences: media extend and translate us, our bodies and our minds. Aristotle is quoted in *Laws of Media*, and so is his idea of the metaphor based on the principle of analogy built on four comparative terms, two always stated and two often implicit. With his tetrad, McLuhan overcomes the purely literary value of the metaphor and elevates it to an operative structure by retrieving the mimetic potentialities that centuries of literacy had denied to words. The fascinating aspect of probing through the tetrad is to play with language until we reach a verbal archetype capable of containing different experiences, therefore bringing cohesion among differences. Once again, it is up to us to make the model resonate.

As stated in the introduction, McLuhan's laws of media do not rely upon an underpinning theory; they rely on us. The tetrad bores us if we lack imagination, knowledge, and curiosity: it is very easy to flatten our observation if we rely on clichés – or accepted ideas – to answer the four questions. Here is another paradox: conceived by a grammarian, the tetrad can become a fantastic tool in the hands of dialecticians whose goal is to classify and conduct a stocktaking of knowledge through notions. If pressed to an extreme, it can, so to speak, reverse into its opposite: no longer a probing instrument but a system of classification for previous knowledge. The tetrad, too, is a human artefact; it is a human medium we can probe.

$$
\begin{array}{cc}
\text{ENH} & \text{REV} \\
& | \\
\text{RET} & \text{OBS}
\end{array}
$$

Knowledge, Participation	Commonplaces, Cliché
Tetrad	
Etymology, Archetype	Accepted ideas, Absolutist truth

As a probing model, the tetrad enhances your knowledge and your participation in the process of discovery; by so doing, it makes accepted ideas or the notion of 'absolutist' truth obsolete. It retrieves archetypical experiences through the rediscovery of etymology; but this retrieval can produce new clichés and commonplaces if approached as an inventory and not as a dynamic act.

Since you are not me but individuals with a different history, understanding, knowledge, or life, you can have another set of answers, and therefore tell a different story, when probing the tetrad as a medium. Certainly, my colleague in Milan would provide other replies to all four questions. The real issue, though, is not to decide if I am right or if my colleague is wrong, but to accept all answers as being possible because we do not experience our world in the same way. To paraphrase Capra, we cannot but consider all tetrads – all probing – as 'approximations which are valid for a certain range of phenomena.'[10] We must also remember that phenomena are processes inside dynamic environments, and that an environment is, in itself, a network of possibilities, of actors and of events which change and adjust through time. Comparing tetrads helps us to extend our knowledge *by approximation*, in search of an archetype capable of bringing us together, or at least closer, rather than dividing us. It is not so important if or when we actually find the archetype; our will to search is what matters. We must pursue that search honestly, though, amusing ourselves by performing the search of 'the great fool,' knowing that ours will be but incomplete approximations, dynamic figures overlapping on a changing ground. As an operative model and a probing technique, the tetrad invites us to playfully explore chaos through language. It's a 'New Science' comparable not only to previous 'New Sciences' pertaining to our humanistic past, but also to more recent 'New Sciences' which are now popular and widely accepted worldwide. In 1987 James Gleick published *Chaos: Making a New Science* and wrote: 'Where chaos begins, classical science stops ... The irregular side of nature, the discontinuous and erratic side – these have been puzzles to science, or worse, monstrosities. But in the 1970s a few scientists in the United States and Europe began to find a way through disorder ... Now that science is looking, chaos seems to be everywhere ... Chaos breaks across the lines that separate scientific disciplines. Because it is a science of the global nature of systems, it has brought together thinkers from fields that had been widely separated.'[11] And a few years later, entomologist E.O. Wilson elaborated his idea of 'consilience,' defining it as 'the jumping together of knowledge by the linking of facts and fact-based theory across disciplines to create a common ground of explanation.'[12] Yes, we all tell stories. And they are even more fascinating if told by different explorers in different fields to find new ways through disorder and complexity, connecting patterns or probing the nature of our man-made environments:

> It makes no difference whatever whether one considers as artefacts or as media things of tangible 'hardware nature' ... or things of a 'software' nature ... All are equally artefacts, all equally human, all equally susceptible of analysis, all equally verbal in structure. Laws of media provide both the etymology and exegesis of these words: it may well turn out that the language they comprise has no syntax. So the accustomed distinctions between arts and sciences and between things and ideas, between physics and metaphysics are dissolved.[13]

Yes, Sir Medawar was right. 'Imagination is the energizing force of science as well as of poetry.'[14] That is why 'we all tell stories.'

I am about to tell you one: my own story of how to apply McLuhan to the study of fictional sources; of how to challenge knowledge to probe hidden patterns underpinning our mediascapes, where individuals, mass media, and technology interplay in a cosmic dance of which we had better be conscious. My story has seven little episodes; each episode is introduced by a simple tetrad I did to probe a concept which constitutes the narrative thread in the following paragraph. The seven little chapters take you along a progression of effect which unveils my own way of applying McLuhan while engaging with his ideas on media.

'Visual Literate' Forms

ENH   REV

$\underline{\quad}|\underline{\quad}$

RET   OBS

Order, Stability   Cliché, Oversimplification

Canon

Hierarchical society   Chance, Disorder

As shown in the case of Ford Madox Ford's *The Fifth Queen,* some works of fiction can be used to enlighten or even confirm media and technological processes theorized by McLuhan and other intellectuals (from literature to media); others can instead contribute to popularizing media theories and making the audience aware of new potentialities and limits (from media to fiction). Think of Douglas Coupland's *Microserfs,* B.W. Powe's *Outage,* or Don DeLillo's *Cosmopolis,* to name but a few. These titles invite a dialogue between different areas of study, which is worth pursuing because it can lead to new perspectives of investigation and analysis. It could also be quite amusing. To assess the potentialities and limits of such a dialogue, I have intentionally chosen as my fictional case studies two 'cult movies' and a 'cult novel,' often associated with McLuhan's media explorations: David Cronenberg's *Videodrome,* J.G. Ballard's novel *Crash,* and the movie of it made by Cronenberg. For those of you who are Canadians and know Toronto, it is even too obvious to consider Cronenberg's *Videodrome* as a parody of Citytv and of its co-founder and former head Moses Znaimer, an admirer of Marshall McLuhan. In the movie, Max Renn is the director of a small TV station named CivicTv who wants to shock his audience with extreme shows. Thanks to an ambiguous collaborator, he discovers 'Videodrome,' a clandestine program showing violent sadomasochist hardcore. Pursuing his own curiosity, Max tries to connect with the 'Videodrome' production, especially after his girlfriend Niki disappears; she suddenly reappears on the TV screen, as a protagonist of 'Videodrome' itself. As we shall see, Max's search becomes a journey blurring reality and hallucinations, real life and mediascapes, the human body and techno-ness. Max has to be reborn to a new life to fully understand what 'Videodrome' is, what it does to the human mind. The various characters he meets during his journey (Brian O'Blivion, his daughter Bianca, Brian Convex, Moses, and many others) are all instrumental to Max's own explorations and understanding of the new media ground, as well as of its lasting and perturbing effects on us. Ballard's novel *Crash*, too, investigates perturbing effects of our consumerist mediascapes. The novel begins with the death of its main character, Vaughan, narrated by a character who is named after the writer, Ballard. A series of flashbacks take us from Ballard's impromptu crash to his puzzling convalescence to his final rebirth as a new adept of a growing underground tribe which gets aroused through violent car crashes. Through Ballard's story, we witness the birth of a new population of individuals whose bodies are continuously reconfigured by violent impacts and whose psyches are driven by sexual perversions and consumerist mythologies: these are prosthetic individuals inhabiting our present, which in the novel appears as a paranoid and dehumanized montage of artificial simulacra. Cronenberg's cinematographic transposition of this novel further explores Ballard's vision, accelerating the progress of grotesque simulations of deviated behavioural patterns which cast an even more ambiguous light on our mass culture.

Only one of my fictional case studies is a novel; the other two are movies by one of my favourite Canadian film directors. What might appear as an inconsistency is instead a precise choice. If we recall McLuhan's definition of the medium 'cinema,' we can challenge our traditional classification of fictional sources; we can, for instance, reclassify them on the basis of their *mode of fruition*. One step at a time. Let's start by recalling how McLuhan defines 'cinema' as a technology. He tells us that cinema is 'the final fulfilment of the great potential of typographic fragmentation,' so much so that 'movies assume a high level of literacy in their users and prove baffling to the non literate.'[15] Following this idea, we can state that, before digital and 3-D techniques turned cinema into a post-secondary orality medium, cinema epitomized the *eye* and its related *civilization*. The paradox is that, before the development of interactive technologies, in spite of the montage technique which obviously characterizes the making of all movies, their mode of fruition was in fact truly *literate*: *light on*, the audience *looking at* the screen from a given distance, each of them engaging in a personal *inner trip*. Not by chance, in *Understanding Media*, films and the stream of consciousness technique are compared, both in terms of techniques and in terms of effects on the spectators/readers.[16]

Hence, a first lesson the humanities can learn from McLuhan's studies is that we could, in fact, try new definitions of *genres* depending not on the artistic code but on the mode of fruition of a work of art: literate or oral, linear or acoustic, intensifying reality or extending it, hot or cool, as per McLuhan's famous 'classifications' in his *Understanding Media*. In the case of *Videodrome*, or *Crash*, or other 'traditional' (from the technological point of view) movies, we can therefore define them as belonging to the category of literate and linear media, intensifying reality, and *hot*. Extending the game, some novels could be classified as acoustic media and not just as literate ones due to the type of interplay they engage in with their readers. For instance, James Joyce's *Finnegans Wake* belongs to the category of oral and acoustic media, extending reality, and cool: it invites participation, 'light through' and not 'light on.' No matter how much it will annoy critics in love with traditional canons and classifications, this is a provocative and fascinating game to play. And quite a fruitful one, too, as it can contribute to a better appreciation of the complexity of our cultural environments through time, revealing the constant juxtaposing presence of counter-environments, as well as the cross-hybridization of different media: in the Age of Reason and Rationalism (literate, linear, and mechanical), Laurence Sterne's *Tristam Shandy* is an acoustic challenge; at the dawn of the Electric Age (oral and acoustic), movies were reassuringly *linear* productions (the new electric medium – cinematography – was applied in fact to the old linear perceptive patterns of the novel). At the same time, the avant-garde writers experimented with acoustic renderings. Isn't this an enlightening paradox? At the turn of the previous century, the new medium – the cinema – was preserving the old environment, whereas the old medium – the novel – was fostering the new one. However, both films and avant-garde novels are extremely powerful forms because they are 'hybrids': they both embed 'a spectacular wedding of the old mechanical technology and the new electric world.'[17]

As we saw earlier, new media do not replace old media: they complicate each other. Hence, to apply McLuhan to the humanities at large, as I want to do, could lead to an epistemological revolution, breaking vessels and redefining cultural maps. What a great and provocative task to pursue! The challenge is cast here: *Videodrome* and *Crash* (the movie) will be approached as *Crash* (the novel), that is, as literate and linear narratives unravelling electric and acoustic phenomena. They will be approached as 'rear-view mirrors' reflecting the electric age, in terms of both content and form.

In the remaining six 'little episodes,' I will not approach these works of fiction to simply discuss McLuhan's grand narrative on media; that would be reducing a grammarian approach into discrete dialectic units. Fun, but a *déjà-vu*. Various critics have in fact discussed *Videodrome*, as well as Cronenberg's and Ballard's new Sci-Fi, along those lines, often in the light of techno-ness to either praise or denounce new technological *revolutions*. I prefer to use Cronenberg and Ballard to complicate McLuhan and vice-versa. It seems to me that such an interplay could help to enlighten cultural matrixes underpinning the electric age witnessed from the dawn of our post-secondary orality age; that interplay could also help to work out the myth-making behind McLuhan's media icon. For instance, *Videodrome* does a great job in visualizing a hybrid zone, juxtaposing literacy and secondary orality, but it does not contribute to the understanding of McLuhan's full persona. While opening up the doors of perception to the complexity of the technological environment, that movie nevertheless cast a mask on McLuhan which limited our appreciation of both the man and his message.

Masking the Guru

ENH   REV

_ | _

RET   OBS

      Group relations   Alienation

Mask

    Role-playing, Tribalism   Personal identity, The self

When I first saw David Cronenberg's movie *Videodrome* (1983), it was already 1997 and I was working on a PhD research project on Marshall McLuhan; as it often happens when you work intensely on a subject, I saw McLuhan anywhere. I found his ideas scattered throughout everything I was reading. All that was around me at the time was *speaking mcluhanese*, including myself. *Videodrome* was not an exception: while watching it, I could not help comparing McLuhan's grand narrative on media with what the various characters were discussing in the movie, as well as with its troubling setting and representations of the new TV arena. I was so convinced that Mr Cronenberg had based his script on McLuhan's works that I took advantage of a common friend, got his phone number, and tried to interview him to discuss my hypothesis. Over the phone, Mr Cronenberg was patient and very polite, but kindly dismissed all charges, maintaining that he did not know much about what I was saying. That conversation remained a private fact; I finished my doctorate and focused on other enterprises. However, as other official interviews have revealed, there is no doubt that *Videodrome* probes ideas floating in McLuhan's wake because, as Cronenberg himself later acknowledged, when he was writing *Videodrome*, McLuhan's *slogans* 'were in the air, but no one had really done anything about them.'[18] Cronenberg did, to the point that his movie could even be considered an illustrated parody of McLuhan's take on the new media environment.

Videodrome exists as a movie inside the intellectual context of the new counter-cultures – from body art to new Sci-Fi waves – questioning the clash between organic and inorganic elements, and the impact of that clash on our daily lives, our behavioural patterns, our established dogmas, and our own physicality. Through his various movies, in fact, Cronenberg has created a narrative that brings together some crucial *imaginative* (I am using this term here following Ford Madox Ford's definition) probings of his contemporary age, from that of William Burroughs's *Naked Lunch* to J.G. Ballard's *Crash* to those of McLuhan's well-known books on media.

In *Videodrome*, not only does Cronenberg, who is a well-read artist, elaborate and expand McLuhan's ideas on the electric universe, but he also ironically creates a character (Brian O'Blivion) based on Marshall McLuhan himself, offering us an ambiguous portrait, half-way between a madman and a much needed prophet. McLuhan does not play himself in *Videodrome*, as he did in Woody Allen's *Annie Hall*, but his fictional alter ego bears witness to his ideas going into the making of McLuhan's mass mythology, that is, his legacy as a media guru, including the opposing attitudes that many held towards him. In the movie, the Brian O'Blivion character looks like a grotesque copy of Marshall McLuhan 'the media oracle' who lives forever *on air* through his video-taped replicas. They are offered to us as technological simulations of a hyper-real simulacrum.

The grotesque is a powerful strategy to show a community in action, as well as a setting for action itself. McLuhan had passed away only three years prior the release of the movie, his legacy being assessed, questioned, and debated in relation to recent developments of new media on the technological landscape. Cronenberg's movie bears witness to that as well, that is, to a moment in media history which still affects us. By so doing, it shows us how (mass) media played a role in casting McLuhan as a media oracle or guru.

Cronenberg's unofficial portrait is not only extremely ironic, but also quite parodic; as previously mentioned, parody is in effect the underpinning strategy of this movie. The name of the fictional media guru itself is revealing: *Brian* is the anagram of *brain*, which is a term McLuhan often employed in his media analysis, whereas *O'Blivion* is the synonym of *forgetfulness*. Both terms refer to sensorial perception, and to our cognitive abilities and inabilities, that is, to our capability of either processing situations or being numbed by them. The combination of name and surname, in fact, can be read either as *reasoning vs. numbness,* or as the indication of a non-functioning body-mind, the *forgetful brain.* Both are paradoxical and parodic definitions cast as a challenge to us: which one will you choose? Which mask will you put on old Marshall-alias-Brian-O'Blivion? And why? And how?

Actual Sci-Fi

ENH   REV

$$\underline{ \mid }$$

RET   OBS

	Reality	Fiction
Sci-Fi	The imagined, Superstition	Non-fiction

As a beautiful fictional work grasping implications of knowledge pertaining to the making of the twentieth-century media world, Cronenberg's *Videodrome*, as well as most of his other cinematic explorations, are in line with the new idea of Sci-Fi that a writer such as J.G. Ballard had started to conceive a few years earlier. As a writer and an artist, Ballard too was fascinated by the side effects of technological progress on human beings and especially on their brain and psyche. Both Cronenberg's and Ballard's works extend McLuhan's exploration by further probing – through an imagination based on real and contingent situations – the long-term side effects and characteristics of the electric age. Ballard's introduction to his 1974 French edition of the novel *Crash* – which about twenty years later Cronenberg himself adapted into a movie – mentioned McLuhan and delineated an operative project which works well also as an introduction to Cronenberg's explorations; it outlines actuality as being constantly reconfigured by powerful technologies and commodities affecting both reality and imagination:

> The marriage of reason and nightmare that has dominated the 20th century has given birth to an ever more ambiguous world. Across the communications landscape move the spectres of sinister technologies and the dreams that money can buy. Thermo-nuclear weapons systems and soft drinks commercials coexist in an overlit realm ruled by advertising and pseudo events, science and pornography. Over our lives preside the great twin leitmotifs of the 20th century – sex and paranoia.[19]

In this apocalyptic vision, the omnivorous present blurs past and future, reality and imagination, and the global theatre folklore moulds around a hyper-representation (if not a fetishist representation) of daily deeds and mythologies. The new Sci-Fi concentrates on the perturbing and underground aspects of our own world, itself paradoxically perceived as a work of fiction. As McLuhan often repeated, our planet has now become an art form and we have to learn how to play with it. We saw that the Canadian critic also thought of *The Mechanical Bride* as a new form of Sci-Fi investigating our daily reality through ads, newspapers, and comic strips, cast as characters by McLuhan. We look at ourselves through these mass icons, and nothing seems to be closer to us; we see each other reflected in each page. But McLuhan unveils aspects of our times that show us how Big Brother gets inside us, unnoticed. It is the same technique displayed by both Cronenberg and Ballard: their works do not fall into the conventionally given definition of Sci-Fi. But, remember: McLuhan published *The Mechanical Bride* as early as 1951, when Sci-Fi itself was still living what Ballard would later define as the 'heroic period' of modern science fiction. McLuhan considered his work as 'a new form of science fiction' well before Cronenberg and Ballard started to publish and release their experimental works; he contributed to the revelation of the atrocity exhibition offered by the coeval mass culture more than a decade before them. The future is now. Isn't it?

Generally speaking, up to the 1970s a standardized morphology of the Sci-Fi genre, both in cinema and in fiction, promoted one major paradigm: the future location of given events mirrored by a more or less futuristic setting. No matter how distant the future is, either a few years or centuries, this futuristic setting is what somehow grants a good margin of relief (and complicity), as the audiences (or readers) know a priori that what is going on, all monsters, cyborgs, aliens, threats, and crashes, is merely fiction. It is the consciousness of this otherness, of this time and space distance, that enables them to be detached and enjoy either the reading or the screen performance. But in the Sci-Fi of the late 1950s and early 1960s, something new began to happen; the present became the new unknown territory to explore and map. Both Ballard's and Cronenberg's works focus on several dark sides of our own age, discussing uneasy themes that, taken together, form a borderline of unresolved questions: the technological extension of the human body, the psychological effects on human beings living in a hyper-consumerist landscape, the blurring of inner and outer self, the subversion of traditional sexual and moral biases. As artists, both Ballard and Cronenberg seem to pursue the same exploratory search as McLuhan: they are digging into the twentieth century's environmental dynamics and its related psychopathologies – neuroses that are perceived as more or less conscious effects of an environment in progress, constantly reshaped by a complex combination of new scientific discoveries and new media-induced psychodynamics. As a consequence, they explore how individuals modify their way of being, their way of perceiving themselves, their inner and outer selves, their bodies and their minds, and end up reconfiguring both the environment and their perception of it. In both Ballard's and Cronenberg's experimental works, the inner and outer landscapes overlap, and merge in quite familiar, yet disturbing, settings which force the audience to face what Cronenberg himself defines as 'a psychology of the future,' something which, paradoxically, is deeply linked to our present. Like McLuhan, they too seem to consider the future an invention of the present. And they too trigger ambivalent responses from their audiences: as a rule, fascination and repulsion have accompanied the reception of all grotesque works Cronenberg or Ballard released. Audiences have always responded controversially, perceiving them either as geniuses or as monsters. But here comes another provocation: in works such as *Crash* and *Videodrome*, Ballard and Cronenberg were not really *exploring* the present. They were *assessing* it.

Rear-View Mirrors

ENH   REV
$$\underline{}\,\Big|\,\underline{}$$
RET   OBS

Hind-sight	Blindness to what's ahead
Rear-View Mirror	
Memories, Recollections	Worries about what's behind

Cronenberg and Ballard started their careers in the 1960s, and offered some of their most accomplished and original explorations in the 1970s. *Videodrome* was released in 1983, during the first post-McLuhan decade. It is the first movie to openly engage with both his figure and his messages. It is a probe into the electric age which, somehow, comes at a time when that age is becoming fully visible. New technologies are expanding it into what will later become our own digital era. The intriguing paradox is that Cronenberg uses a medium which is 'the final fulfilment of the great potential of typographic fragmentation' to show the depth-involving newness of the electric age: it is a rear-view mirror approach which makes us see an environment which was, in fact, already established. But it makes us better understand some of the hidden patterns of its uncanny mechanisms: it completely shows the emperor's new clothes, and, most importantly, *it makes that knowledge accessible to a broader audience.* In 1941, *Citizen Kane* had warned audiences about the side effects of the age of the printing press when radio was in fact a much more powerful medium; in 1983, *Videodrome* warned us about the side effects of television just when personal computers started to become a commodity. Yes, the future is an invention of the past, and the past is only visible in the future.

It seems that we need both grammarians and dialecticians to fully appreciate cultural, historical, and social phenomena. Imagine those phenomena as an unexplored frontier: you need pioneers exploring it and taking some risks; but you also need farmers to domesticate that very land. Needless to say, it is different if you domesticate a land without understanding the spectrum of the explorations, what came through them, how and why. As a grammarian, McLuhan has certainly been followed by many dialecticians who have domesticated his explorations and made them more intelligible to us; they have 'explained' or given a clear-cut meaning to what was instead meant to be a probing approach.

There is a very good visual example of this process in a video-essay which I still consider to be the best introduction to Marshall McLuhan's ideas and modes of communication, that is, to the complexity of his oracular pronouncements as well as to how they can be approached and read: *Marshall McLuhan's ABC*, written and directed by David Sobelman. Alphabetically introducing some of the key terms in McLuhan's grand narrative on media, Sobelman juxtaposes live-footage interviews of McLuhan with comments explaining his pronouncements by his son Eric and Marshall's wife, Corinne. Eric, who has collaborated with his father in the development of their truly grammarian laws of media, here consciously plays the role of the dialectician interpreting the grammarian's insights into media. It's a continuous and very effective montage of the two men, discussing the same questions at different historical stages and through a different sentence construction. In the video, Marshall responds to various questions in his aphoristic and oracular way; the puzzlement on his interviewer's face is incredibly hilarious. Eric is cut in after each of his father's pronouncements; he explains them through his own understanding, his personal knowledge and recollections, by interpreting his father's cultural and technological context. He takes us by hand, so to speak, and guides us along Marshall's broken knowledge. In this video-essay, the juxtaposing of the grammarian and the dialectician makes us aware of the substantial difference between *aphorism* and *method* as Francis Bacon defined it. Marshall's insights on the electric environment are unfinished and take us inside an evolving process of observation which was and still is open and engaging; Eric's accomplished semantic translations of those insights make them more intelligible and help us to better understand Marshall's ideas. However, those explanations also end our process of discovery, as they inevitably historicize it. From *Marshall McLuhan's ABC* we learn that the real goal, for later pioneers, will be to go back to the rag and bone shop of the abandoned clichés and resuscitate them as tools participating in new discoveries. But we could do so only if we act as grammarians, not as dialecticians. The latter, in fact, could only repeat or classify what has already been said or explored. This is also true of O'Blivion in *Videodrome*, is it not? He hints at an environment conceived as an unexplored frontier, the TV world; however, by the 1980s, that world had already achieved the status of mass media commodity. O'Blivion predicts something which has already happened: his oracular pronouncements are 'genuine fakes'! He is not a grammarian; he is a farcical dialectician.

The whole movie is in fact a dialectic story about the technological side effects of television. Cronenberg aims to take us along a journey to show us how individuals *mutate* in an environment dominated by TV; he focuses on the way the individual's body and psyche change, either evolving or imploding. What Cronenberg reveals is not a genetic mutation, as in the most traditional Sci-Fi movies; individuals do not mutate in order to survive or better adapt to their own environment. Instead, the mutation originates from the violent merging of organic and inorganic elements processed *mentally* and *psychologically*. It follows the complex psychodynamic syndrome taking place among individuals, technology, and the environment to which we contribute all together. Cronenberg seems to indicate in his film that individuals and the new media belong to the same landscape; they complete and extend each other; they constitute a new wholeness. This idea of bodyscape and nature is in line with McLuhan's vision: 'The new media are not bridges between man and nature: they are nature.'[20] The shocking, violent, and brutal merging we see in *Videodrome* melts and dissolves organic and inorganic bodies and triggers a series of unpredictable chain reactions, as if finally liberating something which all characters already possessed but did not dare to face. Cronenberg seems to be saying that to get so close to one's own physical limits frees the self from all inhibitions and turns conventional individuals into newborn quasi-human beings consciously pursuing a new life and a new sexuality. Thus, the marriage of reason and nightmare is also a marriage of technology and sex and is elevated to the uneasy paradigm Cronenberg and Ballard have chosen in order to investigate *diverted* and *subterranean* dimensions of their contemporary environment. Inevitably, it is a perverse and disturbing enterprise.

What has made *Videodrome* a *classic* cult movie is revealed almost from the beginning in a dialogue between Masha, a soft-core pornographer, and Max, the main character, who is the president of CivicTv, the little station specializing in sensationalistic programs. It is something which does not simply relate to a medium *per se*, but to its impact on its environmental situations, to the way it plugs into people's brains and changes their way of seeing things:

Masha: *Videodrome ... It's dangerous.*
Max: *Mafia? ...*
Masha: *More political than that ... It does something that you do not have, Max ... It does a philosophy and that's what makes it dangerous.*
Max: *Whose philosophy? ... Give me a name.*
Masha: *... Brian O'Blivion.*

Brian O'Blivion is a cultural analyst, a media critic and philosopher. He is the founder and director of the Cathode Ray Mission, where people are offered both food and long sessions of television viewings (namely, pre-digested 'food-for-thought'). The Mission is now ruled by O'Blivion's daughter, Bianca.. Her father only appears in video; his desert studio looks like a dusty library and sits above the big hall where the Mission's *clients*, mostly homeless people, are being treated. Brian O'Blivion does not engage in dialogues; he only speaks through video-taped mono-logues (a strategy that, as Max ironically underlines, makes conversation difficult) and delivers 'electric oral pronouncements' which sound like parodies of McLuhan's. For example:

> The battle for the mind of North America will be fought in the Videoarena, the TV. The video-screen is the recto ... of the mind's eye, and the TV screen is part of the physical structure of the brain ... Therefore, TV is real-ity and reality is less than TV.

As I said, O'Blivion predicts only something which has already happen, and which today should be all too obvious. In the movie, the TV arena is dominated by this new philosophy, which is translated into a new reli-gion spread through the Cathode Ray Mission and the philosopher's pronouncements. TV proselytes – but they look more like addicts – continue to increase in numbers and now form a growing tribe. Tel-evision is a very addictive medium, as all electric media are, and it is difficult for people to kick the habit. They act as addicts guided by a dream-like logic which numbs and encourages them to fully embrace the new communal corporate credo. As discussed by McLuhan: 'TV favours a world of deep participation in group rituals (ritualistic flow). TV is a very addictive medium ... TV is a very involving medium, a sort of inner trip.'[21] In other words: 'TV removes people's private identity.' The impact of television on human beings is therefore similar to the impact of all other electric media: they reconfigure the body and trans-late it into communal-corporate units. 'You have not a physical body. You are on the air, either on the phone, on the radio, or TV. This mod-ifies the relation with the environment. This is the biggest or at least one of the biggest effects of the electric age ... It has deprived people of their private identity.'[22] Brian O'Blivion is the perfect *incarnation* of such a *discarnate* individual, who puts on his environment and partici-pates in the numbing process which makes people oblivious. After all, O'Blivion is the master of an electric Mission. Apathy and unconscious actions are another two aspects reflecting the new-age body-panic paranoia.

This twentieth-century paranoia is rendered by McLuhan, Cronenberg, and Ballard through a series of mass hallucinations. *The Mechanical Bride* shows people trapped in daily commercial mythologies delivered through newspapers, magazines, and commercials. In *Videodrome* the proselytes of the Cathode Ray Mission are numbed – literally fed – by TV screening sessions, whereas in *Crash*, reality and fiction merge through the most powerful machine of collective illusions: Hollywood. The Hollywood stories, as well as its star system, offer the simulacra which wrap and give shape to the simulations that Vaughan and his proselytes stage maniacally, and that the subterranean tribes endorse ritually. In Ballard's novel, a crucial scene sees the main protagonists going to stock-car races where the major performance is 'The Recreation of Spectacular Road Accidents,' for example, James Dean's fatal crash. The scene is described as a true performance, at once involving all visitors, technicians, and mannequins, all of them sharing a *dream-like logic. Actions* are, therefore, turned into *performances*, and people act as if following a script someone else wrote for them. As narcissists, they live through their narcosis, which cannot but lead to either physical or metaphysical death.

Performing Presence

ENH   REV

$$\_\;{\Large |}\;\_$$

RET   OBS

The human body, Interplay	Reification
Body-Art	
Piercing & tattooing	Art & crafts, The self

The idea of mass hallucinations relates to McLuhan's analysis of the type of body extension which electric media have encouraged. After the initial body extension which the old mechanical media have fostered, the new electric media extend the brain, our central nervous system, and therefore our psyche. The extension electric media encourage is an implosion. McLuhan insisted that people were moving towards the ultimate extension of consciousness and were acquiring a new communal body through electric media: 'In the electric age we wear all mankind as our skin.'[23] Metaphorically speaking, the inhabitants of the global village become *disembodied* human beings, like ethereal angels. That is an uncanny idea which relates to Ballard's and Cronenberg's Sci-Fi investigations of the *new body / new flash* and the *new psyche*, that is, to the investigation of what constitutes today both the individual and the collective identity.

Our physical body is, in fact, a fundamental aspect of our material presence in space and time; to lose our physicality, to live detached from our organic or biological dimension, induces in us new aggressive strategies aimed at reaffirming our individual identity. Inevitably, 'if you have lost your identity, you have to prove that you are somebody and you become tough and violent.'[24] Violence is an issue in *Crash*, as in *Videodrome*. The new sensationalist TV program which Max is trying to acquire for his TV station combines sex with torture and murder. He wants the 'Videodrome' program because he thinks that it is the future of television. Also, he thinks that what he sees are extremely fictionalized situations; when he discovers that what he sees is real, Max starts a nightmarish journey that forces him to go on an inner technological trip through his own body and mind. The trip is a hybrid of TV realities and inanimate objects. The moment new media deprive the human beings of their original bodies, the marriage of reason and virtuality offers them a new form of physical *resurrection*. In Ballard's *Crash*, too, violence is the ultimate issue; in this novel, car crashes are sublimated moments of sexual paroxysmal excitement. Similarly, McLuhan, when discussing violence, considers it as a natural response to all identity loss, and a situation which the extended proximity induced by new media cannot but foster. As *War and Peace in the Global Village* postulates, life is not necessarily quiet in the electrified global theatre.

Quite rightly, Cronenberg has pointed out that in art there is a strong relationship between the idea of truth and the body, because we experience ourselves and our environment mostly through our own physicality. As he says: 'Ultimately you have to go to the body for verification of anything. You go to the body for verification of life. You go to the body for verification of death. That covers everything ... Everything but the body is an abstraction for us. So the sense of touch keeps returning to the body ... So much of what we think, in our understanding of human relations, is totally satellite around the body.'[25] It is not by chance that what we call *body art* was retrieved right when new media were depriving us of our old sense of physicality. In the 1970s, artists such as Gina Pane, Vito Acconci, Annette Messager, Robert Mapplethorpe, and Louise Bourgeois started to investigate the limits and potentialities of the human body through the arts. They were fascinated by its ambiguous relation to technologies, an exploration later continued by artists such as Orlan and Stelarc. It was a provocative way to return to the body. And it is not by chance that horror movies were in great fashion at the time; McLuhan saw them as 'movies in which people are questing for their identity.'[26]

Inevitably, violence is conceived as a way to retrieve one's own body – and therefore one's own true self. Violence has a complex biological and psychological implication which nevertheless can be approached through new artistic patterns. As a matter of fact, the new idea of *art performance* was already embedded in most modernist avant-garde aesthetics, as they aimed at including the observer (or the reader) in the process of artistic construction. When McLuhan was probing the new media of his times, the idea of inclusion was expanding. It no longer simply implied the blurring of all boundaries separating the artists from their audience, but also encouraged the hybridization of organic and inorganic elements and the challenging of biological and virtual limits. The human body became, in fact, not just the medium of artistic expressions, but one among the many elements of the new artificial landscape. It was to be probed, mutilated, extended, and modified. At the centre of the new artistic performances of the late 1960s, 1970s, and most of the 1980s there were indications of '*ultra-bodies* related to a post-world,'[27] which became fully visible to everybody about a decade later:

> The mutation which takes place around and inside our bodies is a total one. Through virtual worlds, the new techniques of communication propose new social relations; the development of biology and medicine is changing the way we relate to reproduction, illness, death; the progress of cognitive digital prosthesis is modifying our intellectual skills.[28]

In this context, body art no longer shocks us today; grotesque *ultra-bodies* are in fact more and more part of our own reality itself, where scars, tattoos, as well as plastic surgery or high-tech medical applications are turning us all into *post-human* beings, into new specimens of *electric brides or grooms* or, better, cyborgs. Interestingly enough, after body art came video art and digital art, which embedded a new *aesthetic of the wireless* in which the body is returned into a bi-dimensional representation, whose presence is, in fact, more a *performance of presence* suspended between a *telemic* and a *proxemic* condition.[29]

What is fascinating to investigate is the development of the reversal of the situation theorized by McLuhan and reflected in the art of his time: while he was theorizing the new *electric bodies*, disembodied human beings, art was returning (often in extreme and violent forms) to the physicality of the body through body art and new kinds of performances. This body-as-art physicality also pervades Ballard's and Cronenberg's works. In *Videodrome* torture and extreme sex are *narrative* and not *decorative* elements; the same is true in *Crash*, where it is the violent marriage between individuals and cars which starts the sexual awakening process of the hallucinated subjects, so much so that all boundaries between what is real and what is inscribed in the dream-like logic blur. Following the crash, the dichotomy between organic bodies (the men and women involved in it) and inorganic bodies (cars, mechanical means *par excellence*, as well as fetishist status symbols of our Western consumer society) is far more ambiguous than it might originally appear. Flesh and plates, humours, fluids, and mechanical components are continuously confused in Ballard's meticulous and almost aseptic descriptions. Scars, bruises, open wounds, and stains of bodily fluids left on the characters' clothes become ominous tracks revealing a dangerous metamorphosis of the human body, which is progressively turned into a sort of blasphemous altar by the main characters: wounds and bruises are, in fact, perceived not simply as disturbing signs, but as erotic symbols which visually and lastingly preserve each *encounter* with the body-car. At the same time, the car becomes the alpha and omega of a new polymorphously perverse perception which seems to correspond to a collective and intense psychopathology that the main characters accept and explore, therefore developing a technologized sexual religion. It could be read as a sort of growing collective awareness culminating in the car crash, and often leading to the ultimate orgasm, the energy released through the hybridization of organic and inorganic elements, which is also an organic death. The car is therefore a carapace the individual puts on as part of him- or herself in a technological mutation which will continue all through the electric age, as later novels will confirm. In DeLillo's *Cosmopolis*, twenty-eight-year-old multi-billionaire Eric Packer has turned his stretch limo into a mediascape of monitors through which he inhabits and perceives the city landscape. He *touches* the world through old and new media, and he himself is the content of both. It is not surprising to me, that, while writing this volume (2011), David Cronenberg has been announced as the film director who will bring DeLillo's novel to the screen: after *Crash*, *Existence*, *A History of Violence*, and others, here comes *Cosmopolis*, in an incessant assessment of our own twentieth-century psychopathologies.

But both *Crash* and *Cosmopolis* belong to the previous century; they both help us to probe what made the global village a globalized one. We are now into a different moment in time.

Moving into the twenty-first century, today we are at the dawn of a new cinematic technology which is carrying a new message that we are still questioning. The paradox is that, to remain in the world of Sci-Fi, we seem to be enjoying a revival of the heroic times, featuring futuristic locations and alien creatures. The real revolution in cinema is not in the stories we watch, but in their technological developments and in the ensuing mode of realization and of fruition. Today, digital technology is retrieving the body in a new way, literally bringing it back through a newly conceived idea of *tactility* inviting human beings to physically engage with machines through *digital touch* and sensor-induced sound; at the same time, video and digital art are now encouraging an aesthetic based less on actual *physical* presence and more on *performances of presence* enhancing lightness, rapidity, exactitude, visibility, and multiplicity.[30] *Avatar* by James Cameron offers, of course, the perfect example of this process, and its stereoscopic filmmaking stands as a breakthrough in cinematic technology. Certainly, with *Avatar*, the marriage of organic and inorganic elements leads to a hybrid melting of the human body and the latest high-tech specimen in the evolutionary chain of electric media: digital technology. Contrary to what happens to the characters in *Crash*, as well as in *Videodrome*, such a melting seems to imply the possibility of transcending physical death, as well as the traditional boundaries of time and space. It is perhaps the most intriguing development of our postsecondary orality age, as it stands as a fascinating and uncanny threshold of new explorations at once merging scientific and mystic or spiritual elements. It indicates a new possibility of recomposing the split between mind and body, somehow implying that human beings can be and can become something more than just the material sum of the two. It is, in fact, the supreme paradox embedded through the new digital convergence, now fully applied also to the human factor: the most sophisticated applied technology, itself the result of rational thought and empirical testing, opens new doors of perception and makes us *see* and *feel* the infinite transcending our finiteness. In Cameron's movie, through technology, human beings (the actual actors) are turned into avatars, their facial expressions carefully digitalized and recorded for later animation; what we see is at once *real* and *unreal*, experienced through our 3-D glasses in movie theatres. Isn't it somehow ironic that the most mechanical of media – spectacles – is in fact the one which still plugs us into the acoustic depth-involving newness of these high-tech virtual *performances of presence* that we enjoy as collective audiences in movie theatres?

Pathological Narcissuses

ENH   REV

— | —

RET   OBS

           Imagination, Vision   Alienation, Hypnosis

                      Hallucination

             Fear, Faith   .   Reason

McLuhan's media theories focus on the human body and on the different sensorial perceptions either enhanced or made obsolete by each new technology. Most of his probes, in fact, are built around images of *eye* and *ear*; they, in turn, are related to his discussion of linear and acoustic space, of the mechanical or the electric age. Each of these percepts in turn relates to a type of extension the probed medium is inducing. Significantly, both Ballard and Cronenberg develop their narrative through symbolic or allegoric renderings of sensorial experience. In *Crash*, photography is our vivisective *eye*, the medium through which we perceive both the surface and the underground world; after all, McLuhan defined photography as 'The Brothel-Without-Walls.' In particular, in *Crash*, Vaughan's continuous use of photography, his reassembling of visual fragments, and Ballard's accurate description of each photo, of each fragment, suggest the author's intention of scientifically vivisecting the given hyperreality in order to recreate it in a surrealistic mosaic. The real world literally explodes into fragments in Vaughan's photos: the result is a weird architecture, where form no longer reveals function, where it is almost impossible to distinguish organic from mechanical bodies, as both entities melt into a new landscape. 'The photograph extends and multiplies the human image to the proportions of mass-produced merchandise.'[31] The photographs that Vaughan takes and assembles to record the various crashes clearly reveal a new architecture, a new physical and psychological permeation between organic and inorganic elements; it is this newly forming landscape which intrigues all the fictional characters (and us), not the mere crashes or sexual performances *per se.* Following a similar attraction, in McLuhan's *The Mechanical Bride*, it is the whole orchestration which attracts us more than the single fragments; we are fascinated by the new landscape created by the overlapping of vivisected images, showing us artificial legs on a pedestal promoting new stockings, gloved female hands displaying a diamond bracelet, or women portrayed as artificial mannequins selling undergarments. 'You never thought of a page of news as a symbolist landscape?' McLuhan asks us in his first chapter discussing the 'Front Page.' If we did not think of it before reading that volume, for sure we would from that moment onward.

Similarly in Cronenberg's *Videodrome*, the story develops around symbols and themes pertaining to the sensorial sphere, often mixing the organic and inorganic as if probing McLuhan's involving newness as a *continuum*, wrapping bio- and infosphere into a single entity: the new electric landscape has finally extended both the human body and the human consciousness, and Cronenberg literally makes us see it. The videotape Bianca gives to Max *bites*, and he must decide what kind of *teeth* it has. Max interacts with Nicky *through the TV screen* and *enters into it* to kiss her enormous lips standing as an expanded metonymical fragment of her body. The TV *arms* Max by giving him a gun which will become *an extension of Max's hand* and which he will literally hide *inside his own stomach*. Most important, once they approach 'Videodrome,' the sensationalist TV program, all characters develop hallucinations and are no longer capable of distinguishing what is real from what is fictional. The words *disease* and *tumour* are used to define what 'Videodrome' does to people, something which Brian O'Blivion has developed himself; however, he tells Max that he does not consider the tumour as something foreign to his brain, but instead as something which is integral to it. Here the tumour is not necessarily an illness in the way we traditionally conceive of illnesses, but an extension wrapping both brain hemispheres in the hallucinations it develops. It is the unexpected point of contact between organic and inorganic, between real and unreal, between consciousness and virtuality. This is the point through which Big Brother comes inside of us.[32] Susan Sontag wrote on illness as metaphor in what remains among the most powerful books on this subject. She started in 1978 comparing tuberculosis and cancer, the former being the paradigmatic disease of the nineteenth century, the latter of the twentieth century. She convincingly argued that 'with the modern diseases (once TB, now cancer), the romantic idea that the disease expresses the character is invariably extended to assert that the character causes the disease – because it has not expressed itself. Passion moves inward, striking and blighting the deepest cellular recesses.'[33] Cancer, which was usually understood as God's punishment or curse, becomes here the metaphor for something for which we are somehow unconsciously responsible, the physical metabolization of our implosion as human beings. So understood, cancer is the perfect metaphor for Brian O'Blivion's *illness*, as he does not perceive it as a punishment or a curse; instead, he considers it as a mutation of his former biological status, which follows a new environmental condition, turning the old human being into either a disembodied or an hallucinated individual, of which he is now aware. Ten years later, Sontag followed her first study with the new volume *AIDS and Its Metaphors* (1989); in that book, she discusses various metaphors employed to present AIDS as an illness, each of them stigmatizing evolving cultural biases. What strikes me, generally speaking, is that cancer is metaphorically represented as a pathology which remains inside the affected individual; consistently, we know about genetic predisposition but cannot predict if, when, or how the illness will eventually manifest itself. AIDS, however, is rendered as a contagious disease which we pass on through physical contact, so much so that Sontag suggests that 'plague is the principal metaphor by which the AIDS epidemic is understood.'[34] We get it through unprotected sexual intercourse, or through infected blood: we get it when we merge as individuals; sadly, the moral issue strikes back. As a metaphor, it works well for the spreading of the new psychopathology which the protagonists of both *Crash* and *Videodrome* develop following their biological and technological merging. They are doomed to a mass hypnosis that turns their narcissism into a sensorial escape; they are affected by the same disease they themselves contribute to spreading, though its spread is also powerfully promoted by invisible plague-spreaders (remember? McLuhan already spoke of 'best trained individual minds,' whose task is to enter our collective mind to control us and generate *heat*, not *light*).[35]

Cronenberg offers a clear allegory of this condition. In his movie, Barry Convex and his staff at the Spectacular Optic Corporation, an eyeglasses company, know quite well that through 'Videodrome' they can induce a great 'Mass Hallucination,' and they are secretly sponsoring test transmissions to achieve their goal: to spread fatal brain tumours to morally punish North American maniacs for their extreme sexual and violent costumes. Convex is the villain in the story, who tries to control Max through 'Videodrome,' making him act as a servo-mechanism to pursue his murderous plan. Bianca O'Blivion is instead the heroine who *reprograms* Max to halt the conspiracy. Curiously, most of the words and names used to define the group of characters recall either *sight* or *vision* (Convex; Spectacular Optic; Bianca, meaning 'white,' a colour which contains all nuances of the electromagnetic spectrum, a colour which is the sum of all that is visible and becomes invisible when juxtaposed with other colours it, in effect, contains). In a crucial scene, we find Convex hosting a trade show whose setting recalls the Italian Renaissance of the Medici family, while showing his new glasses and quoting traditional mottos related to the power of sight (*loves come to the eye, the eye is the window of the soul*). Thinking of McLuhan's theories, we now can appreciate the reference to the Renaissance period and to the image of the eye as subtle metaphors for what is Convex's will to preserve a hierarchical order which he can dominate. In the electric age, consciously knowing how to use new media to control people and induce a 'Mass Hallucination,' Barry Convex operates to keep the collectivity in a hypnotic state. As McLuhan suggested, if one sense dominates the others, then all other senses will be numbed: 'The selection of a single sense for intense stimulus, or of a single extended, isolated or "amputated" sense in technology, is in part the reason for the numbing effect that technology as such has on its makers and users.'[36] The amplification of sight prevents all tactile sensibility and therefore reinforces the individual's dissociation of sensibility. As McLuhan said, propaganda works better on a literate individual, and Convex and his team have put on a show to mesmerize their audience: they *show* them their new spring collection, something which is used to distract them from understanding what Convex intends to do to them. They are hypnotized through their eyes, the rest of their bodies being numbed to all perception. For Lorenzo de Medici and Renaissance people, the eye was not only the window of the soul but also a sun, the window on the world. For the retribalized electric tribe, the amplification of the eye is instead the eclipse of all other senses, that is, sensorial blindness. Far from making people see, hear, and feel, the Spectacular Optic Corporation amplifies irrelevant figures to make everybody forget the ground: Narcissus and his narcosis are back and the dream-like logic is preserved. Until Max strikes back.

Charismatic Flesh

ENH   REV

RET   OBS

Magnetic appeal   Arrogance, Aggressiveness
Charisma
The divine, The spiritual   Inner self

Ballard's novel and Cronenberg's movies use a series of religious metaphors and symbols which must also be read in relation to McLuhan's ideas on the new electric tribe as discarnate human beings. The very idea of a discarnate or disembodied human being leads to some philosophical and even mystical speculations, in turn connecting McLuhan's theories, on the one hand, to the work of Teilhard de Chardin and, on the other hand, to the idea of a mystical body of Christ pertaining to Roman Catholicism. The Thomistic parallel between McLuhan and Teilhard de Chardin is a fascinating one, as they both tried to mediate between faith and reason. In *The Gutenberg Galaxy*, McLuhan quotes Teilhard de Chardin's idea of the Noosphere or technological brain of the world conceived as a unity of planetary dimensions which exists above the biosphere. Teilhard de Chardin was fascinated by the discovery of electromagnetic waves, which he considered as a biological miracle because they enabled each individual to be simultaneously everywhere. McLuhan further developed this concept and associated it to the new electric implosion with all that implies in terms of perception. However, if we consider that both intellectuals were also Catholics, we cannot but suggest a religious reading of both the Noosphere and the Global Village in order to probe if the new media implosion could eventually lead to the electric reconfiguration of the mystical body of Christ.

In the Catholic doctrine, the Verb (which embeds spirituality) incarnates in a Body (which embeds materiality), which is first lost and then collectively retrieved through the Eucharist; through the Holy Communion, the faithful transubstantiate into Christ's body and the Church – which is a community of *souls* (disembodied entities). It then turns into a mystical body, at once spirit and matter. Similarly, the inclusive newness deprives the individuals of their single bodies and offers them a unique electric body which embraces them all. McLuhan said that 'in a Christian sense, this is merely a new interpretation of the mystical body of Christ; and Christ, after all, is the ultimate extension of man.'[37] The idea of Christ being the extreme extension of man suggests how the sacred and the profane have always mutually engaged each other, something which the arts have also registered through time: from Bosch's paintings to Dalì's visionary ones, from Miller's *Canticle for Leibowitz* to the new 'video Christianity.'

Ballard and Cronenberg offer a disquieting representation of the new religions of the new electric tribe. In *Crash*, Vaughan is portrayed as a disturbing guru who unveils his proselytes' inner drives; they follow him in religious adoration, each scar, each wound received through car crashes, turned into the lasting mark of a religious self-scourging. Vaughan's scarified body itself is perceived as a new altar, as a desired relic, a sort of blasphemous Grail, by a crowd of faithful psychopaths who evoke and simulate it while performing extreme rituals. Emblematically, the character Ballard in the novel (and the fact that Ballard names his narrator after himself is already revealing of an ambiguous embodiment) embraces and gently explores his wife's, Catherine's, injured body, brutally hit by Vaughan during an episode of sexual intercourse; so doing, he performs an act of adoration of his wife's mortified body and being, for through its martyrdom she is now reborn to a new physical and psychological life. All characters lose their old body and transubstantiate into Vaughan's body through their violent car crashes or sexual encounters. In *Videodrome*, apart from the symbolic use of biblical names for some minor characters (Moses, Raphael), the idea of the Cathode Ray Mission immediately conveys the idea of a parson's flock to be guided and nourished. And the nourishment which is provided at the Mission is not only food for the body, but also the hypnotic TV food: mesmerized by prolonged TV screening sessions, the electric herd voluntarily annihilates and decentralizes the self. The new electric tribe wears all mankind as its skin. Symbolically, to regain his freedom Max must lose his body, hopefully to be reborn later. 'Long live the new flesh,' he says before pulling the trigger in imitation of a scene he has just watched on a TV screen: his new passion is therefore meant to free himself and humankind from the 'Videodrome' malignant tumour. Cronenberg brings together sexual and religious passion in an all-embracing landscape inside which his spectators are asked to decide if they have been taken into a spiritual journey shifting them from the earth to the air, that is, if their escape from the body is the prelude to a new communal mysticism or if, opposing all that, they have been offered an opportunity to look at their own time from a safe and revealing viewpoint.

Cronenberg evokes 'a super-civilized sub-primitive man' back in an all-embracing acoustic space; he is aware of the fact that 'the new media are not ways of relating us to the old "real" world; they are the real world and they reshape what remains of the old world at will,'[38] including what remains of the human beings who eventually try to resist the new media embrace. Nevertheless, to refuse to conform to a dominant behavioural model – a gesture which is, in itself, a powerful act of rebellion, of assertion of one's own personality, independence, imagination, physicality – does not necessarily free the self, both in its inner (the psyche) and outer (the body) dimensions. The risk is, in fact, simply remodelling the self into new communal 'microcosms,' that is, into newly shared entities combining bodies, physicality, and psychology which do not exist nor acquire a meaning as such, but only if and when they are incorporated into a wider landscape that, even though they intend to oppose it, still proves to be necessary for their own existence. Therefore, it is the hyper-real, social, and technological context that, in the end, somehow even controls transgression, as transgression is an act deeply affected by the simulation of different, but still corporate, simulacra.

In *Crash*, Vaughan is obsessed by performing exact replicas of famous car crashes of Hollywood stars; he dreams of dying in a car crash with actress Elizabeth Taylor, and therefore spends most of his time planning what he sees as his final embrace, maniacally rehearsing the scene along the highways. He is the guru of an underworld new tribe, but he is prisoner of consumerist mythologies. Individuality, personality, and difference are therefore once more homogenized into corporate dreams. The novel is not a hyperbolic rendering of possible scenarios. It is the representation … of our own future, something which was already embedded in the electrified world Ballard was assessing. Don't we look more and more alike these days? What was offered at the time of *Crash* or *Videodrome* as shocking performances was in fact part of our daily landscape. Body-piercing, tattooing, and scarifications are all rituals increasingly shared by new urban groups; they are all signs revealing new, different, and corporate forms of physicality and 'urban psychopathology.' And what about plastic surgery, which makes us all wear the same smile, the same catty eyes, and the same artificial expressions? And can't each of us become like any other Hollywood star by participating in one of the many reality shows? Yes, we can successfully wear all humankind as our own skin; after all, who needs to preserve our *loathsome deformity called self*? As McLuhan wrote in *The Mechanical Bride*: 'Do you have a personality? Our executive clinic will get rid of it for you.'[39] Better to get rid of it, as it is in fact what afflicts us when *rubbing against [our] fellows*. After all, as McLuhan pointed out, in our contemporary age, 'charisma means to look like a lot of other people.'[40]

Epilogue: Witty Fool or Foolish Wit?

Merging Right and Left

'I use the right hemisphere when they try to use the left hemisphere.' That was McLuhan's stock reply to those who said that it was extremely difficult to follow his reasoning.[1] Despite the fact that McLuhan said this in the turbulent 1960s, we now know that it would be a mistake to associate the terms *right* and *left* with a political context. Like the Fool in Shakespeare *All's Well That Ends Well*, McLuhan is speaking 'the truth the next way,' and in effect postulating a verbal trick that hides a more complex meaning, a meaning which both readers and listeners are expected to discern.

In McLuhan's so-called *nonsensical language*, the terms *right* and *left* are linked to the philosophical ideas of *percept* and *concept* respectively; as previously recalled, they are, in turn, adapted from the scientific language used to describe the bicameral structure of our human brain, as indicated in the studies of Julian Jaynes and Robert J. Trotter.

Marshall McLuhan applied the then seminal (but now obsolesced) research done by Jaynes and Trotter as a rhetorical device to convey the communicative processes that he was probing and to encapsulate, in words, the binary opposition of *eye/ear*. In his works, the metaphorical use of such theories on the bicameral structure becomes an axiom for the exploration of old and new communicative psychodynamics.

To McLuhan's way of thinking, the *right* and *left* hemispheres of the brain are therefore fundamental terms, which he often used in a figurative way to exemplify two opposing cultural strategies of perception and knowledge, in turn reflecting different cultural models and environments. The left hemisphere, which controls the right side of our body, is presented as the kingdom of logic, of sequences, of linearity; the right hemisphere, which controls the left side of our body, represents, instead, the palace of intuition, discontinuity, and simultaneity. Furthermore, in this interpretation, the left hemisphere is part of the *visual* and *quantitative* brain, while the right hemisphere is where the acoustic and qualitative side of human nature resides. Thus, in McLuhan's figurative language, the left hemisphere comes to exemplify the Western hemisphere, which is connected to the idea of visual and Euclidean space, that is, to a space characterized by a precise and hierarchical subdivision into centre and margins. By contrast, the right hemisphere stands for the Eastern (or Oriental) hemisphere. It is connected to the idea of acoustic space 'whose centre is simultaneously everywhere and whose margin is nowhere.'[2]

The *corpus callosum*, between the two hemispheres, constitutes the place of dialogue between them: a bridge across which perception creates its balance between linearity and simultaneity, namely, an *interface*. 'Ordinarily, the two hemispheres are in constant dialogue through the *corpus callosum*, and each hemisphere uses the other as its ground except when one (i.e. the left) is habitually dominant.'[3] If one of the two hemispheres prevails upon the other, then the mode of perception will change. *Mode of perception* here means the way tribal and literate cultures relate to their environment (in terms of visual space versus acoustic space). As a consequence, when the *rendering* of our perception changes from visual to acoustic, our culture also mirrors the change. The verbal and written *translation* of each perception will, in fact, reflect into two different and opposing *discourses*. On the one hand, the predominance of the left hemisphere connects to a linear, logical, and sequential form of writing; while, on the other hand, the predominance of the right hemisphere connects to an analogical, intuitive, and discontinuous form of writing.

Following this reasoning, one could say that the right hemisphere is to the left hemisphere as Shakespeare's Feste in *Twelfth Night* is to Malvolio: Feste is, in fact, the *witty fool* whose language – at first glance rather foolish and nonsensical – reveals a subtler mode of perception; whereas Malvolio stands as the *foolish wit* whose apparent wit is nothing but a thinly disguised presumptuousness which is soon revealed and overcome by the other characters. Similarly, the right hemisphere is to the left hemisphere as the apparently *nonsensical* is to *traditional* scholarly language. Playing with metaphors and words, we could therefore say that the Fool is to the Establishment as McLuhan was to Academia.

Coda: Enters the Fool, Exit All Others

I am aware of the risk implicit in this comparison, as McLuhan has often before been associated with the image of the Fool, and not necessarily for the good. For instance, while discussing Marshall McLuhan as a *humanist manqué*, Donald F. Theall dismisses the Fool image in favour of that of the jester, the joker or pseudo-clown: 'McLuhan's clown-like pose is essentially different from that of the more deeply committed humanists'; 'McLuhan appears admittedly ambiguously clown-like, for like a Joycean Jesuit he is a priest-joker; but this is distinct from the follower of folly, the philosopher of jests ...'[4] Theall goes even farther and presents McLuhan as a trickster or, more precisely, as a 'huckster,' his techniques being associated with those 'of a propagandist, the strategies of a con man.'[5] As previously suggested, even though Theall's investigation is particularly rich and interesting, especially in unveiling McLuhan's humanistic roots, it nevertheless seems inscribed in its time-biased polemics, when McLuhan's generalities and uncanny prose were associated more with 'random eclectic choices' than with an intentional montage. As a consequence, even though he offers deep insights into McLuhan's ideas and style, Theall seems to want to compete with McLuhan as a humanist, often juxtaposing McLuhan's approach to knowledge with the one provided by other famous critics of the time (from Joseph Huizinga to Erwin Panofsky and Leszek Kolakowsky) who were acting in a more systematic and disciplined way.

Unlike Theall – who, in short, associates McLuhan's strategy to those of advertisers by suggesting he popularized 'thoughts that have been in circulation for the last half-century or so'[6] – I think comparing McLuhan to the Fool (as he appeared in the Renaissance theatre) provides us with a better focus on McLuhan's strategy of communication.

Face it, McLuhan was a wise guy. Wise enough to play the Fool, and he played it well! He was a pioneer (for better or worse) of the process that, starting from the 1960s, led to the crumbling of the old ivory tower, forcing the academic world to open up to society; he brought the consequences of electric culture into the classroom and openly adopted the method of art analysis to assess society and the educational process. In those days, it was a necessary step taken to open up the education system to a new matrix. But I am afraid that, in the long run, the cultural process that he (as well as other intellectuals) started in order to realign learning and actuality ended by bringing *kulchur* and not only *culture* into the classroom. Foolish wits have taken the place of witty fools, and advertisers and propagandists have started to prevail. *How many pages out of that novel am I suppose to read to pass your exam?*

Renaissance theatre mirrored a well-ordered and hierarchical form of society in which the character of the Fool was the disrupting element breaking all given order. The Fool, through a different use of language, forced a critical attitude towards people and situations. Released from *literal* and *literate* logic, the Fool combined orality and body language, and by so doing, he became on stage a purveyor of both high and low cultural traditions (the literate tradition and the tradition of court jesters, often associated with popular forms of representation linked to the Italian tradition of the *commedia dell'arte*).

The Fool, in effect, became a sort of *corpus callosum*, an interface, triggering a new balance between the two domains of wisdom and wit. He chose his two forms of communication, combining figures and puns belonging to a folk tradition, which in his shattering uttering became reframed within a more complex and wittier rhetorical context, and which different audiences could perceive and understand in various ways, depending on their education.

Similarly, McLuhan opened traditionally conceived forms of scholarly writing to new forms of mass communication and culture that, up to that time, had been rigorously excluded from academic discourse. He overtly combined forms of language and slang, borrowed from late-night radio and racy commercials, from newspapers and television, and translated these encounters between so-called *low* and *high* culture into witty aphorisms, later trivialized as slogans. Just like the Fool's verbal annoyances and disturbances, McLuhan's nonsensical lines were open to different and simultaneous interpretations by different audiences. In both cases, the playful verbal constructions implied a deep awareness and knowledge of the *ars oratoria* through which the rhetorician always pursues a precise goal: to convince and enlighten the listeners/readers. It is also the same goal pursued by Theall's advertisers. But McLuhan's rhetoric was aimed at making his audience aware of their narcosis and somnambulism, whereas all advertisers only care about making the sale – a difference Theall never quite acknowledged.

McLuhan, as a professor of English, was a witness to the growing gap between the world that his students were inhabiting, their language and culture, and the scholarly world of his time.[7] What I can concede to Theall, however, is that, late in his career, McLuhan developed a self-aggrandizing 'self-consciousness of McLuhan about McLuhan' which made many perceive him as an advertiser of his own myth of culture and technology. In retrospect, that triggered a process which blurred the myth of Marshall McLuhan, whose intellectual comet had already started to wane in the mid-1970s.

The act of persuasion, which both McLuhan and the Fool turn into a playful device through an apparently nonsensical use of language, can be retraced through a conscious exegesis unveiling the witty verbal construction. One must be 'wise enough to play the fool' and display 'a practice / as full of labour as a wise man's act'– because it requires not only a subtler perception of things, people, and situations (' … He must observe their mood on whom he jests / the quality of persons, and the time … ') but also the capability of making those perceptions intelligible to others. What is presented as ostensibly an incoherent and playful form of communication is, in fact, rhetorical speech elaborated by a brilliant oratory that amuses, shocks, and reveals a deeply buried truth in accordance with the zeitgeist and in synch with a mode carefully chosen and conceived by the orator ('A prophet I, Madam, and I speak the truth the next way').

The idea of the *corpus callosum* relates well to both the place the Fool takes on stage, and the location McLuhan took when he became a world-famous media guru, a media oracle, a modernist, a brilliant grammarian of media. He was at once a central character in his own play and to his audience. The Fool probes his context in order to 'display the background of discontent hidden by the emperor's new clothes.'[8] The Fool, a 'corruptor of words,' explores the play's conflicts through language and makes use of riddles, puns, and nonsense: he triggers consciousness through paradoxes! This form of communication is, in fact, meta-referential since it requires the audience's complicity for its understanding and fulfilment. The Fool speaks to the audience's benefit as much as to the other characters' understanding, therefore providing a cognitive link: he plays the *corpus callosum* between *ground* (the dynamic experience of being part of an audience in a theatre) and *figure* (the performed action). Also, as suggested, the Fool chooses forms of communication which use figures and puns belonging to a broadly shared popular tradition; he represents the emotions of the multitude, as T.S. Eliot called it, reframed within a wittier rhetorical context to be interpreted in different ways by the multitude in his audiences. The understanding would depend on each individual's learning.

Similar to this role played by the Renaissance Fool, Marshall McLuhan also took his stance between the scholarly world (the university, academia) and the consumer world. His all-embracing explorations were mediated through verbal and written *probes* (a probe being an instrument which enables one to explore an environment all at once, in a tactile manner, and as a whole, rather than through a linear process). A probe intentionally challenges the traditional structure and requires the reader's co-operation to achieve its full meaning. Being compelled to untangle the aphoristic probe or paradox, the reader is, in effect, engaged to play and interact with the author, therefore contributing to the final revelation of meaning.

It is important to underline the playfully serious and active attitude in the communication process of McLuhan, since he considered jokes, puns, and the ease of good humour as a vital cognitive tool: 'We think of humour as a mark of sanity for a good reason: in fun and play we recover the integral person, who, in the workday world or in professional life can use only a small sector of his being.'[9] At the same time, it is important to acknowledge the active role that the reader must take by sharing the responsibility of the discovery and being on the alert for new meanings, new interpretations, new challenges. It is a condition which encourages the reader to acquire a critical attitude as well as to learn to question received opinions and generally accepted ideas.

I hope that by now it has become clear how verbal puns in McLuhan's writing are turned into a probing device to retrieve a harmonic perceptive balance – a balance which we tend to repress in our every-day dealings with world – between play and work, fun and seriousness, and thus return the individual reader or silent listener to the lost whole-ness of perception. Western society (also in its globalized state) is based on specialization, linearity, and logic, and is professionally unbalanced. Individuals do not *play*, they *compete*. In other words, it is a society still dominated (metaphorically speaking, of course) by the left-hemisphere way of thinking. I also hope that by now it has become clear how satire, irony, and a wilful sense of humour become precious tools in the Fool's hands, as they do in McLuhan's uttering, since they make it possible to strike society at its core, turning upside-down shared conventions, feelings, and values, and thereby also revealing their inconsistencies. In McLuhan's writing, this *divertissement* becomes a cheerful weapon, a play-ful effect based precisely on the reversal of well-established patterns: a process by which he created counter-effects and unleashed the forces of new epiphanies.

As a character, the Joker, the Jester, the Trickster, or the Fool is himself a *counter-environment*, someone who constantly stands for *the other*, the *reverse*, providing his listeners with an alternate viewpoint. In other words, he counterbalances the given rules and, through his witty discourse, forces the deconstruction of a given environment – not to 'destroy' it, but to make us *see, hear,* and *feel it.* Similarly, in a context built upon Western and Euclidean models, the Fool is anyone who refuses to act fragmentarily and chooses, instead, an integral mode of observation. Here's how McLuhan put it succinctly in his delightfully creative literary *Counterblast:* 'When the whole man moves into a specialist area he is a clown. Clowns are integral. Every society has an acrobatic area for specialists. The clown in any society is what is left over, unused, from this acrobatic high-wire act. His act is to attempt the high-wire of specialty, using human wholeness. Even walking is made to appear a crazy aberration of a pedantic microbe.'[10]

A borderline character, the Fool lives in Elizabethan plays to make the reader aware, through a disruptive narrative, of the passage leading from the Middle Ages to the Renaissance or, as per McLuhan's grand narrative on media, the transition from an oral to a literate society, that is, the transformation of a choral to an individualistic social norm. To my mind, it is the passage that turned the integral man, still living in a medieval acoustic and inclusive space, into the fragmented Gutenberg individual who is literate but alienated from the tribe.

From the mid-twentieth century, Marshall McLuhan used his *verbo-vocal-visual* mosaic as an early warning system alerting us to changes as society moved from literacy to post-literacy, from mechanical specialization to electric wholeness. As his own Fool, now playing in a global theatre, McLuhan used the mosaic to *shock,* to *amuse,* and to *reveal.* His well-rooted humanistic background enabled him to combine *classic, oral, eastern,* and *modernist* patterns and to elaborate on the complex narrative of the new environment by showing its surprising affinity with the effect of modern forms of *electric* communication. In this way, I find that McLuhan can be approached as a brilliant Fool who displays a clear intention (a well-defined operative project), and who speaks the truth *the next way.* All investigations that approach McLuhan's world of discovery cannot but start from a renewed consciousness of his interior landscape: at core, McLuhan was a humanist who disclosed new cognitive spaces through the retrieval of ancient educational dicta now applied to the 'magic' world of electricity. What he said is continuously tested and debated, refused and celebrated, by scholars from many different fields, using many rear-view mirrors; but *how* he said what he said and *how he came to elaborate* his original form of communication is a more important, consistent, and pervasive legacy. It is a legacy which suggests to us *how* to slow down, *how* to take the time to play with the spirals of constantly evolving, new vortexes. It is a legacy which tells us *how* to retrieve our human factor and wit: through language, dialogue, play, and active interplay. It is a legacy which playfully reminds us that all our explorations are but 'works in progress,' approximations 'valid for a certain range of phenomena': 'I don't necessarily agree with everything I say.'

In other words, to retrieve McLuhan's '*how*' legacy invites us to listen, to question, to engage in depth, and to participate in a process *consciously*. It is a legacy that reminds us that storytelling is a powerful strategy for exploring and rendering a world in progress, that *pen and words are mightier than the sword*. Is that just a revised cliché? Or is it the core of a universal archetype? To answer this question, try to do a tetrad on 'word,' 'pen,' and 'sword'; invite others to do their own tetrads, and then play and compare your stories. You will start to elaborate *your own* verbal probes and experience how to retrieve the exploratory substance of human language *yourself: you will learn by doing*. But be prepared: if you learn the lesson well, you will no longer be able to read and listen as you used to. Your mind will no longer be at rest; you will become a counter-environment yourself, detecting the figure in the carpet and urging others to see it as well. Are you ready to enter the vortex of exploration and ask yourself, not '*how many* pages out of a novel you have to read,' but *how* you have to read that novel to make it resonate? Are you prepared to shake off the reassuring forgetful snow, to blow the dust aside? Be reassured, you will not end like Poe's sailor, whose descent into the maelstrom turned his hairs 'from a jetty black to white' in less than a single day. However, yours, too, will not be an easy task, as Ford Madox Ford warned us: ('The fact is that what humanity desires, passionately and almost before all other things, is a creed. It craves for accepted ideas; it longs more for a mind at rest ...').[11] Since his years at Cambridge, McLuhan's mind was never at rest. It was always 'boiling with new ideas and experiences'; certainly, he did not delegate his public explorations to a 'few specialists.' As we saw, he considered that the only way to be 'worth anything as an educator' was to constantly engage in explorations in literature and communication, even though he 'would vastly prefer dairy-and-orchard culture to this intense mental culture.' He knew that 'the latter is not easy and its results are less certain.'[12] He also knew, as Ford Madox Ford and all other imaginative writers knew, that 'nothing is more trouble than to look things in the face.'[13] McLuhan did not hesitate, and pursued his search all through his life. His verbo-voco-visual probes are his way of wittily invading his readers' and listeners' inner sensibilities, and troubling them. After all, Ford's lesson was clear: 'The word "author" means someone who adds to your consciousness.'[14]

Our journey ends where it began. Poe's sailor, too, returned to the same surface from where he first took off. But, once there, the maelstrom no longer looked the same. At the beginning of Poe's short story, the sailor takes his companion to a 'little cliff' so that he 'might have the best possible view of the scene' of the event he is about to narrate, as he wants 'to tell [him] the whole story with the spot just under [his] eyes.'[15] From there, the narrator and his listener can master at once ground and figure, outer and inner landscapes. As the narrator tells us, in a few minutes he becomes 'aware' of both the horror and the magnificence of the scene of which he is now part. The new perspective makes him see, hear, and feel the environment and himself in a new way. I hope that looking at McLuhan from a different perspective might help you to see him and his garden maze under a different light, as well as your own environment – *our* own environment – through his – *our* – literary landscapes.

Rip off McLuhan's most famous masks. Off goes the media oracle; farewell to the media guru; time out for the media fan. Gently lift the modernist mask and look below it. What do you see? ... Marshall McLuhan's the Professor of English, a witty Fool whose foolish wit helps us shake off the cold cover of forgetful snow, and clean our doors of perception. Literature matters.

Notes

Prologue

1 Eliot, 'The Burial of the Dead,' in *The Waste Land* (1922).
2 McLuhan, Letter to Walter J. Ong, 18 May 1946, *Letters*, 187.
3 While discussing the structure of McLuhan's mosaic, I do not pursue a structuralist approach. Concerning this issue, in his biography of Marshall McLuhan, W. Terrence Gordon addresses the question 'Is McLuhan a Linguist?' and answers it comparing McLuhan's ideas to those developed by scholars pertaining to various fields of research (semiotics, linguistics, structuralism, etc.), with a special emphasis on de Saussure. Gordon's intention is to deconstruct all criticism coming from areas of studies conceived as organized disciplines, maintaining that McLuhan's theories somehow transcend them all and, at the same time, contain them all (see Gordon, *Marshall McLuhan: Escape into Understanding*, 323ff). It is not my intention in this book to take a clear-cut side on McLuhan's belonging to well-defined schools of thought, as I am more interested in approaching Marshall McLuhan's mosaic *per se*, as a form conceived as an operative tool to probe the dynamics of the so-called 'electric age.' It is not so important for me to assess if McLuhan was ahead of, or in contrast with, some school of criticism, as it is to discuss the role played by the humanities (and especially literature and the arts) in the making of his own *forma mentis*, as well as of his own operative project. Our age is moving fast and it is not always easy to understand the hidden pattern of situations which constantly remould our global setting; it seems to me that McLuhan's *mosaic* could still be approached as an interesting *form* to address such a complexity.
4 Dunlop, 'Seeing,' in *Metropolis*.

5 I discuss Poe's short story as a literary paradigm in the following chapter, 'A Renewed Approach to Marshall McLuhan's Poetics.'

6 The list of critics who have commented in favour or against McLuhan's works is a very long one; it includes critics belonging to various fields of research and to different national realities: Tom Wolfe, James C. Morrison, Arthur Kroker, Gianpiero Gamaleri, Enrico Baragli, Robert K. Logan, to name just a few. Their works (together with many others) are acknowledged in the Bibliography. For my study, particularly useful have been those works postulating and exploring McLuhan's literary roots. In particular, Philip Marchand's biography, *Marshall McLuhan: The Medium and the Messenger*, is the book which initiated me to the understanding of McLuhan's own ground. Also relevant have been the works of Donald Theall, Glenn Willmott, and Janine Marchessault as they have further explored (or even criticized, as in the case of Theall) specific aspects of McLuhan's humanistic background. Concerning the broad field of media studies, there are two chapters in two different books which have acknowledged McLuhan's works as groundbreaking. In 'Canonic Anti-text: Marshall McLuhan's *Understanding Media*' (in Katz et al., eds, *Canonic Texts in Media Research: Are There Any? Should There Be? How about These?* 191–212), Joshua Meyrowitz discusses McLuhan's 'Major Principles,' 'McLuhan's Rise and Fall,' and his 'Resurrection.' This essay aims at including McLuhan as part of the canon in the field of communication, tracing back McLuhan's ideas on media and society, as well as some of his most puzzling rhetorical devices (i.e., 'Fuzzy Terminology,' 'Probes versus Scientific Clams,' 'Lack of Methodological Maps,' 'Absolutist Claims'). In particular, the first part of Meyrowitz's essay ('McLuhan's Rejection of Text-Based Analysis') offers some preliminary considerations which are useful for my discussion on the literary roots of McLuhan's media studies in this book. Also, in 'Marshall McLuhan: The Modern Janus' (in Lum, ed., *Perspectives on Culture, Technology and Communication*, 163–200), James C. Morrison positions McLuhan as a founding father of media ecology, articulating his analysis through a series of conceptual staples: 'The New Media Age,' 'Media as Environments,' 'Style and Substance,' 'Synesthesia,' 'Media Hot and Cool,' 'Retrievals of Orality,' 'Nonlinear Causality,' 'Centers and Margins,' 'Summa Medialogica.' All interested readers will find both these essays useful to trace back McLuhan's ideas on media and society, as well as to compare two approaches to McLuhan 'the media scholar' pertaining to different areas of media(ecology) studies.

7 McLuhan, *The Gutenberg Galaxy*, 7.

8 See Feste in Shakespeare's *Twelfth Night* (1.5.29–33).

9 Joyce, *Finnegans Wake*, 98.34–35.

1. A Renewed Approach to Marshall McLuhan's Poetics

1 Carpenter, *Oh, What a Blow That Phantom Gave Me*, 162.
2 'A Candid Conversation with the High Priest of Popcult and Metaphysician of Media' is the subtitle of a famous interview published in the magazine *Playboy*, March 1969.
3 See note 6 in the Prologue.
4 McLuhan, *The Mechanical Bride*, v.
5 Liss Jeffrey in Benedetti and DeHart, eds, *Forward through the Rear-View Mirror*, 10.
6 Eric McLuhan, in ibid., 45.
7 James, *The Figure in the Carpet*, 365.
8 Eco, 'Il problema della definizione dell'arte' (1963), in *La definizione dell'arte*, 142–3.
9 Theall, *The Virtual Marshall McLuhan*, 94.
10 Theall, *The Medium Is the Rear-View Mirror*; Marchand, *Marshall McLuhan: The Medium and the Messenger*; Willmott, *McLuhan, or Modernism in Reverse*; Marchessault, *Marshall McLuhan*; Cavell, *McLuhan in Space: Cultural Geography*.
11 McLuhan, 'The Place of Thomas Nashe in the Learning of His Time' (1943), 447.
12 McLuhan, 'Foreword' to *The Interior Landscape*, xiii–xiv.
13 I have discussed some of the following ideas at various conferences and in several essays. In particular: 'Marshall McLuhan's Critical Writing,' in Dotoli, ed., *Prospettive di Cultura Canadese*, 199–211; 'Marshall McLuhan and the Modernist Writers' Legacy,' in Moss and Morra, eds, *At the Speed of Light There Is Only Illumination*, 63–83; 'Integral Awareness: Marshall McLuhan as a Man of Letters,' in Strate and Wachtel, eds, *The Legacy of McLuhan*, 153–62.
14 See, for instance, Finkelstein, *Sense and Nonsense in McLuhan*.
15 *The Interior Landscape*, vi.
16 *The Mechanical Bride*, v–vi
17 Ibid., v (my emphasis).
18 Ibid.
19 'Marshall McLuhan: A Candid Conversation with the High Priest of Popcult and Metaphysician of Media,' *Playboy*, March 1969, p. 56.
20 Pound, *ABC of Reading*, 29.

21 Ford Madox Ford (Hueffer), quoted in Stang, ed., *The Ford Madox Ford Reader*, 266.

22 See, among others, the various comments in Stearn, ed., *McLuhan, Hot and Cool*; and in Rosenthal, ed., *McLuhan: Pro & Con.*

23 In his volume *The Medium Is the Rear-View Mirror: Understanding McLuhan*, Donald Theall writes critically about McLuhan as a 'humanist manqué,' and compares McLuhan's 'philosophy' to the philosophy of well-known humanists such as Thomas More and Erasmus to prove that while the latter 'had their antennae tuned to their own periods,' McLuhan did not. McLuhan's generalist approach is deconstructed as an assemblage of 'random electric choices,' and his synthesis as far from grasping the complexity of his time's sensibility: 'McLuhan, rather than attempting such a general synthesis, picks and chooses without ever relating what he picks or chooses to some kind of discussion of theoretical orientation' (ibid., 115ff). Theall's discussion of McLuhan as a 'curious universal scholar' is quite an interesting and a sophisticated one; and yet, it is still embedded in the historical context that strongly affected the reception of McLuhan's ideas, including the reception of McLuhan 'the scholar' shifting towards the business world (something that Theall implicitly condemns and uses to trivialize McLuhan's ideas). It is true that Theall's erudite investigation of McLuhan came at a time when the image of the 'pop philosopher' and the 'media guru' was at its peak, and when McLuhan was boldly exploiting his own popularity (as per Theall, 'McLuhan potentially distorts sources as he creates his own popular myth ...' [ibid., xvii ff]). Ambiguously, Theall praises McLuhan's 'fund of history and sense of tradition which few possess these days. He represents a willingness to confront the present and yet not to reject the past' (ibid.); but, he also compares his attitude to that of a propagandist, making him a 'humanist manqué.'

24 Frye, 'Across the River and Out of the Trees,' in *Mythologizing Canada*, 172.

25 Marshall McLuhan often quoted Edgar Allan Poe's 'Philosophy of Composition' as a literary essay offering a clear explanation of how a writer can obtain an effect through a careful development of rhetorical patterns. This essay became his life-long example of full awareness of one's own poetical process and narrative, obtained by unravelling a situation from the final effect to its formal cause – a technique which is also at the basis of the detective story, one of McLuhan's favourite literary genres. (See chapter 7 of this volume, 'McLuhan and Media Studies.') Similarly, as we shall see in Part Two, all the modernist writers praised by McLuhan were both literary critics and conscious authors, interested in the technical and formal aspects of different literary and artistic productions.

26 Pound, 'A Few Don't's by an Imagist,' in *Literary Essays*, 9.

27 The Italian translation is quite a case in point. Written years before other studies on the interplay of mass culture, media, advertising, and sociological issues (e.g., Roland Barthes's *Mythologies* was published in 1957; Umberto Eco's *Il Superuomo di massa*, in 1976), *The Mechanical Bride* was published in Italian only in 1984 (*La sposa meccanica: Il Folclore dell'uomo industriale*, translated by Francesca Gorjup Valente and Carla Plevano Pezzini [Varese: SugarCo Edizioni]). Significantly, in his introduction to the Italian edition, critic Roberto Faenza observes that the editorial 'delays' had consequences: the delay of McLuhan's first book being available to the Italian-speaking audience had allowed the promotion as original interpretations of media and cultural phenomena ideas which were, instead, borrowed from the Canadian thinker. (On this issue, see also Lamberti, *Marshall McLuhan: Tra letteratura, arte e media*, 26ff.)

28 'What Tiresias *sees*, in fact, is the substance of the poem' (T.S. Eliot, notes to *The Waste Land* [1922]).

29 McLuhan, *Understanding Media*, 63.

30 See McLuhan and McLuhan, *Laws of Media*.

31 'Introduction,' in Benedetti and DeHart, eds, *Forward through the Rear-View Mirror*, 45.

32 See Havelock, *Preface to Plato*; Ong, *Orality and Literacy*.

33 McLuhan and Watson, *From Cliché to Archetype*.

34 Marchand, *Marshall McLuhan*, 252.

35 McLuhan, 'The Place of Thomas Nashe in the Learning of His Time' (PhD diss., Cambridge University, 1943). This work has recently been edited by W. Terrence Gordon and published with the title *The Classical Trivium: The Place of Thomas Nashe in the Learning of His Time* (Corte Madera: Ginko Press, 2006).

36 See, for instance, 'American Advertising,' *Horizon*, October 1947, pp. 132–41. *The Mechanical Bride* was published in 1951, even though McLuhan had started to work on it several years before. (See both Marchand, *Marshall McLuhan*, 107–10; and Gordon, *Escape into Understanding*, 153–7.)

37 From the note printed on all issues of *Explorations*.

38 Lum, ed., *Perspectives on Culture, Technology and Communication*, 27.

39 Ibid., 9.

40 In his historiography of media ecology, Lum refers to Thomas Kuhns's idea of 'Theory Groups' (1962), as well as to Belver C. Griffith and Nicholas C. Mullins's, and Stephen O. Murrays's idea of 'Invisible Colleges' (1972, 1993), to demonstrate that the intellectual tradition of media ecology origi-

nated outside the official academic programs, in the works of the so-called 'Post-Industrial Prophets' (Lewis Mumford, Sigfried Giedion, Norbert Wiener, Harold Adam Innis, Marshall McLuhan, Jacques Elul, R. Buckminster Fuller, as per Kuhns's definition in his *The Post-Industrial Prophets: Interpretations of Technology* [1971]). Neil Postman was then the 'Leader' who established the Media Ecology Program at NYU's School of Education (a pioneering phase in the years 1967–70; a PhD program in 1970), while Terence P. Moran and Christine L. Nystrom became the 'Organizer' and the 'Theoretician/Codifier' helping to launch and consolidate the program. (see Lum, ed., *Perspectives*, 19–28). Today, that legacy is pursued by the Media Ecology Association (MEA): 'a not-for-profit organization dedicated to promoting the study, research, criticism, and application of media ecology in educational, industry, political, civic, social, cultural, and artistic contexts, and the open exchange of ideas, information, and research among the Association's members and the larger community' (see http://www.media-ecology.org).

41 Morrison, 'Marshall McLuhan: The Modern Janus,' 194.
42 McLuhan, 'The Place of Thomas Nashe in the Learning of His Time,' 49.
43 McLuhan and McLuhan, *Laws of Media*, 9.
44 Derrick de Kerckhove, 'Techniques d'intuition,' in Kerckhove and Iannucci, eds, *McLuhan e la metamorfosi dell'uomo*, 27 (my translation).
45 Contrary to what is asserted by Theall in *The Medium Is the Rear-View Mirror* (see, for instance, chapter 8), W. Terrence Gordon recalls that in the 1970s Ferdinand de Saussure's manual was one of the books McLuhan engaged with constantly, not to embrace de Saussure's thesis in toto, but to further investigate language potentialities (see Gordon, *Escape into Understanding*, 323 ff).
46 See references to Richards in McLuhan's letters from Cambridge, in *Letters of Marshall McLuhan*, 50, 58, 79.
47 Richards, *Science and Poetry*, 56.
48 Ibid., 55.
49 Willmott, *McLuhan*, 11–24.
50 McLuhan, *Counterblast*, 14.
51 McLuhan, *The Mechanical Bride*, vii.
52 Ibid.
53 *Letters of Marshall McLuhan*, 221 (my emphasis).
54 Willmott, *McLuhan*, 37.
55 Richards, *Science and Poetry*, 58.
56 McLuhan, *The Gutenberg Galaxy*, lxii.
57 McLuhan, *Counterblast* (1954), n.pag.

58 McLuhan, *Understanding Media*, 170.
59 For a discussion of Bacon's ideas in *The Advancement of Learning*, see McLuhan, *The Gutenberg Galaxy*, 117ff.
60 'Marshall McLuhan: A Candid Conversation with the High Priest of Popcult and Metaphysician of Media,' *Playboy*, March 1969, p. 74.
61 Ibid.
62 McLuhan, Florida State University Lecture, 1970, in *Video McLuhan 5*, written and narrated by T. Wolfe.
63 McLuhan, 'James Joyce: Trivial and Quadrivial,' in *The Interior Landscape*, 31–2.
64 Marshall McLuhan, in 'The Art of Wychwood Park,' ed. Albert W.M. Fulton and Keith M.O. Miller, Wychwood Park Library, Toronto; quoted in Nevitt and McLuhan, *Who Was Marshall McLuhan?* 34.
65 McLuhan, *Understanding Media*, 95 (my emphasis).
66 Medawar, *The Hope of Progress*, 25.
67 Ibid., 31.
68 McLuhan, *Understanding Media*, 85.

2. Towards Post-Secondary Orality: The Mosaic

1 Ong, *Orality and Literacy*, 68.
2 'The execution belongs to the author alone; it is what is most personal to him, and we measure him by that. The advantage, the luxury, as well as the torment and the responsibility of the novelist, is that there is no limit to what he may attempt as an executant – no limit to his possible experiments, efforts, discoveries, successes' (James, *The Art of Fiction*, 9).
3 Ford Madox Ford discusses the elaborations of the concepts of 'time shift,' 'progression d'effet,' and 'juxtaposition of situations' in his memoir *Joseph Conrad: A Personal Remembrance* (1924).
4 See, among many, T.S. Eliot, 'Tradition and the Individual Talent,' and the other essays in *The Sacred Wood* (1920).
5 McLuhan, *Understanding Media*, 430.
6 Landow, *Hypertext 3.0*, 1.
7 See Hutcheon, *A Poetics of Postmodernism*.
8 Ong, *Orality and Literacy*, 100.
9 McLuhan, *The Gutenberg Galaxy*, lxii.
10 See, as one among many possible examples, the chapter entitled 'The Phonograph: The Toy That Shrank the National Chest' in *Understanding Media*, where anecdotic and colloquial stories (see p. 371) are constantly juxtaposed with more scholarly dissertations (see p. 373).

11 Shakespeare, *Twelfth Night*, 3.1.59–67.
12 McLuhan, *Understanding Media*, 284.
13 McLuhan, *The Interior Landscape*, xiv.
14 'Marshall McLuhan,' 1-Famous-Quotes.com, Gledhill Enterprises, 2011, http://www.1-famous-quotes.com/quote/565562, accessed 26 July 2011.
15 McLuhan and Fiore, *War and Peace in the Global Village*, 3.
16 Sobelman, Marshall McLuhan, 10. See also McLuhan on interface in his 'Introduction' to H.A. Innis, *The Bias of Communication*: 'Interface refers to the interaction of substances in a kind of mutual irritation. In art and poetry this is precisely the technique of symbolism ... with its paratactic procedure of juxtaposition without connective. It is the natural form of conversation or dialogue rather than of written discourse' (viii). McLuhan returns to this concept in *The Gutenberg Galaxy*: 'Two cultures or technologies can, like astronomical galaxies, pass through one another without collision: but not without change of configuration. In modern physics there is, similarly, the concept of "interface" or the meeting and metamorphosis of two structures. Such "interficiality" is the very key to the Renaissance, as to our twentieth century' (170).
17 'Marshall McLuhan: A Candid Conversation with the High Priest of Popcult and Metaphysician of Media,' *Playboy*, March 1969, p. 54.
18 'Marshall McLuhan,' 1-Love-Quotes.com, Gledhill Enterprises, 2011, http://www.1-love-quotes.com/quote/912500, accessed 27 July 2011.
19 McLuhan, 'The Future of the Book,' in *Understanding Me*, 177–80.
20 See Ong, *Orality and Literacy*, 9.
21 See Marinetti's preface to his *Antologia dei poeti futuristi* (1912).
22 Ong, *Orality and Literacy*, 3.
23 'As we extend our educational operation by television and videotape we shall find that the teacher is no longer the source of data but of insight. More and more teachers will be needed for the type of depth instruction that goes naturally with television, with light through rather than light on' (McLuhan, 'Electronic Revolution – 1959,' in *Understanding Me*, 10).

3. Thus Spoke the Oracle

1 This documentary sums up all the ideas expressed in the volume of the same title, written in collaboration with artist Quentin Fiore. See *The Medium Is the Massage*, with Marshall McLuhan, Long-Playing Record, 1968, produced by John Simon, conceived and coordinated by Jerome Agel, written by Marshall McLuhan, Quentin Fiore, and Jerome Agel.
2 Walter Ong quoted in McLuhan, *Letters*, 94.

3 Ong, *Orality and Literacy*, 15.

4 Ibid.

5 Ibid., 7, 8.

6 Ibid., 36.

7 Ibid., 38.

8 Ibid., 110–11.

9 This idea constitutes an underpinning leitmotiv in McLuhan's doctoral dissertation, 'The Place of Thomas Nashe in the Learning of His Time' (1943).

10 Ibid., 40.

11 McLuhan, 'Media Hot and Cold,' in *Understanding Media*, 39–50.

12 McLuhan, *Understanding Media*, 413, 425–6.

13 Ong, *Orality and Literacy*, 41.

14 To avoid being misunderstood, I invite you to remember that I am not discussing here McLuhan's *private persona* but his *mosaic*, that is, the summa of *all* his various masks, of which the private man is just one (and, no doubt, as a private persona, McLuhan was a conservative).

15 Ong, *Orality and Literacy*, 15.

16 McLuhan, *Understanding Media*, 12.

17 'Marshall McLuhan: A Candid Conversation with the High Priest of Popcult and Metaphysician of Media,' *Playboy*, March 1969, p. 64. These ideas clearly opened the way to the new field of studies offered by media ecology, as well as to Neil Postman's pedagogical concepts as expressed in books such as *Teaching as a Conserving Activity* (1979) See also Strate, *Echoes and Reflections: On Media Ecology as a Field of Study* (2006).

18 Ong, *Orality and Literacy*, 48.

19 Ibid., 44.

20 Ibid., 45–6.

21 Ibid., 42.

22 Ibid., 49.

23 Marshall and McLuhan, *Laws of Media*, 36.

4. Let the Guru Resound

1 See, for instance, McLuhan, Galbraith, Marcuse parlent à *FORCES* (Montreal: Relations publiques de l'Hydro-Québec, 1973).

2 'The fourth world is the electric world that goes around the first, the second and the third. The first is the industrial world of the nineteenth century; the second is Russian socialism; the third is the rest of the world where industrial institutions have not established themselves yet. And the fourth world is a world that goes around all of them. The fourth world is us, the

electric world, is the computer world. The fourth world can come to Africa before the first and the second worlds …' (*Video McLuhan 6,* York University Lecture, 1979).

3 McLuhan, *The Gutenberg Galaxy,* 33, 81.
4 See Heisenberg, *Physics and Philosophy,* 33ff.
5 Hayles, *The Cosmic Web,* 15.
6 McLuhan and Parker, *Through the Vanishing Point,* 2.
7 Ibid.
8 The *DEW Line* is also the name McLuhan gave to a newsletter he edited in collaboration with the Human Development Corporation in New York City from July 1968 to October 1970. He also used this concept during a radio talk for CBC, in May 1927, 'Canada: A Borderline Case,' in relation to the idea of frontier· 'McLuhan spoke of the DEW line as a kind of electronic frontier, a borderline of data and information' (McNamara in *The Interior Landscape,* 181).
9 McLuhan and Parker, *Through the Vanishing Point,* 3.
10 Ibid., 6.
11 McLuhan, *The Gutenberg Galaxy,* 36.
12 See Umberto Boccioni, *Forme uniche della continuità nello spazio* (1913). McLuhan mentions Boccioni in *Understanding Media,* 206.
13 Capra, *The Tao of Physics,* 42–3 (my italics).
14 Heisenberg, *Physics and Philosophy,* 43.
15 As Eric McLuhan further recalls: 'Of course there was rigour and science in it aplenty, but not conventional science. How then could we reconcile the two: satisfy the one without subverting the other? There began the search that led to the present book … Now we were faced with the question of how to make it "scientific." It took my father nearly two full yeas of constant inquiry to find out what constitutes a scientific statement. He asked everyone he encountered – colleagues, students, friends, associates, visitors. Finally, one evening, he found the answer in Sir Karl Popper's *Objective Knowledge* – that it was something stated in such a manner that it could be disproved. That was it' (*Laws of Media,* viii).
16 Heisenberg, *Physics and Philosophy,* 31, 35, 45–50.
17 Ford, *The English Novel,* 24.
18 Capra, *The Tao of Physics,* 33.
19 McLuhan, *The Gutenberg Galaxy,* 40.
20 McLuhan, *Counterblast,* 23.
21 McLuhan and McLuhan, *Laws of Media,* 15.
22 McLuhan, *The Gutenberg Galaxy,* 36.
23 McLuhan and McLuhan, *Laws of Media,* 40.

24 McLuhan, *The Gutenberg Galaxy*, 40.
25 McLuhan and McLuhan, *Laws of Media*, 16.
26 McLuhan, *The Gutenberg Galaxy*, 183.
27 Ibid., 283.
28 Heisenberg, *Physics and Philosophy*, 50.
29 McLuhan and McLuhan, *Laws of Media*, 43.
30 Ibid.
31 Ibid., 6–7.
32 Ibid., 110.
33 Ibid., 76.
34 Ibid., 41.
35 See R.J. Trotter, 'The Other Hemisphere,' *Science News* 109.2 (April 1976); and J. Jaynes, *The Origin of Consciousness in the Breakdown of the Bicameral Mind* (Boston: Houghton Mifflin Co., 1976). McLuhan engages with these studies in his essay 'The Brain and the Media: The Western Hemisphere,' and in *Laws of Media*, 67 ff.
36 Okakura Kazuko's *The Book of Tea*, quoted in *Laws of Media*, 78.
37 McLuhan and McLuhan, *Laws of Media*, 78.
38 Ibid., 49.
39 McLuhan and Parker, *Through the Vanishing Point*, 36–7.

5. A Conscious Modernist Craftsman

1 Perloff, 'Modernist Studies,' in Greenblatt and Gunn, eds, *Redrawing the Boundaries*, 154.
2 Dettmar, 'Introduction,' in *Rereading the New*, 1–24.
3 Pound, *Hugh Selwyn Mauberley*, Part II (1920).
4 Among the most famous books discussing modernism in terms of an ideological and political approach is the highly controversial volume by Paul Carey, *The Intellectuals and the Masses: Pride and Prejudice among the Literary Intelligentsia* (1989), which tries to establish an antithetical and irreconcilable positioning of modernists and masses. As far as I see it, I'd rather stand with a more articulated approach, such as the one offered by Michael Tratner in *Modernism and Mass Politics: Joyce, Woolf, Eliot, Yeats* (1995), or Melba Cuddy-Keane in *Virginia Woolf: The Intellectual and the Public Sphere* (2003).
5 Marchand, *Marshall McLuhan*, 37.
6 Ibid., 56.
7 McLuhan, 'Dos Passos: Technique vs. Sensibility,' in *The Interior Landscape*, 54–5.
8 McLuhan, *The Mechanical Bride*, vii.

9 See Bacigalupo, 'Le poetiche dell'impersonalità: Pound, Eliot, Joyce e Lewis.'

10 Heisenberg, *Physics and Philosophy*, 54, 58 (my italics).

11 'The Communication Revolution,' *Video McLuhan 4*, Ohio State University Panel, 1958,

12 McLuhan, *The Gutenberg Galaxy*, 95.

13 Ibid., 219.

14 McLuhan and McLuhan, *Laws of Media*, 100.

15 See: Fortunati, 'Il metabolismo delle forme narrative nel romanzo impressionista'; Wees, *Vorticism and the English Avant-Garde*; Di Michele, *Le avanguardie artistiche del Novecento*; Bradbury and McFarlane, eds, *Modernism: A Guide to European Literature, 1890–1930*; Cianci, ed., *Modernismo/Modernismi*.

16 McLuhan, *Understanding Media*, 85.

17 McLuhan and McLuhan, *Laws of Media*, 48–9.

18 Lorenzini, Introduction, in *Il paesaggio interiore: La critica letteraria di Marshall McLuhan*, 11.

6. The Hyper-Language of the Media 'Fan'

1 Moss, 'Introduction,' in *At the Speed of Light There Is Only Illumination*, 1.

2 See, for instance, *Video McLuhan 2 – 1965–1970*, written and narrated by Tom Wolfe.

3 Stone, *Marshall McLuhan and the Humanist Tradition: Media Theory and Encyclopaedic Learning*, 100.

4 Ibid., 101.

5 Landow, *Hypertext: The Convergence of Contemporary Critical Theory and Technology* (1982).

6 Landow, *Hypertext 3.0: Critical Theory and New Media in an Era of Globalization*, 1.

7 Ibid., 4.

8 Nelson, *Literary Machines*, 2.

9 'Memex' is an acronym bridging 'memory' and 'index,' a term created by Vannevar Bush for a theoretical prototype (or 'proto-idea') of the would-be hypertext and discussed in his by now classic essay 'As We May Think.'

10 Moos, 'The Hypertext Heuristic: McLuhan Probes Tested (A Case for Edible Spaceship),' in Strate and Watchel, eds, *The Legacy of McLuhan*, 305–22.

11 Ibid., 315.

12 See *Video McLuhan 5*, Florida State University Lecture, 1970.

13 Moos, 'The Hypertext Heuristic,' 316.

14 Ibid., 318.

15 Ibid., 317.
16 McLuhan, 'Introduction,' in *The Bias of Communication*, by H.A. Innis, vii–xvi.
17 McLuhan, *Understanding Media*, 74.
18 Ibid., 63.
19 See also Moos, 'The Hypertext Heuristic,' 308–9.
20 Ibid., 310.
21 McLuhan, 'Introduction,' in *The Bias of Comunications*, by H.A. Innis, ix. See also Logan, 'The Axiomatics of Innis and McLuhan.'
22 Moos, 'The Hypertext Heuristic,' 310–11. The final passage is quoted from McLuhan's 'Introduction,' in *The Bias of Comunications*, by H.A. Innis, vii.

7. McLuhan and Media Studies

 1 Lamberti, 'From Linear to Acoustic Space,' in Liska and Eysteinsson, eds, *Modernism*, 431–48.
 2 Valdivia, ed., *A Companion to Media Studies*, 1.
 3 Katz et al., eds, *Canonic Texts in Media Research*, 154 (my italics).
 4 See the chapter 'L'accusa di determinismo' in Lamberti, *Marshall McLuhan: Tra letteratura, arte e media*, 80ff.
 5 'My theory of communication is a theory of transformation as opposed to the theories on communication based on transportation. Transportation: how you move information from point A to point B to point C … to avoid disturbance, deviation. That's not what I study. Transformation: what do these media do to the people who use them? How people are changed by the instrument they employ? … The medium is the message means a hidden environment of services created by an innovation. It is the environment that changes people, not the technology' (*Video McLuhan 5*, Florida State University Lecture, 1970).
 6 See chapter 6 in this volume, 'The Hyper-Language of the Media "Fan."'
 7 McLuhan, *The Gutenberg Galaxy*, lxii.
 8 See Joshua Meyrowitz's essay in Katz et al., eds, *Canonic Texts in Media Research*.
 9 See Strate, *Echoes and Reflections*.
10 McLuhan, *The Gutenberg Galaxy*, 229.
11 See, for instance, *Video McLuhan 5*, Florida State University Lecture, 1970.
12 As recalled by Philip Marchand in his volume *Marshall McLuhan: The Medium and the Messenger*. 'The contemporary political movement he mentioned with some guarded approval was fascism; aware of their numerous errors, he nonetheless approved of the Fascists' diagnosis of the ills of the modern world. The Fascists, in urging a return to heroic enterprises, in rejecting the

dull, "emasculating" utopias of socialism as well as the rapacious appetites of capitalism, seemed to him to be on the right track' (27).

13 Stearn, ed., *McLuhan, Hot and Cool*, 279. Also in *Video McLuhan 6*, York University Lecture, 1979, he repeats: 'Marx, I'm not trying to undermine him, I'm simply pointing out the obvious, he was a XIX century man who knew nothing about electricity, nothing about the instantaneous … It never occurred to him that perhaps the most important commodity in the XX century would be information and not hardware products.'

14 Grosswiler, *Method Is the Message*, 13.

15 Ibid., vii.

16 See *Video McLuhan 4*, Ohio State University Panel, 1958, 'The Communication Revolution.' (See also p. 101 of the present volume.)

17 McLuhan, *The Gutenberg Galaxy*, 47.

18 McLuhan, *Counterblast* (1954), n.pag.

19 Ibid.

20 Nerone, 'Approaches to Media History,' in Valdivia, ed., *A Companion in Media Studies*, 99.

21 Calvino, *Why Read the Classics*, 4, 8.

22 Ibid., 5.

8. From Literature to Media Studies

1 Valuable accounts of McLuhan's life and education at Cambridge University can be found in Marchand, *Marshall McLuhan: The Medium and the Messenger*, Gordon, *Marshall McLuhan: Escape into Understanding*, and Marchessault, *Marshall McLuhan: Cosmic Media*.

2 McLuhan, *Letters*, 44.

3 Ibid., 84.

4 See McLuhan, *Letters*, 72–3.

5 In a letter to his mother (5 September 1935), McLuhan comments on and explains his conversion to Catholicism, clearly pointing out the role played by Chesterton in the making of his decision; in the same letter, he also underlines that Chesterton was both a spiritual and a literary guide for him. It was Chesterton who opened McLuhan's eyes to European culture, encouraging him 'to know it more closely' (*Letters*, 73).

6 'G.K. Chesterton: A Practical Mystic,' *Dalhousie Review* 15 (1936): 455–64.

7 Chesterton, *The Secret of Father Brown*, 6.

8 Doyle, 'The Science of Deduction,' chapter 1 of *The Sign of the Four*, 90.

9 McLuhan, 'G.K. Chesterton,' 456, 458.

10 Chesterton, *Heretics*, 56.

11 McLuhan, *Letters*, 221.

12 McLuhan, *The Mechanical Bride*, vii.

13 See McLuhan, 'Formal Causality in Chesterton.' This essay is now part of a collection, recently published: Marshall McLuhan and Eric McLuhan, *Media and Formal Cause* (Houston: NeoPoiesis Press, 2011).

14 McLuhan, *Letters*, 18 May 1946, p. 187 (my italics).

15 See McLuhan's letter to Richards, 12 July 1968, *Letters*, 355.

16 McLuhan, *Letters*, 73.

17 See Lamberti, *Marshall McLuhan: Tra letteratura, arte e media*, especially chapter 5, 'Il grammatico McLuhan' (McLuhan the grammarian).

18 McLuhan, 'The Place of Thomas Nashe in the Learning of His Time' (1943), 447.

19 Lewis, *Time and Western Man*, 389.

20 McLuhan, *Letters*, 41–2.

21 McLuhan, *The Interior Landscape*, 91.

22 'Pound, Eliot, and the Rhetoric of *The Waste Land*,' *New Literary History: A Journal of Theory and Interpretation* 10 (1978–9): 557–80. McLuhan's essay 'Mr Eliot's Historical Decorum' has been reprinted in *Renascence* 25.4 (1972–3): 183–9.

23 See, for instance, Tratner, *Modernism and Mass Politics: Joyce, Woolf, Eliot, Yeats*.

24 'Joyce, Mallarmé and the Press,' in *The Interior Landscape*, 5.

25 Ibid., 17–18.

26 See, for instance, Wilson, *Consilience: The Unity of Knowledge*.

27 Carpenter, 'Remembering *Explorations*,' 7.

28 McLuhan, *Letters*, 18 May 1946, p. 187.

29 Ibid., 147.

30 See McLuhan's letter to Father J. Stanley Murphy (9 March 1944), in which McLuhan introduces his course proposal as 'a course in the analysis of the present scene. Advertisements, newspapers, best-sellers, detective fictions, movies, etc. Contrasted with a true pattern of homogeneous culture, rationally ordered. This contrast made in concrete detail by analysis say of section of sixteenth century society – its architecture, literature, music, economics, etc.' (*Letters*, 157).

31 Ibid., 220–1.

9. Ford Madox Ford: 'Not Mere Chat'

1 Ford, *The Critical Attitude*, 28.

2 Ibid., 29.

3 Ford, *Henry James*, 189.

4 Richards, *Science and Poetry*, 58. See chapter 1 of this volume, 'A Renewed Approach to Marshall McLuhan's Poetics.'

5 Bradbury, 'The English Review'; MacShane, *The Life and Work of Ford Madox Ford*; Stang, *The Ford Madox Ford Reader*; Saunders, *Ford Madox Ford: A Dual Life*.

6 See Elena Lamberti, '"Scientific Historian" versus "Social Historian": Ford Madox Ford's Historic Sense,' in Fortunati and Lamberti, eds, *Ford Madox Ford and 'The Republic of Letters,'* 30–40.

7 Goldring, *South Lodge: Reminiscences of Violet Hunt, Ford Madox Ford and the English Review Circle*, 25.

8 Ford Madox Ford, in *the transatlantic review* 1 (April 1924): 169.

9 Ford quoted in Poli, *Ford Madox Ford and the transatlantic review*, 42.

10 Among the sharper criticisms of the young 'protégés' are those by Wyndham Lewis (who kept reminding Ford that 'what people want is me, not you … They want me. A vortex … I … I. The Vortex' (see Ford, *Return to Yesterday*, 400) and Ernest Hemingway (who in his *A Moveable Feast* introduces Ford as the devil's disciple who loved to lie about everything).

11 Wyndham Lewis clearly pointed out the important role played by Ford Madox Ford in relation to Ezra Pound. As he wrote in 1950: 'It was not the fault of England nor was it his, but I hope I shall not seem sensational if I say that looking back I cannot see him [Ezra Pound] stopping here very long without some such go-between as Ford Madox Hueffer' (in Russell, ed., *An Examination of Ezra Pound*, 259). Pound himself acknowledged his debts to Ford Madox Ford, pointing out that the latter forced him to reassess his use of language as a poet: ' I have put down as a personal debt to my forerunners that I had five, and only five, useful criticisms of my writing in my lifetime, one from Yeats, one from Bridges, one from Thomas Hardy, a recent one from a Roman Archbishop and one from Ford, and that last the most vital, or at any rate on par with Hardy's … He [Ford] felt the errors of contemporary style to the point of rolling (physically and if you look at it as mere superficial snob ridiculously) on the floor of his temporary quarter in Giessen, when my third volume displayed me trapped, fly-papered, gummed and strapped down in a jejune provincial effort to learn, mehercule, the stilted language then passed for "good English" … And that roll saved me at least two years, perhaps more. It sent me back to my own proper effort, namely, using the living tongue … though none of us has found a more natural language than Ford did' (Pound in 'Homage to Ford Madox Ford,' *New Direction* 7 [1942]: 480–1).

12 McLuhan, *Letters*, 206.

13 Ibid., 206–7.

14 'Speaking broadly, literature at the present day divides itself into two sharply
    defined classes – the imaginative and the factual – and there is a third type,
    the merely inventive which, if it be not in any way to be codeine, has func-
    tions in the Republic nearly negligible' (Ford Madox Ford, in *The English
    Review* 1 [Dec. 1908]: 159).

15 Ford Madox Ford, 'The Critical Attitude,' *The English Review* 3 (Nov. 1909):
    665.

16 Stang, ed., *The Ford Madox Ford Reader*, 266.

17 Together with Joseph Conrad, Ford is considered as the father of literary
    impressionism, which – progressing within a line Flaubert had begun to
    trace, the symbolist poets had developed, and Henry James refined – leads to
    a renewed poetic, as well as to a new form. 'We saw that life did not narrate,'
    wrote Ford recalling his collaboration with Conrad, 'but made impressions
    on our brains. We, in turn, if we wish to produce on you an effect of life, must
    not narrate but render impressions' (*Joseph Conrad: A Personal Remembrance*,
    18). Critics have investigated Ford's 'metaphysics,' discussing how Ford and
    Conrad developed a new literary 'realism,' and showing how their technical
    experiments were deeply connected with a new sensibility and a subtler idea
    of 'truth' aimed at deconstructing reality in order to rebuild it. The concept
    of 'imaginative writing' is used by Ford himself in order to define a literature
    whose goal is that of putting the readers into contact with the true spirit of
    their time. To do so, sometimes the writer disregards the historical facts and
    develops illuminating visions, which Ford called 'Impressions.' See Hampson
    and Saunders, eds, *Ford Madox Ford's Modernity*; Wiesenfarth, ed., *History and
    Representation in Ford Madox Ford's Writings*; Fortunati and Lamberti, eds, *Ford
    Madox Ford and 'The Republic of Letters.'*

18 Ford, *The Critical Attitude*, 29.

19 'What is relevant here to the art of Coleridge concerns the confessional and
    digressive character of *The Ancient Mariner*. For it is this confessional and
    circuitous character which has penetrated not only Byron's tales but the art
    of *The Ring and the Book*, the novels of Henry James, of Ford Madox Ford,
    and of Joseph Conrad. It is the pattern of Pound's *Mauberley* and the *Cantos*,
    and provides the thread to the labyrinth of Eliot's poems from Prufrock to
    the *Cocktail Party*' (Marshall McLuhan, 'Coleridge as Artist,' in *The Interior
    Landscape*, 131). The second reference to Ford is in the same volume, in the
    essay 'John Dos Passos: Technque vs. Sensibility,' p. 60.

20 McLuhan, *Understanding Media*, 325.

21 Private interview with Father Dewan, at the Dominican College in Ottawa,
    1997.

22 McLuhan, *Letters*, 173.

23 Ibid., 200.
24 Ibid., 202.
25 Ibid., 204.
26 As Pound wrote, the new poetry should have the following qualities: '1) Direct treatment of the "thing," whether subjective or objective; 2) To use absolutely no word that does not contribute to the presentation; 3) As regarding rhythm: to compose in the sequence of the musical phrase, not in the sequence of a metronome' (F.S. Flint, 'A Few Don'ts by an Imagist [Interview with Pound],' in *Poetry*, March 1913).
27 As McLuhan recalled: 'In this century Ezra Pound called the artist "the antenna of the race." Art as a radar acts as "an early alarm system," as it were, enabling us to discover social and psychic targets in lots of time to prepare to cope with them' ('Introduction to the Second Edition,' *Understanding Media*, 16).
28 'Marshall McLuhan: A Candid Conversation with the High Priest of Popcult and Metaphysician of Media,' *Playboy*, March 1969, p. 56.
29 Ford Madox Ford, 'The Critical Attitude,' *The English Review* 4 (Dec. 1909): 102.
30 'Marshall McLuhan: A Candid Conversation with the High Priest of Popcult and Metaphysician of Media,' *Playboy*, March 1969, p. 56.
31 Ford, Preface to *Stories from de Maupassant*, by Elsa Martindale.
32 Ford, *The English Novel: From the Earliest Days to the Death of Joseph Conrad*, 32.
33 'Marshall McLuhan: A Candid Conversation with the High Priest of Popcult and Metaphysician of Media,' *Playboy*, March 1969, p. 56.
34 Ford, *A History of Our Own Time*, 9–10. The edition quoted (1988) is based on a manuscript (dated ca 1930) sold by Janice Biala (Ford's companion at the time of his death and his literary executor) to the Cornell University Library in 1973.
35 McLuhan, *Understanding Media*, 5–6.
36 McLuhan, *The Gutenberg Galaxy*, 36.
37 Marshall McLuhan, 'An Ancient Quarrel in Modern America (Sophists vs. Grammarians),' in *The Interior Landscape*, 223–34.
38 See Ford, *The March of Literature*, 150.
39 Elena Lamberti, 'Reading Ford through Marshall McLuhan: *The Fifth Queen* in the Light of the New Media,' in Rademacher, ed., *Modernism and the Individual Talent*, 45–53.
40 McLuhan, 'Myth and Mass Media,' 344.
41 McLuhan, *The Mechanical Bride*, 87.
42 Newman, 'Ford Madox Ford's Fifth Queen Trilogy: Mythical Fiction and Political Letters.'

43 Ford, *The Fifth Queen*, 590.
44 Ibid., 54.
45 McLuhan, *The Gutenberg Galaxy*, 193.
46 Ford, *The Fifth Queen*, 22.
47 Ibid., 50.
48 Ibid., 55.
49 Ibid., 79.
50 Ibid., 62.
51 Ibid., 190.
52 Ibid., 12.
53 Ibid., 280.
54 Ibid., 524–5.
55 Ibid., 568.
56 'Marshall McLuhan: A Candid Conversation with the High Priest of Popcult and Metaphysician of Media,' *Playboy*, March 1969.
57 Ford, *The Fifth Queen*, 589–90.
58 'Marshall McLuhan: A Candid Conversation with the High Priest of Popcult and Metaphysician of Media,' *Playboy*, March 1969.
59 McLuhan, *The Gutenberg Galaxy*, 28.

10. James Joyce: Vivisecting Society

1 McLuhan, *Letters*, 217.
2 Ibid., 147.
3 Burgess, *One Man's Chorus*.
4 Marchand, *Marshall McLuhan: The Medium and the Messenger*, 94.
5 McLuhan, 'The Place of Thomas Nashe in the Learning of His Time' (1943), 447. See chapter 8 in this volume, 'From Literature to Media Studies.'
6 *The Mechanical Bride* is the first of a series of books in which McLuhan intended to study man's relation to the environment as shaped by new technologies. McLuhan hinted at this 'series' in a letter to Harry J. Skornia written in 1964: 'I am finishing up the successor to the *Mechanical Bride*.' According to the editors of the volume of letters, McLuhan refers to '*Culture Is Our Business* (1970) – on electronic man (McLuhan had previously studied industrial man in *The Mechanical Bride* and typographic man in *The Gutenberg Galaxy*).' The editors describe *Culture Is Our Business* as 'a graphically arresting anthology of advertisements, paired with a series of statements and quotations that they evoked for McLuhan' (*Letters*, 306)
7 McLuhan, *The Gutenberg Galaxy*, 85.
8 Both Barthes and Eco discuss several 'myths' of mass society (Barthes,

Mythologies; Eco, *Apocalittici e integrati*; *Il superuomo di massa*). It is important to recall again that McLuhan's *The Mechanical Bride* was translated into Italian only in 1984. In his introduction to the Italian edition, Roberto Faenza polemically suggests that such a long delay in translating this important book could have been intentional ('editorial omissions do have a meaning, too') in order to be able to present as 'original ... cultural positions which are instead borrowed ones' (see McLuhan, *La sposa meccanica*, 7–10).

9 Umberto Eco, Review of *La sposa meccanica*, in *L'Espresso*, 25 March 1984, p. 99.

10 See McLuhan, *Letters*, 405. In 1971, Jonathan Miller wrote his *Marshall McLuhan* for the Fontana-Collins 'Modern Masters' series, edited by Sir Frank Kermode. The final passage of that book immediately reveals how Miller's take was not in favour of McLuhan's ideas: 'And yet I can rehabilitate no actual truth from what I read. Perhaps McLuhan has accomplished the greatest paradox of all, creating the possibility of truth by shocking us with a gigantic system of lies.' In 1998, I interviewed Sir Kermode on his decision to publish Miller's negative discussion of McLuhan in his series. Surprisingly, the English critic told me that, in fact, Miller had started with a positive approach to McLuhan's works but that he changed his opinion while writing it. Kermode published it nevertheless because he chose not to censor Miller, even though his choice inevitably affected his relationship with McLuhan. This story is confirmed by McLuhan's letters to various friends: his first meeting with Miller was favourably recalled in a letter to Harold Rosenberg, in 1965; similarly, his original correspondence with or on Kermode was on fair terms until Miller's book came out (see *Letters*, 375, 426).

11 McLuhan, *The Mechanical Bride*, v.

12 'Marshall McLuhan,' 1-Famous-Quotes.com, Gledhill Enterprises, 2011, http://www.1-famous-quotes.com/quote/565424, accessed 27 July 2011.

13 McLuhan, *Understanding Media*, 69.

14 Convincing comments on this aspect can be found in Marchessault, *Marshall McLuhan: Cosmic Media*, 55ff.

15 Ballard, Introduction to *Crash*, 4.

16 McLuhan, *The Mechanical Bride*, v.

17 Ibid.

18 McLuhan, Marshall, 'Art as Anti-Environment,' 56.

19 Ruskin, quoted by McLuhan in *The Interior Landscape*, 17–18.

20 On the idea of 'media poetics,' see McLuhan and McLuhan, *Laws of Media*. The now constantly referred to expression of 'media ecology' can be seen as an extension of McLuhan's original idea that 'new media are new languages, their grammar and syntax yet unknown' (*Laws of Media*, 229). On the implications of 'media ecology,' see, among others, Neil Postman's *Teaching*

as a Conserving Activity (1979) (Postman has often acknowledged his 'debt' to McLuhan) and Lance Strate's *Echoes and Reflections: On Media Ecology as a Field of Study* (2006).

21 McLuhan, *The Interior Landscape*, 17.
22 Ibid., 16 (my italics).
23 Ibid.
24 McLuhan, *The Mechanical Bride*, v.
25 See Eric McLuhan, *The Role of Thunder in Finnegans Wake.*
26 McLuhan, *The Interior Landscape*, xiv.
27 McLuhan and McLuhan, *Laws of Media*, 9. It is a kind of 'epiphany' which clearly retrieves the metaphysical poets' rhetorical strategy. Claude Bissell, president of the University of Toronto when McLuhan was a professor at the university's St Michael's College, put it well: 'Marshall liked to describe his ideas as "probes," not firm convictions, although he always seemed to express them with conviction. They were attempts to force a reconsideration of accepted ideas. These probes were like the "conceits" of metaphysical poets, who delighted in yoking two disparate things together, with illuminating results for each part of the conceit and for the conceit as a whole. These probes would often emerge in conversation or in the give and take of an informal group setting' (quoted in Nevitt and McLuhan, *Who Was Marshall McLuhan?* 188).

11. Ezra Pound: Pursuing Persuasion, Translating Cultures

1 McLuhan, *Letters*, 193–4.
2 H. Kenner, *The Pound Era* (Faber: London, 1971).
3 Marshall McLuhan, book review of *The Poetry of Ezra Pound*, by Hugh Kenner, *Renascence* 4.2 (1952): 215–17.
4 The manuscripts and typescripts of both 'Guide to Cahos' and 'Typhon in America,' 'early versions of *The Mechanical Bride*,' are in the Public Archives of Canada. See McLuhan, *Letters*, 191.
5 McLuhan, *Letters*, 173.
6 Ibid.
7 See De Bernardi, *Una dittatura moderna*, especially the chapter 'L'affermazione del progetto totalitario,' 222–74.
8 See, for instance, McLuhan, *Letters*, 201, 202.
9 As discussed in Part One, the idea of the 'ideogram' as a formal model underpins the making of McLuhan's 'mosaic.' Sir Frank Kermode writes about this when commenting on McLuhan's 'insoluble problem of method' in *The Gutenberg Galaxy*: 'Typography has made us incapable of knowing

and discoursing otherwise than by a "metamorphosis of situations into a fixed point of view"; that is, we reduce everything to the linear and successive, as computers reduce everything to a series of either-ors. And since he [McLuhan] himself is unable to proceed by any other method, he cannot avoid falsifying the facts his books set out to establish. Perhaps its difficulty is more fairly put in a letter that Mr McLuhan was good enough to write me, and which I take the liberty of quoting: He says the ideal form of his book would be an ideogram ...' Kermode continues underlining that 'the more linear clarity [McLuhan] gives his book, the more obviously he himself becomes the victim of typographic distortion. His book tells us not to believe it. He fights against this by making each chapter-heading a sort of verbal ideograph; if you read them all quickly you get a sort of strip-cartoon puzzle-summary of the book.' In a witty passage, Kermode offers a comment on McLuhan's *style* which can be taken, at once, as praise and criticism: 'Mr McLuhan's book is a work of historical explanation, and its merits as well as its defects are related to this. [His is] the method of the specula, or of the old hexameral commentaries, which organised an encyclopaedia into a commentary of Six Days of Creation ... In so doing he offers a fresh and coherent account of the state of the modern mind in terms of a congenial myth' (Kermode, in Stearn ed., *McLuhan Hot & Cool*, 173–80).

10 See Bacigalupo, 'Le poetiche dell'impersonalità,' 261ff.

11 McLuhan, *Letters*, 199–200.

12 Ibid., 204.

13 See Kenner, *The Poetry of Ezra Pound* and *The Pound Era*; Emery, *Ideas into Action: A Study of Pound's Cantos*; Mancuso, *Pound e la Cina*.

14 Marshall McLuhan, book review of *The Poetry of Ezra Pound*, by Hugh Kenner, *Renascence* 4.2 (1952): 215–17.

15 Marshall McLuhan, book review of *The Letters of Ezra Pound*, ed. by D.D. Paige, reprinted in McLuhan, *Letteratura e metafore della realtà*, 76–80.

16 Pound, *Guide to Kulchur*, 60.

17 Ibid., 52–3.

18 Pound's approach to literary tradition is therefore comparable to the one expressed by T.S. Eliot in his famous essay 'Tradition and the Individual Talent,' published in *The Sacred Wood* (1920). However, Eliot refers to the domain of artistic creation, whereas Pound extends that approach to his full-scale investigations of historical processes and to his active commitment not only as a poet and critic, but also as a politically engaged citizen.

19 The 'advent' of Berlusconi's commercial TV networks and its impact on Italian life and politics is recalled in a brilliant documentary-movie by Eric Gandini, *Videocracy* (Lorber Films, 2009).

20 McLuhan, 'An Ancient Quarrel in Modern America,' *Classical Journal*, January 1946, pp. 156–62.
21 Pound, *Guide to Kulchur*, 6.
22 Ibid.
23 McLuhan, *Letters*, 18.
24 McLuhan, *The Mechanical Bride*, vii.
25 See the Introduction in Hayles, *The Cosmic Web*.
26 Pound, *Guide to Kulchur*, 48.
27 Ibid., 51.
28 McLuhan, *The Gutenberg Galaxy*, 82.
29 McLuhan and Parker, *Through the Vanishing Point*, 36–7.
30 In Italy since 1924, Pound bore witness to the establishment and consolidation of the Italian fascist regime, which attracted him as a possible alternative to capitalism, on the one hand, and communism, on the other. In particular, Pound seemed to be fascinated by the idea of a 'new order' encouraged by Mussolini, something which, in turn, was based on the idealization of a tradition – the classic and the Roman one – which Pound himself considered as 'the best one.' See Doob, ed., *'Ezra Pound Speaking': Radio Speeches of World War II*; Rizzardi, *Una ghirlanda per Ezra Pound*; Nicholls, *Ezra Pound*; S. Sabbadini, 'Tra eversione e rappel à l'ordre: I percorsi reazionari entre-deux-guerres: Eliot e Pound,' in Cianci, ed., *Modernismo/Modernismi*, 423–46.
31 On this theme, see Doob, ed., *'Ezra Pound Speaking': Radio Speeches of World War II*; Rizzardi, *Una ghirlanda per Ezra Pound*; and Nicholls, *Ezra Pound*.
32 Pound, *Guide to Kulchur*, 27.
33 Morawski, 'The Basic Functions of Quotations,' 704.
34 McLuhan, *Understanding Media*, 102.

12. Wyndham Lewis: Blasting Time, Blessing Space

1 Jameson, *Fables of Aggression*, 3.
2 Ibid., 6.
3 Ibid., 4.
4 McLuhan, 'Wyndham Lewis: Lemuel in Lilliput,' in *The Medium and the Light*, 179.
5 For a recollection of the meeting and friendship between McLuhan and Lewis, in addition to Marchand's and Gordon's biographies, see McLuhan, *Letters*, 129ff.
6 Lewis, *The Enemy of the Stars*, 181.
7 See Hutcheon, *A Poetics of Postmodernism*, x.

8 Ibid., xiii. See also Wyndham Lewis, 'On Canada,' in Woodcock, ed., *Wyndham Lewis in Canada*, 24–9.

9 McLuhan, *Letters*, 165.

10 See, for instance, Wyndham Lewis, 'Nature's Place in Canadian Culture,' in Woodcock, ed., *Wyndham Lewis in Canada*, 49–59.

11 See McLuhan, *Letters*, 137.

12 See ibid., 146–7.

13 Ibid., 160.

14 See comments in footnote 5 in McLuhan, *Letters*, 165.

15 Ibid., 236.

16 Ibid., 85.

17 McLuhan, *The Interior Landscape*, 85.

18 McLuhan, *Letters*, 9 December 1953, p. 241.

19 Ibid., 217.

20 Ibid., footnote 5.

21 Lewis, *Time and Western Man*, 392.

22 Ibid., 393–4, 416–17 (italics in the original).

23 Brett Neilson, seminar at the University of Bologna, academic year 1998–9. These ideas have been further investigated in Brett, 'Wyndham Lewis in Morocco: Spatial Philosophy and the Politics of Race'; and Brett, 'Visioni dal vortice: L'emergere dello spazio sociale in Paul Cézanne e Wyndham Lewis.'

24 See, for instance, McLuhan, *Letters*, 424.

25 McLuhan, *The Interior Landscape*, 85–9.

26 McLuhan, *The Mechanical Bride*, v.

27 See McLuhan, *Counterblast* (1954).

28 McLuhan, *The Mechanical Bride*, v.

29 See Bergson, *Laughter*.

30 Ibid., 3

31 Lewis, *The Meaning of the Wild Body*, 248.

32 On Lewis's and Bergson's ideas on 'laughter,' see also Sheila Watson, 'Canada and Wyndham Lewis the Artist,' in Woodcock, ed., *Wyndham Lewis in Canada*, 76.

33 Lewis, *The Art of Being Ruled*, 24 (italics in the original).

34 Lewis quoted by McLuhan in *The Interior Landscape*, 91.

35 Ibid.

36 McLuhan, *The Mechanical Bride*, v.

37 McLuhan, *Letters*, 242.

38 Ibid.

39 'A World Art and Tradition' (1929), quoted in C.J. Fox, 'The Wild Land:

A Celebration of Globalism,' in Woodcock, ed., *Wyndham Lewis in Canada*, 45.

40 Fox, 'The Wild Land,' in Woodcock, ed., *Wyndham Lewis in Canada*, 45.

41 As noted by Adam Hammond, 'The work of Wyndham Lewis underwent a profound change during the six years he spent in North America during World War II. The metamorphosis of his political ideas is perhaps the most striking: while in the 1930s Lewis had been an ardent exponent of German and Italian nationalism, after leaving North America he published *America and Cosmic Man*, a passionate defense of internationalism. As Lewis described it, his time here 'transformed [him] from a good [*sic*] European into an excellent internationalist.' His stay in North America also marked a turning point in his stylistic development–a change registered in the strikingly dissimilar volumes of his trilogy The Human Age. The first volume, *The Childermass*, published in 1928, is a conspicuously "modernist" work–difficult, disjointed, disorienting–whereas the final two volumes, written after the war, are straightforwardly realistic' (Adam Hammond, paper presented in a panel on 'The Role of the Artist in the Local Landscape: Examining Marshall McLuhan and Sheila Watson's Relationship to Canadian Modernism,' at the MEA Annual Convention, 'Space, Place, and the McLuhan Legacy,' 23–6 June 2011, University of Alberta).

42 'I am no longer able to teach a story of the world which they would find acceptable; they would not let me teach my students the things which I now know, so I have to tell them that there is no longer anything that I can teach … No, the die, I fear, is cast, I have to find other employment. That would be very difficult in England … You may ask, cannot I think differently? Why, can I not purge myself of this order of things? Well, of course there are some things that everyone thinks which hot irons could not burn out of them. It is the circumstances of the time in which we live which have made it impossible for me to mistake my road: there have been signposts or rather lurid beacons all the way along it, leading to only one end, to one conclusion. How anyone, as historically informed as I am, can come to any very different conclusions from my own I find it hard to understand. They must have blind eyes for all the flaming signs' (Lewis, *Self Condemned*, 39–40, 41–2).

43 'The numbers, the mass of strangers, does not matter, they might as well be stones. Indeed, the thicker the mass of stony strangers the deeper the wilderness. Then the fact that Canada is four-fifths an authentic wilderness does not matter. It would be the same emptiness anywhere. The same ghastly void, next door to nothingness … I have no particular reason to go to Canada. I must go somewhere out of sight of what is going to happen because I know so well the reasons which make it impossible for it not to

occur. How disgusting, how maddening, and how foully comic all the reality of death and destruction will be; I just cannot stick around here and watch that going on. Canada is as good, or as bad a place as any other. The problem is, to get out of the world I have always known, which is as good to say of the world. So Canada is to be my grave' (Lewis, *Self Condemned*, 172).

44 Fox, 'The Wild Land,' in Woodcock, ed., *Wyndham Lewis in Canada*, 43.

45 Lewis, *Filibusters in Barbary*, in *Journey into Barbary*, 75.

46 Ibid., 71.

47 'The world-slump that hit America with the velocity of a Tornado, spewed out on to the streets millions of decent people, not necessarily passionately nomad ... So the enthusiastic Frenchmen, who point to Casablanca as the "pearl of the French Renaissance," and emphasize that it is a great city upon the latest transatlantic model, could even, if they wished, adduce the existence of Bidonville, to make the flattering comparison even more apposite! It is a parallelism which is, however, in no way dishonourable for the French, for *their* Hobo-town is the creation of born nomads, who are, by choice, the inhabitants of a tent or a caboose. No capitalist laws could drive them out of these hovels. It is different in the case of War-debt Drive, in the Hobo-town upon the shores of Lake Michigan. *There* our White stock is being forced down into a semi-savage sub-world of the down-and-out, or Untermensch. It is being thrown back into Barbary – not invited to issue out of Barbary into the advantageous plane of the civilized European life' (Lewis, *Journey into Barbary*, 71–2).

48 Eliot, *The Waste Land*.

49 Lewis, *Journey into Barbary*, 56.

50 McLuhan, *Letters*, 245.

51 McLuhan, *Counterblast* (1954).

52 McLuhan, *Counterblast* (1969), 5.

13. Literature and Media: A Round Trip

1 Medawar, *The Hope of Progress*, 31. See chapter 1 in this volume, 'A Renewed Approach to Marshall McLuhan's Poetics.'

2 McLuhan and McLuhan, *Laws of Media*, 7.

3 Ibid., viii. See also chapter 4 of this volume, 'Let the Guru Resound.'

4 Carpenter, 'Remembering *Explorations*,' 7.

5 McLuhan and McLuhan, *Laws of Media*, 128.

6 Ibid., 216.

7 Ibid., 129–30.

8 McLuhan and Watson, *From Cliché to Archetype*, 19–21.

9 See Battistini, ed., *Letteratura e scienza*, 2ff.

10 Capra, *The Tao of Physics*, 43. See chapter 4 of this volume, 'Let the Guru Resound.'

11 Gleick, *Chaos: Making a New Science*, 3–5.

12 Wilson, *Consilience: The Unity of Knowledge*, 7.

13 McLuhan and McLuhan, *Laws of Media*, 3.

14 Medawar, *The Hope of Progress*, 25. See chapter 1 of this volume, 'A Renewed Approach to Marshall McLuhan's Poetics.'

15 McLuhan, *Understanding Media*, 393, 384.

16 See ibid., 395.

17 Ibid., 383.

18 Cronenberg, *David Cronenberg: Interviews with Serge Grunberg*, 66.

19 Ballard, Introduction, in *Crash* (1995), 4.

20 McLuhan, *Counterblast* (1954).

21 *Video McLuhan 3 – 1972–1979.*

22 *Marshall McLuhan: The Man and His Message.* video, dir. Stephanie McLuhan-Ortved, 1984.

23 McLuhan, *Understanding Media*, 70.

24 *Marshall McLuhan: The Man and His Message.* dir. Stephanie McLuhan-Ortved, 1984.

25 Cronenberg, *David Cronenberg: Interviews with Serge Grunberg*, 70–1.

26 *Video McLuhan 6*, York University, 1979.

27 Alfano Miglietti, *Identità mutanti*, 11.

28 Ibid., 13.

29 See Berger, *Téléovision: Le nouveau Golem*; Hall, *The Hidden Dimension*.

30 See Granata, *Arte, estetica e nuovi media*.

31 McLuhan, *Understanding Media*, 257.

32 See McLuhan, *The Gutenberg Galaxy*, 37.

33 Sontag, *Illness as Metaphor*, 45.

34 Sontag, *AIDS and Its Metaphors*, 575.

35 McLuhan, *The Mechanical Bride*, v.

36 McLuhan, *Understanding Media*, 66.

37 'Marshall McLuhan: A Candid Conversation with the High Priest of Popcult and Metaphysician of Media,' *Playboy*, March 1969, p. 72.

38 McLuhan, *Counterblast* (1954).

39 McLuhan, *The Mechanical Bride*, 35

40 *Video McLuhan 3 – 1972–1979.*

Epilogue: Witty Fool or Foolish Wit?

1 In *Video McLuhan 3 – 1972–1979*, McLuhan comments explicitly on his use of 'the right hemisphere.'

2 McLuhan, 'The Brain and the Media: The "Western Hemisphere,"' 54.

3 McLuhan and McLuhan, *Laws of Media*, 70.

4 Theall, *The Medium Is the Rear-View Mirror*, 112, 113.

5 Ibid., xviii.

6 Ibid., xvi.

7 See Schickel, 'Marshall McLuhan: Canada's Intellectual Comet.'

8 Nevitt and McLuhan, *Who Was Marshall McLuhan? Exploring a Mosaic of Impressions*, 187.

9 McLuhan, *Understanding Media*, 315.

10 McLuhan, *Counterblast*, 28.

11 Ford, *The Critical Attitude*, 113–14. (See also p. 165 of the present volume.)

12 McLuhan, *Letters*, 44. See chapter 8 in this volume, 'From Literature to Media.'

13 Ford, *The Critical Attitude*, 8.

14 Ford, Introduction to *A Farewell to Arms*, by Ernest Hemingway, in *Critical Writings of Ford Madox Ford*, 134.

15 Poe, *A Descent into the Maesltrom*, 2–3.

Bibliography

Works by Marshall McLuhan

Books

McLuhan, Marshall. 'The Place of Thomas Nashe in the Learning of His Time.'
    PhD diss., Cambridge University, 1943.
– *The Mechanical Bride: Folklore of Industrial Man.* 1951. Corte Madera, CA: Gingko
    P, 2002.
– *Counterblast.* 1954 edn. Foreword by W. Terrence Gordon. Afterword by Elena
    Lamberti. Berlin and Berkeley, CA: Transmediale / Gingko P, 2011.
– *The Gutenberg Galaxy: The Making of Typographic Man.* 1962. Centennial edn.
    Toronto: U of Toronto P, 2011.
– *Understanding Media: The Extensions of Man.* 1964. Ed. W. Terrence Gordon.
    Corte Madera, CA: Gingko P, 2003.
– *Voices of Literature.* Edited with Richard J. Schoeck. 2 vols. New York: Holt, Rine-
    hart and Winston, 1964–5.
– *Counterblast.* Designed by Harley Parker. Toronto: McClelland and Stewart,
    1969.
– *The Interior Landscape: The Literary Criticism of Marshall McLuhan, 1943–1962.*
    Selected, compiled, and edited by Eugene McNamara. New York: McGraw-Hill,
    1969.
– *Culture Is Our Business.* New York: McGraw-Hill, 1970.
– *La sposa meccanica: Il Folclore dell'uomo industriale.* Trans. Francesca Gorjup
    Valente and Carla Plevano Pezzini. Varese: SugarCo Edizioni, 1984.
– *Letters of Marshall McLuhan.* Selected and edited by Matie Molinaro, Corinne
    McLuhan, and William Toye. Toronto: Oxford UP, 1987.
– *Essays: Media, Research, Technology, Art, Communication.* Ed. Michael A. Moos.
    Amsterdam: OPA, 1997.

- *The Medium and the Light: Reflections on Religion.* Ed. Eric McLuhan and Jacek Szklarek. Toronto: Stoddart, 1999.
- *Understanding Me: Lectures and Interviews.* Ed. Stephanie McLuhan and David Staines. With a Foreword by Tom Wolfe. Toronto: McClelland & Stewart, 2003.
- *The Classical Trivium: The Place of Thomas Nashe in the Learning of His Time.* Ed. W. Terrence Gordon. Corte Madera, CA: Gingko P, 2005.
- *Letteratura e metafore della realtà. II. La critica letteraria.* Ed. Silvia D'Offizi. Roma: Armando Editore, 2010.

McLuhan, Marshall, and Edmund Carpenter. *Explorations in Communication: An Anthology.* Boston: Beacon P, 1960.

McLuhan, Marshall, and Sorel Etrog. *Images from the Film Spiral.* Text by Marshall McLuhan. Toronto: Exile, 1987.

McLuhan, Marshall, and Quentin Fiore. *The Medium Is the Massage.* New York: Bantam Books, 1968.

- *War and Peace in the Global Village.* New York: Bantam Books, 1968.

McLuhan, Marshall, Kathryn Hutchon, and Eric McLuhan. *City as Classroom: Understanding Language and Media.* Toronto: Book Society of Canada, 1977.

McLuhan, Marshall, and Eric McLuhan. *Laws of Media: The New Science.* Toronto: U of Toronto P, 1988.

- *Media and Formal Cause.* Houston: NeoPoiesis P, 2011.

McLuhan, Marshall, with Barrington Nevitt. *Take Today: The Executive as Dropout.* Toronto: Longman, 1972.

McLuhan, Marshall, and Harley Parker. *Through the Vanishing Point: Space in Poetry and Painting.* New York: Harper & Row, 1969.

McLuhan, Marshall, and B.R. Powers. *The Global Village: Transformation in World Life and Media in the 21st Century.* New York: Oxford UP, 1989.

McLuhan, Marshall, and Wilfred Watson. *From Cliché to Archetype.* 1970. New York: Pocket Books, 1971.

Essays and Interviews

'G.K. Chesterton: A Practical Mystic.' *Dalhousie Review* 15 (1936): 455–64.

'Edgar Poe's Tradition.' *Sewanee Review* 52 (1944): 24–33.

'Kipling and Forster.' *Sewanee Review* 52 (1944): 332–43.

'Poetic vs Rhetorical Exegesis.' *Sewanee Review* 52 (1944): 266–76.

'Wyndham Lewis: Lemuel in Lilliput.' *Studies in Honor of St. Thomas Aquinas, Key Thinkers and Modern Thought* [St Louis University] 2 (1944): 58–72.

'American Advertizing.' *Horizon*, October 1947, pp. 132–41.

'Introduction.' In *Paradox in Chesterton*, by Hugh Kenner. London: Sheet & Ward, 1948. xi–xxii.

'Mr Eliot's Historical Decorum.' *Renascence* 2.1 (1949). Reprinted in *Renascence* 25.4 (1972–3): 183–9.

'Joyce, Aquinas, and the Poetic Process.' *Renascence* 4.1 (1951): 3–11.

'Culture without Literacy.' *Explorations in Communications*, 1 December 1953, pp. 117–27.

'From Eliot to Seneca.' *University of Toronto Quarterly* 22 (1953): 199–202.

'Maritain on Art.' Review of *Creative Intuition in Art and Poetry*, by J. Maritain. *Renascence* 6.1 (1953): 40–4.

'Catholic Humanism and Modern Letters.' *The McAuley Lectures*, 1954, pp. 67–79.

'New Media as Political Forms.' *Explorations in Communications*, 3 August 1954, pp. 120–6.

'Notes on Media as Art Forms.' *Explorations in Communications*, 2 April 1954, pp. 6–13.

'Radio and TV vs the ABCED-MINDED.' *Explorations in Communications*, 5 June 1955, pp. 12–18.

'Space, Time and Poetry.' *Explorations in Communications*, 4 February 1955, pp. 56–64.

'The Media Fit the Battle of Jericho.' *Explorations in Communications*, 6 July 1956, pp. 15–21.

'The Effect of Printed Books on Language in the 16th Century.' *Explorations in Communications*, 7 March 1957, pp. 99–108.

'Third Program in the Human Age.' *Explorations in Communications*, 8 October 1957, pp. 16–18.

'Verbo-Voco-Visual.' *Explorations in Communications*, 8 October 1957, p. 11.

'Myth and Mass Media.' *Daedalus*, Spring 1959, pp. 339–48.

'Art as Anti-Environment.' *Art News Annual* 31 (1966): 55–8.

'Cybernation and Culture.' In *The Social Impact of Cybernetics*. Ed. Charles Dechert. South Bend, IN: U of Notre Dame P, 1966. 95–108.

'Marshall McLuhan: A Candid Conversation with the High Priest of Popcult and Metaphysician of Media.' *Playboy*, March 1969, pp. 26–7, 45, 54–6, 61, 63–4, 74.

'Introduction.' In *The Bias of Communication*, by Harold Adams Innis. Toronto: U of Toronto P, 1970. vii–xvi.

'Marshall McLuhan: Une entrevue de Jean Paré.' *Force Hydro-Québec* 22 (1973): 5–26.

'English Literature as Control Tower in Communication Study.' *English Quarterly* [University of Waterloo], Spring 1974, pp. 3–7.

'Formal Causality in Chesterton.' *Chesterton Review* 11.2 (Spring/Summer 1976): 253–9.

'The Brain and the Media: The "Western Hemisphere."' *Journal of Communication* 28.4 (1978): 54–60.

'Letteratura e Media.' With Amleto Lorenzini. *Argomenti Canadesi* (1978).
'Pound, Eliot, and the Rhetoric of *The Waste Land.*' *New Literary History: A Journal of Theory and Interpretation* 10 (1978–9): 557–80.

Works on Marshall McLuhan

Books and Dissertations

Baragli, Enrico. *Dopo McLuhan.* Torino: Elle Di Ci, 1981.
– *Il caso McLuhan.* Roma: Civiltà Cattolica, 1980.
Benedetti, Paul, and Nancy DeHart, eds. *Forward through the Rear-View Mirror: Reflections on and by Marshall McLuhan.* Scarborough, ON: Prentice-Hall Canada, 1996.
Cavell, Richard. *McLuhan in Space: Cultural Geography.* Toronto: U of Toronto P, 2003.
de Kerckhove, Derrick, and Amilcare Iannucci, eds. *McLuhan e la metamorfosi dell'uomo.* Roma: Bulzoni Editore, 1984.
Duffy, Donald. *Marshall McLuhan.* Toronto: McClelland and Steward, 1969.
Finkelstein, Sidney. *Sense and Nonsense in McLuhan.* New York: International Publishers, 1968.
Gamaleri, Gianpiero. *La Galassia McLuhan: Il mondo plasmato dai media.* Roma: Armando, 1976.
Genosko, Gary. *McLuhan and Baudrillard: The Masters of Implosion.* London and New York: Routledge, 1999.
Gordon, W. Terrence. *Marshall McLuhan: Escape into Understanding: A Biography.* Toronto: Basic Books, 1997.
– *McLuhan for Beginners.* London: Writers and Readers, 1997.
Grosswiler, P. *Method Is the Message: Rethinking McLuhan through Critical Theory.* Montreal: Black Rose Books, 1998.
Kroker, Arthur. *Technology and the Canadian Mind: Innis, McLuhan, Grant.* Montreal: New World Perspective, 1984.
Lamberti, Elena. *Marshall McLuhan: Tra letteratura, arte e media.* Milano: Bruno Mondadori, 2000.
Levinson, Paul. *Digital McLuhan: A Guide to the Information Millennium.* New York and London: Routledge, 1999.
Marchand, Philip. *Marshall McLuhan: The Medium and the Messenger.* New York: Ticknor & Fields, 1989.
Marchessault, Janine. *Marshall McLuhan: Cosmic Media.* London: Sage Publications, 2005.

McLuhan, Eric, and Frank Zingrone, eds. *Essential McLuhan*. Concord, ON: Anansi, 1995.

Miller, Jonathan. *Marshall McLuhan*. London: Fontana Collins, 1971.

Moos, Michael A. *Marshall McLuhan Essays: Media Research, Technology, Art, Communication*. Amsterdam: OPA, 1997.

Moss, John, and Linda M. Morra, eds. *At the Speed of Light There Is Only Illumination: A Reappraisal of Marshall McLuhan*. Ottawa: U of Ottawa P, 2004.

Nevitt, Barrington, and Maurice McLuhan. *Who Was Marshall McLuhan? Exploring a Mosaic of Impressions*. Toronto: Comprehensivist Publications, 1994.

Rosenthal, Raymond, ed. and introd. *McLuhan: Pro & Con*. New York: Funk & Wagnalls, 1968.

Sanderson, E., ed. *Marshall Mcluhan: The Man and His Message*. Special issue of the *Antigonish Review*, Summer 1988.

Sobelman, David. *Marshall McLuhan: The Medium Is the Message: Treatment for a Documentary*. Toronto: Rosefire Film Inc., 1997.

Stamps, J. *Unthinking Modernity: Innis, McLuhan and the Frankfurt School*. Montreal: McGill-Queen's UP, 1971.

Stearn, Gerald Emanuel, ed. *McLuhan, Hot and Cool: A Critical Symposium with a Rebuttal by McLuhan*. New York: The Dial P, 1967.

Stone, Blair Francis. *Marshall McLuhan and the Humanist Tradition: Media Theory and Encyclopaedic Learning*. Ann Arbor, MI: UMI Dissertation Services, 1995. [PhD diss., University of Massachusetts, 1974]

Strate, Lance, and Edward Wachtel, eds. *The Legacy of McLuhan*. Media Ecology Book Series. Cresskill, NJ: Hampton P, 2005.

Theall, Donald F. *The Virtual Marshall McLuhan*. Montreal and Kingston: McGill-Queen's UP, 2001.

– *The Medium Is the Rear-View Mirror: Understanding McLuhan*. Montreal: McGill-Queen's UP, 1971.

Willmott, Glenn. *McLuhan, or Modernism in Reverse*. Toronto: U of Toronto P, 1996.

Essays

Barilli, Renato. 'Re-Thinking Modernity.' *McLuhan Studies* 1 (Spring 1991): 117–40.

– 'L'estetica tecnologica di Marshall McLuhan.' In *Tra presenza e assenza*. Milano: Bompiani, 1974.

– 'Estetica e società tecnologica: Marshall McLuhan.' *Il Mulino* 126 (March-April 1973): 264–340.

Bettetini, G. 'Un mistico delle comunicazioni di massa.' *Rivista del cinematografo* 54.2–3 (Feb.-March 1981): 95.

Carpenter, Edmund. 'Remembering *Explorations.*' *Canadian Notes & Queries* 46 (Spring 1992): 3–14.

Eco, Umberto. 'E' morto Marshall McLuhan.' *La Repubblica* 3 (Jan. 1981).

Fulford, R. 'All Ignorance Is Motivated: Re-examining the Feedback of McLuhanism.' *Canadian Notes & Queries* 45 (Autumn 1991): 3–8.

Galbo, J. 'McLuhan and Baudrillard: Notes on the Discarnate, Simulations and Tetrads.' *McLuhan Studies* 1 (Spring 1991): 103–7.

Guardiani, Francesco. 'The Postmodernity of Marshall McLuhan.' *McLuhan Studies* 1 (Spring 1991): 141–62.

Kermode, Frank, 'Marshall McLuhan Interviewed.' *The Month*, April 1969, p. 219.

Kettle, J. 'Marshall McLuhan, Prophet and Analyst of the Age of Instant Knowledge.' *Canada Month*, October 1995.

Kostelanetz, R. 'Marshall McLuhan: High Priest of the Electronic Village.' In *Master Minds*. New York: Macmillan, 1967.

Logan, Robert K. 'The Axiomatics of Innis and McLuhan.' *McLuhan Studies* 1 (Spring 1991): 75–102.

Lorenzini, Amleto. Introduction. In *Il paesaggio interiore: La critica letteraria di Marshall McLuhan*. Varese: Sugarco, 1983. 7–12.

McLuhan, Eric. 'The New Science and the Old.' *McLuhan Studies* 1 (Spring 1991): 27–36.

The Medium's Messenger: Understanding McLuhan. Special issue of *Canadian Journal of Communication* (Fall 1989). [A special issue commemorating the 25th anniversary of *Understanding Media*]

Meyrowitz, Joshua. 'Canonic Anti-text: Marshall McLuhan's *Understanding Media.*' In *Canonic Texts in Media Research: Are There Any? Should There Be? How about These?* Ed. Elihu Katz et al. Cambridge: Polity P, 2003. 191–212.

Morrison, James C. 'Marshall McLuhan: The Modern Janus.' In *Perspectives on Culture, Technology and Communication: The Media Ecology Tradition*. Ed. Casey Man Kong Lum. Cresskill, NJ: Hampton P, 2006. 163–200.

Pietropaolo, Domenico. 'Vichian Ascendancies in the Thought of Marshall McLuhan.' *New Vico Studies* 13 (1969): 55–62.

Powe, Bruce W. 'Apprehensions Now: Canetti and McLuhan.' In *The Solitary Outlaw*. Toronto: Sommerville House, 1996. 179–206.

– 'Marshall McLuhan, the Put-on' and 'McLuhan and Frye, Either/Or.' In *A Climate Charged: Essays on Canadian Writers*. Oakville, ON: Mosaic P, 1984. 17–33, 55–8.

Sanderson, G. 'Towards Cyborgia: Aristotle, Bergson and McLuhan on the Nature of the Soul.' *McLuhan Studies* 1 (Spring 1991): 177–80.

Schickel, R. 'Marshall McLuhan: Canada's Intellectual Comet.' *Harper's*, November 1965, pp. 62–8.

Wain, J. 'The Incidental Thoughts of Marshall McLuhan.' *Encounter*, June 1985.
Wolfe, Tom. 'What If He Is Right?' In *The Pump House Gang*. New York: Farrar, Straus and Giroux, 1968. 129–68.
Zingrone, Frank. 'Laws of Media: The Pentad and Technical Syncretism.' *McLuhan Studies* 1 (Spring 1991): 109–15.

Videos

Marshall McLuhan: The Man and His Message. Dir. Stephanie McLuhan-Ortved. McLuhan Productions, 1984.
Marshall McLuhan's ABC. Written and directed by David Sobelman. TVOntario Production, 2002.
McLuhan's Wake. Dir. Kevin McMahon. Written and co-produced by David Sobelman. Primitive Entertainment, in co-production with the NFBC, 2002.
The Video McLuhan. Written and narrated by Tom Wolfe. Set of six VHS videotapes. McLuhan Productions, 1996.

Other Works Cited

AAVV. *Discorsi sul romanzo*. Firenze: Alinea, 1984.
Adkins, Richardson J. *Modern Art and Scientific Thought*. Urbana: U of Illinois P, 1971.
Albright, Daniel. *Quantum Poetics: Yeats, Pound, Eliot and the Science of Modernism*. Cambridge: Cambridge UP, 1997.
Alfano Miglietti, Francesca. *Extreme Bodies: The Use and Abuse of the Body in Art*. Milan: Skira, 2003.
– *Identità mutanti: Dalla piega alla piaga: Esseri delle contaminazioni contemporanee*. Genova: Costa & Nolan, 1997.
Ardis, Ann. *Modernism and Cultural Conflict, 1880–1922*. Cambridge: Cambridge UP, 2002.
Ashby, Ross. *An Introduction to Cybernetics*. New York: Wiley, 1957.
Auerbach, E. *Mimesis: The Representation of Reality in Western Literature*. Princeton: Princeton UP, 1953.
Bacigalupo, Massimo. 'Le poetiche dell'impersonalità: Pound, Eliot, Joyce e Lewis.' In *Modernismo/Modernismi: Dalla Avanguardia storica agli anni Trenta e oltre*. Ed. Giovanni Cianci. Milano: Principato, 1991. 255–71.
Bacon, Francis. *The Advancement of Learning*. London: J.M. Dent & Sons, 1950.
– *Essays*. London: J.M. Dent & Sons, 1947.
Ballard, J.G. *The Atrocity Exhibition*. New York: Doubleday, 1970.

– *Crash*. London: Vintage, 1995.

Barilli, Renato. *Informale. Oggetto. Comportamento*. Milano: Feltrinelli, 1979.

Barthes, Roland. *Mythologies*. Paris: Seuil, 1957.

– *S/Z*. Paris: Seuil, 1970.

Bateson, Gregory. *Steps to an Ecology of Mind*. New York: Ballantine, 1972.

Battistini, Andrea, ed. *Letteratura e scienza*. Bologna: Zanichelli, 1977.

Baudrillard, Jean. *Simulations*. Trans. Paul Foss, Paul Patton, and Philip Beitchman. New York: Semiotect(e), Inc., 1983.

Bauman, Zygmunt. *Modernity and Ambivalence*. Ithaca, NY: Cornell UP, 1991.

Bell, Ian. *Critic as Scientist: The Modernist Poetics of Ezra Pound*. New York: Methuen, 1981.

Benedikt, Michael. *Cyberspace: First Steps*. Cambridge, MA: MIT P, 1992.

Berger, R. *Téléovision: Le nouveau Golem*. Lausanne: Iderive, 1991.

Bergson, Henry. *Laughter. An Essay on the Meaning of the Comic*. New York: Macmillan, 1914.

Blake, William. *The Poetry and Prose of William Blake*. Ed. Geoffrey Keynes. London: Nonesuch P, 1948.

Bolter, David. *Writing Space: The Computer in the History of Literacy*. Hillsdale, NJ: Erlbaum, 1990.

Bradbury, Malcolm. 'The English Review.' *London Magazine* 8 (Aug. 1958): 46–57.

– *Possibilities: Essays on the State of the Novel*. Oxford: Oxford UP, 1973.

Bradbury, Malcolm, and James McFarlane, eds. *Modernism: A Guide to European Literature, 1890–1930*. London: Penguin Books, 1976.

Brand, Stuart. *The Media Lab*. New York: Viking, 1987.

Brooks, Peter. *Reading for the Plot: Design and Intention in Narrative*. Cambridge, MA: Harvard UP, 1992.

Buick, J., and Z. Jevtic. *Cyberspace*. Cambridge: Icon Books, 1995.

Burgess, Anthony. *One Man's Chorus*. New York: Carroll & Graf, 1998.

Bush, Vannevar. 'As We May Think.' *Atlantic Monthly* 176 (July 1945): 101–8.

– 'Memex Revisited.' In *Science Is Not Enough*. New York: William Morrow, 1967. 75–101.

Calvino, Italo. *Why Read the Classics*. Translated from the Italian by Martin McLaughlin. New York: Pantheon Books, 2003.

Canetti, Elias. *Crowd and Power*. London: Penguin Books, 1984.

Capra, Fritjof. *The Tao of Physics: An Exploration of the Parallels between Modern Physics and Eastern Mysticism*. New York: Bantam Books, 1977.

Carey, Paul. *The Intellectuals and the Masses: Pride and Prejudice among the Literary Intelligentsia*. New York: St Martin P, 1989.

Carpenter, Edmund. 'Eskimo Space Concepts.' In *Explorations: Studies in Culture and Communication* 5 (June 1955): 131–45.

– *Oh, What a Blow That Phantom Gave Me.* New York: Holt, Rinehart and Winston, 1973.

Carruthers, Peter. *Language, Thought and Consciousness.* Cambridge: Cambridge UP, 1996.

Chesterton, J.K. *Heretics.* Rockville, MD: Serenity Publishers Ltd., 2009.

– *The Secret of Father Brown.* Teddington, Middlesex: The Echo Library, 2007.

Cianci, Giovanni, ed. *Modernismo/Modernismi: Dalla Avanguardia storica agli anni Trenta e oltre.* Milano: Principato, 1991.

Clayton, Philip. *Mind and Emergence: From Quantum to Consciousness.* Oxford: Oxford UP, 2004.

Colombo, Furio. *Confucio nel computer: Memoria accidentale del futuro.* Milano: Nuova ERI, 1995.

Cork, Richard. *Vorticism and Abstract Art in the First Machine Age.* Berkeley and Los Angles: U of California P, 1976.

Coupland, Douglas. *Microserfs.* New York: Regan Books, 1995.

Cronenberg, David. *David Cronenberg: Interviews with Serge Grunberg.* London: Plexus, 2006.

Cuddy-Keane, Melba. *Virginia Woolf: The Intellectual and the Public Sphere.* Cambridge: Cambridge UP, 2003.

Culler, J. *On Puns: The Foundation of Letters.* Oxford: Basil Blackwell, 1988.

Czitrom, D.J. *Media and the American Mind: From Morse to McLuhan.* Chapel Hill, NC: U of North Carolina P, 1982.

Dasenbrock, Reed Way. *The Literary Vorticism of Ezra Pound and Wyndham Lewis.* Baltimore: Johns Hopkins UP, 1985.

Davis, Douglas. *Arts and the Future: A History/Prophecy of the Collaboration between Science and Technology and Art.* New York: Praeger, 1973.

De Bernardi, Alberto. *Una dittatura moderna: Il fascismo come problema storico.* Milano: Bruno Mondadori, 2001.

DeFleur M. *Theories of Mass Communication.* New York: Longman, 1989.

De Saussure, Ferdinand. *Course in General Linguistics.* New York: McGraw-Hill, 1966.

Descartes, R. *Discours de la méthode – Les Passions de l'ame.* Paris: Phidal, 1995.

Desiderium Erasmus of Rotterdam. *On Copia of Words and Ideas.* Translated from the Latin with an Introduction by D.B. King and H.D. Rix. Milwaukee: Marquete UP, 1963.

Dettmar, Kevin J.H. *Rereading the New: A Backward Glance at Modernism.* Ann Arbor: U of Michigan P, 1992.

Di Michele, M. *Le avanguardie artistiche del Novecento.* Milano: Feltrinelli, 1966.

Diepeveen, Leonard. *The Difficulties of Modernism.* New York: Routledge, 2003.

Doob, Leonard W., ed. *'Ezra Pound Speaking': Radio Speeches of World War II.* Westport, CT: Greenwood P, 1978.

Dotoli, G., ed. *Prospettive di Cultura Canadese.* Bari: Edizioni Schena, 1998.

Doyle, Arthur Conan. *The Sign of the Four.* 1890. New York: Barnes and Noble Inc.; 1992.

Dunlop, Rishma. *Metropolis.* Toronto: Mansfield P, 2005.

Eco, Umberto. *Apocalittici e integrati: Comunicazione di massa e teorie della cultura di massa.* Milano: Bompiani, 1964.

– *La definizione dell'arte.* Milano: Mursia, 1990.

– *Il nome della rosa.* Milano: Fabbri Editore, 1980.

– *Il superuomo di massa: Retorica e ideologia nel romanzo popolare.* Milano: Gruppo Editoriale Fabbri, 1978.

Edwards, Paul. *Wyndham Lewis: Painter and Writer.* New Haven: Yale UP, 2000.

Eisenstein, E.L. *The Printing Press as an Agent of Change.* Cambridge, MA: Harvard UP, 1979.

Eisenstein, Sergei. *Film Form.* Ed. and trans. Jay Leda. New York: Meridian, 1957.

Eliot, T.S. *Essays Ancient and Modern.* London: Faber & Faber, 1936.

– *The Sacred Wood.* 1920. London: Methuen, 1960.

– *The Use of Poetry and the Use of Criticism.* London: Faber & Faber, 1955.

– *The Waste Land.* Torino: Einaudi, 1993.

Ellmann, Richard. *James Joyce.* Oxford: Oxford UP, 1982.

Emery, C. *Ideas into Action: A Study of Pound's Cantos.* Coral Gables: U of Miami P, 1958.

Empson, W. *Seven Types of Ambiguity.* 1930. New York: Meridian, 1955.

Etrog, Sorel, and J. Cage. *Joyce and the Dada Circus: A Collage / An Irish Circus on Finnegans Wake.* Toronto/Dublin: The Black P/The Dolmen P, 1982.

Eysteinsson, Astradur. *The Concept of Modernism.* Ithaca, NY: Cornell UP, 1990.

Fakete, J. *The Critical Twilight: Explorations in the Ideology of Anglo-American Literary Theory from Eliot to McLuhan.* London: Routledge and Kegan Paul, 1977.

Fenollosa, Ernest. *The Chinese Written Character as a Medium for Poetry.* Ed. Ezra Pound. San Francisco: City Lights, 1936.

Ford, Ford Madox. *The Critical Attitude.* London: Duckworth, 1911.

– *The English Novel: From the Earliest Days to the Death of Joseph Conrad.* Vol. 1. London: Constable, 1929.

– *The Fifth Queen.* Oxford: Oxford UP, 1984.

– *Henry James: A Critical Study.* In *The Ford Madox Ford Reader.* Ed. S.J. Stang. London: Paladin Grafton Books, 1987.

– *A History of Our Own Time.* Edited by Solon Beinfeld and Sondra J. Stang, with a Foreword by Gordon A. Craig. Bloomington and Indianapolis: U of Indiana P, 1988.

– *Joseph Conrad: A Personal Remembrance.* Boston: Little Brown and Company, 1924.

– *The March of Literature: From Confucius to Modern Times*. London: G. Allen & Unwin, 1939.
– Preface. In *Stories from de Maupassant*, by Elsa Martindale. London: Duckworth, 1903.
– *Return to Yesterday*. London: Gollancz, 1931.
Forster, E.M. *The Aspects of the Novel*. London: Penguin, 1970.
Fortunati, Vita. 'Il metabolismo delle forme narrative nel romanzo impressionista.' In *Discorsi sul romanzo*. Ed. Paolo Bagni. Firenze: Alinea, 1984. 81–100.
Fortunati, Vita, and E. Lamberti, eds. *Ford Madox Ford and 'The Republic of Letters.'* Bologna: CLUEB, 2002.
Foshay, Toby. *Wyndam Lewis and the Avant-Garde: The Politics of the Intellect*. Montreal: McGill-Queen's UP, 1992.
Foucault, M. *The Order of Things: An Archaeology of the Human Sciences*. A translation of *Les mots et les choses*, 1970. New York: Vintage, 1994.
Frank, Joseph. 'Spatial Form in Modern Literature' (1945). In *The Idea of Spatial Form*. New Brunswick, NJ: Rutgers UP, 1991. 31–66.
Frye, Northrop. *Anatomy of Criticism*. Princeton: Princeton UP, 1957.
– *The Bush Garden: Essays on the Canadian Imagination*. Toronto: Anansi, 1971.
– *Mythologizing Canada: Essays on the Canadian Literary Imagination*. Ed. Branko Gorjup. New York: Legas, 1997.
– *Reflections on the Canadian Literary Imagination*. Roma: Bulzoni, 1991.
Fuller, Buckminster. *Education Automation*. Carbondale: Southern Illinois UP, 1961.
Fuller, Buckminster, Jerome Agel, and Quentin Fiore. *I Seem to Be a Verb*. New York: Bantam Books, 1970.
Gasiorek, Andrzej. *Wyndham Lewis and Modernism*. Horndon, Tavistock, Devon: Northcote House Publishers, 2004.
Giddens, Anthony. *The Consequences of Modernity*. Stanford: Stanford UP, 1990.
Giedion, Siegfried. *Mechanization Takes Command*. 1948. New York: Norton, 1969.
– *Space Time and Architecture: The Growth of a New Tradition*. Cambridge, MA: Harvard UP, 1965.
Gilson, Etienne. *The Christian Philosophy of St. Thomas Aquinas*. Trans. L.K. Shook. London: Gollancz, 1957.
– *History of Christian Philosophy in the Middle Ages*. New York: Random House, 1955.
Gleick, James. *Chaos: Making a New Science*. London: Penguin, 1987.
Goldring, D. *South Lodge: Reminiscences of Violet Hunt, Ford Madox Ford and the English Review Circle*. London: Constable & Co. Ltd, 1942.
Gombrich, E.H. *Art and Illusion*. New York: Pantheon Books, 1960.
Granata, Paolo. *Arte, estetica e nuovi media: 'Sei lezioni' sul mondo digitale*. Bologna: Fausto Lupetti Editore, 2009.

Green, Jonathon. *All Dressed Up: The Sixties and the Counter-Culture*. London: Jonathan Cape, 1998.

Greenblatt, Stephen, and Giles Gunn, eds. *Redrawing the Boundaries*. New York: Modern Language Association of America, 1992.

Grenet, Abbé Paul. *Teilhard de Chardin: The Man and His Theories*. Trans. R.A. Rudorff. London: Souvenir P, 1965.

Griffith, Belver C., et al. 'Coherent Social Groups in Scientific Change.' *Science* 177 (15 September 1972): 959–64.

Hall, Edward T. *The Hidden Dimension*. Garden City, NY: Doubleday, Anchor Books, 1969.

– *The Silent Language*. Garden City, NY: Doubleday, 1959.

Hampson, Robert, and Max Saunders, eds. *Ford Madox Ford's Modernity*. Amsterdam: Rodopi, 2003.

Hart, Clive. *Structure and Motif in Finnegans Wake*. London: Faber & Faber, 1962.

Havelock, E.A. *Preface to Plato*. Cambridge, MA: Harvard UP, 1963.

Hayles, Katherine. *The Cosmic Web: Scientific Field Models and Literary Strategies in the Twentieth Century*. Ithaca, NY: Cornell UP, 1984.

Heidegger, Martin. *Being and Time*. Trans. John Macuarrie and Edward Robinson. San Francisco: Harper & Row, 1962.

– *Poetry, Language, Thought*. Trans. Albert Hofstadter. New York: Harper & Row, 1971.

Heim, Michael. *Electric Language: A Philosophical Study of Word Processing*. New Haven: Yale UP, 1993.

– *Virtual Realism*. New York: Oxford UP, 1998.

Heisenberg, Werner. *Physics and Philosophy: The Revolution in Modern Science*. New York: Harper & Row, 1958.

Heyer, Paul. *Communication and History: Theories of Media, Knowledge and Civilisation*. New York: Greenwood P, 1988.

Hickman, Miranda B. *The Geometry of Modernism: The Vorticist Idiom in Lewis, Pound, H.D., and Yeats*. Austin: U of Texas P, 2005.

Higginbotham, J., ed. *Greek and Latin in Literature: A Comparative Study*. London: Methuen, 1969.

Huizinga, Johan. *Homo Ludens*. Trans. R.F.C. Hull. London: Routledge & Kegan Paul, 1949.

Hutcheon, Linda. *A Poetics of Postmodernism: History, Theory, Fiction*. London and New York: Routledge,1988.

– *The Politics of Postmodernism*. London and New York: Routledge, 1993.

Innis, Harold A. *The Bias of Communication*. Toronto: U of Toronto P, 1951.

– *Empire and Communication*. Oxford: Oxford UP, 1950.

Intonti, V. *La parabola del modernismo: Saggi sul modernismo letterario*. Bari: Adriatica editrice, 1993.

James, Henry. *The Art of Fiction*. 1884. Oxford: Oxford UP, 1948.

– *The Figure in the Carpet and Other Stories*.1896. Edited with an Introduction and Notes by Frank Kermode. London: Penguin Books, 1986.

Jameson, Fredric. *The Cultures of Globalization*. Durham, NC: Duke UP, 1998.

– *Fables of Aggression: Wyndham Lewis, the Modernist as Fascist*. Berkeley and Los Angeles: U of California P, 1979.

– *The Modernist Papers*. London and New York: Verso, 2007.

– *Postmodernism; or, The Cultural Logic of Late Capitalism*. Durham, NC: Duke UP, 1991.

Joyce, James. *The Critical Writings*. Ed. Ellsworth Mason and Richard Ellmann. New York: Viking, 1959.

– *Finnegans Wake*. London: Faber & Faber, 1939.

– *Ulysses*. London: The Bodley Head, 1949.

Kadlec, David. *Mosaic Modernism: Anarchism, Pragmatism, Culture*. Baltimore: Johns Hopkins UP, 2000.

Kakuzo, O. *The Book of Tea*. Rutland and Tokyo: Charkes E. Tuttle, 1978.

Katz, Elihu, et al., eds, *Canonic Texts in Media Research: Are There Any? Should There Be? How about These?* Cambridge: Polity P, 2003.

Kenner, Hugh. *The Mechanic Muse*. New York: Oxford UP, 1987.

– *Paradox in Chesterton*. London: Sheet & Ward, 1948.

– *The Poetry of Ezra Pound*. London: Faber, 1951.

– *The Pound Era*. London: Faber & Faber, 1971.

– *A Sinking Island: The Modern English Writers*. London: Barrie & Jenkins, 1986.

– *Wyndham Lewis*. Norfolk, CT: New Directions, 1954.

Kermode, Frank. *The Sense of an Ending: Studies in the Theory of Fiction*. New York: Oxford UP, 1967.

Klee, Paul, *The Thinking Eye*. New York: George Wittenborn, 1961.

Klein, Scott. *The Fictions of James Joyce and Wyndham Lewis: Monsters of Nature and Design*. Cambridge: Cambridge UP, 1994.

Kuhn, Thomas. *The Structure of Scientific Revolutions*. Chicago: U of Chicago P, 1962.

Kuhns, William. *The Post-Industrial Prophets: Interpretations of Technology*. New York: Weybright and Talley, 1971.

Landow, George. *Hypertext: The Convergence of Contemporary Critical Theory and Technology*. Baltimore: Johns Hopkins UP, 1982.

– *Hypertext 3.0: Critical Theory and New Media in an Era of Globalization*. Baltimore: Johns Hopkins UP, 2006.

– ed. *Hyper/Text/Theory*. Baltimore: Johns Hopkins UP, 1994.

Lanham, R.A. *The Motives of Eloquence: Literary Rhetoric in the Renaissance*. New Haven: Yale UP, 1976.

Leavis, F.R. *New Bearings in English Poetry: A Study of Contemporary Situation*. 1932. Harmondsworth: Penguin, 1963.

Leavis, F.R., and D. Thompson. *Culture and Environment*. London: Chatto & Windus, 1931.

Lentricchia, Frank. *After the New Criticism*. Chicago: U of Chicago P, 1980.

– *Modernist Quartet*. Cambridge: Cambridge UP, 1994.

Levenson, Michael. *A Genealogy of Modernism: A Study of English Literary Doctrine, 1908–1922*. Cambridge: Cambridge UP, 1984.

Lewis, Wyndham. *America and Cosmic Man*. London: Nicholson & Watson, 1948.

– *The Art of Being Ruled*. 1926. Ed. Reed Way Dasenbrock. Santa Rosa: Black Sparrow P, 1989.

– *Blasting and Bombardiering*. Santa Rosa: Black Sparrow P, 1983.

– *The Enemy of the Stars*. 1914. In *Modernism: An Anthology*. Ed. Lawrence S. Rainey. Malden-Oxford-Carlton: Blackwell Publishing, 2005.

– *Journey into Barbary: Morocco Writings and Drawings*. Ed. C.J. Fox. Santa Barbara: Black Sparrow P, 1983.

– *The Meaning of the Wild Body*. New York: Harcourt, Brace, 1928.

– *Self Condemned: A Novel*. 1954. Introduction by Allan Pero. Toronto: Dundurn P, 2010.

– *Time and Western Man*. 1927. London: Chatto and Windus, 1931.

Liska, Vivian, and Astradur Eysteinsson, eds. *Modernism*. Comparative History of Literatures in European Languages Series. Amsterdam and Philadelphia: John Benjamins, 2007.

Logan, Robert K. *The Alphabet Effect: The Impact of the Phonetic Alphabet on the Development of Western Civilization*. New York: St Martin P, 1986.

– *The Extended Mind: The Emergence of Language, the Human Mind, and Culture*. Toronto: U of Toronto P, 2007.

– *The Fifth Language*. Toronto: Stoddart, 1995.

Lum, Casey Man Kong, ed. *Perspectives on Culture, Technology and Communication: The Media Ecology Tradition*. Cresskill, NJ: Hampton P, 2006.

MacShane, Frank. *The Life and Work of Ford Madox Ford*. London: Routledge & Kegan Paul, 1965.

– ed. *Critical Writings of Ford Madox Ford*. Lincoln: U of Nebraska P, 1964.

Mallarmé, Stéphane. *Oeuvres complètes*. Paris: Gallimard, 1945.

Mancuso, G. *Pound e la Cina*. Milano: Feltrinelli, 1974.

Marinetti, Filippo Tommaso. *Antologia dei poeti futuristi*. Milano: Edizioni Futuriste di 'Poesia,' 1912.

Marrou, H.I. *Saint Augustin et la fin de la culture antique*. Paris: Edition E. De Boccard, 1938.

McLuhan, Eric. *The Electric Language*. Toronto: Stoddart, 1998.

– 'Joyce and McLuhan.' *Antigonish Review* 106 (1996): 157–65.

– *The Role of Thunder in Finnegans Wake*. Toronto: U of Toronto P, 1997.

Mead, George Herbert. *Mind, Self, and Society.* Ed. Charles W. Morris. Chicago: U of Chicago P, 1934.

Medawar, Peter Brian. *The Hope of Progress: A Scientist Looks at Problems in Philosophy, Literature and Science.* London: Methuen, 1972.

Moles, A. *Sociodinamica della cultura.* Rimini: Guaraldi, 1971.

Morawski, S. 'The Basic Functions of Quotations.' In *Sign – Language – Culture.* Ed. Algirdas Julien Greimas et al. The Hague and Paris: Mouton, 1970. 690–704.

Moretti, Franco. *Segni e stili del moderno.* Torino: Einaudi, 1987.

Mosco, Vincent. *The Digital Sublime: Myth, Power, and Cyberspace.* Cambridge, MA: MIT P, 2004.

Mulhall, S. *Heidegger and Being and Time.* London and New York: Routledge, 1996.

Mullini, Roberta. *Corruttore di parole: Il Fool nel teatro di Shakespeare.* Bologna: Clueb, 1983.

Mumford, Lewis. *Technics and Civilization.* 1934. New York: Harcourt, Brace and World, 1983.

Munton, Alan, ed. *Wyndham Lewis: Collected Poems and Plays.* Manchester: Carcanet, 2006.

Murray, Stephen O. *Theory Groups and the Study of Language in North America: A Social History.* Amsterdam and Philadelphia: John Benjamins, 1993.

Negroponte, Nicholas. *Being Digital.* New York: Knopf, 1995.

Neilson, Brett. 'Visioni dal vortice: L'emergere dello spazio sociale in Paul Cézanne e Wyndham Lewis.' In *Il Cézanne degli scrittori, dei poeti e dei filosofi.* Ed. Giovanni Cianci, Elio Franzini, and Antonello Negri. Milano: Bocca, 2001. 165–78.

– 'Wyndham Lewis in Morocco: Spatial Philosophy and the Politics of Race.' In *Anglo-American Modernity and the Mediterranean.* Ed. Giovanni Cianci. Milan: I Quaderni di Acme, 2006. 313–26.

Nelson, Theodor Holm. *Literary Machines.* Swarthmore, PA: Self-published, 1981.

Newman, Judy. 'Ford Madox Ford's Fifth Queen Trilogy: Mythical Fiction and Political Letters.' *Etudes Anglaises* 38.4 (Oct.-Dec. 1985): 397–410.

Nicholls, P. *Ezra Pound: Politics, Economics and Writing: A Study of the Cantos.* London: Macmillan, 1984.

Norris, Christopher, *What's Wrong with Postmodernism?* Baltimore: Johns Hopkins UP, 1990.

Nunberg, Geoffrey, ed. *The Future of the Book.* Berkeley: U of California P, 1996.

Odgart, M. *Satire.* London: World University Library, 1969.

Olson, D.R., and N. Torrance. *Alfabetizzazione e oralità.* Milano: Raffaello Cortina Editore, 1991.

Ong, Walter J. *Orality and Literacy: The Technologizing of the Word.* London and New York: Methuen, 1982.

Poe, Edgar Allan. *A Descent into the Maelstrom.* New York: Powgen P, 1936.

Poli, B.J. *Ford Madox Ford and the transatlantic review.* Syracuse, NY: Syracuse UP, 1967.

Popper, K.L. *In Search of a Better World: Lectures and Essays from Thirty Years.* London and New York: Routledge, 1994.

Postman, Neil. *Amusing Ourselves to Death: Public Discourse in the Age of Show Business.* New York: Penguin, 1985.

– *Teaching as a Conserving Activity.* New York: Delacorte P, 1979.

Pound, Ezra. *ABC of Reading.* 1934. London: Faber & Faber, 1991.

– *'Ezra Pound Speaking': Radio Speeches of World War II.* Ed. Leonard W. Doob. Westport, CT: Greenwood P, 1978.

– *Guide to Kulchur.* 1938. New York: New Directions, 1970.

– *Literary Essays.* Ed. T.S. Eliot. London: Faber & Faber, 1954.

– *Machine Art & Other Writings: The Lost Thought of the Italian Years.* Essays selected and edited with an Introduction by Maria Luisa Ardizzone. London: Routledge and Kegan Paul, 1996.

– *Selected Works, 1908–1959.* London: Faber & Faber, 1975.

Powe, B.W. *Outage: A Journey into Electric City.* Toronto: Random House, 1995.

– *The Solitary Outlaw: Trudeau, Lewis, Gould, Canetti, and McLuhan.* Toronto: Somerville House Publishing, 1996.

Pritchard, W. *Wyndham Lewis.* London: Routledge & Kegan Paul, 1972.

Rademacher, Jörg W., ed. *Modernism and the Individual Talent / Moderne und besondere Begabung: Re-Canonizing Ford Madox Ford (Hueffer) / Zur Re-Kanonisierung von Ford Madox Ford (Hüffer).* Symposium Münster June/Juni 1999. Münster-Hamburg-London: Lit Verlag, Anglistick/Amerikanistik, 6, 2002.

Richards, I.A. *Practical Criticism.* 1929. New York: Harcourt, Brace & World, 1960.

– *Science and Poetry.* London: Kegan Paul, Trench, Trubner & Co., 1970.

Rizzardi, Alfredo. *Una ghirlanda per Ezra Pound.* Urbino: Argalia Editore, 1981.

Rodley, Chris, ed. *Cronenberg on Cronenberg.* Toronto: Alfred A. Knopf, 1992.

Ruskin, John. *Modern Painters.* 5 vols. New York: Thomas Y. Crowell, 1834–85.

Russell, Bertrand. *The Future of Science.* New York: Wisdom Library, 1959.

Russell, Peter, ed. *An Examination of Ezra Pound.* New York: New Directions, 1950.

Russo, John Paul. *The Future without a Past.* Columbia: U of Missouri P, 2005.

– *I.A. Richards: His Life and Work.* Baltimore: Johns Hopkins UP, 1989.

Sanfilippo, M., and V. Matero. *Da Omero al Cyberpunk: Archeologia del Villaggio Globale.* Roma: Castelvecchi, 1995.

Saunders, Max. *Ford Madox Ford: A Dual Life.* 2 vols. Oxford: Oxford UP, 1996.

Scholes, R. *Structuralism in Literature: An Introduction.* New Haven and London: Yale UP, 1974.

Schwartz, T. *The Responsive Chord.* Garden City and New York: Anchor P / Doubleday, 1973.

– *The Second God.* Garden City and New York: Anchor P / Doubleday, 1983.

Shakespeare, William. *Complete Works.* Ed. S. Wells and G. Taylor. Oxford: Oxford UP, 1986.

Snow, C.P. *The Two Cultures and the Scientific Revolution.* Cambridge: Cambridge UP, 1959.

Sontag, Susan. *Against Interpretation, and Other Essays.* New York: Delta, 1966.

– *AIDS and Its Metaphors.* New York: Farrar, Straus & Giroux, 1989.

– 'AIDS and Its Metaphors.' In *Encounters: Essays for Exploration and Inquiry.* 2nd ed. Ed. Pat C. Hoy II and Robert DiYanni. New York: McGraw-Hill, 2000. 574–84.

– *Illness as Metaphor.* New York: Vintage Books, 1979.

Stang, Sondra J., ed. *The Ford Madox Ford Reader.* London: Paladin, 1986.

Strate, Lance. *Echoes and Reflections: On Media Ecology as a Field of Study.* Cresskill: New Hampton P, 2006.

Tassi, R. *Le avanguardie: Cubismo, Futurismo, Astrattismo.* Milano: Fabbri Editore, 1966.

Tratner, Michael. *Modernism and Mass Politics: Joyce, Woolf, Eliot, Yeats.* Stanford: Stanford UP, 1995.

Valdivia, Angharad N., ed. *A Companion to Media Studies.* Oxford: Blackwell, 2003.

Vico, Gian Battista. *La Scienza Nuova.* Milano: Rizzoli, 1977.

Wees, W.C. *Vorticism and the English Avant-Garde.* Toronto: U of Toronto P, 1972.

Weir, Lorraine. *Writing Joyce: A Semiotics of the Joyce System.* Indianapolis: U of Indiana P, 1989.

Wiener, Norbert. *Cybernetics; or, Control and Communication in the Animal and the Machine.* Cambridge, MA: MIT P, 1961.

Wiesenfarth, Joseph, ed. *History and Representation in Ford Madox Ford's Writings.* Amsterdam: Rodopi, 2004.

Wildiers, N.M. *An Introduction to Teilhard de Chardin.* New York: Harper & Row, 1967.

Williams, R. *Culture and Society, 1780–1950.* London: Penguin, 1963.

Wilson, Edward Osborne. *Consilience: The Unity of Knowledge.* New York: Knopf / Random House, 1998.

Wolfreys, Julian, ed. *Introducing Literary Theories: A Guide and Glossary.* Edinburgh: U of Edinburgh P, 2001.

Woodcock, George, ed. *Wyndham Lewis in Canada.* Introd. Julian Symons. Vancouver: University of British Columbia Publication Centre, 1971.

Yates, Frances Amelia. *The Art of Memory.* Chicago: U of Chicago P, 1974.

Zingrone, Frank. *The Media Simplex: At the Edge of Meaning in the Age of Chaos.* New York: Hampton P, 2004.

Index